The Structure and Evolution of Recent U.S. Trade Policy

A National Bureau
of Economic Research
Conference Report

The Structure and Evolution of Recent U.S. Trade Policy

Edited by **Robert E. Baldwin**
and
Anne O. Krueger

The University of Chicago Press

Chicago and London

Robert E. Baldwin, Hilldale Professor of Economics at the University of Wisconsin, Madison, has written extensively on trade theory and has served as a consultant to the Department of Labor, the United Nations Conference on Trade and Development, the Organization for Economic Cooperation and Development, and the World Bank.

Anne O. Krueger is vice president, economics and research, at the World Bank. Her many books include *Trade and Employment in Developing Countries*, volumes 1, 2, and 3, also published by the University of Chicago Press.

The University of Chicago Press, Chicago 60637
The University of Chicago Press, Ltd., London

© 1984 by the National Bureau of Economic Research
All rights reserved. Published 1984
Printed in the United States of America
93 92 91 90 89 88 87 86 85 84   5 4 3 2 1

Library of Congress Cataloging in Publication Data
Main entry under title:

The Structure and evolution of recent U.S. trade policy.

  (A Conference report / National Bureau of Economic Research)
  Includes index.
  1. United States—Commercial policy—Addresses, essays, lectures. I. Baldwin, Robert E. II. Krueger, Anne O. III. Conference report (National Bureau of Economic Research)
HF1455.S85   1984   382.3'0973   84-2560
ISBN 0-226-03604-9

Contents

Introduction

Robert E. Baldwin and Anne O. Krueger

American interdependence with the world economy continues to increase. One in seven manufacturing jobs were export related in 1980, and by 1981 merchandise exports amounted to 8.0 percent of GNP in contrast to only 4.3 percent in 1970. Furthermore, imports have increasingly become a significant determinant of the competitive fate of corresponding American industries. Although this greater interdependence has been widely recognized and subject to considerable attention, there has been a surprising lag in research on specific trade policies, particularly the numerous nontariff measures and specific tariff arrangements that characterize the modern international trading system.

A number of factors have contributed to this gap in economic research. Trade relations were less important historically than they are now, and the extensive use of nontariff trade policies is a comparatively recent phenomenon. But institutional reasons also account for the deficiency of rigorous trade policy analysis.

One such reason relates to the failure to establish an international organization that deals with international trade in a manner comparable to the way the International Monetary Fund (IMF) and the World Bank handle international financial and economic development issues. The economic staffs of both the IMF and the World Bank have for years been leaders both in carrying on research themselves and in stimulating research by others on these issues. The rejection of the third major international economic organization proposed at the end of World War II, namely, the International Trade Organization (ITO), prevented a comparable level of international research from becoming established in the trade field. While the secretariat of the General Agreement on Tariffs and Trade (GATT)—the salvaged part of ITO—carries on high quality research, its comparatively modest size and authority precludes extensive research in the field.

A similar contrast exists within most countries. In the United States, for example, no federal agency dealing with trade issues comes close to matching the research capabilities that the Board of Governors of the Federal Reserve System and the various individual Federal Reserve Banks have in international finance. A perception by academic economists, at least until relatively recently, that there were many more significant problems to study other than trade policy issues may also help to account for the comparative dearth of research in this field.

The National Bureau of Economic Research project on trade relations is directed at reducing this research deficiency. This volume represents an effort to do so particularly with respect to U.S. trade policies. In Parts II, III, and IV of this volume, eight specific import and export-promoting policies affecting U.S. trade are analyzed in institutional, theoretical, and empirical terms. The objective is to better understand how policies operate, how effective they are in terms of their stated purposes, and their economic costs and benefits. The policies covered are the Japanese voluntary export restraint agreement on autos, the Trigger Price Mechanism established to regulate imports of steel into the United States; the Multifiber Arrangement covering textile and apparel imports; the U.S. Trade Adjustment Assistance program; the Generalized System of Preferences; the U.S. Strategic Petroleum Reserve; the U.S. Domestic International Sales Corporation legislation; and the export-credit subsidization undertaken by the U.S. Export-Import Bank.

Part I of this volume traces the shifts in U.S. import policy after World War II and sets the stage for the detailed studies of the particular issues just listed. Part V adopts a global point of view and tries to assess the degree of trade restrictiveness in the industrial countries, including the extent of their protection against the exports of the developing countries. Brief summaries of the papers are given in the introduction to each part of the volume, while comments of the discussants follow each paper.

For financial support of the conference at which the papers in this volume were presented, the National Bureau of Economic Research is grateful to the National Science Foundation for grant PRA-8116459 for International Economic Policy Research, and to the Andrew W. Mellon Foundation and the Alfred P. Sloan Foundation through their support of the four-year project "Productivity and Industrial Change in the World Economy."

I   U.S. Trade Policy since World War II

Introduction

The essay in this section provides a historical perspective for the consideration of the various U.S. trade policy issues analyzed in the other parts of the volume.

As Baldwin notes, although liberalization has been the key feature of U.S. trade policy over the last fifty years, especially with regard to tariffs, there have been significant shifts in political attitudes toward this liberalization, as well as both in the relationships established between Congress and the president for the purpose of implementing trade policy and in the composition of the political and economic groups supporting an open trading system. During the period of ascendancy of the United States as a hegemonic power, U.S. leadership helped to promote the country's international political goals and the economic interests of most domestic groups by establishing an open world trading system. The Democratic party, with strong support from organized labor, and a growing proportion of Republicans, who were backed by internationally oriented business interests, favored substantial trade liberalization. In agreeing to this policy, Congress gave the president considerable discretion in implementing it. However, as the economic power of the United States slipped relative to such countries as the members of the European Economic Community and Japan, trade policy came to be viewed in the United States in more national economic terms, and the doctrinaire support for liberalization by Democrats and economic groups such as organized labor eroded. One manifestation of the increased concern for the economic interests of the United States has been the greater use of selective nontariff measures to deal with particular issues of import competition and export promotion. Furthermore, Congress began to

3

exert much more control over the implementation of trade policy, partly in response to this more self-centered outlook and partly to reclaim some of the powers it had delegated to the president during the economic and military emergencies of the 1930s and 1940s.

1   The Changing Nature of U.S. Trade Policy since World War II

Robert E. Baldwin

1.1   Introduction

Future economic historians will undoubtedly stress trade liberalization as the most distinctive feature of U.S. commercial policy over the past fifty years. As table 1.1 indicates, through a series of thirty bilateral agreements and eight multilateral negotiations, tariffs have been steadily cut to only about 20 percent of their 1930 average level.[1] The increased use in recent years of nontariff protective measures modifies this liberalization picture somewhat, but the trend in protection over the period has clearly been downward.

Although tariff reduction has been the dominant theme of U.S. trade policy since the early 1930s, important changes have taken place in the nature and extent of U.S. support for this trade liberalization. A consideration of these developments is helpful not only to better understand American international economic policy over the period but also to predict possible significant shifts in future U.S. trade policy. To further these objectives, this paper focuses on five closely related trends in or features of U.S. trade policy since the end of World War II. They are: (1) the shift from the use of trade policy in the immediate postwar period as a means of promoting broad international political and national security goals of the United States to its greater use in recent years as a means of advancing national economic objectives and responding to domestic political pressures based on particular economic interests; (2) the continuing efforts by Congress over the period to modify the trade powers of the president to make U.S. international commercial policy more responsive to its wishes; (3) the changes in the positions of the Republican and

Robert E. Baldwin is professor of economics at the University of Wisconsin-Madison and a research associate of the National Bureau of Economic Research.

Table 1.1   Duty Reductions since 1934 under the U.S. Trade Agreements Program

GATT Conference	Proportion of Dutiable Imports Subjected to Reductions	Average Cut in Reduced Tariffs	Average Cut in All Duties	Remaining Duties as a Proportion of 1930 Tariffs[a]
1. Pre-GATT, 1934-47	63.9%	44.0%	33.2%	66.8%
2. First Round, Geneva, 1947	53.6	35.0	21.1	52.7
3. Second Round, Annecy, 1949	5.6	35.1	1.9	51.7
4. Third Round, Torquay, 1950–51	11.7	26.0	3.0	50.1
5. Fourth Round, Geneva, 1955–56	16.0	15.6	3.5	48.9
6. Dillon Round, Geneva, 1961–62	20.0	12.0	2.4	47.7
7. Kennedy Round, Geneva, 1964–67	79.2	45.5	36.0	30.5
8. Tokyo Round, 1974–79	n.a.	n.a.	29.6	21.2

SOURCE: Real Phillipe Lavergne, The Political Economy of U.S. Tariffs, Ph.D. thesis, University of Toronto, 1981.
[a]These percentages do not take account of the effects of either structural changes in trade or inflation on the average tariff level.

Democratic parties concerning the desirability of trade liberalization versus increased protectionism; (4) the shifts in the attitudes of business, labor, and the farm sector toward the liberalization versus protectionism issue; and (5) the increased use of nontariff measures to regulate international trade at the same time that tariffs were being significantly reduced.

Underlying the different shifts in postwar U.S. trade policy outlined above are three more basic economic and political influences that help explain why these changes occurred and the manner in which they affected the U.S. commitment toward a liberal trade policy. They are, first—and most important—the emergence and subsequent decline of the United States as a hegemonic power; second, the persistent pressure exerted over the entire period by a politically significant group of domestic industries (whose composition changed somewhat over time) against trade liberalization and in favor of increased import protection for themselves; and, third, the efforts by Congress to reduce the greatly increased powers granted the president during the economic emergency of the 1930s and the military emergency of World War II.

1.2   U.S. Leadership in Establishing a
Liberal International Trading Regime

Well before the end of World War II, the foreign policy leaders of the Democratic party had concluded that the lack of an open world economy during the 1930s was a major contributory cause of the war[2] and that the United States must, therefore, take the lead after the end of hostilities in establishing an open international trading system to make "the economic foundations of peace . . . as secure as the political foundations."[3] Thus, even before the war had ended, the Roosevelt administration had not only drafted a proposal for a multilateral trade organization but had also requested substantial, new, tariff-reducing powers from Congress.

1.2.1   The Basis of Democratic Support for a
Liberal International Regime

A desire on the part of political leaders for a new international regime is quite different from actually bringing about such a change, especially when—as in this case—there is a lack of strong direct pressures for the change from either the country's electorate or other governments. One factor that helped the Democratic leadership gain the support of members of their own party for the adoption of a liberal international economic order was the compatibility of such a regime with the trade policy position that the party had long supported. Since the late nineteenth century, the Democrats had associated high tariffs with monopoly profits for the rich and low tariffs with low prices for goods consumed by the average citizen.[4] Furthermore, they maintained that low U.S. tariffs encouraged low foreign tariffs and thus indirectly stimulated increases in U.S. exports, especially agricultural goods. This latter argument was crucial in obtaining passage of the Trade Agreements Act of 1934.[5] The gradual recovery during the 1930s in employment and exports as the trade agreements program was implemented served to reinforce this ideological commitment of Democrats to liberal trade policies. Consequently, the greater emphasis in the postwar period by the party leadership on the foreign policy merits of a liberal trade policy, in addition to its domestic benefits, represented an extension of the party's recent position that was not difficult for most Democrats to accept. It was also consistent with the stance adopted by the Wilson administration at the end of World War I. Thus, over 80 percent of the Democrats voting in the House of Representatives supported the party's position on extending the trade agreements program during the 1940s and 1950s.

The fact that implementing an open international trading system did not involve any significant new increase in the powers of the president also was important in gaining domestic support for the regime change. As a consequence of what almost all regarded as the excessive use of logrolling during the enactment of the Smoot-Hawley Tariff of 1930, coupled with the sense of crisis created by the depression that followed shortly thereafter, the Congress in 1934 gave the president the authority to lower U.S. tariffs by up to 50 percent in negotiations with other countries in return for reciprocal cuts in their import duties. Consequently, the 1945 request for another 50 percent duty-cutting power to enable the United States to take a leadership role in international trade liberalization did not entail any basic changes in existing presidential powers.

The most important reason, however, for the success of the Democratic leadership in first gaining and then maintaining support for the U.S. leadership role in creating a liberal international economic regime was the hegemonic trade and payments position that the United States assumed in the immediate postwar period.[6] The United States emerged from World War II with its economic base greatly expanded, while the economic structures of both its enemies and industrial allies were in ruins. Except for Great Britain's position at the outset of the Industrial Revolution, economic dominance of this extent is unique in the history of the industrial nations. Even as late as 1952, the U.S. share of total exports of the ten most important industrial countries was 35 percent whereas it had been only 26 and 28 percent in 1938 and 1928, respectively (see Baldwin 1958). The 1952 U.S. export share of manufactures was also 35 percent in contrast to only 21 percent in both 1938 and 1928. Furthermore, there was an export surplus in every major industrial group (e.g., machinery, vehicles, chemicals, textiles, and miscellaneous manufactures) except metals. These abnormally favorable export opportunities, together with the vigorous postwar domestic economic recovery, served both to mask protectionist pressures from industries whose underlying comparative cost position was deteriorating and to build support for liberal trade policies on the part of those sectors whose international competitive position was strong.

The ability of government leaders to obtain domestic support for trade liberalization was further enhanced by the emergence of the cold war in the late 1940s. The public generally accepted the government view that the communist countries represented a serious economic and political threat to the United States, its allies, and the rest of the market-oriented economic world. The argument that the United States should mount a vigorous program to offset the communist threat by providing not only military aid to friendly nations but also assistance in the form of economic grants and lower U.S. tariffs, therefore, also received public support.

There was still considerable opposition to trade liberalization in the immediate postwar period, however. As in the 1930s, a long list of industries testified during the 1940s and 1950s against giving the president the power to cut duties on imports competing with domestically produced goods. The products covered included textiles and apparel, coal, petroleum, watches, bicycles, pottery and tiles, toys, cutlery, ball bearings, glass, cheese, lead and zinc, copper, leather, and umbrellas. The decision in this period not to apply a liberal trade policy to agriculture significantly weakened the sectoral opposition to liberalization and established a precedent that has been used several times since to offset protectionist opposition.

Pressures to halt further tariff cutting were also strengthened by the opposition of many Republicans to liberalization on doctrinaire grounds. The Republican advocacy for protectionism on the grounds that this policy promoted domestic economic development and high living standards had an even longer tradition than the Democratic position in favor of liberalization.

From the outset of the trade agreements program, the Roosevelt administration assured Congress that no duty cuts would be made that seriously injured any domestic industry. However, in 1945 the administration recognized the possibility that such injury might occur by agreeing to include in all future trade agreements an escape clause permitting the modification or withdrawal of tariff reductions if increased imports resulting from such a concession caused or threatened to cause serious injury to an industry.[7] Furthermore, under prodding from Republican members of Congress, President Truman in 1947 issued an executive order establishing formal procedures for escape clause actions whereby the International Trade Commission (ITC) would advise the president whether such a modification was warranted.

The strength of the early opposition to across-the-board liberalization is further illustrated by the history of the peril point provision that directed the president to submit to the ITC a list of all articles being considered for tariff negotiations and required the commission to determine the limits to which each duty could be reduced without causing or threatening serious injury to import-competing domestic industries. This provision was introduced in the 1948 extension of the trade agreements program when both houses of Congress were controlled by the Republicans. It was repealed in 1949 when the Democrats regained control of the Congress but was then reintroduced in the 1951 extension act, even though the Democrats possessed a majority in both the House and the Senate. The escape clause was also made an explicit part of the law at that time.

These developments indicate that the U.S. trade policy commitment at the beginning of the postwar period was to a policy of liberal trade rather than to a policy of free trade. It was recognized at the outset that protection of particular industries would be permitted if these sectors would otherwise be seriously injured by increased imports. Furthermore, as indicated by the provisions of the charter for an International Trade Organization (ITO) and the General Agreement on Tariffs and Trade (GATT), the commercial policy section of the ITO, pertaining to such practices as dumping and export subsidization, the United States as well as the other major trading nations condemned so-called unfair trade.

The failure of the U.S. Congress to ratify the ITO or even to approve the GATT as an executive agreement is another indication of the early concerns of domestic political interests for import-sensitive U.S. industries.[8] Among other concerns, Congress was fearful that establishing a strong international organization to deal with trade matters would lead to the destruction of many U.S. industries as a result of increased imports. Numerous members of Congress and some of the groups they represented were also concerned about the increase in presidential power that the approval of such an organization might involve. They believed that the division of political powers among the legislative, executive, and judicial branches of government had shifted excessively in favor of the executive branch as a result of the unusual problems created by the depression and World War II and were, consequently, reluctant to extend new authority to the president, especially in an area specifically reserved for Congress under the Constitution.

1.2.2   Gaining International Support for a Liberal Regime

As previously noted, the implementation of the change from an inward-looking to an open international trading regime required the support of other countries as well as of the U.S. electorate. The hegemonic model is the major explanation put forth by political scientists to account for this support.[9] The reasoning behind this model is as follows.

An open international trading (and payments) system has elements of a public good. For example, adopting a mercantilistic viewpoint, if one country reduces its tariffs under the most-favored-nation principle, other countries benefit from the improved export opportunities this action creates even if they do not make reciprocal duty cuts themselves. Consequently, any individual country has an incentive not to reduce its duties and to hope that it will benefit from the cuts made by other nations. This "free rider" problem may well result in the failure to secure a balanced, multilateral set of duty reductions even though they would benefit all participants. As Olson (1965) and other writers on collective goods have pointed out, it is less likely that the public good will be underproduced from a social viewpoint if one member of the concerned group is very large compared to the others. The dominant member is so large that the costs to it of free rides by other members tend to be small compared to its gains. Furthermore, the large member may be able to use its power to force smaller members to practice reciprocity. Thus, proponents of the hegemonic theory of regime change point to both the dominant trading position of Great Britain in the nineteenth century and the United States in the immediate post–World War II period to account for the creation of open world trading regimes in these periods.

More specifically, in the immediate postwar period the United States was willing and able to bear most of the costs of establishing a liberal international economic order. The other major industrial countries were plagued by balance-of-payments problems, and they rationed their meager supplies of dollars to maximize their reconstruction efforts. Consequently, the tariff concessions they made in the early multilateral negotiations were not very meaningful in terms of increasing U.S. exports. U.S. negotiators were fully aware of this point, and they also offered greater tariff concessions than they received, even on the basis of the usual measures of reciprocity (see Meyer 1978, p. 138). In effect, the United States redistributed to other countries part of the economic surplus reaped from its usually favorable export opportunities to enable those countries to support the establishment of an open trading regime.

While the hegemonic model has considerable appeal, it should be noted that just as U.S. domestic support for an open trading system was qualified in several ways (e.g., no industry should be seriously injured by duty cuts), so too was the support of other countries. For example, the British insisted upon a provision in the GATT permitting the use of quantitative restrictions to safeguard a country's balance-of-payments position. Furthermore, they were successful in preventing the complete elimination of imperial preferences and in excluding customs unions and free-trade areas from the nondiscriminatory provisions of the GATT. Other illustrations of the limited support of GATT signatories for free trade are the provisions permitting preferential government purchasing policies, allowing (at the insistence of the United States) quantitative restrictions on primary products, and imposing almost no restraints on domestic subsidies.

1.3 Shifts in Domestic Support for Liberalization

The shifts in traditional party positions on trade policy that became evident in 1951, when the Democrats voted in favor of the peril point provision and the escape clause, and when a surprisingly large proportion of Senate Republicans supported the administration's earlier efforts to establish a liberal world trading system, continued over the next thirty years. They were the consequence of basic reassessments of attitudes toward liberalization versus import protection by the various economic groups making up the two major political parties. Congress also continued to restrict the president's ability to refuse to provide protection to industries judged by the ITC to be seriously injured by increased imports. At the same time, however, Congress granted significant new duty-cutting powers to the president.

1.3.1 Political Parties and Income Groups

When the Republicans gained both the presidency and control of Congress in 1952, some Republicans expected a return to traditional protectionist policies. However, President Eisenhower and his main advisors within the administration and in Congress believed—like earlier Democratic administrations—that trade liberalization was an important foreign policy instrument for strengthening the "free world" against communism. As became apparent with the issuance of the report of a commission established in 1953 by the president to study foreign trade (the Randall Report), Republican business leaders—especially those in large corporations—also had concluded that a liberal trading order was desirable from their own economic viewpoint. Thus, after a standoff period in 1953 and 1954 during which protectionist-oriented Republicans in the House blocked any further tariff cutting, the liberalization trend was renewed in 1955 when, with the help of a Democratic Congress, President Eisenhower succeeded in obtaining a further 15 percent duty-cutting authority. In 1958 he was granted an additional 20 percent tariff-reducing authority.

Just as more and more Republicans came to accept the desirability of a liberal trade policy as a general principle, more and more Democrats began to press for exceptions to this principle. In the late 1940s, the industries requesting import protection tended to be relatively small and not very influential politically. However, by the mid-1950s the politically powerful cotton textile, coal, and domestic petroleum industries, whose employees tended to vote Democratic, were asking for protection. In 1955, the Eisenhower administration, as part of its efforts to obtain the support of the Democrats for its liberalization efforts, pressured the Japanese into voluntarily restricting their exports of cotton textiles to the United States. This did not fully satisfy the textile interests, however, and in 1962 President Kennedy agreed to negotiate an international agreement permitting quantitative import restrictions on cotton textiles as part of his efforts to gain the support of Southern Democrats from textile areas for the Trade Expansion Act of 1962.[10]

The coal and oil industries succeeded in obtaining a national security clause in the 1955 trade act that permitted quantitative import restrictions if imports of a product threatened "to impair" the national security. Voluntary oil quotas were introduced on these grounds in 1958 and made mandatory in 1959.

The most significant change in the nature of the support for protectionism occurred in the late 1960s when the AFL-CIO abandoned its long-held belief in the desirability of a liberal trade policy and supported a general quota bill. Basically, the shift in labor's position was related to the rapid rise in import penetration ratios (and thus to the increase in competitive pressures) that occurred in many manufacturing sectors in the late 1960s. These included wool and man-made textiles and apparel, footwear, automobiles, steel, and electrical consumer goods, such as television sets, radios, and phonographs (see U.S. Congress, Committee on Ways and Means 1973). Workers also believed that large numbers of domestic jobs were being lost because of extensive direct investment abroad by U.S. manufacturing firms.

Still another reason for organized labor's change in view was its disappointment with the manner in which the Trade Adjustment Assistance (TAA) program under the Trade Expansion Act of 1962 had operated. The AFL-CIO had supported passage of this act in considerable part because its leaders believed that the extended unemployment benefits and retraining provisions of the TAA program would greatly ease not only any adverse employment effects of the Kennedy Round tariff cuts but also the job displacement effects of ongoing shifts in the structure of comparative advantage in the world economy. However, not a single decision providing adjustment assistance to workers was made under the program until November 1969. Congressional modifications in the administration's original proposal on adjustment assistance that were not fully appreciated by labor or the Democratic leadership produced this unfortunate effect. As a result of the program's disappointing performance, the AFL-CIO leadership became more and more disenchanted with a liberal trade policy, and in 1970 the organization testified in favor of protectionist legislation.

As would be expected, this change in organized labor's position was reflected in the trade policy votes of Democratic members of Congress. In 1970 Wilbur Mills, the chairman of the Ways and Means Committee and long a strong supporter of liberal trade policies, yielded to the pressures of many of the members of his committee and sponsored a bill establishing import quotas for textiles and footwear and requiring the president to accept affirmative import relief decisions of the ITC if certain conditions relating to the extent of import increases were fulfilled. In the House of Representatives, 137 Democrats voted in favor of the bill in contrast to only 82 against it. Republicans, on the other hand, opposed the bill 82 to 78. Further protectionist features, such as quotas on fresh, chilled, or frozen meats, were added in the Senate Finance Committee, but when the various trade provisions reached the Senate floor as an add-on to a social security benefits bill, the threat of a filibuster by a small group of Democratic senators who strongly supported liberal trade policies forced recommittal of the trade features of the bill to the Finance Committee where they died.

The shift in the positions of the two parties was again demonstrated in the voting pattern on the Trade Act of 1974, which provided an additional 60 percent duty-cutting authority to the president. In the final House vote, 121 Democrats voted against the bill whereas 112 supported it. Republicans favored the bill 160 to 19. Part of the increased Republican support can be attributed to the significant surplus of agricultural exports that began to emerge in the early 1970s. The agricultural sector has become one of the most internationally competitive parts of the American economy, and most farmers, who tend to support Republicans as members of Congress, now press for trade liberalization as a means of reducing foreign trade barriers against their own export products. At the same time, however, because the international competitive position of certain large-scale industries, such as steel and automobiles, began to deteriorate (and continued to do so in the late 1970s and early 1980s), some Republican members of Congress who rely heavily upon the support of big business began to adopt a more selective approach to liberalization.

It is doubtful, however, if the Trade Act of 1974 would have been approved had not the president made certain concessions both to organized labor and to particular industries subject to considerable import pressure. The criteria for obtaining adjustment assistance were made much easier to meet labor's objections, and the multilateral arrangement on textiles was extended to cover textile and apparel products manufactured from man-made material and wool as well as cotton. In addition, the voluntary export restraints agreed upon in 1968 by Japanese and European steel producers were extended in the early 1970s. The shift to a flexible exchange rate system in 1971 was also an important factor enabling the president to obtain new powers to reduce trade barriers.

Although the pattern of congressional voting on trade policy measures in the early 1970s shows that Republicans favored and Democrats opposed liberalization, it is probably not correct to conclude that this represents a permanent shift in party positions. The fact that there was a Republican president at the time considerably influenced the nature of the voting by Republican and Democratic members of Congress. A more accurate description of what has happened is that liberalization versus protectionism is no longer a significant party position. The vote of an individual member of Congress on trade policy is now more influenced by economic conditions in his district or state and by the pressures on him by the president (if they are both in the same party) rather than by his party affiliation. Regression analyses of the voting patterns on the Trade Expansion Act of 1962 and the Trade Act of 1974 (Baldwin 1976, 1981) indicate that party affiliation was significant in 1962 but not in 1974.

1.3.2 Congressional Restraints on the President

From the outset of the trade agreements program, many members of Congress felt that the president was too willing to reduce tariffs in import-sensitive sectors and—along with the ITC—too reluctant to raise them for import-injured industries. Furthermore, they believed that the executive branch was not sufficiently "tough" in administering U.S. laws dealing with the fairness of international trading practices. Consequently, Congress frequently took the occasion of the program's renewal to introduce provisions designed to force the president and the ITC to comply more closely with these congressional views. Much of the pressure for these provisions came from import-sensitive domestic industries and labor groups. However, part of the readiness on the part of members of Congress to limit presidential authority on trade policy matters seemed to stem from a belief that Congress had given the president too much of its constitutional responsibility "to regulate commerce with foreign nations" and to levy import duties.

Restricting the power of the president by introducing the peril point provision and a formal escape clause provision in 1951 has already been mentioned. The peril point provision was eliminated in the Trade Expansion Act of 1962, but the ITC was still charged with making a judgment "as to the probable economic effect of modifications of duties." More important, at congressional insistence, the chairmanship of the interagency committee established to recommend tariff cuts to the president was shifted from the State Department (long regarded by Congress as being insufficiently sensitive to the import-injury problems of U.S. industry) to a new agency, the Office of the United States Trade Representative (USTR), which reports directly to the president.[11] The requirement of the 1974 law that an elaborate private advisory system be established has somewhat further restricted the degree of independence that the president has in selecting items on which cuts are to be made and in determining the depth of those cuts. The creation and subsequent strengthening of congressional delegations to trade meetings and nego-ʹ tiations under the 1962 and 1974 laws have had the same effect. Since 1954 the president has also been specifically directed not to decrease duties on any article if he finds that doing so would threaten to impair the national security. Furthermore, in granting the president the authority in 1974 to permit duty-free imports from developing countries, Congress specifically excluded certain articles, such as watches and footwear, from preferential tariff treatment.

Congress first put pressure on the president to accept affirmative recommendations of the ITC on escape clause cases when this provision was introduced into law in 1951 by requiring the president to submit an explanatory report to Congress if these recommendations were rejected. Since this seemed to have little effect on the president, Congress included a provision in the 1958 renewal act that enabled the president's disapproval of any affirmative ITC finding to be overridden by means of a two-thirds vote of both the House and Senate. This was eased in 1962 to a majority of the authorized membership of both houses and then in 1974 to only a majority of members present and voting.[12]

Congress has also included numerous provisions in the trade laws passed since the end of World War II aimed at increasing the proportion of affirmative import-relief decisions on the part of the ITC. The most obvious way to accomplish this has been to change the criteria for granting increases in protection when an industry is threatened with or is actually being seriously injured by increased imports. For example, the Trade Agreements Extension Act of 1955 narrowed the definition of an industry and required an affirmative decision as long as increased imports contributed "substantially" toward causing serious injury. The 1962 trade act sharply reversed this move toward easier injury criteria as Congress apparently mistakenly believed that the new Trade Adjustment Assistance program would ease the pressures for import protection, but in 1974 the language was again changed to resemble closely what it had been in the 1955 law. Moreover, the requirement that the increased imports be related to a previously granted tariff concession was eliminated.

Less obvious ways that Congress used in trying to make the ITC more responsive to its views were utilizing its confirmation powers to try to ensure that commission members were sympathetic to its views and changing certain administrative arrangements relating to the agency. Beginning in the late 1960s, the chairman of the Senate Finance Committee, Senator Russell Long, and his committee colleagues began to argue forcefully that "it is to the Congress, not the Executive, that the Tariff Commission is expected to be responsive,"[13] and they began to be very critical of nominees whose professional background was largely in the executive branch of the federal government. In the period between 1953 and 1967, five of the thirteen commissioners appointed had extensive employment experience in the executive branch and another two in the commission itself. However, between 1968 and 1980, none of the twelve newly appointed commissioners had either of these backgrounds. Instead, seven of the approved nominees had significant congressional experience, either as a member of Congress (one person) or as congressional staffers. In a further effort to weaken the influence of the president over the commission, Congress in 1974 removed all controls of the executive branch over the commission's budget and eliminated the power of the president to appoint the chairperson of the commission. This latter change was modified in 1977, but the president still cannot appoint either of his two most recent appointees as chairperson.

Similar steps were taken by Congress to try to ensure a stricter enforcement of U.S. trade laws relating to unfair foreign practices. For example, many members of Congress long felt that the Treasury Department was too lax in administering U.S. antidumping and countervailing duty legislation. One step designed to change this was to transfer in 1954 the determination of injury (but not the determination of dumping) from the Treasury Department to the ITC. Furthermore, under pressure from Congress, the president in 1980 transferred the authority to determine both dumping and subsidization from the Treasury to the Commerce Department—an agency that Congress believed would more closely carry out its intent in these areas. The 1974 change in the manner of administering U.S. legislation pertaining to unfair import practices (sec. 337 of the Tariff Act of 1930) is another illustration of the decline in presidential authority over trade matters. Prior to 1974 the ITC conducted the investigations into alleged violations of this law and then transmitted its findings to the president. If the President was satisfied that unfair import methods had been established, he could ban the importation of the relevant products. However, in 1974 Congress gave the ITC the authority to ban imports of the affected products or to issue a cease and desist order to the person practicing the violation. The only power remaining with the president under this law is his ability to set aside the actions of the ITC within sixty days "for policy reasons."

Perhaps the most significant reduction in the president's authority over trade policy concerns his ability to negotiate agreements with other countries covering nontariff measures. When Congress directed the president to seek such agreements under the Trade Act of 1974, it stipulated—unlike it has done with tariffs—that any agreements must be approved by a majority vote in both the House and Senate. This provision was extended in the Trade Agreements Act of 1979 and both gives Congress much greater control over the nature of any agreement and increases its control over the pattern of tariff cuts undertaken by the president in a multilateral trade negotiation, since the tariff and nontariff concessions made by the participants are closely linked.

1.4 The Increasing Importance of Nontariff Trade-Distorting Measures

As the reduction in tariffs by the industrial countries continued during the 1950s and 1960s, greater attention began to be given to nontariff trade-distorting measures, not only because they became more obvious as tariff rates declined, but also because there seemed to be a trend toward their greater use. During the 1960s, the extension in the use of quantitative restrictions from primary product sectors, such as agriculture and petroleum, to manufacturing activities, such as cotton textiles and steel; the greater utilization of various export-rebate and import-deposit schemes to improve a country's balance-of-payments position; and the introduction of many new domestic subsidies aimed at stimulating growth in depressed areas, easing structural adjustments, and promoting high-technology industries, all served to direct attention to the fact that the benefits of tariff liberalization could be offset by nontariff trade barriers (NTBs).

As the above illustrations indicate, the increased use of NTBs, particularly beginning in the 1960s, stemmed both from the efforts of particular sectors to secure protection or special export assistance through these measures and from the concerns of governments with balance-of-payments problems and with various social and economic policy objectives. In the case of the United States, for example, the sharp increase in the lending and guaranteeing authorizations of the Export-Import Bank in the late 1960s and early 1970s and the approval of the Domestic International Sales Corporation (DISC) in 1971 represented efforts to increase the country's exports within the constraints of the then fixed exchange rate system. While the United States also followed other industrial nations during the 1960s in greatly expanding domestic programs directed at improving social and economic conditions for disadvantaged income groups and depressed sectors, most American programs had little direct or indirect effect on the pattern of trade. Such did not appear to be the case in a number of other industrial countries, however. Substantial financial assistance by other governments to specific industries and particular economic activities appeared to public and private officials in the United States to represent a serious threat to U.S. trade competitiveness and to the liberal international order in general. Consequently, widespread support began to develop for a new GATT-sponsored effort to provide more detailed NTB codes that would reduce the injurious effects on others of such measures as a country's domestic subsidies or its rules pertaining to product standards.

U.S. officials did possess the authority to undertake negotiations on NTBs during the Kennedy Round of trade negotiations, and a GATT committee was established to deal with this subject. Agreement on an antidumping code was reached, as well as on eliminating a number of particular nontariff measures, such as the American selling price (ASP) system of customs valuation and European discriminatory road-use taxes. However, reaching agreement on tariff issues proved to be so difficult and time-consuming that negotiations in the nontariff field were not very extensive. Moreover, Congress felt that the president had exceeded his authority by trying to implement the new antidumping code as an executive agreement rather than submitting it to Congress for approval and therefore passed a law directing the ITC to ignore the new code when making its injury determinations. Congress also rejected the proposal to eliminate ASP.

In the markup sessions on the Trade Act of 1974, key members of the Senate were adamant about the necessity of submitting international agreements reached on nontariff matters to Congress for final approval, and, as noted earlier, such a requirement was included in the act. However, once this matter was settled, Congress fully supported the efforts of the president to negotiate new NTB codes in the Tokyo Round, and the set of codes eventually agreed upon was approved without difficulty by the Congress.

At the same time efforts were undertaken to negotiate new agreements that would mitigate the adverse effects of foreign NTBs. U.S. producers were pressuring government officials for stricter enforcement of existing U.S. "fair trade" legislation, such as the antidumping and countervailing laws, and were seeking import protection under these laws to a greater extent than in the past.[14] Furthermore, domestic producers were demanding the greater use of quantitative restrictions (as compared with import duties) as the means of protecting their industries against injurious import increases.

One factor accounting for the greater number of less-than-fair-value cases has been the difficulty of obtaining protection through the traditional provisions pertaining to injury caused by import competition. Despite the 1974 easing of the criteria for determining whether import relief should be granted, only forty-seven cases were decided by the ITC between 1975 and 1982, and in all but twenty-four of these a negative decision was reached. Furthermore, the president rejected import protection in all but ten of the twenty-four cases. The likelihood that the routine acceptance of affirmative ITC decisions would be interpreted by foreign governments as an abandonment of the postwar international economic leadership role on the part of the United States appears to have made the president reluctant to accept more than a relatively small proportion of these decisions. Even the Congress has been hesitant on similar grounds to weaken the import-relief criteria much beyond what they were in the 1950s.

Providing protection to offset alleged unfair trade practices is much less likely to be interpreted as representing a basic shift in policy, either by other governments or domestic interests supporting a liberal trading order. Thus, within reasonable bounds a president can support efforts to achieve "fair trade" through measures that protect domestic producers while still being regarded as a proponent of liberal trade policies.

Not only has a better understanding of this point led domestic industries to utilize U.S. fair trade legislation more extensively in seeking import protection, but legislative and administrative changes relating to these laws have facilitated this shift. Congress, though diluting the president's power to reduce trade barriers and to set aside ITC decisions, has at the same time given him new authority to limit imports on fairness grounds. For example, the 1922 and 1930 tariff acts granted the president the authority to impose new or additional duties on imports or even to exclude imports from countries that impose unreasonable regulations on U.S. products or discriminate against U.S. commerce. The 1962 Trade Act further directs the president to take all appropriate and feasible steps to eliminate "unjustifiable" foreign import restrictions (including the imposition of duties and other import restrictions) and to suspend or withdraw previously granted concessions where other countries maintain trade restrictions that "substantially burden" U.S. commerce, engage in discriminating acts, or maintain unreasonable import restrictions. The Trade Act of 1974 restates these provisions and in section 301 also gives the president the authority to take similar actions in response to "subsidies (or other incentives having the effect of subsidies) on its [a foreign country's] exports . . . to the United States or to other foreign markets which have the effect of substantially reducing sales of the competitive United States product or products in the United States or in foreign markets" and "unjustifiable or unreasonable restrictions on access to supplies of food, raw materials, or manufactured or semimanufactured products which burden or restrict United States commerce." However, Congress could veto any actions taken by the president. In amending this provision, the 1979 Trade Act stressed the president's responsibility for enforcing U.S. rights under any trade agreement and simplified the list of foreign practices against which he is directed to take action. Interestingly, this act also eliminated the authority of Congress to nullify presidential actions taken under this provision by a majority vote of both houses within ninety days.

The extension of the definition of dumping in the Trade Act of 1974 to cover not only sales abroad at lower prices than charged at home but to include sales of substantial quantities at below cost over an extended period (even if domestic and foreign prices are the same) is another legislative change that encouraged the use of fair trade legislation to gain protection. Under this provision, the steel industry filed dumping charges in 1977 covering nearly $1 billion of steel imports from Japan, all the major European producers, and India. However, as Finger, Hall, and Nelson (1982) point out, cases of this magnitude in key sectors attract so much political opposition (both domestic and foreign) that they cannot be disposed of at a technical, bureaucratic level and consequently spill over into the political route for gaining import protection. In this instance, the domestic industry was successful in convincing President Carter that its claims were justified, and the so-called Trigger Price Mechanism for steel evolved as an alternative to pursuing the antidumping charges to the final stage.

A similar political solution was reached in 1982 when the steel industry filed charges that European steel producers were receiving extensive subsidies and therefore should be subject to countervailing duties. The possibility of countervailing duties had such significant economic and political implications that the governments of the parties involved did not wish the matter to be settled on technical grounds and sought a solution at the political level. Eventually the Europeans agreed to quantitative export limits on a wide range of steel products to the United States.

Other important sectors that have been protected in recent years by nontariff barriers are the footwear, television, and auto industries. Voluntary export restraints were negotiated by the president in the first two sectors after affirmative injury findings by the ITC. However, the ITC rejected the auto industry's petition for import relief. Nevertheless, the industry was successful in persuading the administration of the need for import controls, and the Japanese eventually agreed to restrict their sales of cars to the United States.

The increased use of nontariff trade-distorting measures obviously has weakened the liberal international trading regime, not simply because they represent a move toward protectionism, but because many of them have been applied in a discriminatory manner and are negotiated outside of the GATT framework. Some of the political decisions reached at the presidential level have also occurred without the opportunity for all interested parties to be heard, as would be the case if a technical route such as an import-injury petition before the ITC were being followed, or even if a political route at the congressional level were being pursued.

Several of the most important nontariff measures utilized by the U.S. government to restrain imports or promote exports are analyzed in greater detail in other chapters of this volume. Their purpose is not only to explain more fully how these measures operate but also to appraise their effects on trade and economic welfare.

1.5 Declining U.S. Hegemony and the Liberal International Economic Order

The hegemonic model of regime change predicts openness in world trading arrangements when a hegemonic state is in its ascendancy and a shift toward a closed system as this nation declines in power and is not replaced by another dominant state. Although this theory is consistent with the early part of the postwar period, there is general agreement (Krasner 1976; Goldstein 1981; and Lipson 1982) that the model does not perform very well as an explanation of regime change for more recent years.

Most writers (e.g., Whitman 1975; Kindleberger 1981) date the decline in America as beginning in the 1960s. The decline in relative economic power is evident, for example, from the fact that the U.S. share of merchandise exports of the fifteen largest industrial countries fell from 25.2 percent in 1960 to 20.5 percent in 1970, and then to 18.3 percent in 1979.[15] The percentages for exports of manufactures for the same years are 22.8, 18.4, and 15.5. The U.S. share of the GNP of these countries was 57.1 percent in 1960, 50.2 percent in 1970, and only 38.1 percent in 1979. It became quite clear during the long and difficult Kennedy Round negotiations concerning the appropriate tariff-cutting rule to adopt that other industrial countries, especially the European Community, were no longer prepared to continue to accept the U.S. leadership role in a routine manner.[16] As the reduction in cold war tensions during the 1970s reduced the perceived need for U.S. military protection against the Soviet Union, the decline in American economic and political influence became even more evident.

Despite a shift in power from a situation where one country dominated the economic scene to one where there are now three major economic blocs (the United States, the European Community, and Japan), most observers agree that the trade and payments regime continues to be essentially an open and liberal one. As table 1.1 shows, the tariff cuts made in the 1960s and 1970s were actually much deeper than those made in the 1940s and 1950s. Furthermore, the new nontariff codes negotiated during the Tokyo Round, though often very general in their wording, do represent a significant accomplishment in providing the basis for preventing nontariff measures from undermining the liberalization benefits from the postwar tariff cuts. While the GATT ministerial meeting in November 1982 again demonstrated the inability of the United States to dominate international deliberations on trade policy issues, it did reconfirm the continued commitment of the major industrial nations to a liberal international economic order. The increased use of nontariff trade-distorting measures described in the last section represents derogation from this order, but the trading regime still remains essentially an open one.

A consideration of either the economic theory of market behavior or the production of collective goods suggests that the failure of the hegemonic model to predict the continuation of an open system should not be surprising. A single firm that dominates a particular market is likely to stabilize the price of the product at a monopolistic level while still tolerating some price cutting by the smaller firms making up the rest of the industry. However, oligopolistic market theory suggests that the same result is likely if two or three large firms dominate an industry. Similarly, as Olson (1965) pointed out, the free-rider problem associated with collective action by an industry can be overcome if a small number of firms (as well as just one firm) produce a significant share of the industry's output. Thus, the continued support for a stable, open trading order as the distribution of power changed from an almost monopolistic situation to an oligopolistic one is quite consistent with market behavior theory.

The shift from a hegemonic position to one in which the country shares its previous economic and political power with a small number of other nations is, however, likely to alter the country's international behavior somewhat, just as the change in the status of a firm from a monopolist to an oligopolist is likely to change the firm's market behavior. In the U.S. case, the nature of the change has been to initiate trade negotiations mainly to achieve economic benefits for the country rather than to further general U.S. foreign policy and national security goals.[17] This shift in emphasis first became apparent in the Dillon and Kennedy Rounds of negotiations when government leaders stressed to the public the economic gains that would be achieved by lowering the European Community's tariff level and thereby reducing the trade diversion resulting from the formation of this customs union. The usual arguments about the need to strengthen the free world as a means of meeting the threat of communist expansion were also presented, but with less vigor than in the past.

Support for a multilateral trade negotiation based on the view that it was in the economic interests of the United States to participate in such a negotiation was even more evident in the Tokyo Round. In early 1973 President Nixon sent a generally worded bill to Congress that provided the president with the authority to modify tariffs as he thought appropriate and to conclude agreements with other nations on nontariff issues. Congress took the opportunity of a proposed negotiation to reshape the bill so that it dealt with many of its concerns about the nature of the international trading system. In doing so, it soon became apparent that business, labor, and agricultural interests were very fearful that the increasing use of nontariff measures by other countries would significantly curtail U.S. export opportunities and lead to injurious increases in imports. Congress reacted in part by strengthening U.S. fair trade legislation, but its main response was to give the president detailed directions about negotiating new international codes aimed at reduced nontariff trade-distorting measures. In other words, both the Congress and the president agreed that strengthening the liberal international economic order was in the economic interests of the United States, quite aside from its political and national security implications.

As might be expected, the less altruistic behavior on the part of the United States in its international economic relations has resulted in an increased number of trade disputes between the United States and other countries.[18] Many who support a liberal trading order are concerned that these disputes will become so numerous and difficult to solve that the system will collapse with each of the major trading powers pursuing inward-looking trade policies. This is, of course, a possibility. However, most of the trading frictions do not arise because of disagreements on the principles involved in the commitment to an open trading system but on matters of interpretation within these principles. For example, as pointed out earlier, the key parties in the system have always agreed that it was proper to shield an industry from injurious increases in imports. Consequently, when the United States protects the auto and steel industries from import competition or the Europeans subsidize industries as a means of retaining their domestic market shares, this is not regarded by most countries as a departure from the basic liberal trading rules. Disagreements sometimes arise, however, over whether a country is going beyond the intent of the rules and engaging in what in effect are beggar-thy-neighbor policies. The settlement of major disputes at a high political level and the continuing efforts to improve the GATT dispute-settlement mechanism are a recognition by the major trading nations of the damage to the system that could occur from such disagreements.

Krasner (1976) argues in his amendment to the hegemonic model that the abandonment of the commitment to a liberal trading order on the part of the United States (or the other major trading nations) is likely to occur only when some major external crisis forces policy leaders to pursue a dramatic new policy initiative that they believe to be in their country's interests. However, it may be that the existing power-sharing arrangement between the United States, the European Community, and Japan reduces the likelihood of this outcome compared to the case of a declining hegemony in the midst of many smaller states. In this latter situation, the dominant power is tempted in a crisis to take advantage of its monopoly power over the terms of trade. But when power is shared, the recognition both that a country's market power is quite limited and that retaliation is likely to be swift and significant tends to discourage such adventurism. Of greater concern than the possibility of a dramatic abandonment of the liberal international economic order is the likelihood of a continuing gradual erosion in the openness of international trade because of the inability of the major industrial powers to agree on international measures that take into account the economic interrelationships between trade policies and policies in the exchange rate, monetary, fiscal, and social areas.

Notes

1. If the effects of structural shifts in trade and of inflation on specific duties are included along with the negotiated tariff cuts, the average tariff on dutiable imports drops from a 1931 level of 53 percent to about 5 percent after completion of the Tokyo Round cuts.

2. Gardner (1980, p. 9) documents this point and describes the planning activities of the administration for the postwar period.

3. Statement by President Roosevelt to Congress on 26 March 1945.

4. Hull (1948, vol. 1, p. 81) and Dobson (1976, pp. 56–66) describe the traditional Democratic and Republican positions on trade policy.

5. See Wilkinson (1960, chaps. 1 and 5) for an elaboration of this point as well as a discussion of the subsequent postwar shift in emphasis toward foreign policy considerations.

6. Authors who developed this explanation for the postwar establishment of a liberal international economic order under U.S. leadership include Kindleberger (1973, 1981), Gilpin (1975), and Krasner (1976).

7. See Leddy and Norwood (1963) for a detailed discussion of the escape clause as well as the peril point provisions.

8. Diebold (1952) analyzes the reasons why the ITO failed to gain U.S. support.

9. See Lipson (1982) for a succinct statement and analysis of the hegemonic model.

10. For a description of the protectionist pressures from the cotton textile industry as well as the oil and coal industries during the 1950s and early 1960s, see Bauer, Pool, and Dexter (1963, chap. 25).

11. In response to complaints from Congress and the private sector concerning the lack of a unified U.S. trade policy strategy, President Reagan in the spring of 1983 proposed merging USTR and parts of the Commerce Department into a new Department of International Trade and Industry.

12. The June 1983 Supreme Court decision declaring the congressional veto to be unconstitutional presumably means that this provision will no longer apply.

13. Hearings before the Senate Committee on Finance, 23 June 1971. In these hearings, Senator Long explained the actions of the committee during the late 1960s on various presidential nominees to the commission.

14. Between 1955 and 1972, the average number of antidumping reports issued by the ITC averaged less than six per year, whereas this rate increased to thirteen between 1974 and 1979. Similarly, the number of countervailing duty investigations completed by the ITC between 1962 and 1973 was twelve, while the number rose to thirty-seven between 1974 and the end of 1978.

15. These and the following figures are from the Office of Foreign Economic Research, U.S. Department of Labor (1980, chap. 3).

16. This was due in part to the fact that the United States was no longer willing to provide the necessary compensation to these other countries to gain their acceptance of U.S. proposals.

17. Krasner (1979) also makes this point.
18. Cooper (1973) discusses the increase in trade disputes after the mid-1960s and the implications for foreign policy.

References

Baldwin, R. E. 1958. The commodity composition of trade: Selected industrial countries, 1900–1954. *Review of Economics and Statistics* 40:50–68, supplement.

——. 1976. The political economy of postwar U.S. trade policy. *The Bulletin* 1976:4.

——. 1981. The political economy of U.S. import policy. Unpublished manuscript.

Bale, M. D. 1973. Adjustment to free trade: An analysis of the adjustment assistance provisions of the Trade Expansion Act of 1962. Ph.D. thesis, University of Wisconsin, and Report no. DLMA 91-55-73-05-1 of the National Technical Information Service, Springfield, Virginia.

Bauer, R. A., J. Pool, and L. Dexter. 1963. *American business and public policy: The politics of foreign trade.* Chicago: Aldine-Atherton, Inc.

Caves, R. E. 1976. Economic models of political choice: Canada's tariff structure. *Canadian Journal of Economics* 9:278–300.

Cooper, R. N. 1973. Trade policy is foreign policy. *Foreign Policy* 9:18–37.

Diebold, W., Jr. 1952. *The end of the I.T.O.* Essays in International Finance, no. 16. Princeton: Princeton University.

Dobson, J. M. 1976. *Two centuries of tariffs: The background and emergence of the U.S. International Trade Commission.* Washington, D.C.: U.S. International Trade Commission.

Finger, J. M., H. K. Hall, and D. R. Nelson. 1982. The political economy of administered protection. *American Economic Review* 72:452–66.

Gardner, R. N. 1980. *Sterling-dollar diplomacy in current perspective.* New York: Columbia University Press.

Gilpin, R. 1975. *U.S. power and the multinational corporation: The political economy of foreign direct investment.* New York: Basic Books.

Goldstein, J. L. 1981. The state, industrial interests and foreign economic policy: American commercial policy in the postwar period. Paper prepared for the National Science Foundation Conference on the Politics and Economics of Trade Policy, Minneapolis, 29–31 October 1981.

Hull, C. 1948. *The memoirs of Cordell Hull.* 2 volumes. New York: Macmillan.

Kindleberger, C. P. 1973. *The world depression, 1929–1939.* Berkeley: University of California Press.

———. 1981. Dominance and leadership in the international economy: Exploitation, public goods and free rides. *International Studies Quarterly* 25:242–54.

Krasner, S. D. 1976. State power and the structure of international trade. *World Politics* 28:317–47.

———. 1979. The Tokyo Round: Particularistic interests and prospects for stability in the global trading system. *International Studies Quarterly* 23:317–47.

Leddy, J. M., and J. Norwood. 1963. The escape clause and peril points under the trade agreements program. In *Studies in United States commercial policy*, ed. W. B. Kelley, Jr. Chapel Hill: University of North Carolina Press.

Lipson, C. 1982. The transformation of trade: The sources and effects of regime changes. *International Organization* 36:417–55.

Meyer, F. V. 1978. *International trade policy*. New York: St. Martin's.

Olson, M. 1965. *The logic of collective action*. Cambridge, Mass.: Harvard University Press.

U.S. Congress. House. Committee on Ways and Means, prepared by the staff of the U.S. Tariff Commission. 1973. *Comparison of ratios of imports to apparent consumption, 1968–72*. Washington, D.C.: GPO.

U.S. Congress. Senate Committee on Finance. Hearings on the nominations of Will E. Leonard, Jr., of Louisiana, and Herschel D. Newsom, of Indiana, to be members of the U.S. Tariff Commission, Ninetieth Congress, Second Session. Washington, D.C.: GPO.

U.S. Department of Labor, Office of Foreign Economic Research. 1980. *Report to the president on U.S. competitiveness*. Washington, D.C.: GPO.

Whitman, M. 1975. The decline in American hegemony. *Foreign Policy* 20:138–60.

Wilkinson, J. R. 1960. *Politics and trade policy*. Washington, D.C.: Public Affairs Press.

Comment   Richard N. Cooper

Robert Baldwin has given us a masterly summary of the evolution of postwar U.S. trade policy and the forces that have shaped it. I have little quarrel with what he has said. I can perhaps contribute more by making some general observations on trade policy, designed to complement and extend Baldwin's paper.

Liberal trade policy is a triumph of pure reason over common sense. Everyone who is not an economist thinks he knows that imports reduce

Richard N. Cooper is professor of economics at Harvard University.

profits and limit jobs. This view is even attributed, perhaps apocryphally, to President Abraham Lincoln. It is conceded that noncompeting products such as coffee and bananas increase consumer variety, and that competing products may lower prices. But in a work-oriented society based on the Protestant work ethic, jobs are more important than consumption. In any case, what good are lower prices if people have no income to spend?

Much trade is in the form of inputs into the industrial process, such as steel which goes into the production of automobiles and household appliances, and industrial buyers might be expected to press actively for lower tariffs on these inputs. To some extent they do, as is reflected in the escalation of tariffs by stage of processing. But this pressure for lower tariffs on industrial materials is inhibited by the business ethic, which is not to criticize or contradict other businessmen openly. Representatives of business often are extraordinarily quiet on issues of public policy that do not affect them visibly. Opposition takes the form of nonsupport.

Economists know that all this represents partial equilibrium thinking, and that in a general equilibrium framework imports need not reduce profits or eliminate jobs in the absence of special features, such as downwardly rigid factor prices. But the world of ordinary perception is a partial equilibrium world. General equilibrium is an intellectual construct imposed on the normal senses and comprehension of how things actually work.

Despite this, as Baldwin shows, we have had a major move toward more liberal trade over the past half century. Why is this so? It partly represents the strength of ideas over perception. Men of affairs have a vague recollection of learning in college that international trade is a good thing, at least in the long run. The details are forgotten, but the argument seemed compelling at the time and is not easily abandoned.

But the move toward liberal trade is mainly the result of history and of foreign policy. High tariffs are associated with the Great Depression of the 1930s, and indeed the Hawley-Smoot tariffs were a major contributing factor to the depression. Furthermore, the then secretary of state, Cordell Hull, thought that tariffs, and especially tariff discrimination, led to war. He worked single-mindedly to build a postwar system of low, nondiscriminatory tariffs.

This political motivation for liberal trade was reinforced by the necessity to rebuild Europe following World War II, a task which, it was early realized, could best be accomplished on a multilateral basis rather than by each nation acting on its own. Thus trade liberalization became a major feature of postwar foreign economic policy both within Europe and between the United States and Europe, and a major plank of overall foreign policy.

Congress has periodically objected to the dominance of foreign policy considerations with respect to trade policy. In the early 1960s it insisted that negotiations on tariffs be removed from the Department of State and moved to a newly created special trade representative in the executive office of the president. More recently, we have seen strong congressional sentiment for creating a new Department of International Trade and Industry, on the model of Japan's Ministry of International Trade and Industry (MITI), to absorb the function of trade negotiations and give them a more clearly commercial orientation. But from a presidential perspective, an ultimate unity exists between national security and foreign economic policy because our principal allies are so heavily dependent on foreign trade for their economic well-being, and hence for their security. Maintenance of a liberal trade policy by the United States *is* national security policy in the broadest sense.

The Roosevelt administration during the Great Depression was able to begin the process of trade liberalization by introducing the notion of reciprocity: the reduction of U.S. import tariffs was necessary to persuade foreigners to reduce their import tariffs, and that in turn was necessary to stimulate U.S. exports, which in turn created jobs. Without reciprocity, trade liberalization almost certainly could not have occurred, despite the persistent argument by well-trained economists that even unilateral trade liberalization is good for the country undertaking it. Economists have introduced two qualifications to this argument for unilateral tariff reduction. The first concerns the terms of trade; if a country reduces its tariffs unilaterally, the resulting worsening of its own terms of trade may more than offset the efficiency gains resulting from the tariff reduction. Reciprocal tariff reductions could avoid this worsening of the terms of trade. (The argument in any case does not apply to a country so small that it cannot influence its terms of trade.) The second qualification concerns adjustment costs. A country that unilaterally reduces its tariffs may worsen its balance of payments and have to take demand-deflating corrective action to deal with it. Thus a cost is imposed on the country that unilaterally reduces its tariffs. Again, reciprocal reductions in tariffs can avoid this temporary deterioration in the balance of payments, or at least reduce it to a second-order effect.

But if we are realistic observers of the political scene, we economists must recognize that neither of these arguments were responsible for the success of reciprocity. Rather, the motivation was primarily mercantilistic. The public was persuaded that tariff reductions would increase exports at least as much as competitive imports, and this in turn would create profits and employment.

The advocates of liberal trade have managed to secure the semantic high ground in the debate. No one wants to be a "protectionist" these days. It is a bad word. (It was not always so. In the 1920s and even in the late 1940s some politicians were avowedly protectionists.) This is perhaps one favorable consequence of years of teaching results that were complex to absorb in detail, but whose general flavor got through. As a result, those who favor protectionist policies must dress in the semantic clothing of liberal traders. They argue for "fair trade," and now especially they are pushing for true "reciprocity" in trading relationships, a phrase that has been associated for the last fifty years with the liberalization of trade, not with protectionism. But many draft pieces of legislation and other proposals that are dressed in the guise of innocuous terms or even terms with favorable connotations are protectionist underneath. Economists are remiss by not looking at these proposals in detail and by leaving the field to lawyers. Perhaps the current proposals for protectionist action can be beaten back one by one, each defeated on the dubiousness of its merits.

But in trade policy, as in other areas of life, the best defense is to take the offensive. Protectionist trade legislation is unlikely to be enacted if the United States is actively engaged in trade negotiations with other countries, or even in preparing for such negotiations. Liberal trade policy has been likened to a bicycle: one must continue to move forward to avoid falling over. The partial equilibrium perceptions will dominate policy unless the executive branch can stay in motion, keeping the foreign policy aspects of trade policy as well as the nation's economic interests in the forefront. This general wisdom does not automatically dictate the next policy moves, however, since tariff reductions have already proceeded very far. The next logical step in that direction would be free trade in industrial products. U.S. Trade Representative Brock's emphasis on liberalization of trade in services can be interpreted as a move to take the offensive. The same can be true of the current administration's initiatives in agriculture, although that is treacherous territory and could lead to a morass rather than to clear forward movement.

The liberal trading system is in peril at present (late 1982). High unemployment and a strong dollar, leading to a large trade deficit, both contribute to the strong protectionist pressures. Both are consequences of the tight monetary policy that was introduced to fight inflation. Paradoxically, the major casualty in this fight against inflation may be the liberal trading system—a possibility that did not enter the calculations either of monetarists or of central bankers.

Comment   Alfred Reifman

Baldwin's paper on the changing nature of U.S. trade policy is an excellent and thoughtful appraisal. However, despite the well-advertised de-

Alfred Reifman is Senior Specialist in International Economics at the Congressional Research Service, Library of Congress, Washington, D.C.

cline in U.S. hegemony, the United States remains the single most important economy in the world and the only country that can take a constructive initiative:
- The European Community is not a country, though it has some of the attributes of one. Despite the Treaty of Rome, important economic decisions require unanimity. This obviously is a brake on its potential leadership role.
- Japan ought to be a leader in world economic affairs since it has a large and persistent balance-of-payments surplus and a much higher rate of economic growth than the other industrial countries. But it shows no signs of moving to the head of the parade.
- In short, the United States must continue to lead, though it will need to elicit the cooperation of the European Community and Japan.

The reciprocity legislation in the Congress is in part an attempt to get the attention of Japan and the European Community on trade questions and not necessarily a retreat to protectionism.

As today's issues in international trade move from measures taken at the border (tariffs and quota restrictions) to domestic policies reflecting the increased role of government in the economy (industrial policy, state-owned enterprises, domestic subsidies, regulation of industry, etc.), the universal rules of GATT (nondiscrimination and reduced barriers at the border) become inapplicable or, if not, more difficult to apply. This, as much as the decline in U.S. hegemony, raises serious problems for GATT.

Baldwin notes that U.S. trade policy is shifting its objective from broad political and security goals to economic or mercantilist ones. This is certainly correct. But he does not ask how much of the shift is temporary because of (a) slow growth, (b) the stage of the business cycle, (c) the overvalued exchange rate, and (d) the growth of interdependence.

The economic profession can be credited for making liberal trade the basic objective of the U.S. bureaucracy in both Republican and Democratic administrations and making protectionism the deviant behavior.

Finally, the appointment of Cordell Hull as FDR's secretary of state was a lucky accident. Hull, a Southerner, firmly believed that free trade was good economics—a Southern tradition—and important for peace. Thus the reciprocal trade program became his prime interest over the other subjects a secretary of state normally has on the top of his agenda.

Baldwin –

usual surveys US

to prove pro per int public

int small physical process

items as regards on free trade

(items & protec, regret = 116) — to pl where

int party int small processes of voting

just on the legisla P.15

II Industry-Specific Nontariff Trade Barriers

Introduction

This section analyzes three nontariff measures aimed at easing the competitive problems of particular U.S. industries. They are the agreement by the Japanese to limit their exports of automobiles to the United States, the dumping problems of the U.S. steel industry and the resulting Trigger Price Mechanism for steel imports, and the Multifiber Arrangement for quantitative import restrictions covering textile and apparel products.

Feenstra focuses on the quality, employment, and welfare effects of the Japanese voluntary export restraint agreement (VER) in automobiles. Using hedonic regressions to determine changes in the quality-adjusted prices of U.S. and Japanese cars, he concludes that two-thirds of the inflation-adjusted 8.4 percent rise in the price of imported cars in the two years following the VER is due to quality improvements and one-third to an increase in the quality-adjusted price of Japanese cars. Consequently, there was about a 3 percent rise in price for which consumers were not compensated by improved quality. Under the assumption that a reduction of (say) $1 million spent on Japanese imports due to a price change leads to an extra $1 million spent on American cars, Feenstra then estimates that the increased employment resulting from the VER amounted only to between 5,000 and 22,000 workers. As he notes, these figures compare with indefinite layoffs in the auto industry of over 200,000 workers in early 1982.

Eichengreen and van der Ven concentrate on the U.S. steel industry in analyzing dumping from both a theoretical and empirical point of view. Using the Trigger Price Mechanism (TPM) introduced by the U.S. government in 1978 as an illustration, they show how trade policies often evolve that make good sense politically but not economically. They then develop a model of dumping that emphasizes the existence of imperfect competition in both domestic and foreign markets and utilize it to estimate the effects of the TPM in 1979. In raising the price of imported steel by, in effect, establishing a minimum import price, the TPM increased the income of U.S. steel producers but reduced the economic welfare of consumers. However, as Eichengreen and van der Ven demonstrate, it is possible for total welfare to increase as a result of the TPM because of the initial distortion associated with imperfectly competitive domestic markets. Their welfare estimates vary from a net gain of $6 billion to a net loss of $.03 billion. Of course, as they note, if antidumping policies can be welfare improving because of distortions in domestic markets, first-best policies aimed at promoting competition can raise welfare even more.

Pelzman traces the long and complicated history of international regulation of textile and apparel imports and indicates how the structure of the U.S. textile industry has changed since World War II. He then tries to ascertain empirically whether the Multifiber Arrangement (MFA) had a positive effect on the industry's profit rates. Using the percentage of imports subject to quantitative restrictions to proxy for the MFA and controlling for such factors as the degree of market concentration, the growth of domestic demand, and the extent of import penetration, Pelzman finds evidence that the MFA did indeed appear to raise profit rates by limiting domestic competition.

2 Voluntary Export Restraint in U.S. Autos, 1980–81: Quality, Employment, and Welfare Effects

Robert C. Feenstra

2.1 Introduction

On 1 May 1981 the Japanese agreed to limit their exports of automobiles to the U.S. market. Since the voluntary export restraint (VER) applies to the *number* of autos exported to the U.S. (and not their total value), we expect that Japanese auto producers will shift the composition of exports toward higher priced, higher quality cars (Gomez-Ibanez et al. 1983). In this way they are able to maintain the maximum profit per unit sold, while staying within the quantity restraint. Such a response to quota restrictions can be obtained from simple theoretical models (see section 2.4) and has been observed within the textile and shoe industries (Baldwin 1982).

This quality shift has important implications for the employment and welfare effects of the VER. It is reasonable to assume that consumers demand the *services* of automobiles, where services are measured by automobile size, horsepower, comfort, and so forth. For a single car, the services provided are a measure of quality. Then a change in the price of Japanese automobile services will lead to a welfare loss for consumers and a substitution toward American models. For example, if due to the VER the average price of Japanese auto imports rises by 10 percent, but in addition the average quality of imports improves by 7 percent, then we would conclude that the price of services obtained from these imports has increased by only $10 - 7 = 3$ percent. This 3 percent effective price rise would determine the consumer welfare loss and the extent of substitution

Robert C. Feenstra is assistant professor of economics at Columbia University.

The author would like to thank Joseph Harary for outstanding research assistance and discussions throughout the course of this project, and Mordechai Kreinin and Ronald Jones for their comments as discussants.

away from Japanese models. Clearly, from this example, only looking at the change in purchase price, with no adjustment for quality, can be quite misleading in assessing the impact of the VER. A precise empirical measure of automobile quality is thus essential to our study.

After reviewing background data on the U.S. auto industry in section 2.2, a preliminary inspection of the VER is given in section 2.3. The number of imported Japanese autos met the restriction, and a substantial price increase—quite unprecedented by recent historical standards—occurred following the export restraint. In section 2.4 we review relevant theory concerning import restrictions and quality shifts. By focusing on the aggregate price of services obtained from Japanese imports, our analysis goes beyond the traditional framework which relates consumer welfare to the purchase price, unadjusted for quality. However, like the traditional framework, we relate consumer welfare to the *aggregate* import price. Thus, we do not attempt to measure the consumer loss or gain from a shifting composition of import models within an aggregate level of services. Such an exercise would be beyond the scope of the present study.

To measure the quality shift in imports, we have collected data on retail price and characteristics (e.g., length, horsepower, etc.) of twenty-two Japanese models for 1980, 1981, and 1982. The quality of automobiles is measured as the predicted price from hedonic regressions in which model prices are regressed on characteristics (see Griliches 1971). The quality-adjusted or service prices, which determine consumer demand and welfare, are measured by the residuals from the hedonic regressions. Using this method, in section 2.5 we identify three Japanese models which experienced substantial retail price, quantity, and quality increases following the VER with reductions in quality-adjusted price: Toyota Cressida, Toyota Celica Supra, and Datsun 810 Maxima.

In section 2.6 we apply hedonic regressions to eleven small and thirty-three large U.S. models for 1980 and 1981. Among the U.S. small cars, there is very little quality change and lower price rises than for other U.S. models. By comparing the results for Japanese imports and U.S. small cars, we conclude that about *two-thirds of the import price rise following the VER is due to quality improvement, with the remaining one-third a de facto price increase.* This is a major conclusion of our study.

In section 2.7 we apply the results of earlier sections to estimate the U.S employment and welfare effects of the VER. Since a major part of the import price rise is explained by quality improvement, the employment and welfare effects are both quite small. We estimate that between 1980 and 1981 the welfare loss was approximately 3 percent of revenue spent on Japanese imports. In the first year of the VER, unemployment in U.S. autos was reduced by 5 percent or less of existing layoffs, with the exact magnitude depending on the import elasticity of demand.

2.2 Recent Experience in U.S. Autos

On 1 May 1981 the Japanese government announced a three-year system of "voluntary export restraints" (VER) on the export of automobiles to the U.S. market. For the period from April 1981 to March 1982 these exports would not exceed 1.68 million units, while for the second year (April 1982 to March 1983) the export ceiling would be raised by 16.5 percent of the growth in the U.S. market. At the end of the second year, a decision about whether to extend the export restraint for a third year would be made. Later the Japanese government announced that the exports of certain "utility" vehicles (e.g., the Subaru Brat, Toyota Land Cruiser and Van) would be limited to 82,500 units over the initial year, and exports to Puerto Rico would not exceed 70,000. Thus, total Japanese exports for all these vehicles in the initial year would not exceed 1,832,500 units. On 29 March 1982 it was announced that the system of VER in place during the first year of the agreement would be extended without change to the second year (presumably because of the lack of growth in the U.S. market). The export limits are administered by the Japanese Ministry of International Trade and Industry (MITI), which allocates fixed proportions of the total export quantity to the Japanese producers; this method of restricting exports does not violate U.S. antitrust law.

These actions were made against a background of falling production and high unemployment in U.S. autos, along with several legislative attempts to curb imports. For example, on 5 February 1981 Senators Danforth and Bentsen introduced a bill (S.396) to impose quotas on the import of automobiles from Japan of 1.6 million units during 1981, 1982, and 1983. Indeed, this bill was scheduled for markup (line-by-line revision) in the Senate Finance Committee on May 12 and no doubt contributed to the specific action announced by the Japanese on May 1. Other outstanding bills include more stringent import quotas and domestic content requirements which specify the minimum content of American-made parts for autos sold in the United States.

An earlier legislative action was the petition for import relief made by the UAW in June 1980 to the U.S. International Trade Commission (ITC). In August 1980 the Commission received a petition for similar import relief from the Ford Motor Company. Under this legislation a recommendation for relief can be given only if the "increased imports of an article are a substantial cause of serious injury, or threat thereof, to the domestic industry." The statute defines the term "substantial cause" as "a cause which is important and not less than any other cause." The ITC determined that, while imports of autos into the United States had increased and the domestic industry was in fact injured, the recession in the United States was a greater cause of injury than the increased imports. Accordingly, import relief was not given. The shift in consumer preferences toward small, fuel-efficient autos (due in part to rising gasoline prices) was also found to be an important cause of injury, but less important than the recessionary conditions.

Recent data on imports of passenger autos (including the "utility" vehicles referred to above) are reported in table 2.1. In the first row, first column it can be seen that actual Japanese imports for April 1981 to March 1982 essentially met the limit of 1,832,500 units. This represents a fall in quantity of 9 percent from the previous year and can be contrasted with an average annual rise of 14 percent in imports over 1978–80. Comparing the April 1981 to March 1982 imports with those of the previous year, and noting that imports had been rising, we certainly expect that the VER restricted imports by *at least* 180 thousand units. The actual extent of restrictions may be significantly higher and will be estimated in section 2.7.

Data on U.S. factory sales, consumption, and import market shares (ratios of imports to consumption) are also shown in table 2.1. Note that consumption fell continually over the years with a larger fall from 1979 to 1980, whereas import market shares show an abrupt rise in 1979–80 but only small changes in other periods. The rising import market share over 1979–80 is largely attributable to Japanese imports. Despite this larger share, the ITC found that the decline in U.S. consumption over the same period was a more important cause of injury to the domestic industry.[1] As factory sales have been reduced, employment has decreased at a slightly slower rate, resulting in a fall in the average product of labor shown in table 2.1 (eighth row). Along with the reduction in sales, of course, profits of the auto manufacturers have been cut dramatically.

2.3   Effect of the VER

To determine the employment effect of the VER during its first year of operation, an initial calculation could proceed as follows. Suppose that for each unit of import reduced by the VER, U.S. production rises by one unit. (We shall argue below that this assumption is false, however, due to imperfect substitution and quality change in imports.) Then if the VER reduced Japanese imports by at least 180 thousand units, as discussed above, this could lead to a rise in U.S. employment of at least $180/9.5 = 19$ thousand workers, where we have used a middle value (9.5) of the average product of labor appearing in table 2.1. The increased employment of 19,000 can be compared with indefinite layoffs in the auto industry approaching 200,000 in late 1981 (see U.S. Department of Transportation 1982). Thus, the VER could affect at least one-tenth of the unemployment in autos during its first year. Of course, additional jobs would also be created in the rest of the economy.[2]

However, the employment impact of the VER may have been less than this estimate due to a shift of Japanese exports toward higher valued cars. Thus, at the bottom of table 2.1 we show the total value of Japanese imports and the average value (or price) obtained as the ratio of value to quantity. Over the period 1978–80 the average price of Japanese auto imports rose at an average rate of 6 percent, below the general rate of inflation. However, in the first year of the VER the price jumped by 17.4 percent as compared with the previous year. Annual inflation over the April 1980 to March 1982 period (as measured by the consumer price index) was 9.6 percent, which leaves a real increase of $17.4 - 9.6 = 7.8$ percent in import prices. Alternatively, we can compare the rise in prices from April 1980 to March 1982 with earlier years and obtain an unexpected increase of $17.4 - 6 = 11.4$ percent in import prices. In any case, it is clear from the data that the rise in average value during the initial year of the VER was quite unprecedented by recent historical standards and can be assumed to be a direct result of the export restraint. The average price of U.S. autos for some periods are shown for comparison; more recent figures will be computed in section 2.6.

The rise in average import prices may be achieved by (a) a simple rise in prices reflecting scarcity in the market; (b) a shift of Japanese exporters toward higher priced existing models which are larger, heavier, have greater horsepower, and so forth; (c) the introduction of new, or modified, models which are also larger, heavier, and the like. We shall refer to the specific features of a model such as weight and horsepower as "characteristics" and the bundle of characteristics embodied in a particular car as the "quality." With this terminology, the rise in average import price following the VER may be decomposed into a rise in quality (either within or across models) and a residual change in the price after adjusting for quality.

To evaluate the effect of the VER on consumer welfare, we shall have to measure the extent of quality change in Japanese imports. This shall be done in section 2.5 using hedonic regressions. In the following section we briefly review relevant theory concerning quality shifts in response to quota restrictions.

2.4 Theory of Import Restrictions and Quality Shifts

The theoretical impact of tariffs and quotas on import quality has been examined in Falvey (1979), Rodriguez (1979), and Santoni and Van Cott (1980). Falvey analyzes the case of fixed quality for each imported good but a shifting composition of imports. His analysis can be briefly summarized as follows.

Consider two import goods with unit costs c_1 and c_2, where $c_1 > c_2$ so that good 1 is the higher cost, higher quality item. In the absence of trade

Table 2.1   New Passenger Automobiles

	April 1981 to March 1982	April 1980 to March 1981	1980	1979	1978
	Quantity (thousands of units; thousands of employees)				
Japanese imports	1,833.3	2,012	1,992	1,617	1,563
Total imports	2,840	3,037	3,116	3,006	3,025
U.S. factory sales	5,602[a]	6,220[b]	6,400	8,419	9,165
Apparent U.S. consumption	7,962	8,684	8,904	10,643	11,505
Ratio of Japanese imports to U.S. consump. (percent)	23.0	23.2	22.4	15.2	13.6
Ratio of total imports to U.S. consump. (percent)	35.7	35.0	35.0	28.2	26.3
Average employment[c]	642	662	691	904	922
Ratio of U.S. factory sales to employment	8.7	9.4	9.3	9.3	9.9

Value (millions of dollars) and Average Price

Japanese imports	9,421	8,804	8,229	6,471	5,771
Ratio of Jap. import value to quantity	5,139	4,376	4,131	4,002	3,692
Ratio of U.S. production to quantity[d]	—	—	6,097	6,014	5,829

SOURCES: Bureau of Labor Statistics, 1981, *Supplement to Employment and Earnings: Revised Establishment Data*, August and later issues; U.S. International Trade Commission, 1982, *The U.S. Automobile Industry: Monthly Report on Selected Economic Indicators*, Publication 1244, May, Washington, D.C., tables 1, 2, 4; U.S. International Trade Commission, 1981, *Automotive Trade Statistics, 1964–1980*, Publication 1203, December, Washington, D.C., tables 1, 2, 3; U.S. International Trade Commission, 1980, *Certain Motor Vehicles and Certain Chassis and Bodies Therefor*, Publication 1110, December, Washington, D.C., table 19.

[a]Domestic production, May 1981 to April 1982.

[b]Domestic production, May 1980 to April 1981.

[c]Employment in SIC 3711 (motor vehicles and car bodies) plus SIC 3714 (motor vehicle parts and accessories).

[d]Producer's shipments; 1980 figure is for January to June. Later data were not available.

restrictions and assuming competition (Falvey also considers the monopoly case), we have $p_1 = c_1 > p_2 = c_2$, where p_i is the price of good i. In the presence of an ad valorem tariff of rate t, we could have $p_i' = (1 + t)c_i$, for $i = 1$ and 2, which implies $p_1'/p_2' = p_1/p_2$, so the relative price of the goods is unchanged. In this case we expect that the relative quantities imported are also unchanged. However, in the presence of a quota or VER on the *sum* of imports (over both goods), suppliers would ensure that the profits earned per unit imported are equalized in either good. That is, $p_1' - c_1 = p_2' - c_2$, where p_i' are the postquota domestic prices. But an equal increase in the price of each good implies a lower *percentage* increase in the price of good 1, since $p_1 > p_2$ initially. In other words, $p_1'/p_2' < p_1/p_2$, so the relative price has *decreased* for the higher quality good. Correspondingly, we expect a larger relative quantity imported of this good.

Rodriguez, on the other hand, considers a single import good where competitive firms choose the optimal quality. He assumes that the import demand applies to the *services* the good provides, where services equal

(1) $$S = xQ,$$

and S = import demand for services; Q = number of physical units imported; and x = amount of services provided per physical unit, or the unit quality content.

Rodriguez demonstrates that an ad valorem tariff will not affect the quality level x chosen by producers. However, in the presence of a binding quota or VER on imports, the quality content x will be *increased*.

The welfare cost from the VER is shown in figure 2.1. DD' is the import demand curve for services, p denotes the price of services, and the free-trade equilibrium is at E_0. As demonstrated by Rodriguez, the export restraint will lead to a rise in the price of imported services, with a new equilibrium such as E_1. Since the *exporting* country receives the higher price and thus the quota rents, the loss to the importing country is given by the entire shaded region under the import demand curve. This loss is approximately measured by

(2) $$L_S = (p_1 - p_0)S_1 + (1/2)(p_1 - p_0)(S_0 - S_1).$$

It is interesting to compare the appropriate measure of loss (L_S) with that obtained if the change in quality were not considered. That is, suppose we incorrectly measure the loss by the change in physical quantity imported and corresponding price. Since x is the quality content of a physical unit, px is the price per physical unit. Then the quantity measure of loss would be

(3) $$L_Q = (p_1 x_1 - p_0 x_0)Q_1$$
$$+ 1/2(p_1 x_1 - p_0 x_0)(Q_0 - Q_1),$$

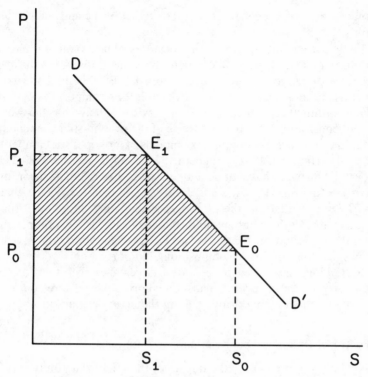

Fig. 2.1   Effect of VER on services.

where the subscript 0 (or 1) refers to pre- (or post-) VER. It can be shown that

$$(4) \qquad L_Q - L_S = (1/2)(x_1 - x_0)(p_0 Q_1 + p_1 Q_0).$$

With unit quality rising after the VER, $x_1 > x_0$, so the physical quantity measure of loss L_Q overstates the actual loss L_S. Indeed, relative to the total income spent on importables, the extent of overstatement is approximately equal to the percentage increase in unit quality.

We have been implicitly assuming that the imported good is a perfect substitute for the domestic product. If instead they are *imperfect substitutes*, then the change in the imported services price from p_0 to p_1 will shift the entire domestic demand curve, and a new equilibrium domestic price would be obtained. Let us suppose that the import demand curve DD' in figure 2.1 is drawn while *allowing* the domestic price to adjust to its new equilibrium levels. Then it can be argued (see Tarr 1980, pp. 11–15) that the shaded area in figure 2.1 is still an appropriate measure of welfare loss. This result is obtained essentially because the change in consumer surplus in the domestic market is exactly offset by a change in producer surplus.

Finally, we should mention an important qualification to our measure of welfare loss (L_S). We shall estimate this welfare loss using the *aggregate* price of services from Japanese imports. By this method, we are ignoring any consumer gain or loss from a shifting composition of import models within the aggregate level of services. Measuring the welfare component would be beyond the scope of the present study but could be initiated using the recent theoretical models of monopolistic competition and trade (Helpman 1981, Krugman 1979, 1980, Lancaster 1980). Only recently, however, have these models been extended to incorporate import restrictions (Feenstra and Judd 1982, Lancaster 1982, Venables 1982). One result from these models is that only under very special assumptions will the market equilibrium lead to a socially optimal quantity and range of product varieties (see Feenstra and Judd 1982, sec. 1). It follows that the shift in the composition of import models induced by the VER, holding the aggregate level of services fixed, can raise or lower consumer welfare in general. Thus, by ignoring this welfare component we may be understating or overstating the actual welfare loss.

2.5 Model Data and Quality of Japanese Imports

To analyze more closely the impact of the VER, data on twenty-two Japanese models over the calendar years 1980, 1981, and 1982 were obtained fom the annual *Automotive News Market Data Book*. These data included quantity imported into the United States (except for 1982), suggested retail price in March or April for the base version (i.e., without options) of each model, and characteristics including length, weight, horsepower, miles per gallon, and others. The twenty-two imported models were comprehensive except that: (a) "utility" vehicles (e.g., the Subaru Brat), referred to in section 2.2, were omitted; (b) import quantities of individual models included both station wagon and nonwagon quantities (e.g., Toyota Corolla sedan plus wagon), whereas only the price and characteristics of nonwagon imports were obtained.[3]

Summary information for the Japanese imports is shown in table 2.2 (upper portion). The quantity imported fell by 57,000 units from calendar year 1980 to 1981. In addition, the average price (computed as a ratio of total value to quantity) shows a substantial increase of 19.8 percent over this period. Thus, while the calendar year periods do not correspond exactly to those of the VER (i.e., April 1981 to March 1982), the qualitative behavior of the aggregate data is similar to that in table 2.1. Accordingly, we feel that a careful study of the model data will be useful in assessing the impact of the VER.

Table 2.2   **Sample of Automobiles**

	1981	1980	Percent Change from 1980 to 1981[a]
Japanese imports:			
Quantity (1,000)	1,721	1,778	−3.3
Price ($)[b]	5,950	4,881	19.8
Quality ($)[c]	5,250	4,943	6.0
U.S. small car production:			
Quantity (1,000)	1,321	1,449	−9.3
Price ($)	5,673	5,064	11.4
Quality ($)	5,258	5,220	0.7
U.S. large car production:			
Quantity (1,000)	2,663	3,010	−12.3
Price ($)	8,233	6,962	16.8
Quality ($)	7,420	7,078	4.7

[a]Difference in the natural logarithms.
[b]1982 average price computed using 1981 quantities is $6,306.
[c]1982 quality computed using 1981–82 regression and 1981 quantities is $5,236.

A scatter plot of the quantity change from 1980 to 1981 for individual models is shown in figure 2.2. The greatest percentage increase was obtained by the Toyota Cressida and Datsun 810 Maxima, the second and third most expensive models. (Note that the Toyota Starlet is an outlier, since this model was just introduced in 1980 leading to a high quantity increase in 1981.) The most expensive 1980 model was the Toyota Supra, a luxury sports version of the Celica. While this model experienced an import decline from 1980 to 1981, during the first seven months of 1982 Supra imports had substantially exceeded import sales during all of 1981.[4] Indeed, on an annual basis the import gain from 1981 to 1982 can be computed as 105 percent, placing the Supra up with the Cressida and Maxima as obtaining the largest import gains.

A glance at the other models in figure 2.2 certainly confirms our hypothesis that, due to the VER, the composition of imports shifts toward higher quality models. Next to the Cressida and Maxima, the next highest quantity gain is 30 percent (excluding the Starlet). The great majority of models are priced below $7,000, where there is no discernable trend in quantity changes. The model with the worst quantity decline— the Toyota Corona—will appear as an extreme point in following figures.

In figures 2.3 and 2.4 the price increases for 1980–81 and 1981–82 are shown. Most interestingly, the Cressida and Maxima (for 1980–81) and

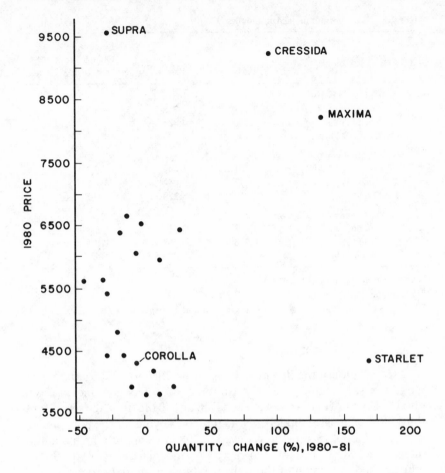

Fig. 2.2   Quantity change in Japanese imports, from 1980 to 1981.

Supra (for 1981–82) record some of the largest price rises. The question then is how the import gains were accomplished in the face of higher prices. One possibility is that these three models experienced significant quality improvements, making them attractive to buyers despite the price increases. We shall examine this possibility now, using hedonic regressions. (The basic reference on this technique is Griliches 1971; see also Triplett 1975.)

In hedonic regressions we attempt to explain the variation in automobile prices using information on model characteristics. Specifically we shall regress the natural logarithms of Japanese model prices on their length, weight, horsepower, gas mileage, and dummy variables for five-speed transmission, air-conditioning, and year. The results of these re-

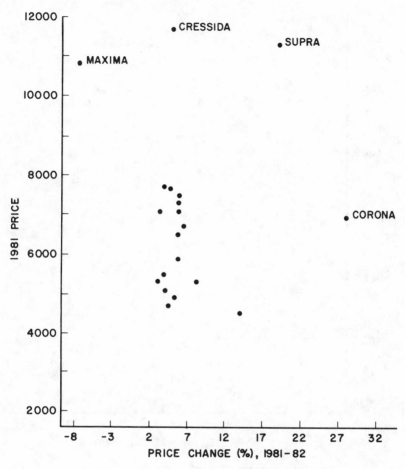

Fig. 2.3   Price change in Japanese imports, from 1980 to 1981.

gressions for 1980–81 and 1981–82 are shown in the first two columns of table 2.3.

Since the dependent price variable is measured as a natural log, the coefficients in the regressions can be interpreted as the proportionate change in price from a unit change in the independent variable. For example, in the 1980–81 regression for Japanese imports, an increase in length of one foot reduces the model price by an estimated 16 percent. Similarly, an increase in weight of one ton increases the model price by 77 percent. It can be seen that the presence of a five-speed transmission or air-conditioning as standard features are positively related to price, whereas gas mileage is negatively related. The standard errors of the estimates are shown in parentheses, and the gas mileage coefficient is

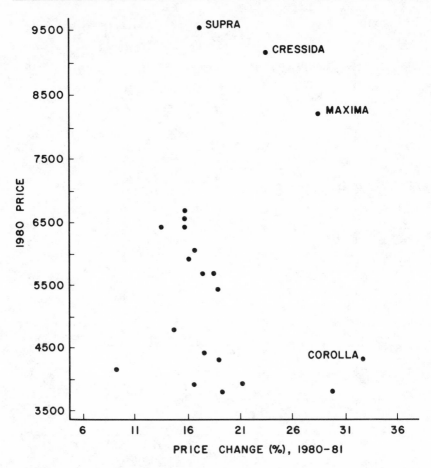

Fig. 2.4   Price change in Japanese imports, from 1981 to 1982.

insignificantly different from zero. Overall, the regression is able to explain 90 percent of the variation in model prices with a total of forty-four observations over the two years.

The regression for Japanese imports in 1981–82 is similar to that of 1980–81. In either case, additional explanatory variables were considered, including interior room area, turning circle, number of doors, hatchback, and others.[5] However, these variables were generally insignificant and of the "wrong" sign. One useful explanatory variable that was not available is dealer discounts, which were used extensively in 1981 (see U.S. Department of Transportation 1982).

The last variable in each regression is a dummy for the next year. The coefficient of this variable can be interpreted as the average rise in model prices *not* explained by the improvement in characteristics. Thus, for

Table 2.3   Hedonic Regressions (dependent variable: natural logarithm of model price)

	Japanese 1980–81	Japanese 1981–82	U.S. Small 1980–81	U.S. Large 1980–81
	Obs. = 44 R^2 = 0.90	Obs. = 44 R^2 = 0.93	Obs. = 22 R^2 = 0.80	Obs. = 66 R^2 = 0.95
Intercept	9.56* (0.82)	9.28* (0.69)	7.96* (0.55)	8.99* (0.44)
Length (feet)	−0.16* (0.069)	−0.10 (0.054)	0.14* (0.040)	−0.16* (0.023)
Weight (tons)	0.77 (0.41)	0.47 (0.30)	−0.48 (0.26)	1.48* (0.16)
Horsepower (100 HP)	0.74* (0.23)	0.54* (0.17)	−0.20 (0.30)	−0.27 (0.093)
Gas mileage (100 MPG)	−0.78 (0.76)	−0.57 (0.64)	−2.29* (1.08)	1.84* (0.80)
Dummy variables:				
Five-speed	0.080 (0.041)	0.15* (0.038)	—	—
Automatic	—	—	—	0.090* (0.040)
Power brakes	—	—	0.12* (0.042)	—
Air-conditioning[a]	0.21* (0.066)	0.26* (0.054)	—	0.43* (0.050)
Year 1981	0.13* (0.034)	—	0.089* (0.035)	0.11* (0.024)
Year 1982	—	0.057* (0.025)	—	—

*Significant at 5 percent level. Standard errors are in parentheses.
[a]For Japanese models this variable indicates air-conditioning and automatic transmission, which were nearly perfectly correlated.

1980–81 the suggested retail price rose by 19.8 percent, but after adjusting for quality improvements, such as greater horsepower, air-conditioning, and the rest, the residual price rose by only 13 percent. The difference between these two figures is the rise in quality content. More precisely, the total import of Japanese automobile *services* can be measured as the predicted price from the hedonic regression times the quantity, summed over all models.[6] The *quality* of imports is then obtained as the total services divided by total quantity. As shown in table 2.2, we measure the quality content of imports as $4,943 and $5,250 in 1980 and

1981, respectively, obtained using the 1980–81 regression. The difference between these figures gives a 6 percent rise in quality.

The sensitivity of this quality measurement to specification of the hedonic regression can be checked by examining the "year 1981" coefficient. For various additional explanatory variables considered, the 1981 dummy coefficient was between 0.126 and 0.136, indicating an average rise in model prices not explained by quality improvement of approximately 13 percent, as found in table 2.3. For example, when variables for roominess, maneuverability, and axle ratio (a measure of durability) are added to the Japanese regression in table 2.3, the year 1981 coefficient is 0.132 for 1980–81. This compares with an estimate of 0.126 for 1980–81 when these three additional variables are excluded. If engine displacement and horsepower/weight are used in place of horsepower and weight, while retaining room, maneuverability, and axle ratio, then the 1981 dummy coefficient is 0.136 for 1980–81. Other combinations and additional explanatory variables result in a coefficient between these bounds. The measure of quality improvement can be approximately obtained as the difference between the retail price increase (19.8 percent) and the year 1981 coefficient (13 percent). Since the latter is not very sensitive to the regression specification, our measure of quality improvement appears to be quite robust.

The scatter plots of the residual, or quality-adjusted, price changes for 1980–81 and 1981–82 are shown in figures 2.5 and 2.6. Comparing figures 2.3 and 2.5 we can see substantial difference in the price changes for the Supra, Cressida, and Maxima, relative to the other models. Thus, while the retail price increases for these models over 1980–81 were well above average, the quality-adjusted price increases were well below average. From the raw data the quality improvement of the Supra can be identified as an increase in horsepower and the introduction of a five-speed transmission; the Cressida became heavier with greater horsepower; and the Maxima increased in weight with air-conditioning and automatic transmission added as standard equipment.

A similar pattern of high retail price increase with much smaller quality-adjusted price change can be seen for the Supra over 1981–82 in figures 2.4 and 2.6. These overall results neatly confirm the hypothesis that the quantity gain in the highest priced Japanese imports was brought about by a significant improvement in the quality content, as expected from the theory. Aside from the Cressida, Maxima, and Supra models, no general pattern of price or quality change is identified.

2.6 Model Data and Quality of U.S. Production

In addition to the data on Japanese imports, data on prices and characteristics of forty-four U.S. models were also obtained from the same

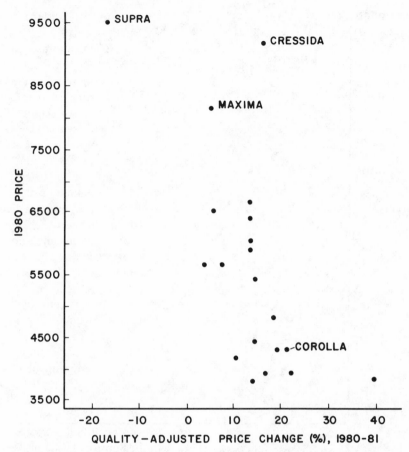

Fig. 2.5   Quality-adjusted price change in Japanese imports, from 1980 to 1981.

source for the calendar years 1980 and 1981. Station wagons and several other models were omitted from the sample because of lack of information. The sample will be used to make comparisons with the Japanese imports and to establish general conclusions in section 2.7.

The data for U.S. small cars and large cars are summarized in table 2.2. (Note that the large car category includes both intermediate and large models.) The small cars experienced a lower price rise than large cars. This difference is explained in part by a changing composition *within* the large car category. In particular, the price of intermediate-sized cars (below $8,000 in price) rose substantially more in percentage terms than the price of very large cars (above $8,000 in price). The general price rise, then, partially reflects a quantity shift toward more expensive models within the large car category. Overall, U.S. large cars experienced a

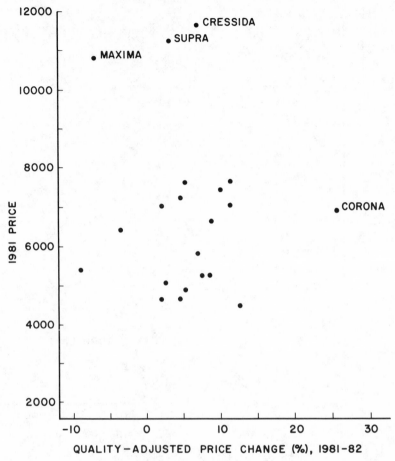

Fig. 2.6   Quality-adjusted price change in Japanese imports, from 1981
                  to 1982.

greater percentage quantity decline than small cars, as reported in table
2.2.

One conclusion to be drawn from the summary information is that U.S.
small car prices do not appear to include a significant monopolistic
increase over the 1980–81 period, in contrast to the prediction of traditional theory (see, e.g., Lindert and Kindleberger 1982, appendix E).
That is, despite the export restriction, those models which compete most
directly with Japanese imports—U.S. small cars—experienced lower
price increases than intermediate and large cars. One possible explanation for this result is that, faced with limited availability of lower priced,
lower quality Japanese imports, U.S. consumers did not substitute toward small U.S. models. Instead they could have substituted toward

intermediate U.S. models, used cars, or they could have decided to defer their purchases.[7] To the extent that substitution did *not* take place toward U.S. cars, the employment impact of the VER is reduced.

Hedonic regressions were also run for U.S. small and large cars, using similar explanatory variables as in the analysis of Japanese imports described in section 2.5. The results are shown in table 2.3. The U.S. small car regression contains several unusual signs, with less explanatory power than for U.S. large cars.[8] In the latter case, all estimated coefficients are significant at the 5 percent level, with length having a negative and gas mileage a positive relation to price.

As with the Japanese imports, the predicted prices from the hedonic regressions can be used to construct an estimate of total *services* produced (predicted price times quantity, summed over all models). When divided by the quantity of small or large cars, we then obtain a measure of *quality*, as shown in table 2.2. The quality content of U.S. small cars increased only slightly from 1980 to 1981, in contrast to the substantial quality change of Japanese imports. For U.S. large cars, quality increased by 4.7 percent. This is partially explained by the quantity shift from intermediate to very large cars as discussed above.

2.7   Effects of the VER within the Sample

We shall now derive general conclusions about the effect of the VER within our sample of Japanese imports and U.S. production. In particular, we shall investigate the U.S. employment and welfare impact. Recalling that our sample covers the calendar years 1980 and 1981, whereas the initial year of the VER was April 1981 to March 1982, our quantitative results do not directly measure the effect of the VER in its first year. But we certainly expect that our general conclusions will carry over to other, similar time periods.

Returning to table 2.2, we must first decide what portion of the 19.8 percent rise in retail import prices is a general inflationary effect across producers from cost increases and simple price leadership but not related to the VER. We noted above that the U.S. small car prices do not appear to include a significant monopolistic increase in 1981, rising by less than intermediate and large car prices, so it seems reasonable to regard the 11.4 percent increase in small car prices as the general inflationary effect. It follows that the difference between the retail price increases of Japanese imports and U.S. small cars, or *19.8 − 11.4 = 8.4 percent, is the increase in import prices directly caused by the VER*, after correcting for the inflationary effect across producers. The next question is what portion of this price increase is directly the result of quality improvement. From table 2.2, we see that the quality improvement of the Japanese imports exceeded that of U.S. small cars by $6.0 - 0.7 = 5.3$ percent. That is,

5.3/8.4 or about *two-thirds of the rise in import prices can be attributed to quality improvement*. The remaining 8.4 − 5.3 = 3.1 percent, or one-third of the total, is a de facto price increase for which the consumer is not compensated by a change in quality.

To obtain further conclusions, we must begin to introduce some assumptions and parameters. In table 2.4 we give alternative values of the elasticity of U.S. demand for Japanese automobile services, ranging from 2 to 5. Using these elasticities and the 3.1 percent residual price increase obtained above, we can readily compute the value of imported services restricted by the VER. In the absence of this restraint we would have expected the 1981 Japanese quality to be approximately the same as in 1980. Accordingly, we can compute the extent to which the VER restricted auto imports in the second row of table 2.4. For demand elasticities of 2 and 3, the extent of import restrictions is measured as 220,000 and 277,000 units, respectively.

From the estimates reported in Toder (1978, chap. 3), a value of 1 to 2 for the short-run elasticity of demand for imported autos is expected, while the value of 3 is somewhat high. In assessing the employment impact of the VER during its first year, we shall thus focus on the first two columns of table 2.4. The last column, with an elasticity of 5, would be relevant for periods exceeding one year when consumers show greater adjustment to a price increase.

Let us make the strong assumption that the *overall* U.S. demand elasticity for domestic and Japanese autos is unity. That is, a fixed proportion of total income is spent on these autos, and a reduction of $1 million spent on Japanese imports because of a price change will imply exactly $1 million extra spent on U.S. models. This assumption is supported by the empirical evidence (see Toder 1978, p. 44 and the references cited there) that the price elasticity for *all* cars purchased in the United States is approximately one. By excluding European imports, we may be overstating the income which consumers continue to spend on Japanese and American models after a price rise. The assumption of an overall demand elasticity of unity, combined with specific import elasticities, permits us to model the degree of substitution between Japanese and U.S. models, as follows.

For the various import elasticities in table 2.4 we can readily compute the additional income spent on U.S. autos because of the VER as being equal to the reduced income spent on Japanese imports. Dividing this revenue by an average 1981 price of $6,000 for cars which substitute quite closely with Japanese imports, we obtain the additional U.S. production (fourth row). These production gains can be contrasted to the number of auto imports restricted, with the differences due to imperfect substitution. Further dividing the production gain by the average product of labor, we obtain the additional U.S. employment (fifth row). With import elasticities of 2 and 3, the employment gains are 5,600 and 11,100 workers, respectively. These figures can be compared with indefinite layoffs in the auto industry exceeding 200,000 in early 1982.

Thus, the employment impact of the VER during its first year was 5 percent or less of existing layoffs. Further evidence would be required to assess the employment impact over later years, though the last column of table 2.4 suggests that the reduction in unemployment would be larger.

In the last row of table 2.4 we give the correct welfare loss L_S derived in section 2.4 and the incorrect loss L_Q which ignores the quality change in imports. These magnitudes can be compared with 1981 expenditures on Japanese imports of $10,240,000. Thus, the correct welfare loss is approximately 3.1 percent of 1981 expenditures, while the incorrect welfare loss is approximately 8.4 percent. These amounts are just the quality-adjusted and unadjusted rise in import prices, respectively, since the welfare loss from the VER is the entire reduction in consumer surplus (see figure 2.1)

Table 2.4   **Effects of the VER from 1980 to 1981**

	Elasticity of Demand for Japanese Automobile Services		
	2	3	5
Japanese services restricted[a] ($ mill)	560	840	1400
Japanese autos restricted[b] (1,000)	220	277	390
Additional U.S. revenue[c] ($ mill)	317	635	1270
Additional U.S. production[d] (1,000)	53	106	212
Additional U.S. employment[e] (1,000)	5.6	11.1	22.3
Welfare loss:			
L_S ($ mill)[f]	327	332	342
L_Q ($ mill)[g]	915	929	958

[a]0.031 × elasticity × 1981 Japanese services. Services = quality × quantity.
[b](1981 Japanese services + services restricted)/1980 Japanese quality − 1981 Japanese auto imports.
[c]0.031 × (elasticity − 1) × 1981 Japanese import value.
[d]Additional U.S. revenue/$6,000.
[e]Additional U.S. production/9.5.
[f](0.031 × 1981 Japanese services) + 1/2 × (0.031 × 1981 Japanese service price × Japanese services restricted). Service price = nominal price/quality.
[g](0.084 × 1981 Japanese import value) + 1/2 × (0.084 × 1981 Japanese price × Japanese autos restricted).

with quota rents accruing to Japanese producers. The specification of the import elasticity only modestly affects the loss. The correct measure of welfare loss is about one-third of the incorrect measure.

2.8 Conclusions

Our major conclusion is that two-thirds of the increase in Japanese import prices following the VER was due to quality improvement, with the remaining one-third a de facto price rise for which the consumer is not compensated by a change in quality. This result was found to be quite insensitive to the specification of the hedonic regressions used to measure quality (section 2.5). It also depends on the general inflationary price increase across producers, not related to the VER. Since U.S. small car prices rose by less than the intermediate or large car prices (section 2.6), we chose the former as a measure of the general inflationary increase. We then took the *difference* between the Japanese import and U.S. small car price rise and regarded this amount as the increase in import prices directly caused by the VER. Two-thirds of this price increase could be explained by quality improvement in Japanese imports.

The residual import price rise not accounted for by quality change was measured as 3.1 percent. It followed that the loss to American consumers in 1981 from the VER was approximately 3.1 percent of expenditure on Japanese imports. The exact welfare loss depends only slightly on the import demand elasticity, since most of the loss comes from the quota rents obtained by Japanese producers. It is also observed that three Japanese models experienced substantial retail price, quantity, and quality increases following the VER, with reductions in their quality-adjusted prices: the Toyota Cressida, Toyota Celica Supra, and Datsun 810 Maxima. The increased imports of these luxury models neatly confirm the theoretical predictions.

Our conclusions about the effect of the VER on employment in U.S. autos are subject to greater qualification. Clearly, we have not considered the general equilibrium response of wages to unemployment in one industry, or the extent to which decreased U.S. imports would result in lower demand for U.S. exports. More specifically, we have not been able to consider imports from countries other than Japan or the introduction of new U.S. models following the VER. Including European imports into our analysis could decrease the employment impact of the VER because of substitution by U.S. consumers toward these models. On the other hand, introduction of new U.S. models, such as the General Motors J-car (and earlier the Chrysler K-car), could present desirable alternatives for limited Japanese imports. While a consideration of these factors would be useful, our general conclusion that the employment impact of the VER was small during the first year due to quality improvement and imperfect substitution between Japanese and U.S. autos does not seem to be overstated.

Notes

1. Thus, suppose the import market share were held *constant* at its 1979 value. Then 1980 factory sales could be estimated as $6,400 + 3,116 - (8,904 \times 0.282) = 7,005$, where the first figure is actual 1980 sales and the next figures are actual and estimated 1980 imports. Factory sales in 1979 were 8,419, so the extent of decline due to falling consumption (i.e., recessionary conditions) is $(8,419 - 7,005)/(8,419 - 6,400) = 70$ percent. The remaining 30 percent of falling sales can be attributed to import competition. Precisely this type of simple calculation was instrumental in leading to the ITC decision.

2. For example, the Council of Economic Advisors (submission to Senate, 3 April 1980) reports that the production of 50 autos creates 10 jobs in the economy, with 2.3 workers employed directly in autos and 7.7 employed elsewhere. These data are from the Department of Labor (apparently based on a study referenced in submission to the House of Representatives, 7, 18 March 1980). However, the average product of labor in autos implicit in these figures is extremely high ($50/2.3 = 22$). I have been unable to account for the difference between this estimate and those reported in table 2.1.

3. Dealers were contacted to try and separate the station wagon and nonwagon import quantities, but this proved unsuccessful. In addition, note that the imported models include those built for U.S. firms, such as the Chrysler-Mitsubishi Challenger, Champ, and Colt. Imports into Puerto Rico are not included.

4. Imports of the Toyota Celica Supra during 1980, 1981, and the first seven months of 1982 were 21,542 units, 16,146 units, and 19,266 units, respectively. Ward's Communications, Inc., kindly supplied this information. Due to its overall performance, the Supra was chosen as *Motor Trend* magazine's 1982 Import Car of the Year.

5. The occurrence of air-conditioning was very highly correlated with the occurrence of automatic transmissions in the Japanese imports, so these were combined into one dummy variable. Also, the prices were adjusted so that all models excluded a radio.

6. The predicted price used in this calculation does not include that portion of the model price explained by the year dummy in the regression, since the year dummy captures that portion of the price *not* related to the physical characteristics (i.e., services) of the model.

7. Since the 1981 U.S. small and large car prices were collected on April 10, it is of course possible that the small car prices had not responded to the VER simply because it was not announced until May 1. On the other hand, the evidence is quite strong that at least the Japanese had anticipated the VER in setting their prices as of 6 April 1981, which are used in our sample. But whether the VER was anticipated by U.S. producers or not, we still obtain the result that the U.S. small car price rise over 1980–81 does not appear to include a monopolistic increase, and this result will be used in section 2.7.

8. At a later stage of our research we also pooled the Japanese import and American small car models to test for equality of the regression coefficients. By the usual F-test, the test statistic for the null hypothesis that the regression coefficients were equal, was computed as 1.55. The 95 percent significance point of the F-distribution with degrees of freedom (5, 60) is 2.37, so we cannot reject the null hypothesis. In future research it would be useful to pool these data.

References

Automotive news market data book. 1980, 1981, 1982. Detroit: Automotive News.

Baldwin, Robert E. 1982. The efficacy (or inefficacy) of trade policy. Frank Graham Memorial Lecture, Princeton University.

Falvey, Rodney E. 1979. The composition of trade within import-restricted product categories. *Journal of Political Economy* 87, no. 5 (October):1105–14.

Feenstra, Robert C., and Kenneth L. Judd. 1982. Tariffs, technology transfer, and welfare. *Journal of Political Economy* 90, no. 6 (December):1142–65.

Gomez-Ibanez, Jose A., Robert A. Leone, and Stephen A. O'Connell. 1983. Restraining auto imports: Does anyone win? *Journal of Policy Analysis and Management* 2:196–219.

Griliches, Zvi. 1971. Hedonic price indexes for automobiles: An econometric analysis of quality change. In *Price indexes and quality change*, ed. Zvi Griliches. Cambridge: Harvard University Press.

Helpman, Elhanan. 1981. International trade in the presence of product differentiation, economies of scale and monopolistic competition: A Chamberlin-Heckscher-Ohlin approach. *Journal of International Economics* 11 (August):305–40.

Krugman, Paul R. 1979. Increasing returns, monopolistic competition, and international trade. *Journal of International Economics* 9 (November):469–79.

———. 1980. Scale economies, product differentiation, and the pattern of trade. *American Economic Review* 70 (December):950–59.

Lancaster, Kelvin J. 1980. Intra-industry trade under perfect monopolistic competition. *Journal of International Economics* 10 (May):151–75.

———. 1982. Protection and product differentiation. Columbia University. Mimeo.

Lindert, Peter H., and Charles P. Kindleberger. 1982. *International economics.* Homewood, Ill.: Richard D. Irwin.

Rodriguez, Carlos Alfredo. 1979. The quality of imports and the differential welfare effects of tariffs, quotas, and quality controls as protective devices. *Canadian Journal of Economics* 12, no. 3:439–49.

Santoni, Gary J., and T. Norman Van Cott. 1980. Import quotas: The quality adjustment problem. *Southern Economic Journal* 46, no. 4 (April):1206–11.

Tarr, David. Federal Trade Commission 1980. *Effects of restrictions on United States imports: Five case studies and theory.* Washington, D.C.: GPO.

Toder, Eric J., with Nicholas Scott Cardell, and Ellen Burton. 1978.

Trade policy and the U.S. automobile industry. Charles River Associates Research Report. New York: Praeger Publishers.

Triplett, Jack E. 1975. Consumer demand and characteristics of consumption goods. In *Household production and consumption*, ed. Nestor E. Terlecky. Conference on Research in Income and Wealth: Studies in Income and Wealth, vol. 40. New York: Columbia University Press for the National Bureau of Economic Research.

U.S. Congress. Senate. Committee on Banking, Housing, and Urban Affairs. Subcommittee on Economic Stabilization. 1980. *The effects of expanding automobile imports on the domestic economy*. 96th Cong., 2d sess., 3 April.

U.S. Congress. House. Committee on Ways and Means. Subcommittee on Trade. 1980. *World auto trade: Current trends and structural problems*. 96th Cong., 2d sess., 7, 18 March. Serial 96-78.

U.S. Department of Transportation. 1982. *The U.S. automobile industry, 1981*. May. Washington, D.C.: GPO.

Venables, Anthony J. 1982. Optimal tariffs for trade in monopolistically competitive commodities. *Journal of International Economics* 12 (May):225–42.

Comment   Ronald W. Jones

Voluntary export restraints have recently attained prominence in the portfolio of techniques used in exercising U.S. commercial policy, and this stimulating paper by Feenstra analyzes the possible effects of such a program on welfare and employment in the currently depressed U.S. automobile industry. Believing as I do in the advantages of division of labor and in the doctrine of comparative advantage, I leave to my codiscussant from the state of Michigan remarks as to the nuances of the automobile industry and concentrate, instead, on some points of more theoretical interest suggested by the paper.

The application of VER instead of, say, a U.S. tariff or quota has the obvious welfare disadvantage that foreigners are invited to capture the rents created by the restraint. As Feenstra carefully points out, however, if the composition of the limited imports is altered in favor of higher quality products, the welfare loss would be incorrectly expressed in the price rise. Indeed, economic theory associated with the work of Alchian and Allen (1972) suggests that it is in the producers' best interest to adjust the product mix in favor of higher quality. (In their classic example,

Ronald W. Jones is professor of economics at the University of Rochester.

transport costs are shown to lower the *relative* price of the higher quality apples in distant markets, thus explaining, for Western apple growers, why the "good apples move East"). Recently Falvey (1979) has harnessed this logic to the case of quantity restrictions to argue that, unlike the case of ad valorem tariffs, the price rise associated with quotas will be relatively less for higher quality products. Feenstra estimates that a full two-thirds of the price rise on imported Japanese automobiles was due to an improvement in quality and should thus not be counted as a welfare loss.

This argument about quality changes does alter the traditional measure of welfare loss, but what can be said about employment? To the extent that a restriction on imports of Japanese automobiles shifts demand toward home-produced autos, local employment can be expected to rise. However, Feenstra emphasizes that much depends on the elasticity of demand. Suppose demand for Japanese cars is inelastic, although, say, demand in the aggregate for all cars is unit elastic. Then the VER could cause a reduction in the value of demand for American-made autos (neglecting the effect on European imports), which, assuming no price fall in this area, translates into a loss of output and jobs. Thus, argues Feenstra, it is not clear that the VER will raise employment of U.S. autoworkers.

I concur with this result and merely add two observations. First, the argument concerning employment need not rest on changes in quality, as does the argument concerning welfare. What is required is inelastic demand for auto imports, and this can be expressed either in quality or quantity units. Thus Feenstra used the Rodriguez (1979) concept of import demand related to the *services* of a good, so that

$$S = xQ,$$

where Q measures the quantity of auto imports, x is a measure of services provided per physical unit, and S is the demand for services (from imports). If p_Q represents the price of autos and p_S the price of services, and if demand for autos is inelastic so that a rise in p_Q results in:

$$-\hat{Q} < \hat{p}_Q,$$

it must be the case that

$$-\hat{S} < (\hat{p}_Q - \hat{x}).$$

Since p_s equals p_Q/x, demand for services would also be inelastic. Expressed either way, the VER could lower employment.

A general equilibrium approach, however, shifts the focus of the argument. If trade stays roughly balanced, a rise in the value of imports may reduce employment in import-competing sectors, but it would be matched by a rise in the value of exports (and employment in exporting sectors). Similarly, if a VER cuts back on import spending, there are negative employment effects in exportables to be considered in conjunction with any employment gains in the protected sectors. Net employment effects depend both on a comparison of labor intensities in various sectors of the economy as well as on the issue raised by Feenstra as to the expansionary or contractionary effect in the import-competing sector. In any case Feenstra's conclusion that the employment effects of the VER are less obvious than the welfare effects seem supported at the economy-wide level as well as in the U.S. auto industry.

References

Alchian, A., and W. Allen. 1972. *University economics*, 3d ed. Belmont, Calif.: Wadsworth.

Falvey, R. 1979. The composition of trade within import-restricted product categories. *Journal of Political Economy* 87:1105–14.

Rodriguez, C. 1979. The quality of imports and the differential welfare effects of tariffs, quotas, and quality controls as protective devices. *Canadian Journal of Economics* 12:439–49.

Comment   Mordechai E. Kreinin

This is an excellent paper, employing an imaginative approach to an important problem. At issue is the effect of the Japanese Voluntary Export Restraint in autos on U.S. welfare and employment.

Product upgrading is a well-known outcome of any quantitative import restriction (import quotas, VERs) limiting the importation of a product to a specified number of units without distinction between brands, grades, or other product attributes. Because such quantitative limitations are equivalent to a specific tariff, they raise the price of cheap brands proportionately more than the price of expensive brands. This constitutes an incentive on the part of buyers and of exporters to upgrade the product. Upgrading occurs in all cases where product differentiation exists.

Using hedonic regressions, Professor Feenstra estimates the degree of product upgrading that occurred in Japanese cars exported to the United States as a result of the VER. Because of the many features of product differentiation that exist in autos, I suspect that somewhat less than the entire degree of upgrading could have been so captured; but the author competently demonstrates that the "leftover" bias could not have been large. The author's estimated U.S. welfare loss due to the VER, after

Mordechai E. Kreinin is professor of economics at Michigan State University.

taking into account the product upgrading, is only one-third of the estimated loss when the quality upgrading is ignored. He then proceeds to estimate the rise in U.S. auto output and the additional U.S. employment attributable to the VER under alternative elasticity assumptions. Both effects are very small under the assumptions of import-demand elasticities of 2, 3, or 5.

Having revealed my general admiration for the paper, I shall proceed with specific criticisms. They were made orally on an earlier draft, but the author merely recognizes them without adjusting his calculations. Some of the following points have offsetting effects on the results, but the extent of the net bias cannot be determined without further calculations. Table C2.1 is computed from the author's table 2.1 and will be useful in highlighting some of the criticisms.

1. *How effective was the VER?* The first VER year spanned the months from April 1981 to March 1982, and it is the only period for which data were available at the time of the author's calculations. Under the VER agreement, total Japanese exports were not to exceed 1,832,500 units. And indeed the last column (first row) in table C2.1 shows that their exports were held to that number. By subtracting that figure from 2,012,000—Japanese exports to the United States in the previous year—

Table C2.1   New Passenger Cars (thousands of units)

	1980		April 1980 to March 1981		April 1981 to March 1982 (VER period)
Japanese imports	1,992		2,012		1,833
Percentage change		1.0		−9.8	
Total imports	3,116		3,037		2,840
Percentage change		−2.6		−6.9	
Non-Japanese imports[a]	1,124		1,025		1,007
Percentage change		−9.7		−1.8	
U.S. factory sales	6,400		6,220		5,602
Percentage change		−2.9		−11.0	
Apparent U.S. consumption	8,904		8,684		7,962
Percentage change		−2.5		−9.1	
Ratio of Japanese import to U.S. consumption	22.4%		23.2%		23.0%
Ratio of total import to U.S. consumption	35.0%		35.0%		35.7%
Ratio of non-Japanese imp. to U.S. consumption	12.6%		11.8%		12.7%

[a]Obtained by subtraction of row 1 from row 2 in the author's table 2.1.

the author suggests that the VER restricted imports by at least 180,000 units. But total U.S. car output and consumption also declined by 9 and 11 percent, respectively, over the same period. Indeed the ratio of Japanese imports to U.S. consumption was reasonably stable, at 23 percent, over the two years. Can one attribute the entire 9.8 percent drop in Japanese imports to the VER? It is probably an overestimate, which is then reflected in the final results.

2. *The role of European imports.* Following comments on the original version of the paper, the author now recognizes the existence of European imports but does not incorporate them in his calculations. By subtracting row 1 from row 2 in the author's table 2.1, row 3 in table C2.1 shows that non-Japanese imports account for about one-third of total imports. Although the author does not explicitly say so, I am assuming that (following convention) Canadian imports (governed by the U.S.-Canada auto treaty) are excluded. Thus non-Japanese imports are essentially European models.

Imported European cars cover the entire range of quality and price. And the product upgrading by the Japanese means that they compete with the Europeans in the U.S. market in the entire product range, certainly at both ends of the price spectrum. Because the VER was limited to Japan, one might expect some substitution of European (rather than American) models for the excluded Japanese cars. That such substitution may have been important is clear from table C2.1. European imports declined by only 1.8 percent from 1981 to 1982, while Japanese imports declined by 9.8 percent, and U.S. auto consumption by 9.1 percent. By making some simple assumptions about market shares (as the author does in other cases, such as in section 2.2), one may tentatively infer that over one-third of the "slack" created by the VER was picked up by European rather than American-built cars.

The exclusion of European cars from his calculations may have a profound effect on the results, especially on the estimated welfare and employment effects of the VER. Substitution from European models is likely to have scaled down the effect of the VER on U.S. employment. In fact, such possible substitution must be incorporated into the author's own calculations because his accompanying assumption of a fixed proportion of consumer income spent on cars applies to *all* cars, including European ones.

In sum, the assumption of U.S.-Japanese substitution, ignoring European imports, affects results throughout the paper. It is possible to indicate the direction of the bias so created. For example, the rise in U.S. employment due to the VER is overestimated. Furthermore, by making certain credible assumptions, the estimates themselves could have been revised to more realistic levels.

3. Is a constant share of income spent on automobiles? That assumption crops up in various places. As stated above, at best it should be applied to all cars, including European.

How realistic is that assumption? Although there are not a priori grounds for making it, the assumption is supported by data not cited by the author.[1] But that evidence relates only to the 1960s and 1970s. In view of the profound changes that have taken place in the industry over the past three years, the assumption cannot be accepted on its face value for 1980–82, the main period under study. The author needs to check explicitly the validity of the assumption (critical to parts of his discussion) for the 1980s. The possibility must be recognized that if consumers spend more (less) on cars they have less (more) money to spend elsewhere.

4. To what extent was the rise in U.S. auto prices triggered by (resulted from) an increase in Japanese prices? There is evidence of such pricing behavior by U.S. automakers from episodes of devaluations or depreciations of the dollar. This may partly account for the rise in the price of intermediate-sized cars. The failure of small car prices to rise may have been due to depressed market conditions and to European competition rather than to market structure.

5. Effect of exchange rate changes. The sharp 1982 appreciation of the dollar could have depressed the dollar price of Japanese models, so the price rise embodied in the calculations (attributed to the VER) may be biased.

6. The hedonic regressions. Although the results appear robust, the regressions may not have captured all quality characteristics (e.g., improved carpeting or seat covers) and need to be regarded as a lower bound.

A few words beyond the scope of this well-crafted paper are in order. What is the cause of the decline in the competitive position of the U.S. auto industry that triggered demands for VERs and domestic content legislation?

Wrong management decisions in the 1970s, especially concerning the product mix and perhaps the introduction of new technology, are well-known. But a recent study[2] shows that during the 1970s there had been a distinct increase in unit labor costs in the auto industry *relative to that in U.S. manufacturing in general*: Labor compensation in autos rose at a faster rate than its counterparts in all manufacturing, while output per worker rose in tandem with all manufacturing. No such change occurred in Japan, where both compensation and productivity in autos rose at a faster rate than in all Japanese manufacturing, so that unit labor costs rose in tandem. Indeed, in 1980 labor compensation in the U.S. auto industry was 60 percent above that of the U.S. manufacturing average. In Japan and Germany that excess is only 25 percent, while in other European countries it is even lower than that. Apparently the U.S. comparative advantage in autos has eroded.

Notes

1. U.S. Department of Transportation, *The U.S. Automobile Industry, 1980*, Washington, D.C., January 1981, fig. 2-1.

2. Mordechai E. Kreinin, "United States Comparative Advantage in Motor Vehicles and Steel," in *Michigan Fiscal and Economic Structure*, ed. H. E. Brazer and D. S. Laren. (Ann Arbor: University of Michigan Press, 1982), chap. 6.

3   U.S. Antidumping Policies: The Case of Steel

Barry Eichengreen and Hans van der Ven

Few aspects of international economic relations are as contentious as the allegation of dumping and the enforcement of antidumping statutes. Recently, attention has been focused on allegations by U.S. producers of foreign violations of U.S. trade law, most notably in the steel sector. The controversy surrounding these allegations clearly has captured the attention of foreign governments, which have threatened to retaliate against the United States if antidumping duties are assessed. To defuse a potentially explosive situation, the United States has experimented with a new form of administered protection, the Trigger Price Mechanism for steel, and has made several formal and informal attempts to negotiate orderly marketing arrangements with foreign governments and producers.

Dumping complaints certainly are not limited to steel. Indeed, recent allegations are notable for their catholicity: in the United States alone, dumping complaints have ranged from trade in basic agricultural commodities to sophisticated high-technology products, encompassing exports from developed and developing countries alike. Neither are dumping allegations new; such complaints have been prevalent in the

Barry Eichengreen is professor of economics at Harvard University, and a faculty research fellow of the National Bureau of Economic Research. Hans van der Ven was affiliated with the Harvard Business School at the time this study was prepared.

The authors are indebted to Susan Houseman for exceptionally capable research assistance and to Barbara Sloan of the European Community Information Service for help with the statistics. They are grateful to Alan Auerbach, Richard Caves, Wesley Cohen, Gene Grossman, Elhanan Helpman, Joseph Kalt, Hans Mueller, Joel Mokyr, Barbara Spencer, Peter Suchman, and Lars Svensson for comments, and to the conference discussants, Wilfred Ethier and Gary Horlick, for their helpful remarks. Eichengreen's research draws on work supported by the Social Science Research Council. Van der Ven's research was made possible by a Paul Henry Spaak Fellowship through the Harvard Center for International Affairs. The views expressed and any errors that remain are the authors' alone and should not be attributed to any above-mentioned individuals or organizations.

international steel trade for more than a century. However, not since the 1920s, in the environment of mutual suspicion and costly structural adjustment that followed World War I, have these allegations been so widespread. Indeed, dumping complaints and the use of antidumping policies to protect industries claiming injury from "unfair competition" are prototypical of the "new protectionism" of the post-Bretton Woods era. In contrast to the operation of traditional trade restrictions, which typically entails the imposition of specific or ad valorem tariffs at well-defined rates or quotas at well-defined levels, the new protectionism is characterized by trade restrictions administered on a contingent basis by complex bureaucracies exercising a considerable degree of discretion. Antidumping duties generally, and the Trigger Price Mechanism in particular, can be seen as instances of this phenomenon.

In part, recent interest in U.S. antidumping policies has been stimulated by changes in the popular connotation attached to the term "dumping." Under the provisions of the U.S. Antidumping Act of 1921, the primary definition of dumping was export sales at a price below that of sales in the home market. Following Viner (1923), economists generally adhered to this criterion, defining dumping as price discrimination between national markets and explaining it with familiar theories of monopolistic behavior. This definition encompasses both the standard case of export prices below domestic prices and the opposite configuration, known as "reverse dumping." However, the 1921 antidumping act also included a provision to be invoked in the absence of comparable sales in foreign markets. In such instances, dumping was said to occur when export prices failed to cover a statutory measure of foreign producers' production costs. Nearly half a century ago, Haberler (1937) noted that this "rival" definition had gained considerable currency. The U.S. Trade Act of 1974 and the Trade Agreements Act of 1979 further broadened the applicability of these constructed value provisions. As dumping allegations increasingly have come to revolve around the relation of prices to production costs, the literature has extended beyond reasons for price discrimination to encompass also the motivation for sales at prices that fail to cover costs (e.g., Ethier 1982; Davies and McGuinness 1982).

In this paper, we analyze dumping from both theoretical and empirical points of view.[1] The following four sections take four quite distinct views of dumping and recent U.S. antidumping policies. Section 3.1 describes the evolution of U.S. antidumping policies, emphasizing the changing definition of dumping and the development of administrative procedures. Section 3.2 focuses on the application of these procedures to the international steel trade, taking as a case study the most noteworthy of recent innovations: the Trigger Price Mechanism (TPM). We analyze the administrative and procedural conventions that caused the TPM to be attractive in the first place but contributed ultimately to its demise, and we examine its economic effects. Given recent events, this analysis has the appearance of an extended postmortem, but we think it serves an important function in illuminating some general principles about the effects of administered protection.

Section 3.3 formulates a model that can be used to analyze dumping. We discuss both the "traditional" definition of dumping as price discrimination among national markets and the "modern" definition of dumping as pricing below costs. Evidence presented below indicates the presence of substantial price discrimination persisting for extended periods in markets for steel products, such as cold rolled sheet and concrete reinforcing bars. For this and other reasons, in our theoretical and empirical analyses we concentrate on the traditional definition of dumping as price discrimination in international trade. Section 3.4 calibrates the model and uses it to illustrate how the extent of dumping and the TPM's effects depend on the model's parameters. The final section presents some concluding remarks.

3.1 The Evolution of U.S. Antidumping Policies

Current U.S. antidumping statutes can be traced to the Antidumping Act of 1921.[2] The avowed purpose of the 1921 act was to deter predatory pricing in international trade in order to prevent foreign monopolization of domestic markets.[3] Its provisions, as incorporated into the Tariff Act of 1930, remained little changed until the 1950s. The secretary of the Treasury was to investigate dumping complaints by comparing U.S. import prices with the "fair value" of imports. Upon finding that fair value exceeded U.S. import prices, Treasury was to calculate the difference (known as the dumping margin) and, finding evidence of material injury to U.S. producers, to assess an antidumping duty. Measurement of U.S. import prices was straightforward: the FOB factory sales price could be used except when the transaction between foreign supplier and U.S. purchaser was not at arm's length, in which case U.S. market price, net of import charges and costs of transportation and preparation for the market, could be substituted. From the law's inception, the calculation of fair value was ambiguous, since the concept was not defined by statute. From 1921 through 1954, Treasury used as a standard for fair value a commodity's foreign market value or, in its absence, constructed value. Foreign market value was a transactions price, preferably observed in the exporter's home market but otherwise in third markets. Constructed value was a complex measure made up of allowances for production costs, costs of preparing the good for shipment, and statutory minima for general expenses and profits.

Before 1955, Treasury calculations of fair value and foreign market value rarely proved problematic. Most dumping cases simply were disposed of either on the grounds that injury was absent or on the acceptance of price assurances. In 1954, however, an amendment to the antidumping act assigned responsibility for determining injury to the Tariff Commission and instructed that injury decisions be deferred pending Treasury ruling that dumping was present, thereby subjecting the Treasury's decisions to public scrutiny. In addition, the growth of trade with centrally planned economies for which market prices were not readily observed increased Treasury's reliance on constructed value. Repeatedly, Treasury was forced to revise its procedures as new complications arose. On several occasions between 1958 and 1974, antidumping regulations were modified to bring them into conformance with established practice.

The amendments to the antidumping act contained in the Trade Act of 1974 culminated this process of revision. Of greatest consequence was section 205(b) which defined new circumstances under which the constructed value criterion could be substituted for foreign market value.[4] In instances where sales "over an extended period of time and in substantial quantities" were made in the foreign producer's home market at prices below costs of production, those foreign market prices were to be disregarded and constructed value calculations were to be substituted. Despite ambiguity about the meaning of "an extended period" and "substantial quantities," this revision of the law represented a significant shift in the design of U.S. antidumping policies from an emphasis on dumping as price discrimination to an emphasis on dumping as sales below cost.

The economic effects of the constructed value provisions in U.S. antidumping statutes have been the subject of considerable discussion.[5] According to U.S. antidumping law, constructed value should be a guide to prices which permit the recovery of raw material and fabrication costs, plus a 10 percent minimum allowance for general expenses and an 8 percent minimum allowance for profits.[6] Other than the "extended period" clause, the act makes no provision for the profit margin to vary over the business cycle. Thus, the law makes it difficult for firms to cut prices when market conditions are unfavorable and increases the likelihood that marginal cost pricing during recessions will be construed as dumping. Moreover, the 8 percent profit allowance, which makes no provision for variations in corporate finance, requires a higher return on equity for firms with higher debt-equity ratios, and the 10 percent allowance for general expenses makes no provision for variations in cost structure.

These provisions provided a considerable incentive for U.S. producers to file antidumping suits. In the case of the steel industry, other factors also contributed to the growing incidence of dumping complaints. The United States had been a net importer of steel products since 1959, and by 1968 the import share of the U.S. market had risen to nearly 17 percent.

In 1969 the first of two successive voluntary export restraint agreements with the European Community and Japan went into effect. When the second of these agreements expired in 1974, coincident with the end of the 1972–74 steel market boom, U.S. producers pressed with growing vigor for further voluntary restraints, but without success.[7] From 1975 through 1977, the industry's position worsened: three consecutive years of exceptionally low shipments by domestic producers culminated in a serious profit squeeze. In 1977 the Carter administration suggested that the U.S. steel industry drop its campaign for quantitative import restrictions in return for strict enforcement of the provisions of the 1974 trade act providing protection from unfair foreign competition. As the proceedings of the Gilmore case (filed in early 1977) seemed to indicate, this approach was highly promising. When the industry initiated twenty-three dumping complaints, the European Community threatened to retaliate against the United States, while Treasury and the International Trade Commission were confronted by the difficulty of processing the petitions within required time limits.

The administration had already established a Treasury task force to study the problem. Its recommendations included a reference price system to facilitate rapid initiation of steel dumping complaints.[8] In the event that steel was imported at a price below reference prices based on the constructed value of Japanese steel (Japan was assumed to be the world's most efficient producer), a Treasury dumping investigation automatically would be triggered. Hence the term "Trigger Price Mechanism." Claiming insufficient resources both to administer the TPM and to investigate independent dumping complaints, Treasury warned the industry that the TPM would be maintained only so long as producers refrained from filing antidumping petitions. Eventually, the steel industry complied and withdrew most of its complaints.

The Trade Agreements Act of 1979 represented an attempt to limit the discretion of administrative authorities, to enhance the prospect of relief for petitioners, and to strengthen opportunities for judicial review. Title I of the 1979 act replaced the Antidumping Act of 1921. Its central provisions shortened the time limits within which an antidumping determination must be reached. Under the new law, the preliminary determination of sales at less than fair value must come within 140 or 190 days of the initiation of an investigation, depending on a case's complexity. This compares with 180 or 270 days under previous law. In exceptional circumstances, the preliminary determination now may be announced within ninety days.[9]

In addition to these changes, the 1979 act marks the continued ascendancy of the constructed value criterion. Previously, when price comparisons with the exporters' home markets were appropriate but impossible, the authorities were permitted to use constructed value only when price comparisons with third-country markets were infeasible. Under the 1979 act, they are allowed further discretion in the use of either third-country or constructed value comparisons. Although Treasury initially was instructed to continue its use of third-market comparisons wherever possible, the Department of Commerce now has the option of using constructed value not just when there is evidence that sales fail to cover costs "over an extended period of time and in substantial quantities," but whenever necessary to meet the shortened time limits.[10] Even the possibility that constructed value calculations might be substituted for third-market comparisons has elicited objections from U.S. importers and foreign producers.[11]

Once again, the modifications in the new act provided an inducement to file antidumping petitions. In March 1980 the U.S. Steel Corporation filed a major dumping complaint against European producers, leading to the suspension of the TPM. This and subsequent petitions eventually were withdrawn after a new set of trigger prices was adopted in October. However, this second understanding was even less durable than the first. In January 1982 the steel industry lodged a new round of 132 complaints under the provisions of both countervailing duty and antidumping statutes, marking the second suspension and apparently the demise of the TPM.

In summary, the evolution of U.S. antidumping policies can be seen as a response to economic and administrative exigencies. As markets have grown increasingly integrated, criteria and procedures for determining dumping have been modified to expedite the decision-making process. Statutory and procedural changes have led to growing dependence on the constructed value criterion for dumping. Dissatisfaction with earlier procedures has provided the impetus to reduce the discretion of administrative agencies and to place greater reliance on legalistic procedures, leaving less room for negotiated solutions and encouraging the emergence of adversarial relationships. The Trigger Price Mechanism provides a clear illustration of these phenomena.

3.2 The Trigger Price Mechanism

The TPM was based on the following principles: (1) Treasury was to calculate for each product the average cost of production in Japan, which was assumed to be the world's most efficient producer. (2) Customs was to collect and analyze data on production costs and prices in major steel-exporting countries and to monitor imports by means of a special invoice for steel products, alerting Treasury to substantial or repeated shipments below trigger prices. (3) In such instances, Treasury was to initiate an antidumping investigation without waiting to receive a complaint. (4) While officially the TPM did not prevent domestic producers from exercising their rights under U.S. trade law, in fact the TPM was based on an understanding that existing dumping complaints would be dropped and no major new ones would be initiated. (5) Equally, the TPM did not prevent foreign producers from exercising their rights under U.S. antidumping statutes. Preclearance (assurance that exports under trigger price levels would not lead to the initiation of antidumping procedures) would be granted if they demonstrated that prices were not below fair value. (6) If sales at less than fair value were found and injury was established, countervailing duties were imposed on all shipments of the product by the offending producer. The level of the duty was determined by the difference between either foreign market price or constructed value and U.S. market price; that is, without reference to trigger prices.

The trigger price for each product was made up of three components: a "base price" for each product category, "extras," and transport charges. The base price reflected estimates of the average cost of production in Japan. Treasury, and later Commerce, based their average cost estimates on confidential data supplied by Japan's Ministry of International Trade and Industry (MITI). "Extras" were added to base prices to account for additional costs associated with specifications for width, thickness, chemistry, or surface preparation differing from the base product. To these figures were added transport costs, including charges for Japanese inland freight, loading, ocean freight, insurance, and wharfage. These charges differed for East Coast, Gulf Coast, Pacific Coast, and Great Lakes shipments. Importers' sales commissions were excluded, since trigger prices were based on cost to importers, assuming that transactions were at arm's length. If the importer was related to the exporter of the steel mill product and the transfer price did not reflect an arm's-length transaction, then the first sales price by the importer to an unrelated U.S. buyer was compared with the trigger price.

Trigger prices were calculated in dollars per metric ton (2,205 lbs) or net ton (2,000 lbs), with quarterly adjustments for changes in estimated production costs, transport charges, and yen-dollar exchange rates. To provide the authorities with some discretion in light of the extent of exchange rate fluctuations, a 5 percent "flexibility band" was introduced to permit trigger prices to fluctuate around landed cost estimates. With the reinstatement of the TPM in 1980, the preclearance procedure and the exchange rate conversion factor were altered, and an "antisurge" provision was added, setting quantitative rules for a special review of imports in periods when steel imports were increasing and domestic capacity utilization was low.[12]

3.2.1 Calculating Trigger Prices

Calculating Japanese production costs is a difficult task. (A representative estimate is shown in table 3.1.) We focus on four problematic aspects

Table 3.1   Estimated Japanese Cost of Production (1981 IV, dollars per metric
                   ton finished product)

Basic raw materials	166.60
Other raw materials	86.90
Labor	106.62
Other expenses	26.01
Depreciation	35.86
Interest	28.67
Profit	30.57
Scrap-yield credit	30.89
Total	467.74

Source: Department of Commerce, International Trade Administration.

of the cost calculation: estimating normal capacity utilization rates, adding an allowance for profits, estimating yield ratios, and converting costs in yen into trigger prices in dollars.

Estimates of normal capacity utilization rates mattered for calculating Japanese costs because the fixed cost component of total costs was divided by normal capacity utilization rather than current capacity utilization in constructing fixed costs per ton of production. For the second and third quarters of 1978, cost estimates were based on an 85 percent capacity utilization rate, the average for Japanese facilities over the previous twenty years. In 1978 IV, Treasury switched to the average operating rate over the previous five years. Given Japan's relatively low capacity utilization rates in the mid-1970s, this change raised trigger prices by approximately $18 per net ton.[13] This effect became even more significant as the high capacity utilization years 1973–74 left the five-year reference period. Capacity utilization assumptions significantly affected estimated Japanese costs because not only 90 percent of depreciation and 75 percent of interest expenses, but 50 percent of labor costs and other expenses were included in fixed costs.

In accordance with U.S. trade law, under the TPM an allowance for normal profits was added to Japanese costs in the amount of 8 percent of raw material costs, labor costs, and other expenses. Like fixed costs, this allowance was divided by normal capacity utilization rather than actual capacity utilization in calculating profits per ton of production. Compared to the constructed value provision of U.S. antidumping law, there was little tendency for the profit margin to rise as the level of activity declined. However, this provision still prevented foreign firms from emulating their domestic competitors by reducing their markups and accepting lower profit margins in periods of stagnant demand.

The production cost data submitted by MITI were based on an 86.5 percent yield ratio (tons of finished steel per ton of crude steel). U.S. producers, whose older facilities generated lower yields, claimed that some of the products that were regarded as finished by the Japanese were scrap by U.S. standards. Consequently, the 86.5 percent yield was lowered to 80 percent. Only from 1978 IV, after a mission by the Steel Task Force to Japan, was the extent of Japanese superiority in steel processing and finishing recognized and incorporated into higher yield ratios of 82.7 percent and into higher yield credits, together reducing estimated Japanese costs by as much as $15 per net ton.[14]

While trigger prices were expressed in dollars, production costs, with the exception of most raw materials, were denominated in yen. Since exchange rates were considerably more variable than production costs, initially yen were converted to dollars using a sixty-day average exchange rate for the period prior to announcement of the current quarter's trigger prices. After reinstatement, this sixty-day average was replaced by a thirty-six-month moving average "to minimize the impact of exchange rate fluctuations on TPM levels."[15] This change in the exchange rate used to convert yen to dollars significantly affected trigger price levels.[16]

Table 3.2 illustrates the extent to which exchange rate conversion factors affected estimated Japanese production costs. For example, had Japanese production costs been based on current exchange rates, the average base price would have fallen from $395 in 1978 IV to $356 in 1979 IV instead of rising by $16 over the period. Had a thirty-six-month average been used in this period, it is likely that the TPM would have been stillborn, because the first base price would have been $293 instead of $328, a difference of 11 percent.

In the first year of the TPM, the base price rose 18 percent, not withstanding a 2.8 percent downward adjustment under flexibility band provisions. This rise was almost exclusively attributable to appreciation of the yen. It is not surprising that a one-year review of the TPM by the Steel Tripartite Committee regarded it as a highly successful mechanism.[17] In 1979 I the yen began its steep decline, which was reflected in trigger prices beginning with 1979 II. Rising Japanese production costs were almost entirely offset by the higher yen/dollar exchange rate: the 1980 I base price was less than 2 percent above its 1979 I level. Again, it is not surprising that the U.S. industry grew increasingly dissatisfied with the TPM's operation. The U.S. Steel Company filed its March 1980 antidumping suits in reaction to these developments more than anything else.[18] Thus, exchange rate fluctuations play a major role in explaining the suspension of the TPM.

Following reinstatement, the thirty-six-month average was substituted for the sixty-day average. This reduced the risk that further depreciation of the yen would reduce base prices in the immediate future. The choice of exchange rate conversion factor had major implications. The most extreme instance was in 1979 I when the difference under the two exchange rate conversion factors was 20 percent. If in the first two years of

Table 3.2   **Influence of Exchange Rates on Trigger Prices**

Quarter	Current Rate[b]	Yen/Dollar Exchange Rate — 60-Day Average[c] Used in TPM	60-Day Average[c] Calculated	36-Month Average[d] Used in TPM	36-Month Average[d] Calculated	Japanese Cost of Production[a] (dollars per metric ton) — Based on Current Exchange Rate Hypothetical[e]	Based on 60-Day Average Exchange Rate Actual	Based on 60-Day Average Exchange Rate Hypothetical[e]	Based on 36-Month Average Exchange Rate Actual	Based on 36-Month Average Exchange Rate Hypothetical[e]	Base Prices — Average Base Trigger Price (dollars per metric ton)	Difference between Base Prices and Japanese Cost of Production[f]
1978 II	221	240			286	347	328.23			293	328.26	—
III	193	226			281	386	346.30			301	346.30	—
IV	190	215			274	395	363.12			311	363.12	—
1979 I	201	187			265	370	399.59			321	388.54	−2.8%
II	218	197			256	359	383.94			325	388.54	+1.2
III	219	212			248	367	375.97			340	383.09	+1.9
IV	239	217			241	356	378.86			354	383.09	+1.1

1980 I	244	227		236	362	379.63	370	394.97	+4.0
1980 II									
1980 III	} Suspension of TPM								
1980 IV	211	223	223	460	443	442.83		442.83	—
1981 I	206	211	221	468	461	446.83		446.63	—
1981 II	220	204	218	442	467	446.22		466.22	—
1981 III	232	218	216	446	465	467.81		466.22	-0.3
1981 IV	225	234	217	457	445	467.74		466.22	-0.3
1982 I	234	227	221	446	455	463.60		466.22	+0.6

SOURCES: Calculations based on International Monetary Fund, *International Financial Statistics*, various issues; Department of Commerce, International Trade Administration, *Announcement of Trigger Price Levels*, various issues; Department of Treasury, *News*, various issues.

[a] Base prices, which are for illustrative purposes only, do not include "extras," transport costs, and importation charges.

[b] Average exchange rate for the quarter.

[c] The sixty-day average was based on a period terminating between one and two months before the quarter's start. In calculating the sixty-day average exchange rate applied to a quarter, we average the exchange rate for the first two months of the previous quarter.

[d] Average of thirty-six months terminating two months before the quarter's start.

[e] For purposes of these calculations, base prices are corrected for flexibility band effects. One-third of Japanese costs are assumed to be expressed in dollars to allow for dollar-denominated raw material imports.

[f] Japanese production cost estimates may differ from base trigger prices due to use of the flexibility band. A "plus" indicates an upward adjustment due to the flexibility band.

the TPM a thirty-six-month average had been used, Japanese production costs in dollars would have been 12 percent lower on average. In contrast, following the reinstatement of the TPM, the difference under the two methods was comparatively small.

The TPM's first suspension was partly the result of the depreciation of the yen and the strength of the dollar; its second suspension and demise were partly a consequence of inflation in the United States combined with stable Japanese production costs, in yen, and a virtually constant thirty-six-month average exchange rate. At the same time, fluctuations of the European currencies against the dollar and the yen contributed to disintegration of the second stage of the TPM. Appreciation of the yen against most European currencies increased European producers' ability to export below trigger prices (see table 3.3). Although the impact of these exchange rate changes was mitigated to some extent by raw material prices being quoted in dollars, it resulted in a proliferation of preclearance requests by European producers; for example, preclearance procedures on behalf of Hoogovens of the Netherlands indicated that they were capable of exporting under trigger prices without exporting below fair value. With the realization that prospects for extensive antidumping actions were dim, the U.S. steel industry's focus shifted increasingly to the issue of foreign government subsidization, and the TPM's days were numbered.

3.2.2   Economic Implications of the TPM

The shipping cost of Japanese exports to the United States differs substantially by region (see table 3.4). Since different trigger prices were calculated by region, owing to differences in Japanese transport costs and related factors, the system significantly distorted established trade and

Table 3.3   **Exchange Rates under the Second Stage of the TPM, 1980 IV–1982 I***

	Against Yen[a]	Against "TPM-Yen"[b]	Against $[a]
Belgian franc	−18%	−27%	−35%
German mark	−10%	−19%	−23%
French franc	−18%	−27%	−36%
Italian lira	−20%	−29%	−39%
British pound	−14%	−23%	−29%

SOURCES: Department of Commerce, International Trade Administration, *Commerce News*, various issues; International Monetary Fund, *International Financial Statistics*, various issues.

[a]Quarter averages.

[b]Thirty-six-month average used in calculating Japanese production costs in dollars.

*A minus indicates an appreciation of the yen.

Table 3.4   **Importation Charges on Japanese Steel Products, 1978 II**
                   (dollars per metric ton)

Product	Freight	Insurance	Interest	Handling	Total
Hot rolled carbon bars to:					
Lakes	40.83	3.49	11.18	3.63	59.13
East	28.13	3.36	8.77	3.63	43.89
Gulf	23.59	3.32	8.66	4.54	40.11
Pacific	22.69	3.31	6.68	2.72	35.40
Cold rolled sheet to:					
Lakes	31.76	2.42	7.77	3.63	45.58
East	24.50	2.34	6.14	3.63	36.61
Gulf	20.87	2.31	6.05	4.54	33.77
Pacific	20.87	2.31	4.68	2.72	30.58

SOURCE: *Treasury News*, 3 January 1978.

production patterns. The use of Japanese transport costs in the calculation of trigger prices reversed the traditional geographic relationship of relatively low Great Lakes prices to relatively high West Coast prices.[19] The implications for foreign producers, other than the Japanese, depended on whether their major export market was the East Coast and the Great Lakes or the Gulf Coast and the West. Regional differences in trigger prices penalized European producers whose markets were in the East relative to those whose markets were in the West. The effects were analogous for domestic firms: West Coast producers were penalized relative to East Coast and Great Lakes producers, since they faced lower priced import competition. Both the 30 percent rise in imports on the Pacific Coast between 1977 and 1978, in a period when imports into the Great Lakes region were declining by 15 percent, and the losses experienced by Kaiser Steel (a leading West Coast producer) in an otherwise profitable year may have reflected these phenomena.[20] Similarly, domestic steel-using industries in Ohio were put at a disadvantage relative to their competitors in California and the Southwest. European opposition to generous trigger prices in their major regional markets led Treasury to adjust downward the freight allowance to the Great Lakes, but distortions of established trade patterns remained.

In addition to regional price differentials, the product mix of imports was altered by the TPM. For some products, differences between trigger prices and U.S. mill list prices were substantial, while for others they were minor. Compare the margins (which disregard American discounting) reported in table 3.5. A comparison of trigger prices and American list prices suggests that the trigger-price/list-price differential varied substantially. Foreign producers specializing in relatively sophisticated, ex-

Table 3.5   Trigger Price–U.S. List Price Differentials, 1978

	Trigger Price 1978 II, Plus Estimated Duties East Coast (1)	U.S. Steel Co. List Price January 1978 (2)	(1) − (2) in % of (1) (3)	U.S. Steel Co. List Price February 1978 (4)	(1) − (4) in % of (1) (5)
Hot rolled sheet	$262	$288	−9	$300	−15
Plate	301	324	−7	323	−8
Cold rolled sheet	329	333	−1	358	−9
Hot rolled bar	373	359	+4	345	+8
Tin plate	500	481	+4	na	na

SOURCE: *Iron Age*, 16 January 1978, p. 29.
na: not available.

pensive products objected most strenuously to large positive differentials.

Another effect was a shift by foreign producers to the sale of fabricated steel products which were exempt initially from the TPM. Imports of fabricated standard shapes were 71 percent higher in December 1978 than in the previous year. In contrast to large increases in the price of basic steel products, the prices of TPM-exempt fabricated standard shapes increased on average by only 3.5 percent from the previous year.[21] The wire and wire rod segment of the market provides a graphic example of incomplete coverage: the fact that initially the TPM covered wire processors' inputs but not their outputs led them to complain of negative effective rates of protection. Subsequent extensions of the TPM's coverage from 65 percent of imports initially to 85 percent in 1979 II reflected the administration's recognition of this problem.

The establishment of a single reference price for a particular steel product, independent of origin, affects all foreign suppliers similarly only if products are homogeneous. In fact, significant quality differences exist in products that appear superficially to be homogeneous.[22] Prior to the TPM, foreign suppliers of low-quality steel could use low prices to compete with suppliers of higher quality products. This was more difficult under the TPM, which tended, other things equal, to divert trade from suppliers of low-quality steel to suppliers of high-quality products.

In theory, the TPM was based on prices charged by exporters to unrelated U.S. customers, or by related importers to subsequent unrelated customers. However, when the exporting and importing companies were related, the proper measure of compliance often was difficult to observe. Domestic customers could delegate steel purchases to a foreign branch or open an offshore trading firm to buy foreign steel below trigger prices and export it to the United States above trigger prices. Similarly, foreign producers with downstream investments in steel processing in the United States could respect trigger prices in sales to U.S. subsidiaries, merely transferring profits from the U.S. subsidiary to the foreign base without affecting any physical transactions. The rise of related party transactions from 40 to 60 percent of total imports in the first year of the TPM is suggestive of the extent of these practices.[23] In response, Commerce changed its related party monitoring procedures to include an ex mill price monitoring policy and new rules to evaluate unrelated resale prices.

Economic considerations provided importers and exporters with obvious incentives to circumvent the Customs Bureau's policing mechanism. The indictment of the Japanese trading company, Mitsui, for defrauding the United States provides an indication of the techniques available to an importer.[24] To circumvent the TPM and the antidumping act, Mitsui admitted reporting falsely inflated invoice prices and reducing actual payments by customers by arranging false contract cancelation confirmations, which entitled the customer to cancelation penalties; by providing refunds for false damage claims, misproductions, or other debit memoranda; by paying commissions to a foreign parent company of an American customer; and by making "currency adjustment" payments based on a secret "yen/dollar exchange rate agreement." It also admitted predating contracts to shift the apparent sales date into the period when the TPM was suspended.

We have no way of estimating the prevalence of such practices, but it is clear that insuring compliance is one of the major problems confronting architects of schemes for administered protection such as the TPM. To understand these problems better, it may help to look more closely at the motivation for dumping itself.

3.3 Models of Dumping

Although a number of explanations for dumping, defined either as price discrimination in international trade or as sales below costs of production, are current in policy circles, few of these arguments have been subjected to formal analysis. In this section we first review the popular explanations, starting with the "modern" definition of dumping as sales below costs of production, before proceeding to the alternative definition of the practice as international price discrimination. Finally, we present a theoretical model of what seems to us a particularly important explanation for dumping in the international steel trade: international differences in industry structure and conduct in imperfectly competitive, segmented markets.

Until recently there have been few formal models of reasons why firms may persist in exporting at prices below production costs. It is well known, of course, that in perfectly competitive markets where firms equate price with marginal cost, it may be optimal to continue operating at a loss during periods of depressed demand so long as revenues cover variable costs. However, this does not seem to be quite what those who criticize sales below costs have in mind. Rather, they seem to be objecting to practices which imply that firms have departed from their cost curves and are engaged in questionable practices, possibly predatory in nature. Ethier (1982) has presented a model in which competitive firms not only export at prices below costs but appear to depart from their supply curves when demand is unusually depressed. He assumes that firms are constrained to negotiate wage contracts before the state of demand is known, and that they are incapable of responding to a demand shortfall by renegotiating wages. Their only option is to lay off laborers whose contracts can be terminated. Since they are not permitted to accumulate inventories, firms may have no choice but to sell output at prices below average cost when demand is unfavorable. The unique feature of the model is that there are circumstances in which it is optimal for firms to practice restraint in laying off workers even when labor's wage exceeds its marginal product. Ethier assumes that employers and employees share knowledge of the shape of the wage-employment trade-off. Firms which retain some workers when demand is depressed despite the fact that labor's wage exceeds its marginal product are able to pay lower wages, other things being equal, when demand is buoyant. Thus, firms engage in practices that bear little resemblance to a strategy of minimizing losses in the face of fixed costs and that therefore can be construed as predatory dumping. In fact, they are merely acting in their perceived long-run interest, given conditions in factor and product markets.

Other explanations for the persistence of pricing below apparent variable costs are based on dynamic considerations. In Eichengreen (1982) we analyze several dynamic models. We formalize the claim that firms dump intermittently to attract other firms' loyal customers, referred to by Stegemann (1980) as the "short-sighted buyer" argument. The firm's problem is formulated in standard dynamic optimization terms, where the number of customers to whom it can sell is a slowly adjusting variable that depends on the firm's past pricing policy. In response to disturbances, the firm may find it optimal to reduce price below variable cost in order to augment its stock of customers. At each point in time, the firm equates current marginal cost with marginal revenue from current sales plus the present value of future sales to customers acquired as a result of current pricing policy. This practice, which in fact equates marginal cost with shadow marginal revenue, resembles dumping nonetheless.

We also formalize the argument that firms may price below the standard markup and perhaps below current variable cost in periods of depressed demand due to additional costs of adjusting the level of production. Again, the dynamic optimization problem is standard, except that we include an adjustment cost term, specified as an increasing function of the percentage change in output. The optimal response to a permanent decline in demand is fairly intuitive. As the unanticipated demand shortfall occurs, the firm must sharply reduce its price, since it is costly to cut production in response to the exogenous decline in demand. Over time, the firm reduces production at the optimal rate, given adjustment costs, permitting it to increase the price charged for its output. Although the firm is simply equating marginal revenue with shadow marginal cost, the initial price cut again resembles dumping.

Another popular dynamic argument is that dumping results from firms' concern with the economics of learning by doing. If firms wish to move down their learning curves, they may sell output at prices where current marginal costs are more than current marginal revenues. If higher output now reduces costs of production later, then the solution to a firm's dynamic optimization problem is to set current marginal cost equal to the sum of current marginal revenue plus the present value of the indirect saving on future production costs. Spence (1981) has analyzed this problem for the closed economy, and Krugman (1982) has extended the analysis to the case of international competition.

The other explanations for dumping we have labeled the "traditional" view. In textbooks, dumping is explained as price discrimination between national markets by foreign producers facing a price elasticity of demand in the export market that exceeds the price elasticity of demand in their own market.[25] Permitting foreign suppliers to discriminate in favor of domestic consumers reduces the surplus captured by domestic rivals but by less than the increase in the surplus captured by domestic consumers. Domestic competitors have an incentive to lobby for restrictions on price discrimination by foreign suppliers, while policymakers seeking to maximize national welfare have an incentive to resist.[26]

A limitation of the textbook explanation of dumping as monopolistic price discrimination is that different price elasticities of demand are assumed to arise arbitrarily from taste differences among residents of home and foreign countries. As Brander and Krugman (1983) note, this explanation provides little guidance as to when we should expect to observe dumping rather than reverse dumping or no price discrimination at all.

We proceed by analyzing the textbook explanation for dumping as price discrimination in international trade. However, instead of assuming arbitrary differences in demand, we emphasize systematic differences in supply. Specifically, we focus on aspects of market structure and conduct that can lead to price discrimination in favor of overseas customers. To highlight these factors, we assume, until explicitly stated to the contrary, that commodity demands in the home and foreign countries are identical. Thus, dumping cannot arise from arbitrary differences in tastes. To further simplify the exposition, we assume throughout the theoretical analysis that the common price elasticity of demand ϵ is constant and exceeds one in absolute value.

We analyze a model made up of two regions (or "countries"): the importing and exporting, or domestic and foreign, countries. As the nomenclature suggests, the model does not admit of trade-pattern reversals or two-way trade in identical products. It is necessary to rule out reexports by assumption, for in their presence price discrimination (net of transport costs) is impossible. Any one of several restrictions is sufficient to preclude this possibility; for simplicity we assume that the exporting country's market is protected by prohibitive trade restrictions. We consider a number of specific market structures under which dumping may occur. Market structure is taken as parametric in that entry and exit are not permitted. Models of dumping as entry deterrence are considered in

Eichengreen (1982), but such considerations are omitted here as not being essential to a relatively short-run analysis of the steel industry.

The implication of the analysis is the same in each case: dumping will occur when firms producing for sale to customers in the importing country find it relatively difficult to restrict output to the joint-profit-maximizing level. The incidence of dumping will depend on the number of firms producing for each national market, their costs, their market shares, and the degree to which they recognize and exploit their mutual dependence.

Assume initially that a homogeneous commodity Z is produced at home and abroad by identical single-product firms, subject to a fixed cost F and a constant variable cost c.

(1)
$$C_\ell = F + c(y_\ell).$$
$$C_i^* = F^* + c^*(x_i + x_i^*).$$

$C(C^*)$ is total cost of domestic (foreign) firms;[27] asterisks denote foreign values throughout; y_ℓ is domestic firm ℓ's production for the domestic market; and x_i and x_i^* are foreign firm i's production for the domestic and foreign markets, respectively. The constant variable cost assumption is dispensable, but it makes for expository simplicity. Its realism is addressed below.

The industry in each country is comprised of a small number of oligopolistic rivals. Initially, we assume that all such firms abide by the Cournot rule, setting quantities under the assumption that rivals' supplies to each market are fixed. A variety of richer strategies are available to the firm, but this assumption provides a reasonable starting point. Here and below, we consistently assume that second-order and stability conditions are satisfied. Each firm maximizes profits $\pi(\pi^*)$ subject to its rivals' behavior. It is possible that firms owned or operated by government agencies pursue other objectives, but we restrict our attention here to the implications of profit maximization. For a representative foreign firm:

(2) $\pi_i^* = p(z)x_i + p^*(z^*)x_i^* - c_i^*(x_i + x_i^*) - F_i^*,$

where z is total supply to the domestic market ($z = \Sigma_{i=1}^{k} x_i + \Sigma_{\ell=k+1}^{m} y_\ell$), and z^* is total supply to the foreign market ($z^* = \Sigma_{i=1}^{k} x_i^*$). There are k foreign firms and $m - k$ domestic firms; p and p^* are the domestic and foreign prices of Z. $\partial\pi_i^*/\partial x_i^*$ implies that:

(3) $p^* - (p^*/\epsilon)(x_i^*/z^*) = c_i^*,$

where $\epsilon = (-dz/dp)(p/z)$ is the price elasticity of market demand. Multiplying by x_i^*/z^* and summing over the k firms which produce for sale to foreign customers yields:

(4) $p^* - (p^*/\epsilon)H^* = \hat{c}^*,$

where $\hat{c}^* = \Sigma_{i=1}^k (x_i^*/z^*)c_i^*$ is the share-weighted average of the variable costs of foreign firms, and $H^* = \Sigma_{i=1}^k (x_i^*/z^*)^2$ is the Herfindahl index of foreign sales concentration.[28] Since the markup over marginal cost is an increasing function of H^*:

(5)
$$\frac{p^*}{\hat{c}^*} = \frac{\epsilon}{\epsilon - H^*},$$

the ratio of foreign to domestic prices (the "dumping ratio") is:

(6)
$$\frac{p^*}{p} = \frac{\hat{c}^*}{\hat{c}} \cdot \frac{\epsilon - H}{\epsilon - H^*}.$$

Here $\hat{c}$ is a share-weighted average of variable costs for firms selling to the domestic market, and H is the Herfindahl index of domestic sales concentration, defined over both domestic and foreign firms. Note that the Herfindahl index measures the extent to which sales to customers in a given country (as distinct from production by firms located in that country) are concentrated among a small number of rivals. The first term in equation (6) indicates that price will be lower in the market where, on average, suppliers produce subject to lower variable costs. The second term in (6) indicates that the domestic price/cost ratio will be lower than the foreign one when the domestic market is less concentrated than the foreign market as measured by the Herfindahl index. The greater the degree of concentration in sales, the closer the oligopolists are able to approach the joint-profit-maximizing solution.

The intuition for this result is apparent. Equation (3), from which the dumping ratio is derived, indicates that a firm sets perceived marginal revenue equal to marginal cost. Perceived marginal revenue depends not only on market price and market elasticity of demand but also on the individual firm's market share. A smaller market share increases the elasticity of a firm's perceived marginal revenue function by reducing its loss of revenue on inframarginal sales.

A special case is where all firms produce subject to identical costs. In this case, all firms selling in a particular market have identical market shares, and the Herfindahl index is simply the reciprocal of that number of firms. Dumping occurs when more firms produce for sale to the domestic market than to the foreign one, which is necessarily the case in this instance, given our other assumptions. The sales of each domestic firm are z/m, so profits of each firm are $[p(z) - c]z/m - F$. Thus, while our model focuses on the price discrimination definition of dumping, it is compatible with the sales below cost criterion analyzed by Ethier (1982) and others, for it is entirely possible in our model for profits to be negative during periods of depressed demand.

It is straightforward to generalize the dumping ratio to allow firms to anticipate the reactions of rivals and to introduce a competitive fringe in each market. To introduce the fringe firms, define:

$$x^* = \sum_{i=1}^{k} x_i^* + \sum_{\ell=k+1}^{n} x_\ell^*,$$

(7)
$$x = \sum_{i=1}^{k} x_i + \sum_{\ell=k+1}^{n} x_\ell,$$

$$y = \sum_{q=n+1}^{s} y_q + \sum_{u=s+1}^{w} y_u,$$

where there are $n - k$ members of the foreign competitive fringe and $w - s$ members of the domestic competitive fringe. Each domestic oligopolist maximizes the expression:

(8)
$$\pi_q = p(z)y_q - c_q(y_q) - F_q.$$

The first-order condition is:

(9)
$$p + y_q \frac{\partial p}{\partial z} \left(\frac{\partial z}{\partial y_q} + \sum_{i=1}^{n} \frac{\partial x_i}{\partial y_q} + \sum_{q \neq r}^{w} \frac{\partial y_r}{\partial y_q} \right) = c_q.$$

We assume that oligopolists neglect the reaction of fringe firms ($\sum_{u=s+1}^{w} [\partial y_u/\partial y_q] = \sum_{\ell=k+1}^{n} [\partial x_\ell/\partial y_q] = 0$) and that members of the fringe act as price-takers, setting price equal to marginal cost. For algebraic simplicity, we assume that each firm's conjecture about the reaction of each rival is identical.[29] Multiplying by y_q/z (or by x_i/z) and summing over firms producing for the domestic market yields an expression that can be rearranged to read:

(10)
$$\frac{p}{\hat{c}} = \frac{\epsilon}{\epsilon - \tilde{H}(1 + \delta)},$$

where $\tilde{H}$ is the truncated Herfindahl index for the $k + s - n$ largest firms selling to the domestic market, and δ is the conjectural variation on rivals' domestic sales.[30] The dumping ratio is:

(11)
$$\frac{p^*}{p} = \frac{\hat{c}^*}{\hat{c}} \cdot \frac{\epsilon - \tilde{H}(1 + \delta)}{\epsilon - \tilde{H}^*(1 + \delta^*)},$$

where $\tilde{H}^*$ is the truncated Herfindahl index for foreign firms, defined over shares of foreign sales, and δ^* is the conjectural variation on foreign rivals' foreign sales. Thus, the dumping ratio depends on costs, on market demand elasticities, and on (truncated) Herfindahl indices, now adjusted for conjectural variations. The dumping ratio is a decreasing function of the conjectural variation in the domestic market, since the larger the conjectural variation, the greater the perceived threat of retaliation by rivals to an individual firm's price reduction.

It is a small step to derive the analogous expression when domestic and foreign outputs are imperfect substitutes. Let $p' = p'(y, p)$, where p' is the price of home output in the domestic market, and p is the price of foreign output in the domestic market. For simplicity of exposition, we retain the assumption that the foreign market is closed to imports; thus $p^* = p^*(x^*)$. It will be necessary to consider two price ratios. Denote the market share of the domestic fringe θ. Each domestic oligopolist maximizes the expression:

$$(8') \qquad \pi_q = p'(y, p)y_q - c_q(y_q) - F_q.$$

The first-order condition is:

$$(9') \qquad p' + y_q \frac{\partial p'}{\partial y}\left(\frac{\partial y}{\partial y_q} + \sum_{q \neq r}^{s} \frac{\partial y_r}{\partial y_q} + \sum_{u \neq v}^{w} \frac{\partial y_v}{\partial y_q}\right)$$

$$+ y_q \frac{\partial p'}{\partial p} \frac{\partial p}{\partial y_q} = c_q.$$

For algebraic simplicity, we again assume that each domestic oligopolist's conjecture about the reaction of each domestic rival is identical. It is convenient to impose two further assumptions: that each domestic oligopolist makes the same conjecture about the response of foreign suppliers to a percentage change in its output ($\psi = [\partial p/\partial y_q][y_q/p]$ is the same for all q), and that each domestic oligopolist forms the same estimate of the ratio of cross- to own-price elasticities in the demand for its output (that is, each makes the same estimate of $\alpha = [\partial p'/\partial p][p/p']$). Recalling that oligopolists neglect the fringe's reaction ($\sum_{u=s+1}^{w}[\partial y_u/\partial y_q] = 0$) and that members of the fringe act as price-takers, multiplying by y_q/z and summing over domestic firms yields:

$$(10') \qquad \frac{p'}{\hat{c}'} = \frac{\epsilon'}{\epsilon'(1 + \sigma) - \tilde{H}_y(1 + \delta)},$$

where $\sigma = (1 - \theta)\alpha\psi$, $\hat{c}'$ is the share-weighted average of variable costs for domestic firms, and ϵ' is the elasticity of demand for the domestic good, as distinct from the elasticity of demand for the foreign good (still denoted ϵ). $\tilde{H}_y$ is the truncated Herfindahl index for the $s - n$ largest domestic firms, and δ is now the conjectural variation on domestic rivals' behavior. Making the same assumptions about foreign firms, the dumping ratio is:

$$(11') \qquad \frac{p^*}{p} = \frac{\hat{c}^*}{\hat{c}} \cdot \frac{\epsilon(1 + \sigma^*) - \tilde{H}_x^*(1 + \delta^*)}{\epsilon - \tilde{H}_{x^*}^*(1 + \delta^*)},$$

and the ratio of imported to domestic steel prices is:

$$(11'') \qquad \frac{p}{p'} = \frac{\hat{c}}{\hat{c}'} \cdot \frac{\epsilon}{\epsilon'} \cdot \frac{\epsilon'(1 + \sigma) - \tilde{H}_y(1 + \delta)}{\epsilon(1 + \sigma_x^*) - \tilde{H}^*(1 + \delta^*)},$$

where $\tilde{H}_x^*(\tilde{H}_{x^*}^*)$ is the truncated Herfindahl index defined over shares of sales of the k largest foreign firms in the domestic (foreign) market. Again, the dumping ratio depends on (truncated) Herfindahl indices adjusted for conjectural variations. The ratio p/p' is a decreasing function of the conjectural variation in the domestic market, since the larger the conjectural variation, the greater the extent of retaliation anticipated by firms contemplating a price reduction. Now, however, the dumping ratio also depends on market demand elasticities adjusted for the effects of σ^*. The term σ^* reflects foreign firms' estimates of the substitutability of national outputs α and foreign firms' conjectures on their domestic rivals' reactions to import price cuts ψ. The larger foreign firms' conjectures on the reaction of domestic firms to an import price reduction, the less the temptation to cut prices.

The welfare effects of antidumping actions are illustrated in figures 3.1 and 3.2, with zero subscripts denoting initial prices and quantities. We consider the case where domestic and foreign outputs are imperfect substitutes for one another and analyze the effects of an antidumping action which effectively places a floor p_1 beneath the price of imports (fig. 3.1). Income effects are neglected throughout. Before any antidumping action, there is a distortion in each market due to the presence of imperfect competition. When the price of the importable is raised from p_0 to p_1, rents accruing to foreign suppliers change by areas $E - B$. $E - B$ may be positive, in part since foreign producers were incapable previously of restricting output to joint-profit-maximizing levels. Even in this

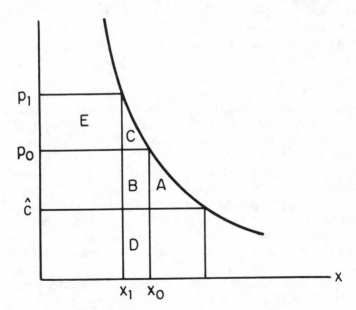

Fig. 3.1   Imported Steel

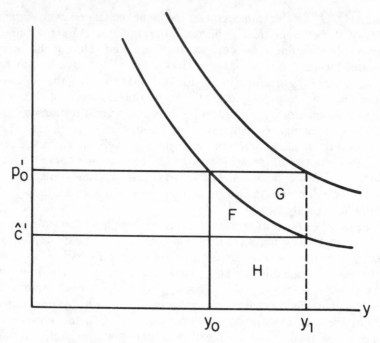

Fig. 3.2   Domestic Steel

case, however, foreigners may object to antidumping initiatives, since under the assumptions of the model any one foreign producer expects to increase its profits by expanding supply and driving down prices. It is possible for $E - B$ to be negative if $p_1 - p_0$ is large and if the demand for imports is depressed sufficiently below the joint-profit-maximizing level.

The rise in the price of imports shifts the demand curve for domestic output to the right (see fig. 3.2). However, due to our assumption of a constant demand elasticity and no change in firms' conjectures, domestic producers do not raise prices in response to the shift in domestic demand. In this model, if domestic rents are zero initially, they remain zero. In this case import restraints do not increase the profitability of domestic production, and domestic producers derive little if any benefit from the imposition of antidumping duties or similar trade restrictions. In general, the change in domestic rents equals $F + G$.

The implications for domestic consumers are straightforward. Consumers suffer a loss of surplus in the market for imported steel amounting to areas $C + E$. Since the marginal utility of y equals the price consumers pay, there is no change in consumer surplus in the market for domestic steel.

To measure the welfare loss associated with an antidumping action which raises the price of x from p_0 to p_1, we employ Harberger's (1974) standard formula $-\Delta W = 1/2\Sigma_i \Delta T_i \Delta Q_i + \Sigma_i T_i \Delta Q_i$, where ΔW is the change in welfare, Q_i is the quantity demanded, and T_i is the distortion due to the divergence of price from marginal cost. The first term in this summation approximates area C in figure 3.1; $\Sigma_i T_i \Delta Q_i$ approximates areas $F + G - B$. B is the extra loss in the market for x due to the presence of a previous distortion also working to restrict demand. $F + G$ is the welfare gain in the market for y, since raising the price of imports stimulates demand for another good whose production is depressed by the presence of a second distortion. Thus, for the welfare loss we have the expression $-\Delta W = (B + C) - (F + G)$.

3.4   Some Numerical Estimates

In this section we calibrate the model of section 3.3 to illustrate how the extent of dumping and the TPM's effects depend on the model's parameters. We calibrate the model for 1979, the latest year for which the necessary data are available and the TPM was in effect. Readers familiar with previous efforts along these lines will note the resemblance of our approach to those of Crandall (1981) and Tarr (1982a). Our framework differs from theirs, however, in that we highlight the presence of imperfect competition.

One way to proceed is to estimate pricing equations with time-series data. The results of section 3.3 indicate that the dumping ratio should be a function of the market demand elasticities, Herfindahl indices, and conjectural variations. Using time-series methods to estimate this relationship is appealing, but in this instance there are a number of impediments to implementing this approach. Consistent time series on the value and volume of precisely defined categories of European steel exports can be constructed only from 1960 or 1966. The small size of the sample is problematic when the pricing equation is nonlinear, as is the case in section 3.3. A further difficulty is that certain variables of interest, such as the conjectural variation, are unobservable. While the use of proxies is feasible, it is unlikely in practice to yield definitive conclusions. In preference to time-series estimation, we choose to examine what data are available and to use them as a basis for calibrating the model. The parameter values imposed are best thought of as informed guesses of the relevant magnitudes. Given that our model is highly simplified and that our parameter values are certainly not above dispute, we would prefer our estimates to be viewed as numerical illustrations of how the extent of dumping and the TPM's effects depend on particular parameters.

3.4.1   Data

A number of sources provide information on the domestic and foreign prices of steel products. However, there are difficult and well-known problems in establishing a concordance between U.S. statistics and those of other nations. In this section we examine data on the price of European steel exports to the United States relative to the price of the same goods in Europe, since European producers were among the exporters most heavily affected by U.S. trigger prices. While official base prices for European steel products are readily available, the prevalence of discounting in the European steel market renders them a poor proxy for transactions prices. We choose instead to examine unit value figures derived from international trade statistics. Thus, for the price of European steel in Europe, we use unit values of intra–European Community (EC) trade. By implication, we neglect discounting by European producers in sales to their favored domestic customers. Unit values are themselves imperfect proxies for transactions prices; a number of authors have shown that changes in calculated unit values tend to lag behind changes in transactions prices. While this problem should be borne in mind, it is more important in other applications than when trade figures are annual totals and when one set of unit values is deflated by another.

Calculated unit values for European exports have been employed previously by Tarr (1979, 1982b) and Takacs (1982). However, their figures are not appropriate for our purposes, since they do not distinguish European exports to the United States from European exports bound for other destinations. Our figures for unit values of European steel exports to the United States and intra-EC steel trade, drawn from the European Community's *Analytical Tables of Foreign Trade*, are available at a low level of aggregation, permitting us to present statistics for relatively homogeneous product categories. For example, we consider only concrete reinforcing bars, eliminating other bars from that category, and remove hot rolled sheet and plate from the figures for sheet and plate less than 3 mm used by Tarr and Takacs. While product-mix effects may not be eliminated entirely, their influence should be minimized by our use of narrow product categories.

Table 3.6 presents the ratio of domestic to export prices for four categories of European steel products: rails, wire rod, concrete reinforcing bars, and cold rolled sheet. The dumping ratios exhibit a striking degree of variation. Regressing the unit value of exports destined for the United States on a constant term and the intra-EC export unit value leads in every case to rejection of the joint hypothesis of a zero constant and a slope coefficient of unity.[31] Interestingly, the dumping ratios in table 3.6 are similar to the price differentials of up to 40 percent reported by Kravis and Lipsey (1977) for German-American trade in bars and in tube and pipe fittings.

3.4.2 Dumping Ratios

Our calculated dumping ratios will differ greatly depending on whether U.S. and imported steel products are treated as perfect or imperfect

Table 3.6   Relative Price of European Steel Exports to United States
                   ("domestic" unit value relative to export unit value)

	Rail[a]	Wire Rod[b]	Concrete Reinforcing Bars[c]	Cold Rolled Sheet[d]
1961	.703	1.012	—	—
1962	.695	1.059	—	—
1963	.668	1.056	—	—
1964	.792	1.099	—	—
1965	.713	1.082	—	—
1966	.942	1.079	1.121	1.403
1967	.779	1.035	1.171	1.290
1968	.806	1.082	1.099	1.259
1969	.731	1.064	1.349	1.279
1970	.812	1.000	1.290	1.297
1971	.902	1.086	1.239	1.159
1972	1.077	1.083	1.144	1.242
1973	1.529	1.176	1.066	1.497
1974	.839	.877	1.027	.948
1975	.956	.895	.833	1.185
1976	1.085	1.108	1.040	1.218
1977	1.104	1.256	1.179	1.287
1978	1.183	1.104	1.066	1.287
1979	1.161	1.027	1.212	1.318
1980	1.079	.957	na	1.425

SOURCE: European Community, *Analytical Tables of Foreign Trade*, various issues.
NOTE: Values greater than one indicate price discrimination in favor of the United States.
na: not available.
[a]NIMEXE 7316.14, 7316.16
[b]NIMEXE 7310.11, 7363.21, 7373.23, 7373.24, 7373.25, 7373.26, 7373.29.
[c]NIMEXE 7310.13.
[d]NIMEXE 7313.43, 7313.45, 7313.47, 7313.49, 7313.50, 7313.92, 7365.55, 7365.81, 7375.63, 7375.64, 7375.69, 7375.83, 7375.84, 7375.89.

substitutes. Evidence on this issue is far from conclusive. Many carbon steel products appear undifferentiated—concrete reinforcing bars being perhaps the best instance in our sample. At the same time, as noted in section 3.2, subtle quality differences are cited frequently in studies of import penetration. The imperfect substitutes assumption is supported by all recent empirical studies, so we adopt it here.

Prices are assumed to be set in accordance with a generalized version of equation (11'). For European steel:

$$(12) \qquad \frac{p^*}{p} = \frac{\hat{c}^*}{\hat{c}} \cdot \frac{\epsilon^*}{\epsilon} \cdot \frac{\epsilon(1 + \sigma^*) - H_x^*(1 + \delta)}{\epsilon^* - H_{x^*}^*(1 + \delta^*)} .$$

In contrast to (11'), market demand elasticities $\epsilon(\epsilon^*)$ are allowed to differ, and we consider standard Herfindahl indices. For price elasticities of demand, we draw on work by Stone (1979). For iron and steel semimanufactures, Stone reports import demand elasticities of 2.83 and 1.66 for the United States and the European Community, respectively. We use 1.66 as the market demand elasticity for Europe and 2.83 as the own-price elasticity of demand in U.S. import demand functions.

In constructing Herfindahl indices, we treat each national European industry as a joint-profit maximizer. While it is a drastic simplification, we impose this assumption in recognition of the extent of nationalization and pervasive government involvement in the various national industries. Thus, the Herfindahl indices measure the extent to which sales by European producers, either to the U.S. market or within the European Community, are concentrated nationally. For 1979, values for $H_{x^*}^*$ and H_{x^*}, calculated as in table 3.6 and weighted by product shares, are .335 and .215, respectively. Relaxing the assumption of joint-profit maximization would tend to lower the Herfindahl indices and reduce the price-cost margins. For the conjectural variations, we consider the Cournot and constant market share values of zero and unity. σ^* is calibrated at 0 and -0.1. In the absence of contrary evidence, we set $\hat{c}^*/\hat{c}$ to unity.

The dumping ratios for 1979 generated by equation (12) are presented in table 3.7. For the parameter values considered, the dumping ratio falls within the range of values in table 3.6.

3.4.3 The TPM's Effects

For purposes of our calculations, it is necessary to consider the supply response of Japan and other exporting nations against whom the TPM was not primarily directed. If, for example, trigger prices restrict exports by the European Community and other suppliers whose costs are high relative to those in Japan, the incipient change in U.S. import prices may

Table 3.7   **Calculated Dumping Ratios (p^*/p)**

		δ^*	
$\sigma = 0$		0	1
δ	0	1.158	1.549
	1	1.063	1.409
		δ^*	
$\sigma = -0.1$		0	1
δ	0	1.033	1.382
	1	0.937	1.314

SOURCE: See text.

elicit increased exports by suppliers whose costs are relatively low. The effect will be smaller the larger the supply response of the so-called restrained suppliers, to use the terminology of Tarr (1982a).[32] In our view, while restrained suppliers possessed considerable excess capacity both prior to and in the period of the TPM, they resisted the temptation to increase exports to the United States. Hence, we assume no supply response by restrained suppliers to the imposition of trigger prices. In the welfare calculations that follow, we treat their supply curves as inelastic and their markets as undistorted. In this and other respects, our analysis is partial equilibrium.

In what follows, we distinguish three categories of steel: steel produced domestically, steel imported from Europe, and steel imported from other countries. Each of our demand functions has their three respective prices as arguments. As a first approximation, we treat foreign producers other than European as restrained suppliers.

We model the TPM as simply placing a floor under the price of U.S. imports at the 1979 average trigger price of $350 per net ton. Thus, we neglect problems of noncompliance and related complications discussed in section 3.2. To quantify the TPM's effects, we use equations such as (12) to calculate the prices that would have obtained in the mechanism's absence. To do so, it is necessary to select specific values for $\hat{c}$ and $\hat{c}'$. The ratio of domestic to foreign costs is a fiercely debated issue which cannot be resolved here; we set $\hat{c}/\hat{c}'$ equal to 1.2, and for upper and lower bounds we calibrate $\hat{c}$ at $230 and $290 per net ton.[33] We do not distinguish U.S. exports from domestic sales. U.S. exports are small in volume and value; adding this distinction would only modify our measures in minor ways at the cost of further complexity. In the absence of precise estimates, we set the own-price elasticity of demand for domestic steel to unity and all cross-price elasticities to half the value of own-price elasticities, thereby insuring that demands are homogeneous of degree zero in prices. Given the manner in which U.S. mill list prices appear to have hovered around trigger prices, we set the price of domestic steel at $350 per net ton.

The results of our numerical calculations are shown in table 3.8 for the cases where the TPM would be binding. As indicated above, the magnitude of the effects and the sign of the net change in welfare depend largely on whether the initial distortion in domestic markets is large relative to the rise in import prices caused by the TPM. In cases (1) through (4), the domestic distortion is large and the welfare effects are easily interpreted. European producers suffer a loss of surplus, while U.S. producers and foreign restrained suppliers receive additional rents. Since the markup charged by domestic producers is relatively large, so is the transfer they receive. Thus, domestic producers receive the largest portion of the incremental rents. The estimated efficiency gain ranges from $1931.4 million to $5985.6 million.

Table 3.8   Illustrative Effects of the TPM, 1979 (in $ million)

	Change in Welfare	Change in Consumer Surplus	Transfer to U.S. Producers	Transfer to European Producers	Transfer to Other Producers
(1)	+5985.6	$\hat{c} = 230$ −853.0	$\delta = 0$ +6396.0	$\sigma = 0$ −87.7	+530.3
(2)	+4222.3	$\hat{c} = 230$ −657.4	$\delta = 1$ +4600.1	$\sigma = 0$ −135.2	+414.8
(3)	+3617.5	$\hat{c} = 230$ −616.2	$\delta = 0$ +4001.0	$\sigma = -0.1$ −140.1	+372.8
(4)	+1931.4	$\hat{c} = 230$ −380.1	$\delta = 1$ +2205.5	$\sigma = -0.1$ −119.8	+225.8
(5)	−29.7	$\hat{c} = 290$ −240.2	$\delta = 0$ +49.0	$\sigma = 0$ −27.5	+189.0
(6)	−5.3	$\hat{c} = 290$ −51.8	$\delta = 1$ +13.1	$\sigma = 0$ −8.6	+42.0

Source: See text.

When the domestic distortion is relatively small, as in cases (5) and (6), the sign of the welfare effect is reversed. On balance, the loss to consumers outweighs the gain to producers. Foreign firms capture the largest share of transfers to producers, and there is an overall loss of efficiency which ranges from $5.3 million to $29.7 million. These effects resemble what we referred to in section 3.3 as the standard textbook case.

The unusual welfare effects in cases (1) through (4) provide a graphic illustration of the theory of the second best: when distortions in the market for domestic steel are severe relative to distortions in the market for imports, it is possible to reduce the deadweight loss by adding distortions on the import side. Having mentioned this possibility compels us to close on a cautionary note. If antidumping action can be welfare improving because of distortions in domestic markets, first-best policies addressed at those domestic distortions are still to be preferred. In our case, promoting competition can alleviate the domestic distortion without causing any loss on the import side.

Although we have attempted to extend simple welfare calculations in a number of directions, our model ultimately remains partial equilibrium. We have already seen how effects that are usually dismissed as second order can be crucially important in an imperfectly competitive setting.

Among the effects we have suppressed are distortions in factor markets, changes in the extent of collusion, dangers of foreign retaliation, and rent seeking by domestic factors of production; this last possibility, for example, greatly diminishes the likelihood that the additional distortion will enhance welfare. Many of these extensions are readily incorporated into our framework. Even without these complications, however, our analysis suggests that governments must be able to estimate a relatively large number of parameters with considerable accuracy before they can be assured that this form of intervention is welfare improving.

3.5 Concluding Remarks

In this paper we have analyzed dumping and U.S. antidumping policy from a number of different perspectives. While attempting to address a broad range of questions in a relatively few pages, we recognize that each of these issues warrants more extensive treatment. The first sections of the paper analyze the evolution of U.S. antidumping policy and the design of the Trigger Price Mechanism. To understand the evolution of antidumping policy, we have argued, it is necessary to analyze how policy is adapted in response to political pressures; the TPM provides a dramatic illustration of these considerations. From the point of view of its architects, who felt pressure from all sides, the TPM was a political masterpiece. Economically, it was perhaps less masterful; its exponents may have incompletely anticipated how administered protection could distort established patterns of trade and production. An analysis of the TPM demonstrates also how administrative decisions on seemingly minor points—such as the exchange rate to use in computing costs—can have major economic effects.

The latter sections of the paper use theoretical models to explain the sources of dumping and to illustrate the magnitude of its effects. The models of most relevance to the practices currently at issue in the steel industry seem to us models of oligopolistic rivalry in imperfectly competitive, segmented markets. Basing our analysis on the traditional economic definition of dumping as price discrimination in international trade, we have attempted to identify a number of crucial variables on which the incidence of dumping will depend: the number of firms producing for each national market, their costs, their market shares, and the extent to which they recognize and exploit their mutual dependence. Finally, we have used these models of imperfect competition to illustrate how the size of the dumping ratio and the incidence of the TPM depend on certain crucial parameter values. Much remains to be done to establish the generality of our framework, but we hope that we at least have stimulated some of our readers to think along these lines.

Notes

1. In this paper we are concerned solely with dumping and U.S. antidumping policies. We do not discuss countervailing duties imposed in response to foreign government subsidization of exports. However, see note 27 below.

2. Antidumping measures also were included in the Revenue Act of 1916, whose provisions proved difficult to administer.

3. U.S. Senate (1934) discusses the origins of the 1921 act.

4. The immediate impetus for the change was a complaint that Canadian sulfur was being sold in both U.S. and Canadian markets at prices below cost. The 1974 act also authorized the Treasury to base constructed value calculations on data for comparable market economies when production costs in state-controlled economies proved difficult to measure.

5. See, for example, Crandall (1978, 1980), U.S. General Accounting Office (1979), and Kawahito (1981).

6. Section 206(a) of the Trade Act of 1974 defined constructed value as the sum of (1) "The cost of materials . . . and of fabrication or other processing . . . at a time preceding the date of exportation of the merchandise under consideration which would ordinarily permit the production of that particular merchandise in the ordinary course of business." (2) "An amount for general expenses . . . not less than ten percent of material and of fabrication costs." (3) "An amount for profit not less than eight percent of the sum of material and fabrication costs and general expenses." (4) "The cost of all containers and coverings . . . and all other expenses incidental to placing the merchandise . . . in condition . . . ready for shipment to the United States."

7. The debate over voluntary restraint agreements is recounted by Takacs (1976), Mueller and Kawahito (1979), and Adams and Dirlam (1980).

8. In the words of its architects, the system was to "expedite relief from unfair import competition, but to do so in a manner which would not preclude competition in the U.S. market." See Solomon (1977, 8).

9. Treasury must acquire sufficient information on which to base a determination within seventy-five days, and the complainant must waive his right to verify the exporter's submission. In a related action, responsibility for enforcing U.S. antidumping statutes was transferred from Treasury to the Department of Commerce.

10. In practice, the constructed value provisions do not appear to have been invoked on these grounds.

11. American Importers Association (1979, 21); Sato and Hodin (1982, 37).

12. U.S. Department of Commerce (1980, 5).

13. *Treasury News*, 20 July 1980, p. 3.

14. *Ibid.* If the yield ratio is 80 percent, the other 20 percent is scrap. A credit in the amount of the value of the scrap was applied to production cost estimates for finished steel. The yield credit was raised in 1978 IV on the grounds that Japanese scrap was actually a higher valued secondary material.

15. U.S. Department of Commerce (1980, 4).

16. We neglect feedback from trigger prices to exchange rates, and from there to domestic costs. The assumption that such feedback was negligible is crucial to our interpretation of table 3.2. On these effects, see Eichengreen (1981, 1983).

17. Steel Tripartite Committee (1979, 8).

18. Mueller (1980, 1).

19. Dirlam and Mueller (1981, 13).

20. McCormack (1981, 313). See also American Iron and Steel Institute (1978).

21. See *Treasury News*, 13 April 1978.

22. For a recent analysis, see U.S. General Accounting Office (1980, chap. 3; 1981, chap. 3). Similar points were made some years ago by Jondrow et al. (1976).

23. U.S. General Accounting Office (1980, 21). See Dirlam and Mueller (1981) and Walter (1982) for discussions of these allegations.

24. See United States versus Mitsui (1982).

25. See, for example, Caves and Jones (1973, 212–14), or Corden (1974, 235–47).

26. This is not to imply that there is no role for policy toward industries facing import competition. For analyses of the arguments for adjustment assistance, see Bhagwati (1982).

27. It would be straightforward to introduce production and export subsidies at this point. However, as noted above, we feel that the subsidy question is logically distinct from the issues analyzed here, so we make no attempt to incorporate it into our model. For a similar approach to analyzing subsidies, see Brander and Spencer (1982). It would also be straightforward to introduce transport costs. Although we do not treat such costs explicitly, they can be thought of as a component of c. See also Brander (1981) and Brander and Krugman (1983).

28. See Rader (1972), Dansby and Willig (1979), and, for an elegant application to the Japanese steel industry, Yamawaki (1982).

29. In other words, we assume $\Sigma_{i=1}^{k} (dx_i/dy_q) = \Sigma_{q \neq r}^{s}(dy_r/dy_q)$ for all i, q, and r. Dixit and Stern (1982) argue that this assumption captures the case where oligopolists are in the industry on broadly equal terms.

30. If the oligopolists take fringe firms' reactions into account, then we get the standard Herfindahl index in place of the truncated index. The conjectural variation is the firm's estimate of the slope of rivals' reaction functions. It can be heuristically interpreted as the perceived probability of retaliation. Thus, $\delta = 0$ is the Cournot case, and $\delta = 1$ is the case where each firm believes that other firms will try to preserve market shares. Cases of $\delta < 0$, while conceivable, are not considered here. Firms' conjectures are taken as constant throughout. Modeling conjectures as rational makes it difficult to characterize industry equilibrium, so we follow standard practice by taking conjectural variations as exogenous. On rational conjectural variations, see citations in Kamien and Schwartz (1981).

31. Variables are in logs. Such tests of the 'law of one price' are surveyed by Crouhy-Veyrac, Crouhy, and Melitz (1982).

32. Were national outputs perfect substitutes and market imperfections absent, one could visualize a scenario in which U.S. antidumping policy administered under the TPM caused European steel formerly destined for the United States to be diverted to Japanese markets or to remain in Europe and a corresponding quantity of Japanese production to be diverted to the United States. In fact, allegations of this type of activity on part of European and Japanese producers have recently been made by the U.S. steel industry. Neglecting transport costs, in this case U.S. antidumping policies would have no efficiency or distributional effects. When steel products produced in different countries are imperfect substitutes, the analysis is more complicated but the implication is the same.

33. Mueller and Kawahito (1978) review the available evidence and present estimates of their own. For example, for 1976 their estimate of the ratio of European to U.S. costs is 1.17. In this paper we present no evidence on the constancy of variable cost. Since Takacs (1976) finds marginal costs to be slightly declining, while others such as Crandall (1981) treat them as rising, this seems to be a judicious compromise. Our estimates of $\hat{c}^*$ for 1979 are constructed by adjusting Mueller and Kawahito's figure of $205 in 1976 for the change in prices of industrial goods. We think of these figures as including costs of variable labor, coal, fuel oil, natural gas, electricity, iron ore and scrap, plus transportation and related expenses. For a number of reasons, including the fact that their calculations exclude the United Kingdom, there is reason to treat $230 as a lower bound; we use $290 as an upper bound. We recognize, however, that we have suppressed the large cost differentials that exist among producers in a given location.

References

Adams, Walter, and Joel B. Dirlam. 1980. Unfair competition in international trade. In *Tariffs, quotas, and trade: The politics of protectionism*, ed. Walter Adams *et al.* San Francisco: Institute for Contemporary Studies.

American Importers Association. 1979. *Analysis of the Trade Agreements Act of 1979*. New York: American Importers Assn.

American Iron and Steel Institute. 1978. *Annual report*. Washington, D.C.: AISI.

Bhagwati, J. N., ed. 1982. *Import competition and response*. Chicago: University of Chicago Press for the National Bureau of Economic Research.

Brander, James. 1981. Intra-industry trade in identical commodities. *Journal of International Economics* 11:1–14.

Brander, James, and Paul Krugman. 1983. A "reciprocal dumping" model of international trade. *Journal of International Economics* 13:313–22.

Brander, James, and Barbara Spencer. 1982. Export subsidies and international market share rivalry. Paper presented to the NBER International Studies Program. Mimeo.

Caves, Richard, and Ronald Jones. 1973. *World trade and payments*. Boston: Little, Brown.

Corden, W. M. 1974. *Trade policy and economic welfare*. Oxford: Clarendon Press.

Crandall, Robert W. 1978. Competition and "dumping" in the U.S. steel market. *Challenge* 21:13–20.

———. 1980. Steel imports: Dumping or competition? *Regulation* 4:17–24.

———. 1981. *The U.S. steel industry in recurrent crisis*. Washington, D.C.: The Brookings Institution.

Crouhy-Veyrac, L., M. Crouhy, and J. Melitz. 1982. More about the law of one price. *European Economic Review* 18:325–44.

Dansby, R. E., and R. D. Willig. 1979. Industry performance gradient indexes. *American Economic Review* 69:249–60.

Davies, S. W., and A. J. McGuinness. 1982. Dumping at less than marginal cost. *Journal of International Economics* 12:169–82.

Dirlam, Joel B., and Hans Mueller. 1981. *Import restraints and reindustrialization: The case of the U.S. steel industry*. Middle Tennessee State University Business and Economic Research Center Conference Paper no. 67.

Dixit, A., and N. Stern. 1982. Oligopoly and welfare: A unified presentation with applications to trade and development. *European Economic Review* 19:123–45.

Eichengreen, Barry 1981. A dynamic model of tariffs, output and employment under flexible exchange rates. *Journal of International Economics* 11:341–59.

———. 1982. *The simple analytics of dumping.* Harvard Institute of Economic Research Discussion Paper no. 943.

———. 1983. Effective protection and exchange rate determination. *Journal of International Money and Finance.* 2:1–15.

Ethier, Wilfred. 1982. Dumping. *Journal of Political Economy* 90:487–506.

Haberler, Gottfried. 1937. *The theory of international trade with its application to commercial policy.* New York: Macmillan.

Harberger, Arnold C. 1974. Taxation, resource allocation, and welfare. In *Taxation and welfare,* ed. A. C. Harberger. Boston: Little, Brown.

Jondrow, James, et al. 1976. *Forms of competition in the steel industry.* Arlington, Va.: Public Research Institute.

Kamien, M. I., and N. L. Schwartz. 1981. *Conjectural variations.* Northwestern University Center for Mathematical Studies in Economics and Management Science Discussion Paper no. 466S.

Kawahito, Kiyoshi. 1981. *Economic implications of U.S. antidumping statutes, with special reference to the steel trade.* Middle Tennessee State University Business and Economic Research Center Conference Paper no. 63.

Kravis, I. B., and R. E. Lipsey. 1977. Export prices and the transmission of inflation. *American Economic Review Papers and Proceedings* 67:155–63.

Krugman, Paul. 1982. Import protection as export promotion: International competition in the presence of oligopoly and economies of scale. Massachusetts Institute of Technology. Mimeo.

McCormack, Garry P. 1981. The reinstated steel Trigger Price Mechanism: Reinforced barrier to import competition. *Fordham International Law Journal* 4:289–339.

Mueller, H. 1980. *The competitiveness of the U.S. steel industry after the new Trigger Price Mechanism.* Middle Tennessee State University Business and Economic Research Center Monograph no. 25.

Mueller, H., and K. Kawahito. 1978. *Steel industry economics.* New York: Japan Steel Information Center.

———. 1979. *Legal and economic aspects of the steel import issue.* Middle Tennessee State University Business and Economic Research Center Conference Paper no. 42.

Rader, Trout. 1972. *Theory of microeconomics.* New York: Academic Press.

Sato, Hideo, and M. W. Hodin. 1982. The U.S.-Japanese steel industry issue of 1977. In *Coping with U.S.-Japanese economic conflicts,* ed. I. M. Destler and H. Sato. Lexington, Mass.: Heath.

Solomon, Anthony M. 1977. Report to the president: A comprehensive program for the steel industry. Mimeo.

Spence, A. M. 1981. The learning curve and competition. *Bell Journal of economics* 12:49–70.

Steel Tripartite Committee. 1979. Steel Trigger Price Mechanism. A one year review for the Steel Tripartite Committee. Washington, D.C., June 25. Mimeo.

Stegemann, Klaus. 1980. *The efficiency rationale of antidumping policy and other measures of contingency protection.* Queen's University Institute for Economic Research Discussion Paper no. 387.

Stone, J. A. 1979. Price elasticities of demand for imports and exports: Industry estimates for the U.S., the E.E.C. and Japan. *Review of Economics and Statistics* 59:306–12.

Takacs, Wendy E. 1976. Quantitative restrictions on international trade. Ph.D. diss., Johns Hopkins University.

———. 1982. Cyclical dumping of steel products: Comment. *Journal of International Economics* 12:381–84.

Tarr, David G. 1979. Cyclical dumping: The case of steel products. *Journal of International Economics* 9:57–63.

———. 1982a. Estimation of the costs to the U.S. economy and to consumers of the imposition of countervailing duties on the steel products under investigation at the Department of Commerce. Mimeo.

———. 1982b. Cyclical dumping of steel products: Another look. *Journal of International Economics* 12:377–80.

U.S. Department of Commerce. International Trade Administration. 1978–79. *Announcement of trigger price levels*, various issues. Washington, D.C.

———. 1980. *Reinstatement notice.* 45 F. R. 66833, ret. 8.

———. 1981. *Steel Trigger Price Mechanism procedures manual.* 46 F.R. 22738, April 20.

U.S. General Accounting Office. 1979. *Report to the Congress: U.S. administration of the Antidumping Act of 1921.* ID7915. Washington, D.C.: GPO.

———. 1980. Report to the Congress: Administration of the steel Trigger Price Mechanism. ID8015. Mimeo.

———. 1981. *Report to the Congress: New strategy required for aiding distressed steel industry.* EMD8129. Washington, D.C.: GPO.

U.S. Congress. Senate. 1934. *Antidumping legislation and other import regulation in the United States and foreign countries.* 73d Cong., 2d sess. S. Doc. 112.

United States versus Mitsui, et al. 1982. Filed 20 July 1982 with the United States District Court for the Northern District of California.

Viner, Jacob. 1923. *Dumping: A problem in international trade.* Chicago: University of Chicago Press.

Walter, Ingo. 1982. *Structural adjustment and trade policy in the international steel industry.* Institut für Volkswirtschaftslehre und Statistik der Universität Mannheim Discussion Paper no. 220/82.

Yamawaki, Hideki. 1982. Market structure, capacity expansion and pricing. Ph.D. diss., Harvard University.

Comment   Wilfred J. Ethier

This excellent paper is notable both for its contribution to the theory of dumping in general and for its discussion of the Trigger Price Mechanism in particular. The paper opens with a historical overview of U.S. policy. The central theme is the evolutionary rise in importance of the sales-below-cost criterion of dumping relative to the price-discrimination criterion. I agree with this conclusion and would only add that the steel industry itself apparently played a significant role in the process by alleging sales below cost in its 1977 complaints, which led to the Gilmore case and to the TPM. Basic characteristics of the U.S. steel industry appear to have been relevant here; I discuss this in more detail below.

The paper's discussion of the actual operation of the TPM is a detailed and perceptive case study that makes fascinating reading. I wish both that the authors had supplied background information on the steel industry (the U.S. industry in particular), since the nature of that industry is central to the dumping issue, and that they had discussed government subsidies, which were important in the demise of the TPM. But I do understand the strict adherence to their topic.

In the formal model and its calibration, the basic assumption is made that dumping (of steel) is in essence a matter of price discrimination, presumably in contrast to sales below cost. (Though the latter are not inconsistent with the model, as Eichengreen and van der Ven note; they are tangential). This contrasts sharply with the earlier parts of the paper emphasizing the gradually increasing relative importance of the sales-below-cost criterion and describing in detail the operation of a system based, at bottom, on that criterion. This assumption is defended on the grounds that oligopolistic rivalry in segmented markets seems to be a prominent characteristic of the steel industry. I concede the validity of this observation, and also that of the persistence of dual pricing in the industry about which this paper offers interesting evidence of its own. But accepting the practical validity of the assumption basic to this paper's

Wilfred J. Ethier is professor of economics at the University of Pennsylvania.

model is hardly the same as conceding that it captures what is central to dumping in the steel industry.

An alternative is available. Many observers would point instead to a large ratio of fixed to variable costs, a great sensitivity to cyclical fluctuations in demand, factor-market rigidities, worldwide excess capacity, and, especially in the U.S. industry, a downward inflexibility of domestic steel prices as the characteristics most intimately related to the issue of dumping. Similar characteristics do seem widely prevalent in industries where dumping is an issue (e.g., see Lloyd 1977), and steel is an interesting special case precisely because the characteristics are thought to be especially pronounced there. They are central to the view that antidumping efforts of the U.S. steel industry—and that industry's concern with the cost of production criterion and with subsidies—are motivated at bottom by the desire to prevent imports from destroying the industry's traditional practice of maintaining domestic price levels during periods of depressed demand (e.g., see Dale 1980). If this alternative view has validity, the model of this paper, though not inconsistent with this alternative, completely misses the essentials of antidumping actions in the steel industry. This paper therefore requires a detailed defense of the proposition that the characteristics embodied in its model are in fact more central to dumping than are those characteristics emphasized by this alternative view. Merely pointing to the existence of oligopolistic rivalry in segmented markets, as the authors do, is no substitute for such a defense.

Turn now to the actual structure of the formal model. Price discrimination theories must all cope with the problem of explaining why firms face different elasticities of demand in different markets and why the differences should induce dumping rather than reverse dumping. Eichengreen and van der Ven dispose of this problem in a simple and ingenious fashion. Essentially, if a fixed number of foreign oligopolists export to the home market, but domestic oligopolists are prevented from also exporting, then there will be more competition in the domestic market and consequently a lower price, other things being equal. Note the crucial role of the imposed entry asymmetry: this model assumes without explanation that the United States is the dumping ground of the world steel industry.

The model is used only to devise a formula for the dumping ratio. The formula is then shown to easily adapt to many complicating amendments, and this is certainly one of the attractions of the model. But the welfare analysis of antidumping actions is then conducted in the usual geometric fashion, completely divorced from the model. It would have been desirable—and easy—to embed the model in a simple general equilibrium framework and to use that to derive explicit analytic formulas for the welfare effects.

The empirical material is, as the authors point out, a "calibration" of the model and not an estimate of its parameters or, in any sense, a test of its validity or relevance. It is rather a very useful "what if" exercise. Note that what distinguishes this exercise from the standard ones involving commercial policy is *not* the policy tool: the special features of the TPM play no role at all in this part of the paper. Rather it is the particular price-discrimination context in which the protection is hypothetically applied. The resulting useful discussion of possible welfare consequences brings out very nicely—and quite sharply—the inherent "double distortion" situation. But note that this makes even more crucial the unfortunate lack of justification for the basic assumption about dumping that underlies the formal model.

References

Dale, Richard. 1980. *Anti-dumping law in a liberal trade order.* New York: St. Martin's Press.
Lloyd, Peter J. 1977. *Anti-dumping actions and the GATT system.* Thames Essay no. 9. London: Trade Policy Research Centre.

Comment   Gary N. Horlick

Eichengreen and van der Ven have undertaken an ambitious and difficult task: explaining the evolution of U.S. antidumping policies in general (and specifically for steel) and evaluating the effects of those policies. I found the results very interesting and useful. The dumping model presented, which may fit many product sectors well, may be too general to deal with a category as varied as steel. The analysis of the effects of the steel Trigger Price Mechanism rests on some published materials that are not entirely accurate. Finally, the analysis of the evolution of dumping policies is sound enough in general outline, but somewhat exaggerates the degree of the shift toward use of constructed value as the measure of fair value.

The authors are correct in noting a shift toward the use of constructed value as the basis for fair value in dumping cases after passage of the Trade Act of 1974 and the Trade Agreements Act of 1979. They believe that speeding up the decision-making process was a spur behind the move to constructed value; in fact, as the authors note, the 1974 amendment responded to the perceived facts of one specific case. While constructed

Gary N. Horlick was deputy assistant secretary for Import Administration, U.S. Department of Commerce, Washington, D.C., from 1981 to 1983; he now practices law with the firm of O'Melveny and Myers in that city.

value cases have turned out to be less difficult than they were at first thought to be, particularly when the alternative is to make extremely complex adjustments for differences in merchandise, they are still more time-consuming than a "normal" price-to-price comparison.

We have found increasing numbers of cases in which merchandise is produced specifically for export to the United States, or, particularly in steel, where home market sales have been below the cost of production for a sustained period. In these cases, we have been forced to use constructed value.

Nevertheless, our preference is for home market prices—in fact, we are *required* to use home market prices if they are sufficient in quantity and above cost. Only if adequate home market sales are not available do we consider using third-market sales or constructed value, and our preference then is for third-country sales prices; that preference is codified in our regulations (19 C.F.R. 353.4 [c]). Where prices are available, they are a simpler and, I believe, more accurate measure of fair value, in part for reasons identified by the authors (e.g., the 10 percent statutory minimum general expense). Our preference for home market or third-country prices as the basis for fair value extends to state-controlled economy cases as well. Constructed value has been used in only one of the seven post-1979 through 1982 state-controlled cases (when there was no other non-U.S. seller). During the most recent period for which full data are available (1 January 1982 to 30 June 1982), forty-one of our antidumping determinations were based on home market or third-country sales, seven were based on constructed value, and three were a combination of the two.

To the paper's brief history of the TPM, I add one insight concerning the reasons for the demise of the second TPM. Certainly the shift of exchange rates that made the U.S. market more lucrative to EC producers and reduced the probability of sales below fair value was important—it gave an illusion of safety from unfair trade cases to those EC producers who actively sought such an illusion and provided those producers with an undeniable incentive to boost sales to the United States, particularly given the dismal state of the EC market. More important, however, was the shift of the likely battleground from dumping to unfair subsidization, a shift several EC producers deliberately chose to ignore.

The growth of subsidies to steel producers in the European Community since 1977, when TPM was first conceived, was breathtaking, and by 1981 several large EC producers had become quite vulnerable to countervailing duty action. Because countervailing duty law is concerned with pricing only as it bears on injury, whether or not the shift in exchange rates had erased sales at less than fair value became increasingly irrelevant; the only way for heavily subsidized EC producers to avoid the filing, much less the losing, of countervailing duty cases was to moderate export quantities to avoid injuring U.S. producers. When August 1981 imports of steel from the European Community hit a record 860 thousand tons, it was clear that TPM's usefulness had been overtaken by events. Quantity, not price, had become the issue, a change that was recognized in the ultimate settlement of the hundred-plus cases filed against EC producers in 1982. (It should be noted that because of the need to allocate over several years many of the large capital-equipment subsidies received, several EC producers will be vulnerable to countervailing duty cases for years to come).

One specific problem with this paper is the analysis of the results of the TPM both in the text and in the calibration of the dumping model. While a clear theoretical incentive existed under TPM to move steel to the West Coast because trigger prices were lower there (allowing more undercutting of U.S. prices), the theoretical incentive to sell to the Great Lakes where trigger prices were higher provided an opposite motivation. Only empirical evidence can reveal what TPM's effects were, and the analysis must consider other factors that might have influenced shifting patterns of imports, such as divergent demand trends in the several regions of the United States, the closure of U.S. plants on the West Coast, and the emergence of steel exporters in South Korea and Taiwan.

As table C3.1 indicates, the percentage of total steel imports into the West Coast market did not change significantly after TPM's introduction in 1978. In fact, the relative size of West Coast imports was largest in 1980, when the TPM was suspended from March to October, and again in the third quarter of 1982, after TPM had been terminated. There was a shift of EC producers to the West Coast in 1978, but again, the proportion of West Coast sales to total EC imports was greatest during periods of TPM suspension.

A General Accounting Office report is cited as evidence that TPM

Table C3.1   U.S. Imports of Basic Steel Mill Products on the West Coast as Percent of Total U.S. Basic Steel Mill Products Imports, from the European Community, Japan, and Total, 1975–1982

Year	EC	Japan	Total
1975	6.3%	30.9%	19.4%
1976	9.1	28.5	20.0
1977	5.9	30.7	17.1
1978	12.6	35.3	20.4
1979	10.0	35.1	20.1
1980	16.2	38.9	24.7
1981	12.6	37.1	20.4
1982 I	11.2	32.5	18.9
II	10.8	32.8	18.2
III	17.4	41.1	26.4

caused a shift of steel imports from independent to foreign-related importers. Our research, based on data not available to Eichengreen and van der Ven, reveals that if there was such a shift, it was extremely small (on the order of 5 percent). U.S. steel imports have been predominantly through importers related to the exporters since long before the TPM was implemented.

I strongly agree that both fraud and legal manipulations posed a threat to TPM's integrity as a monitoring system and offer our experience to anyone contemplating price regulation of imports. Throw up a barrier and the marketplace will usually find a way around it, with some cost in efficiency.

The authors' dumping model strikes me (a lay person) as a useful mathematical model of a common sense concept. Differential market power, supported by protection of the home market, may account for a substantial portion of dumping. In the case of steel, however, it seems to me that the actions of the foreign governments should be at the center of the model rather than as a mere side assumption to rule out reexportation (which transport costs effectively rule out). In the absence of specific modeling of the effects of EC regulation of prices, output, and imports, Eichengreen and van der Ven are forced to make an insupportable assumption about the behavior of EC steel producers.

Each national European industry is treated as a single firm in constructing Herfindahl indices, their measure of oligopolistic strength. They argue that this assumption of national unity is in "recognition of the extent of nationalization and pervasive government involvement in the various national industries." National governments in the European Communities are primarily involved in steel through the provision of subsidies; regulation of competition, output, prices, and imports are overwhelmingly the responsibility of the European Communities. EC regulation has been of variable intensity over the time period of this study, reaching its peak in the 1980 declaration of a "manifest crisis" and the setting of mandatory production quotas for most products. A model of oligopolistic competition cannot capture the economic arbitrariness of politically based price and output adjustments.

To treat the German firms of Thyssen and Klockner as a joint-profit maximizer or the supercompetitive Bresciani of Northern Italy as a single firm is inappropriate, even if necessary for simplifying the model. Similarly, a single Herfindahl index for "steel" ignores the critical variation of concentration by product. For example, cold rolled sheet production is quite concentrated, while rebar production is distributed among dozens of producers.

The approximated "dumping margins" for aggregated steel product categories which the authors rely on to calibrate their model do not provide a reliable measure of dumping. As an attorney defending alleged dumpers and as a government official conducting dumping investigations, I can testify to the need for exact product comparisons, consideration of circumstances of sale, and all the other details that make dumping investigations so complicated. Unit value comparisons of categories of steel products cannot reveal dumping. For example, product differences within the category of cold rolled sheet can result in wide price variations—the last trigger price for the base product of cold rolled sheet was $416 per ton, while the same cold rolled sheets after special treatment could cost another $60. In addition, U.S. imports of rebar from the European Communities are too small to make any unit value comparisons reliable.

An accurate model of steel dumping, with empirical estimation of parameters, would require a much more complex model and data set than currently available. Changes in exchange rates, protection of home markets, imperfect availability of information, and firm cost structures (particularly fixed versus variable cost) all need to be taken into account, and the data must be based on precise product comparisons with necessary adjustments. I doubt that anyone will make available the necessary resources for such a complete data set for steel; I would be interested in seeing Eichengreen and van der Ven's model applied to a more discrete and manageable product.

The study of dumping, which is merely price discrimination across borders, needs to blend in more completely with a study of domestic price discrimination and to focus on how the interposition of a border, with attendant government interventions of various sorts, affects firm behavior. The border effects have led to the dramatically different treatment of domestic and international price discrimination; a fuller understanding of what those effects are could help policymakers reevaluate whether that differential treatment is justified in light of the rapid integration of national economies since the first dumping law (Canada's, aimed at U.S. Steel!) was written in 1904.

4   The Multifiber Arrangement and Its Effect on the Profit Performance of the U.S. Textile Industry

Joseph Pelzman

4.1 Introduction

Over the past two-and-a-half decades trade in textile and apparel products has evolved from a trade environment, encumbered only by high tariffs, to a system of regulations that includes both high tariffs and ever more restrictive bilateral import quotas. This multifaceted trade management system regulating textile-apparel trade is of considerable interest because it has been credited with providing both a certain degree of market certainty and, consequently, an environment in which the U.S. textile industry has found it profitable to undertake major structural changes, which have transformed it from a small-scale, unintegrated, predominantly family-owned sector to a large-scale, more concentrated, capital-intensive, technologically advanced, and internationally competitive industry.[1] As such, the experience of the U.S. textile and apparel industries in repeatedly requesting and obtaining continued protection, as well as in implementing major structural adjustments, may be an important precedent for other so-called crisis industries who are now attempting to restructure U.S. trade policy in favor of greater protection.

A number of basic policy issues are raised by the Multifiber Arrangement (MFA) and its predecessor agreements. Primary among these issues is the degree to which the existence of the MFA has resulted in a misallocation of resources in both the developed and developing countries. For example, what portion of the average annual capital investment

Joseph Pelzman is professor of economics at George Washington University.

The author is indebted to Robert E. Baldwin, Joseph J. Cordes, and John E. Kwoka, Jr., for very helpful discussions and comments. Valuable discussions at the conference with David G. Tarr and Martin Wolf are gratefully acknowledged. Thanks are due to Greg Barker for providing particularly efficient research assistance.

in the textile and apparel industries of $1144.5 and $425.7 million, respectively, during the 1970–80 period was attributable to the existence of the MFA? At a more general level, what impact has the MFA had on industry output, employment, prices, and profits? Another important issue concerns the magnitude of the economic cost of such an elaborate quota system. Clearly many significant issues are raised by the existence of this trade management system. A study of all of them would require resources far beyond those available for this project. Consequently, this paper focuses on just one important question raised by U.S. textile and apparel quotas, namely, whether these import quotas have served to improve the profit performance of the domestic industry.

Section 4.2 briefly outlines the history of textile trade regulation. The restructuring of the U.S. and West European textile industries is discussed in section 4.3. The methodology by which the marginal impact of the MFA on the profitability of domestic producers will be tested is explained in section 4.4. The empirical results are presented in section 4.5. Concluding remarks are given in section 4.6, and data sources are in the appendix.

4.2 International Regulation of Textile Trade

For the United States, trade in textile products has always been extremely important. In part this was and still is because of the size of the industry, its geographic concentration, its level of employment, and the political power it can wield.[2] The voluntary export controls agreed to by Japan in 1957 mark the beginning of a long list of international agreements (in the postwar period) designed to manage the trade of both textile and apparel products.[3]

4.2.1   Early Textile Trade Regulation

In the early 1950s the U.S. textile industry was faced with market adjustment problems precipitated by excess capacity in cotton textiles, a shift to synthetic fibers, technological changes, and increased imports of certain cotton textile products from Japan. As a partial solution to these problems the industry began to seek protection from import competition.[4] The primary exporter targeted by the industry was Japan. In response to escape clause actions and fearing legislation authorizing import restrictions, Japan in 1957 agreed to a voluntary control of its exports of cotton textiles and apparel to the United States. While this agreement was successful in limiting Japanese exports of cotton products to the United States, it encouraged increased imports from new entrants, such as Hong Kong, Portugal, Egypt, and India. It soon became obvious to the U.S. administration that a more comprehensive solution was necessary to adequately control imports. In particular, the government desired to avoid legislated import restrictions, preferring instead a legitimatized system of trade restrictions whereby the world market would be divided so that both the developing countries and the industrialized countries would share the responsibility of an "orderly" market suitable for the expansion of developing countries and yet minimizing the damage to the U.S. market.[5]

Multilateral discussions, initiated by the United States and designed to reorder textile trade in accordance with these objectives, were held under the auspices of the GATT beginning on 16 June 1961. These discussions led in July 1961 to the first of a series of multilateral arrangements, known as the Short-Term Cotton Textile Arrangement (STA), which went into effect for one year beginning 1 October 1961. A more comprehensive agreement, known as the Long-Term Arrangement on Cotton Textiles (LTA), went into effect for five years on 1 October 1962 and was extended twice through 1973. Under the LTA cotton textile imports were controlled on an item-by-item basis.

The signing of the LTA initiated a departure from GATT rules for manufactured goods.[6] Under this agreement importers could apply restraints selectively without compensation to exporters. Furthermore, under LTA provisions, unilateral action against an exporter could be implemented to cover all cotton exports regardless of whether there was any evidence of market disruption in the importing country.[7] As an import restricting measure the LTA worked well initially. By 1967 the United States had restrained the supply of specific cotton textile and apparel products under article 3 of the LTA from seventeen of its major suppliers. Later that year these same countries accepted bilateral agreements with the United States under article 4 of the LTA. By 1972 the United States had concluded similar restraining agreements with thirteen other countries, bringing the total restraints to thirty suppliers.

Imports of man-made fiber textiles and apparel, unlike cotton textiles, increased more than ten-fold over the eleven-year life of the LTA. In response to the developing countries' success in expanding exports of man-made apparel, the United States attempted to widen the scope of the LTA. In 1971 the United States reached bilateral agreements with its principal suppliers, Japan, Hong Kong, Taiwan, and Korea, designed to control the flow of wool and man-made textile and apparel products. However, these restrictions were not justified under the LTA framework, and subsequently the United States focused on amending the LTA so that it would cover textile and apparel products of all three fibers.[8]

4.2.2 The Multifiber Arrangement

Such an expanded agreement was reached on 20 December 1973 by some fifty governments. This multilateral agreement, known as the Arrangement Regarding International Trade in Textiles or more commonly the Multifiber Arrangement (MFA), became "the statement of principle and policy" regarding international textile trade.[9] The MFA initially covered the period from 1 January 1974 to 31 December 1977 and was later extended, with some major modifications, first through 31 December 1981 and later through 31 July 1986. The primary goal of the MFA was the fulfillment of two conflicting objectives: to foster the expansion of world trade in textiles with particular emphasis on developing countries' exports while, at the same time, preventing disruption of developed country markets.

These MFA objectives are clearly stated in its articles. Article 1 provides that the basic objective of the MFA be: "to achieve the expansion of trade, the reduction of barriers to such trade and the progressive liberalization of world trade in textile products while at the same time ensuring the orderly and equitable development of this trade and avoidance of disruptive effects . . ." Another principal aim of the MFA, also set forth in article 1, is "to further the economic and social development of developing countries and secure a substantial increase in their export earnings from textile products and to provide scope for a greater share for them in world trade in these products."

Article 1 goes further to state that the safeguards provision of the MFA is to be applied in "exceptional circumstances" and is designed to "assist any process of adjustment which would be required by the changes in the pattern of world trade in textile products."

The extent to which a particular country can impose unilateral control is limited to "market disruption," which is defined in annex A of the agreement as serious damage to the producing industry. Along the general lines of the LTA, initial quotas were to be based on past import levels with the exception that these quotas were to grow at a minimum of 6 percent per annum (annex B of the agreement). Furthermore, provisions were made for a transfer of unused quotas among categories (the so-called swing provision) and between years (the so-called carry-over and carry-forward provisions).[10]

The MFA further provides in article 6 for special and more favorable treatment of new entrants and small suppliers. It also provides for surveillance procedures by the Textile Surveillance Body composed of both developed and developing country members. By 1 October 1977, the United States had negotiated bilateral agreements with eighteen countries limiting their principal textile exports. Furthermore, through its consultation mechanism, the United States had authority to unilaterally control imports of other textile categories considered disruptive.

While the MFA provides the framework for an "equitable"[11] regulation of trade in textile products, the specific implementation of this agreement is dependent on a set of bilateral agreements drawn according to article 4 of the MFA. The United States interpreted this article to imply that bilateral agreements should provide a more liberal treatment of developing country suppliers "on overall terms." Consequently, under most of the bilaterals, within each aggregate limit specific quota levels for subgroups and specific quotas for items within subgroups were established. In the event that a particular item was perceived to be "very sensitive," specific levels were negotiated that held import growth to less than 6 percent for the duration of the agreement. For example, for the very sensitive wool industry U.S. bilaterals under the MFA have provided for growth of no more than 1 percent annually for both subgroup and specific item ceilings.

When the MFA came up for renewal at the end of 1977, the European Community (EC) pressed for greater control over developing country exports. Unlike the United States who had actively pursued bilateral agreements during the first MFA, the Europeans had no consistent textile trade policy.[12] Consequently, developing country suppliers increased their sales of textile and apparel products to the EC markets. In large part to satisfy EC concerns, the extension protocol renewing the MFA contained an amendment allowing "jointly agreed reasonable departures" from the 6 percent growth rate in quotas as well as from the agreement's "flexibility provisions," thus allowing not only growth at less than 6 percent but for zero or negative growth in those products considered sensitive by importing countries.[13]

While never formally invoking the "reasonable departures" clause, the U.S. government did respond to industry pressure threatening to hinder U.S. participation in the Multilateral Trade Negotiations (MTN) by reducing some of the flexibility in existing agreements. On 15 February 1979 the government issued its Administration Textile Program, referred to as the White Paper (U.S. Department of Commerce 1979).[14] As part of this program, provision was made to limit the use of the carry-over provisions. Specifically, the program states that a "year to year increase . . . should not normally exceed the previous year's shipments plus one-half of the unfilled portion of the previous year's quota but in no event more than the current year's quota." Furthermore, the administration program promised closer monitoring of import quotas and a renegotiation of bilateral agreements to prevent "surges,"[15] and provided a "snapback clause" so that tariff concessions negotiated in the MTN would revert to pre-MTN levels if the MFA was not renewed.

Under the provisions of the second MFA (MFA II), the United States concluded bilateral restraint agreements with twenty supplying countries and agreements with consultative mechanisms with eleven other countries. These bilateral agreements resulted in over 80 percent of total U.S. imports of textile and apparel products being subject to control by 1980.[16]

Under MFA II, the United States negotiated bilateral agreements whereby quotas were set at three levels: at the aggregate level covering all textile and apparel products, in two to four broad groups of products, and at commodity specific levels. Within these commodity specific limits, the quota could be established as either a specific quantitative limit, a minimum consultation level, a consultation category, an agreed limit, or a designated consultation limit.[17] These quantitative restraints for 1981 are listed in table 4.1 for all twenty countries with which the United States had such agreements during MFA II. As the data show, the three major suppliers (Hong Kong, South Korea, and Taiwan) had the largest share of the U.S. market.

The present Multifiber Arrangement (MFA III) is in its third life cycle. As such it represents a culmination of repeated increases in its restrictiveness. According to this latest agreement, future bilaterals will be allowed to limit the aggregate growth rate of textile imports to the growth rate of the domestic textile market, defined as the growth in the per capita consumption of textiles and apparel (estimated by the industry to be 1.5 percent). In addition, this MFA allows for the globalization of quotas[18] and attempts to continue preferential treatment of smaller developing countries at the expense of the larger developing country exporters. The effects of these provisions will be felt most by Hong Kong, Taiwan, and South Korea, who combined accounted for 53 percent of total U.S. restricted textile and apparel imports in 1981. Under the recently completed bilateral agreements with one of these large exporters, sensitive items bound by specific limits have been limited to growth rates between 0.5 and 2.0 percent per annum. Smaller exporters, on the other hand, have been allowed growth rates exceeding 6 percent.[19]

Most industry specialists would agree that the protection provided under the MFA and its predecessor agreements has achieved its intended purpose, namely, a reduction in the growth of imports from restricted suppliers. The growth of textile and apparel imports in quantity is presented in table 4.2 for the United States and in table 4.3 for the European Community. The data in both tables demonstrate the relative success of the various trade restrictions, in that the rate of growth of textile and apparel imports has been remarkably small. In the post-MFA period, 1974–81, total textile imports grew at less than 2 percent per year. For the United States, textile imports measured in square-yard equivalents were actually lower in 1981 than in 1971. During the same period, the composition of U.S. imports changed radically from textiles toward apparel and from industrial countries toward imports from the developing countries.

In the European Community a concerted effort to control imports began only after 1976 and in particular during MFA II. Thereafter, both total imports and those from the developing countries grew at very modest rates. While total imports during 1976–80 grew at 4.9 percent per annum, imports from countries with bilateral agreements grew at only 2.2 percent per annum.

To dramatize the degree to which the commodity composition of textile imports have shifted in favor of apparel in the United States, the ratio of imports to domestic production for selected textile and apparel categories is presented in table 4.4. Comparing these ratios for various commodities representing yarn, fabrics, apparel, and made-up goods, the degree of import penetration in apparel is substantially higher. Among the apparel products, imports of sweaters, especially those made of wool, and shirts and blouses, predominantly for women and girls, rank among the highest. In contrast, imports of man-made yarn, broadwoven fabric, and knit fabric were quite modest. It would appear that this elaborate trade management system is quite successful in its ability to limit the market access of textile products where the industrialized countries possess comparative advantage, yet far less successful in the apparel area where the low-wage, developing countries have a stronger comparative advantage.

4.3   The Restructuring of the Textile Industry

Traditionally the apparel industry and (to a lesser degree) the textile industry have been dominated by a large number of small and medium sized, mostly privately held companies. The minimum scale for efficient operation was low. Consequently there were few significant barriers to entry, and concentration levels, while varying by subcategory, were far below the average for all manufacturing. In the postwar period, both the textile and apparel industries underwent a series of major, structural, demand-and-cost-related changes. The resulting characteristics of these industries are presented in table 4.5. Despite all the changes discussed below, both the textile and apparel industries have fairly low concentration rates (41 and 28 percent, respectively, in 1979). Furthermore, in both industries the import penetration ratio, measured in dollars, is less than 10 percent, in part because of the success of the quota system in restricting import growth.

Of the numerous factors having an impact on these industries in the postwar period, six factors seem most important. First, with the mass introduction and consumer acceptance of man-made fibers, firms using man-made fibers rapidly increased their share of textile output at the expense of those firms processing natural fibers. Second, changes in technology, especially in the conversion of fibers into yarn and yarn into fabrics, led to an increase in the minimum efficient size of textile plants. Similar advances in the apparel stage have been absent primarily because of technical constraints. Consequently, the apparel industry is still composed of many small and medium-sized plants with relatively low scales of operation. Third, international trade created new opportunities for expanding scale economies. In Europe, the formation of the European

Table 4.1 U.S. Bilateral Quotas and Fulfillment Levels under MFA II for 1981 (in thousand equivalent square yards)

Country	Aggregate Limit	Group 1 Limit	Group 2 Limit	Group 3 Limit	Group 4 Limit	Specific Limits	No. of Items on Specific List	Total Imports Restricted by Specific Limits	Total Imports	Restricted Imports as a Percent of Total Specific Limits	Restricted Imports as a Percent of Total Imports	Country Share of Total Imports
Brazil	158990	56102	68725	35063	100854	100854	17	69084	75963	68.5	90.9	1.65
China	—	—	—	—	—	98920	8	111160	593564	112.4	18.7	12.94
Costa Rica	—	—	—	—	—	7892	1	7854	21769	99.5	36.1	.47
Egypt	—	—	—	—	—	—	—	—	5939	—	—	1.24
Haiti	—	—	—	—	—	26619	6	10685	44041	40.1	24.3	.96
Hong Kong	1140630	313719	712647	70839	43422	789572	33	622317	872064	78.8	71.4	19.01
India	228110	184740	—	43370	—	83242	7	33696	76911	40.8	44.2	1.68
Japan	—	—	—	—	—	—	3	—	469356	—	—	10.23
South Korea	703173	173978	547037	15860	—	470614	30	439513	706440	93.4	62.2	15.40

Macau	45570	44200	1516	—	—	—	29438	22	37499	43351	127.4	86.5	.95
Malaysia	—	—	—	—	—	24139	14	19896	38185	82.4	52.1	.83
Mexico	—	—	—	—	—	80803	14	33307	127488	41.2	26.1	2.78
Pakistan	188038	162966	27579	—	—	153573	3	127798	206687	83.2	61.8	4.51
Philippines	278772	24552	—	—	—	232841	104	133017	157617	57.1	84.4	3.44
Poland	53753	—	41685	2215	802	45594	22	14018	14018	30.7	100.0	2.46
Romania	—	—	32294	28000	—	16947	7	11332	28917	66.9	39.2	.63
Singapore	278251	62355	213351	3543	—	111203	18	77004	109857	69.2	70.1	2.39
Taiwan	903915	197728	701034	5713	—	561810	24	525008	834688	93.4	62.9	18.20
Thailand	—	—	64927	—	—	66367	20	42946	112267	64.7	38.3	2.44
Yugoslavia	—	—	—	—	—	816	1	4	4	0.5	100.0	—

SOURCE: U.S. Department of Commerce, Office of Textiles, Expired Restraints, 7 June 1982.

NOTES: A line (—) indicates no limit imposed.

Textile groups are normally defined as:

Group 1 — Yarns of cotton, wool, and man-made fibers.

Group 2 — Fabrics, made-up goods, and miscellaneous nonapparel products of cotton, wool, and man-made fibers.

Group 3 — Apparel of cotton, wool, and man-made fibers.

Group 4 — Special made-up goods and miscellaneous textile and apparel. For Hong Kong the categories are: 435, 436, 438, 443, 445/6, 447/8, 633/4, 635, 638/9, 641, 648.

Table 4.2 United States Imports of Textile and Apparel Products by Source, 1971–81 (in million equivalent square yards)

Year	Apparel	Textiles	Total	Hong Kong, Taiwan, South Korea	Latin America	Other Developing Countries[a]	Japan	China	Europe and Others
1971	2,098	3,853	5,951	1,762	293	383	1,691	0.2	1,822
1972	2,226	4,010	6,236	1,810	369	559	1,249	11	2,238
1973	2,090	3,035	5,125	1,523	453	635	813	33	1,668
1974	1,937	2,473	4,410	1,475	422	571	861	84	998
1975	2,077	1,751	3,828	1,559	362	432	536	141	758
1976[b]	2,578	2,560	5,138	2,134	463	708	832	153	848
1977[b]	2,466	2,511	4,977	1,978	418	552	943	91	995
1978	2,905	2,835	5,740	2,247	605	776	853	201	1,058
1979	2,671	1,977	4,648	1,930	512	812	492	231	681
1980	2,884	3,000	4,884	2,210	461	820	461	325	608
1981	3,136	2,626	5,762	2,460	543	993	503	562	702
Average annual growth rates:									
1971–81	3.6	−3.4	−0.3	3.0	5.4	8.1	−9.8	18.2	−8.1
1971–73	−0.1	−7.9	−4.9	−4.8	14.3	16.5	−23.4	65.9	−2.9
1973–81	4.4	−1.6	1.3	5.2	2.0	4.9	−5.2	19.8	−9.1
Percentage share:									
1971	35.2	64.8	100.0	29.6	4.9	6.4	28.4	n.a.	30.6
1973	40.8	59.2	100.0	29.7	8.8	12.4	15.9	0.6	32.5
1981	54.4	45.6	100.0	42.7	9.4	17.2	8.7	9.8	12.2

SOURCES: International Trade Commission, *The History and Current Status of the Multifiber Arrangement, 1978*, Washington, D.C., 1978; International Trade Commission, *The Multifiber Arrangement, 1973 to 1980*, Washington, D.C., 1981; International Trade Commission, *U.S. Imports of Textile and Apparel Products under the Multifiber Arrangement, 1976 to 1981*, Washington, D.C., 1982.

[a]Defined here as Asia and Africa (except Israel and South Africa).

[b]Minor changes in conversion factors for converting garments, yarns, etc., into equivalent square yards took place between 1976 and 1977 when the system of product categories was changed.

Table 4.3   European Community Imports of Textile and Apparel Products, 1973–80 (thousand metric tons)

Year	Industrial Countries	Countries Covered by the MFA			Total
		Countries with Agreements	Preferential Countries[a]	Total	
1973	254	n.a.	n.a.	572	826
1974	334	n.a.	n.a.	752	1,086
1975	306	n.a.	n.a.	855	1,161
1976	356	651	n.a.	1,093	1,449
1977	332	598	301	1,001	1,333
1978	354	598	366	1,072	1,426
1979	472	697	421	1,225	1,697
1980	526	709	396	1,227	1,753
Annual growth rates:					
1973–76	11.9	n.a.	n.a.	24.1	20.6
1976–80	10.3	2.2	9.5[b]	2.9	4.9

SOURCES: Commission of the European Community, *The European Community's Textile Trade*, Europe Information no. 44/81, Brussels, 1981, and unpublished data from the Commission of the European Community.

[a]Includes the products of the 46 countries of Africa, the Caribbean, and the Pacific (ACP) who receive duty free access to the European Economic Community.

[b]For 1977–80.

Table 4.4   Imports as a Percentage of Domestic Production for Selected Textile and Apparel Categories

Item	1972	1973	1974	1975	1976	1977	1978	1979	1980
Yarn:									
Cotton	4.1	2.9	1.8	1.8	3.6	1.9	4.1	1.7	2.6
Wool	3.1	2.8	5.5	3.6	5.0	7.2	6.8	4.4	4.9
Man-made, textured	11.8	7.3	3.2	2.3	2.2	3.1	1.4	0.8	0.6
Man-made, spun noncellulosic	1.5	1.6	0.8	0.6	0.9	2.1	3.4	2.2	2.8
Broadwoven fabric:									
Cotton	12.2	13.3	13.4	11.2	16.8	11.8	18.2	14.3	16.0
Wool	11.7	13.2	10.7	10.1	12.5	15.4	15.0	12.7	10.0
Man-made	3.5	2.7	2.8	3.0	3.3	3.3	3.9	3.4	2.8
Knit fabric:									
Cotton	0.1	0.1	0.1	0.1	0.2	0.1	0.1	0.0	0.1
Wool	17.5	3.9	2.2	4.0	4.3	3.5	1.2	0.9	0.8
Man-made	3.4	1.8	0.7	0.7	0.6	0.6	0.5	0.3	0.2

Rugs, carpets:									
Cotton	28.3	31.3	58.7	40.1	58.9	26.8	26.5	20.2	49.3
Wool	10.3	19.8	34.6	43.7	63.4	61.5	64.0	58.9	102.9
Man-made	1.1	0.7	0.5	0.5	0.6	0.5	0.4	0.4	0.4
Sweaters, total:	77.3	74.8	79.0	89.0	115.2	106.8	119.4	122.1	162.6
Men's and boys'	35.8	42.1	37.0	43.3	61.5	60.6	86.8	75.8	68.9
Women's and girls'	101.1	95.1	107.4	111.0	141.2	129.1	136.7	148.3	219.3
Wool	110.5	156.7	139.7	187.5	390.2	426.5	201.0	214.6	436.7
Man-made	103.3	96.0	108.2	107.0	129.3	112.3	131.9	134.0	188.2
Shirts and blouses:									
Woven	33.8	29.4	31.4	35.3	48.1	49.3	67.5	70.1	70.1
Shirts and blouses, knit	41.3	40.6	41.1	47.3	46.9	39.5	46.7	42.9	40.8
Men's and boys'	23.9	24.7	15.8	19.0	18.1	17.3	24.8	23.0	23.2
Women's and girls'	62.5	60.1	74.4	79.1	82.8	65.4	72.5	66.2	65.6
Suits, total:	6.1	6.6	11.8	12.4	13.0	11.4	14.1	12.2	11.6
Trousers and slacks, total:	22.3	21.4	17.0	20.9	23.1	24.1	31.3	26.3	26.7
Men's and boys'	9.8	9.1	7.5	11.7	13.5	14.3	18.2	15.4	14.9
Women's and girls'	43.2	41.1	31.2	33.2	37.7	38.7	53.2	43.5	46.1

SOURCE: U.S. Department of Commerce, International Trade Administration, *Cotton, Wool and Man-Made Fiber Textiles and Apparel*, June 1982.

Table 4.5   Profile of the U.S. Textile and Apparel Industries, 1979 (in million of dollars except as noted)

	Textile Mill Products (SIC 22)	Apparel and Other Textile Products (SIC 23)
Number of establishments in 1977	7,100	26,000
Value of shipments	46,850	47,276
Total employment (000)	858.2	1,331.0
Production workers (000)	742.6	1,151.1
Average hourly earnings	4.87	4.38
Capital expenditure	1,423	524
Simple four-firm concentration ratio:		
1965	38%	21%
1979	41%	28%
Average 1965–79	39%	23%
Import penetration ratio:[a]		
1965	6.77%	3.23%
1979	8.16%	9.35%
Average annual growth in domestic demand:[a]		
1965–73	.031%	.039%
1974–79	.042%	.056%
Average annual growth in imports:[a]		
1965–73	.287%	.100%
1974–79	− .942%	− .989%

Source: U.S. Department of Commerce.
[a]Valued in dollars.

Economic Community and the European Free Trade Association aided the industry by providing a larger market. The large internal U.S. market together with the Canadian market had already provided U.S. firms with the opportunities for exploiting scale economies. Fourth, many of the smaller, less capital-intensive textile enterprises, faced with this new internal competition, were absorbed by larger, more affluent conglomerates. Fifth, the introduction of cotton dust standards in 1974 led to intraindustry changes that forced marginal cotton textile firms to close down as a result of the proposed new regulations. Finally, the entire process of structural change was undertaken under the protective umbrella of the MFA and its predecessor agreements. These agreements were aimed at preserving the market share of domestic textile and apparel producers by limiting the growth of specific imports.

The resulting change in the composition of raw materials consumed by the textile and apparel industries is well known. Whereas in 1963 man-made fibers accounted for 36 percent of all fibers consumed by the U.S. textile industry, by 1980 man-made fibers rose to 75 percent of total fibers consumed. A similar development occurred in the European Community and Japan where man-made fiber consumption rose from 26 and 43 percent to 60 and 67 percent, respectively. This interfiber competition had a very pronounced effect on the structure of the textile industry. It created a substantial barrier to entry by raising the cost of a minimum efficient plant, especially in the primary stages of production, namely weaving and knitting.[20]

The shift toward man-made fibers can be attributed to both domestic and trade-related factors. First, the advances in polymer technology led to lower and more stable man-made fiber prices in contrast to higher natural fiber prices. Second, imports of man-made fiber products began to be restricted as early as 1971. Third, consumer tastes shifted in favor of easier care fabrics. This combined with technological changes in the use of man-made fibers contributed to the slow but steady collapse of the smaller textile firms primarily producing cotton textiles.

As mentioned above, the public introduction of proposed cotton dust standards in December 1974 also may have caused some intraindustry changes in the textile industry. While the actual rules did not take effect till the end of 1980, some analysts believe that the impending rules did encourage some textile firms to stop processing cotton. In a recent article, Maloney and McCormick (1982) point out that starting in 1974 a redistribution of wealth took place within the textile industry, where larger firms capable of adapting to the new cotton dust standards continued cotton production while smaller, more marginal firms were driven out of the cotton business.

For many years the textile sector was composed of three major activities: the treatment and transformation of raw fibers into yarn, the conversion of yarn into fabric, and the assembly of fabric into apparel. In large part as a result of the introduction of man-made fibers, technological changes introduced in the 1960s and 1970s have blurred the distinctions between this troika production process. In cases such as nonwoven fabrics, the processes of yarn and fabric production have merged. In cases such as seamless hosiery, certain sweaters, and sheets, yarn is transformed directly into the finished product. In addition to combining the production processes of certain products, technological changes have also altered the way each of these processes is carried out. In particular, the speed with which each operation is performed and the amount of automatic transfer between operations has increased. All this has lead to a reduction in inventory requirements and in labor usage. It has, on the other hand, led to a substantial increase in capital requirements.[21]

In both the United States and Europe, increased investments in both textiles and apparel have been primarily influenced by steady increases in the capital intensity of the textile operation and by industry expectations of increased textile demand. From the data presented in table 4.6, the

Table 4.6   Volume of Gross Fixed Investment in the Textile and Clothing Industries, 1970–78 (annual averages, million $)[a]

Country	Textile Industry		Apparel Industry	
	1970–74	1975–78	1970–74	1975–78
Germany	615.7	428.0	155.7	130.0
Belgium	107.0	117.2	46.2	25.7
Denmark	37.9	21.4	8.8	7.6
France	545.1	318.6	96.1	92.3
Ireland	24.3	32.2	3.2	4.1
Italy	440.8	412.0	97.8	84.8
Netherlands	92.9	59.4	19.6	13.5
United Kingdom	437.4	311.1	79.0	71.1
Total EEC	2364.1	1699.9	506.4	429.1
Austria	79.6	59.7	22.9	18.5
Spain	149.5	119.6	44.6	24.9
Finland	45.4	27.7	21.3	17.9
Greece	122.9	172.7	8.3	16.4
Norway	22.1	18.8	4.6	5.3
Portugal	155.6	66.1	16.3	6.8
Sweden	50.2	46.9	13.0	12.2
Total Europe	2989.4	2211.4	637.3	531.1
Canada	147.4	107.4	21.9	18.6
United States	1278.9	1068.1	447.1	388.4
Total North America	1426.3	1175.5	469.0	407.0
Japan	1320.0	627.9	161.7	135.9
Australia	64.8	32.6	17.8	8.9
Total OECD	5800.5	4047.5	1285.8	1082.9

SOURCE: Organization for Economic Cooperation and Development (OECD), *Textile Industry in OECD Countries*.
[a]At 1975 prices and 1975 exchange rates.

investment boom in the industry appears to have started in the early 1970s and culminated in 1974. In the post-1975 recession, investment in the textile and apparel industries dropped off substantially from a prerecession annual average of $5.8 billion to a post-1975 level of $4.0 billion for the entire Organization for Economic Cooperation and Development (OECD).

The pattern of OECD textile/apparel investment is generally assumed to be motivated by a number of factors.[22] First, the anticipation of a boom in consumer demand combined with an anticipated reduction in the growth of imports led to the creation of highly capital-intensive excess capacities in the production and processing of man-made fibers. Second, advances in the quality of equipment combined with rising labor costs induced many enterprises to renew their capital stock more rapidly. Since 1975 the emphasis of investment activity has been concentrated on new processes and on the elimination of bottlenecks. While gross fixed investment has declined in the post-1975 period, the capital stock of the industry does not appear to have declined. In fact, the textile industry in the OECD, and especially in the United States, has transformed itself over the past twenty to twenty-five years from a labor intensive, small-scale industry to one that is far more capital-intensive and above all more profitable. The same cannot be said, however, for most of the apparel industry, which is still predominantly labor and low-skill intensive.

Based on the above discussion, the restructuring of the textile (and to a lesser extent the apparel) industry apparently can be attributed to a variety of factors that are not all trade related. Yet the role of the MFA cannot be discounted. While it may not have played the major role, it did in fact preserve the market share for the domestic apparel industry, which is the largest (40 percent) customer of the U.S. textile industry.

4.4   Measuring the Impact of the MFA

A central proposition of economic theory is that, in long-run competitive equilibrium, resources will be allocated efficiently when prices equal marginal cost and producers earn only normal rates of return. Departures from this norm because of either imperfect competition or government intervention (e.g., trade restrictions) should result in an inefficient allocation of resources or rates of return above the competitive norm. A major area of industrial organization research has therefore focused on differences in market characteristics as determinants of above-competitive-equilibrium profits. The literature in this area has generally confirmed that the size distribution of sellers, the rate of growth of demand, and barriers to entry are important determinants of industry profitability.[23] More recently this literature has incorporated the impact of foreign trade on the performance of U.S. manufacturing industries.[24] The central proposition of this literature is quite simple. Actual and potential import competition increases the strength of the competitive process in the domestic market, in effect reducing seller concentration and resulting in competitively determined prices and normal profits. Conversely, one could argue that the existence of fewer foreign competitors or the expectation of fewer foreign competitors leads to higher domestic concentration and consequently to higher than competitive levels of profitability.

While existing studies have taken into account the role of import competition (Esposito and Esposito 1971), the role of exports (Caves, Khalizadeh-Shirazi, and Porter 1975), and the role of foreign direct investment (Pagoulatos and Sorensen 1976), an examination of the impact of Orderly Marketing Agreements, such as the MFA, on industry profit performance has not been carried out. By focusing on whether

U.S. textile and apparel quotas have served to improve the profit performance of the domestic industry, the following analysis attempts to fill this gap in the literature.

4.4.1 The Empirical Framework

The industrial organization literature uses multiple regression analysis to estimate the relationship between industry profitability, market structure, and foreign competition. These equations ordinarily include seller concentration, geographic dispersion, economies of scale, capital requirements, and market growth of demand as the major structural determinants of profitability and, at a minimum, the import penetration ratio as the foreign variable.[25] The theoretical justification for both the domestic structural variables and the international factors along with a thorough explanation of the model are more than adequately discussed in the substantial industrial organization literature cited earlier. Consequently, only a brief explanation of the theoretical rationale for each of the conventional variables is presented here.

Competitive Performance

The dependent variable used in the analysis to represent competitive performance is the price-cost margin (PCM) which has been successfully used in previous industrial organization studies (see, for example, Collins and Preston 1968, 1969, Kwoka 1977, Mann 1970, and Weiss 1974). This proxy of profitability equals profits plus capital costs (calculated as value added minus payroll) divided by value of shipments. Consequently, part of the cross-industry variability in profitability will reflect differences in capital intensity. To control for this variation in capital costs, the capital output ratio is used as an independent variable. The PCM can therefore be viewed as an approximation of a percentage margin of revenue over direct cost.[26]

Economic theory would argue that in a competitive equilibrium, ceteris paribus, interindustry profit rates should equalize. That is, the PCM for a perfectly competitive industry in long-run equilibrium would be zero, regardless of the level of import competition. The state of competition in the textile and apparel industries represents a continuum from industries nearly perfectly competitive to industries where the joint-profit-maximization outcome is approached. Consequently, inequality of industry profit rates may indicate differences in the state of actual and expected competition. Lower actual or expected competition should, ceteris paribus, result in higher profits for that industry. In an open economy, Marvel (1980) has demonstrated that an expansion in preimport profitability induces imports to increase, while increases in imports tend to reduce ex post domestic profitability.

Capital Intensity

Because most of the subsectors of the textile and apparel industries differ in capital intensities and because the dependent variable (PCM) subtracts only direct factor costs, one must take account of implicit capital cost differences between subindustries. A capital output ratio (KO), calculated as the gross book value of fixed assets divided by value of shipments, is therefore included as an independent variable to control for the opportunity cost of capital. One would expect the KO ratio to be positively related to the price-cost margin.

A major weakness of the KO ratio is that in rapidly growing industries it may not reflect the steady-state equilibrium level of KO. To minimize this problem, value added per production worker (VAP) was added as a further independent variable. VAP will further distinguish the varying impact of changes in productivity occurring in both industries during the 1965–79 period.

Geographic Dispersion

To take into account differences in regional concentration of manufacturing activity within the United States, a particularly successful index used is one developed by Collins and Preston (CPIN; 1968). This index of regional concentration is calculated as the sum of the absolute differences between the percentage of a particular industry's domestic shipments and the population across census regions. Assuming that per capita demand for a given industry's product is distributed at a constant population share rate across regions, a high concentration of an industry in one region would imply that the industry product is tradeable. Consequently, increases in the CPIN index are associated with increased international trade and lower price-cost margins. The sign of CPIN is therefore expected to be positive for industries like textiles and apparel where manufacturing is not concentrated in one region of the United States.

Growth of Domestic Demand

Growth in industry demand (GROWD), calculated as the annual percentage change in industry shipments, should, ceteris paribus, exhibit an independent and positive relationship with industry profits. Theory and past empirical evidence support the proposition that when an industry experiences high growth in demand, firms may secure above-competitive profits. When growth is slow or declining, firms may be compelled to reduce profit margins to maintain adequate levels of sales.

Seller Concentration

The measure of seller concentration most often used is the four-firm concentration ratio (CR4). A generally accepted proposition is that the greater the share of industry output controlled by a few firms, the greater the probability that these firms will tacitly collude to raise prices above long-run average costs. Thus, industry profit rates are likely to be positively related to seller concentration.[27]

Economies of Scale

Oligopoly theory suggests that the greater the output of an entrant's minimum efficient plant relative to industry output, the higher the barrier to entry. Consequently, an economies of scale variable (ECSC) is calculated as the ratio of the average plant size among the largest plants producing 50 percent of the industry's value of shipments to total value of shipments of the industry. One would expect profits to be positively associated with the level of scale economies.

Foreign Competition

Empirical implementation of the structure-conduct-performance paradigm of industrial organization without foreign variables is straightforward. However, when foreign trade is introduced as a further constraint on above-competitive returns, one must take into account the simultaneity between industry profitability and international trade. As Marvel (1980) and White (1974) have pointed out, above-competitive profits by domestic manufacturers encourage imports, and a large import share, expost, reduces profits.[28] To deal with this simultaneity problem, an expected import penetration ratio ($\widehat{\text{IMPR}}$) is added to the set of independent variables commonly used to explain variations in rates of return among industries.

Following the lead of Marvel (1980), the expected values for the import penetration ratios are estimated from the following equation:

$$(1) \qquad \text{IMPR} = \beta_0 + \beta_1 \, \text{CR4} + \beta_2 \, \text{KO} + \beta_3 \, \text{AHE} + \beta_4 \, \text{NPWP} + \beta_5 \, \text{CPIN},$$

where AHE is average hourly earnings of production workers, and NPWP is nonproduction workers payroll as a percent of total payroll. Because the import penetration ratio (IMPR) is bounded by zero, ordinary least squares is inappropriate. Consequently, the import penetration equation is estimated using a maximum likelihood Tobit procedure.[29]

A second, equally important problem when introducing international trade is how to demonstrate that the restraining effect of imports depends on the domestic structure of the textile and apparel industry. That is, of one considers these industries to be imperfectly competitive, then increased imports should restrain above-competitive levels of profitability. On the other hand, if these industries are viewed as inherently competitive, then price will already equal marginal cost and, hence, there will be no restraining effect from imports. To capture these differential effects of imports due to differences in industry concentration, we have followed the lead of Pugel (1980) in assuming that the impact of import competition varies interactively with the industry's concentration ratio. Consequently, the measure of import competition used is $\widehat{\text{IMPR}} \cdot \text{CR4}$. One would expect that in those cases where concentration ratios are high $\widehat{\text{IMPR}} \cdot \text{CR4}$ would be negatively related to the price-cost margin.[30]

In addition to incorporating the expected import penetration measure, we have also added two variables to reflect barriers to foreign competition. The first measure is the ad valorem, trade-weighted, nominal tariff rate (AVE); the second is a proxy for the MFA. The measure for the quota system (MFASL) is calculated as the percent of an individual four-digit-SIC industry's imports subject to specific quantity limits at the textile category level. The higher (lower) the percentage of trade subject to a ceiling, the greater (lower) the barriers to foreign suppliers, and the higher (lower) the price-cost margin would be. That is, if a large portion of a four-digit industry's output is covered by specific import limits under the MFA, then it is assumed that the firms in the industry can be quite confident, based on the history of textile trade regulations, that imports will not be allowed to grow above the designated quota ceilings and therefore not grow as a percentage of the domestic market. Consequently, domestic textile and apparel firms may be more likely and willing to raise prices and increase profits above the competitive norm.

These arguments suggest an empirically useful estimating equation for the structure-conduct-performance paradigm in the following general form:

$$
\begin{aligned}
\text{PCM} = \alpha_0 &+ \alpha_1 \,\text{KO} + \alpha_2 \,\text{CPIN} + \alpha_3 \,\text{ECSC} + \alpha_4 \,\text{GROWD} \\
&+ \alpha_5 \,\text{CR4} + \alpha_6 \,\text{VAP} + \alpha_7 \,\text{AVE} \\
&+ \alpha_8 \,(\widehat{\text{IMPR}} \cdot \text{CR4}) + \alpha_9 \,\text{MFASL};
\end{aligned}
\tag{2}
$$

$$
\alpha_1, \alpha_3, \alpha_4, \alpha_5, \alpha_6, \alpha_7, \alpha_9 > 0; \ \alpha_8 < 0; \ \alpha_2 \gtrless 0.
$$

4.5   Empirical Results

In the present study the textile and apparel industries are defined at their respective four-digit SIC levels. As such, our entire sample is composed of twenty-nine, four-digit textile SIC categories and thirty-three, four-digit apparel SIC categories over the fifteen-year period of 1965–79.[31] The major drawback of such a limited sample, apart from the lack of universal applicability, is the high degree of homogeneity of the four-digit categories within each industry.[32] Furthermore, given that our primary concern is the impact of the MFA on both the textile and the apparel industries in the six-year period of 1974–79, a consistent set of observations over time series and cross sections is not sufficient for an efficient estimate of either a time-series or a cross-section equation. Therefore, the estimation of equation (2) can only be obtained by pooling cross-section and time-series observations for the pre-MFA period (1965–73) and the post-MFA period (1974–79) for each of the industries.[33] The pooling procedure used is commonly termed a cross-sectionally correlated and time-wise autoregressive model. The behavioral characteristics of this model are well known and need not be restated here.[34]

Parameter estimates for both the textile and the apparel industries for the pre- and post-MFA periods are presented in table 4.7. In general, the results based on MFASL (the quota variable) suggest that the existence of the MFA did in fact improve the profit performance of the protected textile and apparel sectors.

4.5.1 Foreign Factors

The central concern of this paper is to determine whether the MFA had a positive impact on the profit performance of the domestic textile and apparel industries. The results as demonstrated by the coefficient of MFASL (α_9) presented in table 4.7 suggest that for both industries the MFA had a positive and significant impact on industry performance.[35] One can therefore argue that by providing market certainty for the domestic textile and apparel industries the MFA did improve their profit performance during 1974–79.

Two other foreign variables of some concern are the trade-weighted, ad valorem, nominal tariff rate (AVE) and the proxy for import competition ($\widehat{IMPR} \cdot CR4$). The empirical results of these two variables were far short of expectation. While the coefficient of AVE (α_7) was positive in three out of four cases, it was significantly different from zero only during the post-MFA period for the textile industry and only during the pre-MFA period for the apparel industry. The proxy for import competition was insignificant in all cases and of the wrong sign in three out of four cases. These results suggest that an increase in import penetration did not have a negative impact on the profit performance of either the textile or apparel industries. On the other hand, the positive and significant results of the tariff measure (in two cases) suggest that in addition to the positive influence of the MFA on the textile industry, high tariff rates also contributed positively to the profit performance of the industry. The most surprising aspect of these results was that while the MFA positively contributed to the profit performance of the apparel industry during 1974–79, high nominal tariffs significantly detracted from the industry's profit performance.

Table 4.7   Determinants of Textile and Apparel Industry Performance Using Pooled Cross-Section, Time-Series Data for the Pre- and Post-MFA Periods

	Textiles		Apparel	
Variables	Pre-MFA (1965–73)	Post-MFA (1974–79)	Pre-MFA (1965–73)	Post-MFA (1974–79)
Constant	0.063 (2.65)	0.220 (4.19)	−0.020 (1.07)	0.166 (3.88)
KO	0.010 (1.58)	−0.063 (4.75)	0.014 (0.76)	0.061 (2.20)
CPIN	0.024 (1.12)	0.014 (0.31)	0.016 (0.89)	0.081 (1.09)
ECSC	0.009 (0.86)	0.018 (0.67)	0.015 (2.47)	0.001 (0.11)
GROWD	0.007 (1.72)	0.051 (3.01)	−0.004 (0.87)	0.021 (1.39)
CR4	−0.001 (3.49)	−0.002 (1.78)	0.016[a] (0.56)	0.001 (0.82)
VAP	0.011 (35.1)	0.001 (1.79)	0.015 (21.7)	0.001 (3.34)
AVE	0.003 (1.26)	0.001 (3.10)	0.003 (8.84)	−0.001 (3.47)
$\widehat{\text{IMPR}}$ · CR4	−0.002[a] (1.20)	0.004[a] (0.88)	0.003[a] (1.48)	0.003[a] (1.13)
MFASL	— —	0.001[a] (2.11)	— —	0.001[a] (2.23)

NOTES: t-values are in parentheses. Summary of goodness-of-fit statistics, especially R^2, are not reported because an interpretable R^2 when using generalized least-squares estimation does not exist.
[a]The estimated coefficient is multiplied by 100.

4.5.2 Domestic Factors

For the most part, the domestic market structure variables did not perform as expected. The coefficients of the capital output ratio (KO) for the textile and apparel industries in the pre-MFA period are not statistically significant, although positive as is generally predicted. In the post-MFA period for the textile industry the coefficient is negative and statistically significant. For the apparel industry it is positive and statistically insignificant. Part of the explanation for this result rests on the low variation in the KO variable.

A somewhat more interesting result can be seen in the geographic dispersion variable (CPIN). In general, past empirical evidence supports the proposition that the higher the geographic dispersion index, the more likely the given commodity will be traded internationally, and the lower the price-cost margin. However, for the textile and apparel industries where production in the United States has not been concentrated in a single region, the coefficient on CPIN is of the expected sign (positive) for both the pre- and post-MFA periods, although insignificant in all four cases. Therefore no inference can be drawn from this variable.

The results of the economies of scale (ECSC) and the value added per production worker (VAP) variables are mixed. It is generally accepted that in the 1970s the scale of operation in both the textile and the apparel industries was increasing with the significant improvements in labor productivity. This is reflected, in part, in the industry-specific results. For both industries the coefficient on VAP is positive and significant in both the pre- and post-MFA periods. The coefficient on ECSC is positive for both industries, although significant only in the pre-MFA period for the apparel industry.

A further mixed result is that the coefficient on the growth of domestic demand variable (GROWD) is positive, although statistically significant only for the textile industry in the post-MFA period. Finally, given the low level of concentration in the two industries, it is not surprising that the four-firm concentration ratio (CR4) is not significantly different from zero in three out of four cases. However, a negative sign was unexpected. The low variation in the data may be one explanation, but not the overriding one.

4.6 Conclusion

The MFA was only one factor among many others impacting the U.S. textile and apparel industries. Nevertheless, the MFA's role stands out because it is distinct from the other factors in its attempt to secure the market for the domestic textile and apparel industries. As such, one would expect that by limiting competition the MFA would positively affect the performance of the U.S. textile and apparel industries. The results suggest that in fact that was the case. This positive impact arises from the MFA's ability to control the growth in imports, as was its intention. Having determined that the MFA was indeed a successful protective instrument of the United States, the next important question to be answered is: What has this success cost?

Appendix

Annual observations for our domestic and foreign variables by four-digit, output-based Standard Industrial Classification (SIC) categories over the period 1965–79 were taken from generally available published sources. Data on the quota enforcement were obtained from the U.S. Department of Commerce, Office of Textiles. Our entire data base consisted of twenty-nine, four-digit textile categories (combining SIC 2257 and 2258 after 1972) and thirty-three, four-digit apparel categories over fifteen years, or a total of 930 observations. The variables are:

PCM = (VA − PA)/VS: Price-cost margin; where VA = value added, PA = payroll, and VS = value of shipments; obtained from *Census of Manufactures* (CM) and the *Annual Survey of Manufactures* (ASM), various years.

KO = GBVFA/VS: Capital output ratio; where GBVFA = gross book value of fixed assets; obtained from CM. The values for the intercensus period were derived by interpolation.

CPIN = $\Sigma_{i=1}^{4} |(VS_i/VS) - (Pop_i/Pop)|$: Geographic dispersion; where i = the four census regions, and Pop = population; derived from CM. The values for the intercensus period were derived by interpolation.

GROWD = % Δ VS: Growth in domestic demand; derived from both ASM and CM.

VAP = (VA/Prod): Value added per production worker; where Prod = the number of production workers; obtained from the Bureau of Labor Statistics (BLS).

AVE: Ad valorem, trade-weighted, nominal tariff rates; obtained from the U.S. Department of Labor.

CR4: The four-firm concentration ratio; obtained from both ASM and CM. The values for the intercensus period were derived by interpolation.

ECSC: Economies of scale derived as AVS/VS, where AVS = average plant size among the largest plants producing 50 percent of the industry's value of shipments; obtained from CM. The values for the intercensus period were derived by interpolation.

IMPR = VM/VS + VM − VX: Import penetration ratio; where VM = value of imports and VX = value of exports; obtained from BLS and the Office of Foreign Economic Research (OFER), computer tapes.

$\widehat{\text{IMPR}}$: The expected import penetration ratio estimated from equation (1).

GROWD = % ΔVM: Growth in imports; derived from trade data provided by BLS and OFER.

MFASL: Share of an individual four-digit-SIC industry's imports subject to a specific quota. The quota levels by country and textile category were obtained from the U.S. Department of Commerce, Office of Textiles. These textile categories are defined by the United States for monitoring imports of textile and apparel products. They were converted to seven-digit TSUSA items using U.S. Department of Commerce, Industry and Trade Administration, Office of Textiles, *Correlation: Textile and Apparel Categories Tariff Schedules of the United States, Annotated.* Washington, D.C.: GPO, 1979. The individual TSUSA items were then converted to output-based SIC categories using a concordance provided by the U.S. Department of Labor, Office of Foreign Economic Research. While this concordance process is theoretically correct, the addition and deletion of both textile categories and SIC categories in the mid-1970s may have created some problems. Furthermore, for 1965–1973 no attempt is made to include the quota on cotton because there the concordance is far less reliable.

Notes

1. A recent survey of such changes is presented in Pelzman (1982). Note, however, that the degree of change varies considerably across the textile and apparel industries.
2. Despite the shrinking of the U.S. textile industry between 1910 and 1955, it still remained an important industrial sector. In the late 1950s and early 1960s it represented 6.0 percent of manufacturing employment and 4.0 percent of manufacturing output. Combined with the apparel industry, which accounted for an additional 7.0 percent of manufacturing employment and 3.6 percent of manufacturing output, the enlarged textile complex represented a substantial interest group. In 1980 the same complex represented 10.6 percent of manufacturing employment and 5.6 percent of manufacturing output. In addition to these economic facts, the enlarged complex when combined with fiber producers represented a well-organized political pressure group, with strong influences in the industrial Northeast in the 1960s and in the low-wage areas of the Southeast in the 1970s and 1980s.
3. For an in-depth discussion of the MFA and its development, see Keesing and Wolf (1980), Pelzman (1980), and U.S. ITC (1978). All of the agreements beginning with the Japanese voluntary export controls cover both textile and apparel products.
4. In 1957 Japanese cotton textile and apparel exports accounted for over 60 percent of total U.S. imports. These exports were concentrated in cotton ginghams and velveteens. In response to these increased imports, the U.S. textile industry filed four escape clause petitions with the U.S. Tariff Commission between January and June 1956. For more details see U.S. ITC (1978, 1–5).
5. By "orderly" the administration meant a system whereby the developed country producers would not be subjected to competition from lower-cost producers.
6. The bilateral agreements negotiated under the LTA were contrary both to the principles of nondiscrimination of article I and to the safeguards provision of article XIX of the GATT.

7. Under the LTA, quotas could be either agreed on jointly or be imposed by the importing country. The usual course by which quotas were imposed by the United States was to first set specific limits on a limited set of items under article 3 (whether unilateral or negotiated) and then to follow up with a more comprehensive bilateral agreement under article 4. Quotas imposed under article 3 were initially set at the actual level of imports during the year ending three months prior to the consultation call. These quotas were generally increased by 5 percent a year. Under article 4 a much more comprehensive agreement was possible, thus limiting the imports of cotton from major developing country exporters even more.

8. Two major events occurred during 1961–72 which affected the operation of the LTA. First, there was a very rapid increase in the use and trade of man-made fibers which were not covered under the LTA. Second, new entrants into the market were heavily concentrated in apparel which also was not very well protected under the LTA.

9. The text of the MFA can be found in U.S. ITC (1978, appendix A).

10. The disposition of unused quotas is determined by the individual bilateral agreement. In general countries are allowed to borrow a total of 11 percent against a commodity-specific limit or aggregate limit. The distribution of that 11 percent between forward and backward borrowing is determined by the bilateral. In most cases it is 6 percent forward and 5 percent backward.

11. By "equitable" the authors of the MFA meant that it provided for a small but guaranteed 6 percent expansion in the exports of developing countries. By all accounts, this quota system was and remains highly inequitable because it denies market access to efficient producers.

12. The delay to negotiate bilateral agreements by the EC member states was in part due to their lack of agreement over the allocation of imports within the European Community. Furthermore, the EC debate over comprehensive or selective agreements delayed an EC trade position vis-à-vis textiles.

13. In the original MFA there was flexibility for switching quotas among years (carry-over and carry-forward) as well as among textile categories (swing). This flexibility provision was under attack both in the United States and the European Community for providing the potential for "surges" in developing country exports of so-called sensitive products. In MFA II the major suppliers were induced to give up these flexibility provisions in their most important categories. In addition, in those categories where the quotas were not filled, the new bilaterals eliminated specific quotas, substituting instead consultation provisions whereby the United States could impose quotas at levels below the original quotas but higher than existing trade.

14. The Administration Textile Program or the so-called White Paper was issued on 15 February 1979.

15. By limiting "surges" the administration intended to: (a) limit the carry-over provisions, (b) impose designated consultation levels, and (c) list categories considered to be sensitive and subject to a consultation or to an agreed limit.

16. It is difficult to determine what in fact the quota system has controlled. While it is true that over 80 percent of total U.S. textile and apparel imports in both 1980 and 1981 were controlled by the aggregate limit, imports in both years under specific limits represented slightly over 50 percent of total imports.

17. The difference between these limits is very subtle. Quotas set as either specific limits or agreed limits are for all practical purposes specific quotas. Items designated by minimum consultation levels are threshold markers which when crossed allow the United States to call a consultation for the purpose of setting a quota limit. Categories designated consultation categories do not have quotas set, but are considered sensitive items subject to a quota.

18. "Globalization of quotas" means a system where the importing country sets a maximum quantity for the level of imports based either on growth of imports vis-à-vis domestic demand or on some threshold import penetration rate. Given this maximum, in

the bilateral negotiations the importing country can allocate shares based on the premise, for instance, that new entrants (with no proven comparative advantage) be given greater access to the U.S. market. The above scenario was presented as a viable option by Shelley Appleton, secretary-treasurer, International Ladies' Garment Workers' Union, before the Trade Subcommittee, Committee on Ways and Means, U.S. House of Representatives, 21 July 1980. During MFA II the European Community did in fact impose such a global system for what they considered very sensitive items.

19. The recent bilateral agreement with Hong Kong imposed specific limits on twenty-seven categories, limiting growth rates between 0.5 percent to 2.0 percent per annum. Of these twenty-seven categories, nineteen will allow for only the minimum 0.5 percent growth. On the other hand, bilateral agreements with Pakistan, Mexico, and Singapore limit the growth of specific limits to 7 percent, 7 percent, and 5 percent per annum respectively.

20. These developments are discussed at some length in both Pelzman (1980) and OECD (1981).

21. For an excellent discussion of the adjustment process in the textile and apparel industries as it applies to trade and protection, see Glismann et al. (1983). The subject of technological change is presented in great detail in Boon (1981).

22. Some of these factors are noted in OECD (1981, 72–77). Note that without detailed data or an appropriate investment model, these factors are merely speculative.

23. See, for example, Collins and Preston (1968, 1969), Kwoka (1977), Mann (1970), Miller (1967), Rhoades and Cleaver (1973), and Stigler (1964). An extensive bibliography is included in Weiss (1974) and Scherer (1980).

24. See, for example, Esposito and Esposito (1971), Pagoulatos and Sorensen (1976), and more recently Pugel (1980) and Marvel (1980).

25. Other variables commonly used to explain interindustry differences in profitability include: consumer-producer distinctions, advertising/sales ratios, inventory/sales ratios, and buyer concentration. A full list of variables and the relevant literature is presented in Scherer (1980, chap. 9). These variables were excluded from this analysis primarily because they do not apply to our particular industry sample.

26. One can think of the PCM variable as a good proxy for the Lerner measure of monopoly power. That is, PCM = (TR − TVC)/TR, where payroll plus the cost of materials is a good proxy for variable cost (TVC). Value added is defined by census as the value of shipments plus services rendered minus cost of materials, supplies and containers, fuel, purchased electrical energy, and contract work. Therefore, TR − TVC can be approximated by VA − Payroll. Accounting rates of return, such as rates of return on assets and equity, are frequently used as alternative indices of monopoly power and market performance. However, as Fisher and McGowan (1982) have shown, using accounting rates of return is valid only to the extent that profits are indeed monopoly profits or are economic profits. Given the fact that the actual state of competition in the textile and apparel industries is between these two polar cases, it was decided to use PCM as a proxy of domestic industry profitability.

27. Other measures of concentration including individual firm market shares, eight-firm concentration ratios, and the Herfindahl-Hirschman index have been used with some strikingly different results. Given our concern with the impact of the trade variables and in particular the impact of the MFA, it was decided to use the four-firm concentration ratio. This debate concerning different measures of concentration is presented in Scherer (1980, chap. 9).

28. Assuming that the domestic industry is not perfectly competitive and that foreign firms are not subject to entry limitations which result in domestic market power, White (1974) has shown that import shares are expected to be positively related to above-competitive profit rates earned by domestic firms. In a perfectly competitive environment

one would expect that above-normal profits would encourage entry from domestic sources as well, resulting in lower concentration and hence lower profits.

29. Related work by Marvel (1980) and DeRosa and Goldstein (1981) have successfully used a similar specification to predict import penetration. The results of this estimated equation are not reported here, but they are available from the author.

30. Some would argue that in the textile and apparel industries concentration rates are low, implying that domestic competition is high. In this case import competition may not affect profit rates but may rather drive marginal firms out of business.

31. Data sources for all the variables are presented in the appendix.

32. The impact of that homogeneity is that the variance in the PCM as well as in the independent variables is small.

33. One could argue that the MFA actually started in 1971 when the United States signed bilateral agreements with Japan, Hong Kong, Taiwan, and Korea designed to control not only the exports of cotton but also of wool and man-made textile and apparel products. However, given the lack of data on the level of constraints in these agreements during 1971–73, it was decided to date the MFA as of the 1974 agreements for which data were available.

34. One should not ignore the fact that pooling cross-section and time-series data has its own set of problems. In particular, difficulty arises because the disturbance term is likely to consist of time-series-related disturbances, cross-section disturbances, and a combination of both. The particular pooling procedure used here allows cross-section disturbances to be mutually correlated and heteroskedastic and allows time-series disturbances to be autoregressive. See Kmenta (1971, 512–14).

35. Throughout the paper statistical significance is taken to be at the 5 percent level.

References

Boon, Gerard K. 1981. *Technology transfer in fibers, textile and apparel.* The Netherlands: Sijthoff and Noordhoff.

Cannon, C. M. 1978. International trade, concentration, and competition in U.K. consumer goods market. *Oxford Economic Papers* 30:130–37.

Caves, Richard, J. Khalilzadeh-Shirazi, and M. E. Porter. 1975. Scale economies in statistical analyses of market power. *Review of Economics and Statistics* 57:133–40.

Collins, Norman, and Lee Preston. 1968. *Concentration and price-cost margins.* Berkeley: University of California Press.

———. 1969. Price-cost margins and industry structure. *Review of Economics and Statistics* 51:271–86.

DeRosa, Dean A., and Morris Goldstein. 1981. Import discipline in the U.S. manufacturing sector. *International Monetary Fund Staff Papers* 28:600–634.

Esposito, Louis, and Frances Ferguson Esposito. 1971. Foreign competition and domestic industry profitability. *Review of Economics and Statistics* 53:343–53.

Fisher, Franklin M., and John J. McGowan. 1982. On the misuse of accounting rates of return to infer monopoly profits. Mimeo.

Glismann, Hans-Hinrich, Dean Spinanger, Joseph Pelzman, and Martin Wolf. 1983. *Trade, protection and employment in textiles.* London: Trade Policy Research Centre.

Jacquemin, A., E. deGhelling, and C. Huveneer. 1980. Concentration and profitability in a small open economy. *Journal of Industrial Economics* 39:131–44.

Keesing, Donald B., and Martin Wolf. 1980. *Textile quotas against developing countries.* London: Trade Policy Research Centre.

Khalilzadeh-Shirazi, Javad. 1974. Market structure and price-cost margins in United Kingdom manufacturing industries. *Review of Economics and Statistics* 54:258–66.

Kmenta, J. 1971. *Elements of econometrics.* New York: Macmillan.

Kwoka, John E., Jr. 1977. Large firm dominance and price-cost margins in manufacturing industries. *Southern Economic Journal* 44:183–89.

Maloney, Michael T., and Robert E. McCormick. 1982. A positive theory of environmental quality regulation. *Journal of Law and Economics* 25:99–123.

Mann, H. Michael. 1970. Asymmetry, barriers to entry, and rates of return in 26 concentrated industries, 1948–57. *Western Economic Journal* 8:86–89.

Marvel, Howard P. 1980. Foreign trade and domestic competition. *Economic Inquiry* 18:103–22.

Miller, Richard. 1967. Marginal concentration ratios and industry profit rates. *Southern Economic Journal* 34:259–68.

Organization for Economic Cooperation and Development. Directorate for Science, Technology, and Industry. 1981. *Structural problems and policies relating to the OECD textile and clothing industries.* Paris: OECD.

Pagoulatos, Emilio, and Robert Sorensen. 1976. International trade, international investment and industrial profitability of U.S. manufacturing. *Southern Economic Journal* 42:425–34.

Pelzman, Joseph. 1980. *The competitiveness of the U.S. textile industry.* Columbia: University of South Carolina, College of Business Administration.

———. 1982. The textile industry. In *The internationalization of the American economy*, ed. J. Michael Finger and Thomas D. Willett. The Annals of the American Academy of Political and Social Science, 460:92–100.

Pugel, Thomas A. 1980. Foreign trade and U.S. market performance. *Journal of Industrial Economics* 29:119–29.

Rhoades, Stephen, and Joe Cleaver. 1973. The nature of the concentration price/cost margin relationship for 352 manufacturing industries: 1967. *Southern Economic Journal* 39:90–102.

Scherer, F. M. 1980. *Industrial market structure and economic performance.* Boston: Houghton Mifflin.

Stigler, George. 1964. A theory of oligopoly. *Journal of Political Economy* 72:44–61.

Turner, Phillip P. 1980. Import competition and the profitability of United Kingdom manufacturing industry. *Journal of Industrial Economics* 39:155–66.

U.S. Department of Commerce. Bureau of the Census. 1978–79. *Annual survey of manufactures, industry profiles.* Series M76 (AS)-7. Washington, D.C.: GPO.

———. 1963, 1967, 1972, 1977. *Census of manufactures.* Washington, D.C.: GPO.

U.S. Department of Commerce. International Trade Administration. 1979. Administration Textile Program. News release, February 15.

U.S. International Trade Commission. 1978. *The history and current status of the Multifiber Arrangement.* Washington, D.C.: GPO.

Weiss, Leonard. 1974. The concentration-profits relationship and antitrust. In *Industrial concentration: The new learning*, ed. Harvey Goldschmid, H. Michael Mann, and J. Fred Weston. Boston: Little, Brown.

White, Lawrence J. 1974. Industrial organization and international trade: Some theoretical considerations. *American Economic Review* 64:1013–20.

Comment   David G. Tarr

The Pelzman paper is divided into descriptive and model sections. I found the descriptive section of the paper informative and useful. For example, his description of the industry noted that the minimum efficient size of textile firms has increased such that a restructuring of the industry has occurred. Textiles and apparel are now very different in that we now export textiles, and textiles are regarded as an internationally competitive industry. One question I have is, since much of U.S. exports are to Europe, would our net export position change significantly if Europe did not have restraints on imports from the developing countries?

The problems I have with the Pelzman paper are that the paper does not provide estimates of the variables its title leads one to expect and that

David G. Tarr is with the Federal Trade Commission, Washington, D.C.

The views expressed are those of the author and do not necessarily reflect those of the Federal Trade Commission or any individual commissioner.

no model of the industry is developed. In fact the paper is a test on the textile industry of the structure-conduct-performance paradigm of industrial organization. In this context the paper is a reasonable effort, but problems remain.

What estimates did I expect this paper to provide? I expected among other things to find estimates of the changes in output, employment, and profit in the textile industry induced by the MFA. I hoped that estimates of costs to consumers and deadweight losses to the economy would be provided. To my surprise, no such estimates were either provided or attempted. The reason no such estimates were provided or attempted is that no industry model is developed, in any real sense, from which these estimates may be derived.

Let me be more specific. If you were interested in determining the effects of the MFA on output, employment, profit, and price in the textile industry, how would you proceed? I would start with specification of a supply equation and a demand equation for the industry. One would hypothesize how the MFA affects the demand equation and enter it accordingly. (I call this an "industry" model.) Solving for the reduced form and estimating would yield estimates of the relevant parameters, including the coefficient for the effect of the quota. With the parameters estimated (and successfully tested), one could estimate (or simulate) the effects of the quota by recalculating the new equilibrium with different quota values plugged in. The changes in output, employment, profit, and prices attributable to the MFA could be calculated. Admittedly, this is not an easy process. It is also not the only way to proceed; but I had hoped to see something along these lines.

Pelzman states early on that resource constraints precluded the development of such a model in his paper. Instead he attempts to estimate the effect of a number of variables, including the MFA, on price-cost margins in the textile and apparel industries. In taking this approach, he precludes himself from answering what I believe to be the most important questions regarding the effects of the MFA.

Instead of a true industry model, Pelzman tests the structure-conduct-performance (SCP) paradigm of industrial organization on the textile industry. Price-cost margins are regressed on about ten variables traditionally employed in SCP tests. How the parameter estimates relate to any underlying structure is unknown, because no structural equations are specified. (That is, no SCP structural model, as opposed to an industry model as mentioned above, is developed.) Indeed why some variables enter the model at all or enter with the hypothesized sign is a point of confusion. This problem manifests itself very strongly when the parameters are estimated.

More fundamentally, there appears to be confusion regarding the purpose of the paper. If one is interested in testing the SCP paradigm of industrial organization (with international variables), then why restrict oneself to the textile industry? Presumably the purpose of such an exercise is to make conclusions about whether concentration, or imports, or barriers to entry affect price-cost margins or profits. Restricting oneself to the textile industry severely limits the size of the sample and the range of the variables, such as the four-firm concentration ratio.

Before discussing the empirical results, I should add that Intrilligator and Weston (1975) have shown that it is possible to specify and estimate a simultaneous-equations model of the SCP paradigm of industrial organization. Without going into details, their results show that there are a number of important differences between single-equation and multiequation estimation techniques in this field, which suggest that the failure of single-equation methods to account for simultaneity bias casts serious doubt on single-equation studies of the SCP paradigm. Pugel (1978) has also done a simultaneous-equations model test of the SCP paradigm in which he explicitly incorporated international trade variables. Thus reasonable multiequation SCP models, starting with a structural specification and including most of the important variables modeled by Pelzman, exist in the literature, suggesting that a fuller model in this instance is not an impossible task.

Regarding the empirical results, I shall interpret them in the context of a test of the SCP paradigm on the textile industry rather than as evidence of resource allocation shifts due to the MFA. For the reasons I have mentioned, this is the only way the results can be meaningfully interpreted.

The capital output ratio was included as a measure of barriers to entry and was hypothesized to have a positive coefficient. The estimated coefficient was found to be insignificant. First, I note that Intrilligator and Weston (1975) have found that the capital intensity variable is especially susceptible to simultaneity bias.

But part of the problem is at the theoretical level. I believe that a high capital output ratio is not very reflective of barriers to entry. Following the recent work of Fisher (1979), a barrier to entry is said to exist if and only if entry would be socially beneficial but is somehow prevented. This is a definition of a barrier to entry in terms of the results one would like to see obtain. A high capital output ratio is reflective of the necessity of making a large investment to enter. Is that a barrier to entry? Assuming firms can borrow at rates that correctly reflect perceptions of risk, firms will enter depending on whether long-run anticipated profits will justify their initial large investments. This is the calculation one would make on behalf of society, so the capital output ratio is not a barrier to entry. Regarding the empirical results, if it is not a barrier to entry, it does not preserve abnormally high profits or prices, so we should not expect to find high price-cost margins dependent in a positive way on capital intensity.

Pelzman finds that the four-firm concentration ratio either had the wrong sign or was not statistically significant. He argues, with reason, that given the low levels of concentration among the industries sampled, this is an unsurprising result.

Regarding the foreign non-MFA variables, perverse results were obtained. An increase in imports was found to be either insignificant or to increase price-cost margins. Similarly the variable measuring, interactively, the influence of imports and concentration achieved mixed and nonsupporting results regarding its influence on price-cost margins. Although Pelzman follows Pugel (1978) by including an interactive relationship between import share and concentration (i.e., a competitive or unconcentrated industry would already have low price-cost margins that would not be significantly lowered by a higher share of imports), Pelzman uses the change in the share of imports rather than the import share directly. Since a country could have a large change in imports starting from a small base and have little effect on the price-cost margins, it is the latter measure which would seem to have the most relevance. Moreover, if one believes that imports must only enter interactively, then why include a separate variable for noninteractive imports? This is a manifestation of the more general problem mentioned above: One would like to know what structural model the author has in mind that leads to this form of the estimating equation. A properly specified model would almost certainly yield a different estimating equation and might find, as did Pugel (1978) and Marvel (1980), that imports restrain price-cost margins in concentrated industries.

Pelzman finds that the MFA restrictions result in higher price-cost margins. This is the most important result of the paper, but, lacking an industry model, we do not know the effect on output, employment, and profits.

In conclusion, I found the descriptive sections useful, but I believe it is necessary to specify and estimate a model of the *industry* if one wishes to obtain estimates of the effects of the MFA on resource allocation in the textile and apparel industries. As a test of the structure-conduct-performance paradigm of industrial organization, it is a useful addition to the literature; but the lack of a structural SCP model here as well leads to problems that cause the paper to fall short of being a very significant contribution in this limited area.

References

Fisher, Franklin. 1979. Diagnosing monopoly. *Quarterly Review of Economics and Business* 19:7–33.
Fisher, Franklin, and John McGowan. 1982. On the misuse of accounting rates of return to infer monopoly profits. Mimeo.

Intrilligator, Michael, and J. Fred Weston. 1975. An econometric approach to industrial organization. Paper read at the Third World Congress of the Econometric Society, August, Toronto. Mimeo.

Marvel, Howard. 1980. Foreign trade and domestic competition. *Economic Inquiry* 18:103–22.

Pugel, Thomas. 1978. *International market linkages and U.S. manufacturing: Prices, profits and patterns*. Cambridge, Mass.: Ballinger.

Comment   Martin Wolf

These remarks will cover three areas: first, the paper itself; second, issues that could have been discussed in the paper but were not; and, finally, the wider implications of the Multifiber Arrangement (MFA).

Analysis of the Paper

Professor Pelzman's paper is divided into three principal sections: a discussion of the MFA; a review of the evolution of the textile and clothing industries; and an econometric analysis of the impact of import restrictions and other factors on the profitability of the various branches of the textile and clothing industries. The paper hypothesizes that "by limiting competition the MFA would positively affect the performance of the U.S. textile and apparel industries." It concludes that "the results suggest that in fact that was the case." The discussion below concentrates on the econometric analysis, but begins with the historical sections.

History of the MFA

The paper provides a good account of the evolution of the MFA and brings out two important points: first, the primary role that the United States has played in its creation and development; second, the central place of bilaterally agreed export quotas. The latter feature ensures that exporters have some leverage in bargaining as well as the opportunity to extract the scarcity rent created by the quotas.

Only one point needs qualification. In general, as Professor Pelzman notes, imports of apparel from developing countries have grown much more rapidly than those of textiles. The main reason for this is the stronger comparative advantage of developing countries in the former than in the latter (Keesing and Wolf 1980, chap. 2). Thus, textile imports grew more slowly than those of apparel not so much because the trade management system is "quite successful" in this area, as the paper

Martin Wolf is director of studies at the Trade Policy Research Centre, London.

suggests, but because of a lack of developing country competitiveness in most textile products. It would probably be more accurate to conclude that the system curbed but—at least until recently—did not prevent the consequences of developing countries' comparative advantage in clothing, while it was largely redundant in the case of textiles, at least after the mid-1960s.

Restructuring of the Textile Industry

Professor Pelzman's discussion brings out the rapid technical change in the textile industry but the much slower change in the clothing industry. This itself suggests that protection had a modest effect on technical change, since it was in the relatively less protected textile sectors rather than the generally more protected—because more vulnerable—clothing sectors that the increases in capital intensity were greatest.

Impact of the MFA

The empirical technique employed in an investigation of the effects of a number of independent variables, including import restraints, on the profitability of segments of the textile and apparel industries. A number of methodological issues arise, but the remarks made below are concerned almost exclusively with the specification of the model:

(a) The price-cost margin (PCM) is not a logical measure of profitability. It is rather the rate of return on capital across sectors that might be distorted from a hypothesized equality by the factors enumerated in the paper. The PCM variable should, therefore, have been divided by the capital output ratio (KO).

(b) Value added per worker (VAP) presumably captures comparative advantage. As such it is important, but in the present equation its high significance may be because profits are included in both the dependent and this independent variable. Furthermore, there is presumably collinearity between this variable and the capital output ratio. Wages per worker might have been a better variable to use as a proxy for human capital intensity when the physical capital output ratio is also included as an independent variable.

(c) Concentration may lead to higher wages rather than higher profits, which could be one reason why the concentration variable (CR4) performs poorly. More seriously, the relevant factor is, of course, potential competition. If barriers to entry are fairly low throughout the industries, measured concentration ratios may be of little economic significance.

(d) The import penetration ratios do not work well as explanatory variables. While the two-stage estimation technique used is a sensible way of dealing with the simultaneous relation between import penetration ratios and profitability, the equation for import penetration ratios in terms of the exogenous variables is puzzling. Particularly striking in the context of this paper is the fact that the MFA variable is used independently of the import penetration variables in equation (1) and is not included in equation (2), although one would expect the effect of these restrictions to be via their impact on import penetration ratios. However, an additional simultaneity problem is involved in the use of the MFA variable, since low profits are likely to lead to the imposition of restrictions, which then raise profits ceteris paribus. A further equation explaining the imposition of MFA restraints in terms of the exogenous variables is needed.

(e) Finally, it is difficult to argue that the appropriate break between the two periods for the United States is after 1973. The United States had effective restraints on major suppliers in all three fibers by 1971.

In sum, while the analysis comes up with the desired result that MFA restraints raised profitability, there is sufficient doubt about the specification to throw similar doubt on the conclusion.

Issues That Need To Be Considered

Because of the limited focus of the paper, a number of important questions remain to be explored:

(a) According to the paper, average annual capital investment in textiles and clothing between 1970 and 1980 was $1.5 billion in the United States. Is a large proportion of this explained by protection?

(b) What was the social rate of return on the resources invested?

(c) What effect did protection have on the factor intensity of the industry and especially on technical change?

(d) Finally, to what extent did technical change and capital-labor substitution nullify the purported employment benefits of the restraints?

These questions need further exploration by analysts interested in the impact of the MFA on the protected industries.

Implications of the MFA

The present MFA is the heir of export restraints on textiles imposed in the 1950s. This treatment of textiles used to be considered exceptional, but as similar devices have sprouted in other sectors—steel, automobiles, consumer electronics, and footwear, for example—the "exception" has become less exceptional. In fact, the MFA is beginning to look increasingly like a precedent rather than an exception. This raises two questions: First, why did the U.S. government get involved in constructing export cartels against its own citizens? Second, what general lessons can be learned from the evolution of the textile restraint arrangements toward their current convoluted state (Wolf 1982)?

Why Export Restraints?

In trying to understand how the system of export restraints grew up within textiles and then spilled over into other sectors, one learns a great deal about the weak elements in the liberalization of commercial policy after World War II. Three points are relevant:

(a) The goal of successive administrations has been conservative, namely, to preserve the core of the agreements to liberalize trade from the infection of overly powerful lobbies. By creating such special arrangements, it has been hoped that domestic textile interests and subsequently those of other industries would be politically "sterilized."

(b) Another objective of successive administrations has been to preserve executive autonomy in trade policy matters by avoiding a request to Congress for authority to control imports directly, which is thought to have incalculable consequences.

(c) Finally, the device used buys off all existing significant producers in both importing and exporting countries. This, in turn, makes it politically the easiest form of protection to maintain.

In effect, the system is the consequence of taking the path of least political resistance over a long period.

What Are the Lessons?

There are two points, the first is relevant to the longstanding discussion of selectivity in safeguard protection, the second concerns the evolutionary tendencies of sectoral arrangements of this kind.

The MFA was intended to provide a balance of advantage between importers and exporters. It certainly embodied many explicit restraints on the actions of the former. Yet over time these restraints have been steadily whittled away, each derogation acting as a precedent for the next, with the result that the previously almost unthinkable notion of cutbacks in quotas is now completely acceptable. The experience suggests that restraints on the way that selective protection can be implemented decay over time, largely because of the imbalances of power between the importers and the particular exporter against whom action is taken. The crucial step then is the grant of international legitimacy to selective action. Once this had been given in the case of textiles, the proliferation of restraints and the erosion of safeguards against their abuse seem to have acquired an irresistible momentum.

This experience also says something about sectoral systems, especially those involving discrimination. Over time the exclusion of outsiders is increasingly successful, as a dense network of bureaucrats and industry lobbyists construct an independent and extremely complex structure of protection. Within the system there is something for almost everyone, at least when compared with other systems of protection. The exceptions are the governments of importing countries, who are happy to sacrifice the potential tariff revenue to obtain the acquiescence of exporters, and the governments of potentially successful, restricted exporters with small current quotas, who usually have little weight. In consequence, such systems will not be liberalized from inside and are not allowed to be liberalized from outside. A recent paper which I coauthored asks whether the MFA will last indefinitely (Curzon et al. 1981). The only plausible answer is in the affirmative.

References

Curson, Gerard, José de la Torré, Juergen Donges, Alasdair I. Mac-Bean, Jean Waelbroeck, and Martin Wolf. 1981. *MFA forever? Future of the arrangement for trade in textiles*. International Issues no. 5. London: Trade Policy Research Centre.

Keesing, Donald B., and Martin Wolf. 1980. *Textile quotas against developing countries*. Thames Essay no. 23. London: Trade Policy Research Centre.

Wolf, Martin. 1983. Managed trade in practice: Implications of the textile arrangements. In William R. Cline, ed., *Trade Policy in the 1980s*, pp. 455–82. Washington, D.C.: Institute for International Economics.

III Trade Policies to Facilitate Domestic Adjustment, Promote Developing Country Exports, and Meet Strategic Concerns

Introduction

The three papers in Part III focus on the use of trade policies to assist workers in adjusting to increased import competition and to promote certain foreign policy goals of the United States. The first appraises U.S. efforts to deal with the worker adjustment problems associated with injurious import increases by granting financial and retraining assistance rather than greater import protection to those in injured industries. The second analyzes the U.S. Generalized System of Preferences (GSP) under which exporters from developing countries are favored in tariff terms over those from other developed nations. The last paper in this section considers the desirability of the U.S. government holding "strategic reserves" of oil.

As Aho and Bayard point out, there are efficiency, equity, and political grounds for the government's involvement in the Trade Adjustment Assistance (TAA) program. Efficient adjustment under free market conditions may be impeded by the existence of market imperfections; losers from economic change in the highly uncertain foreign sector deserve to be compensated for their income losses, especially when the government's action in lowering protection is the reason for the losses; and socially beneficial trade liberalization will be blocked politically by those who lose from this liberalization unless they are compensated for their losses.

Drawing upon several empirical studies of the TAA program, they point out that the scheme has not encouraged very much labor market adjustment and has actually led to longer durations of unemployment. Furthermore, while permanently displaced TAA recipients suffered significantly higher wage losses than other permanently displaced workers, this group tended to be a fairly small subgroup of all TAA recipients. Most TAA recipients in the late 1970s returned to their old positions in industries paying wages above the national average. Nevertheless, Aho and Bayard conclude that on balance the TAA program has probably been economically beneficial because of the national welfare gains resulting from the liberalization that otherwise might never have materialized because of political opposition from those compensated by the program.

Instead of dealing with the usual problem of trying to determine how successful an import policy has been in restricting trade, Sapir and Lundberg measure the import-increasing effects of a particular trade policy. Specifically, they estimate the trade and employment effect of the U.S. GSP scheme introduced in 1976. Their methodology is to include the actual margin of tariff preferences granted different products and countries as one determinant (among such others as physical capital/labor ratios and measures of human capital) of post-GSP changes in U.S. import shares by product and country groups. They find that the program has increased trade flows for products that have enjoyed large preference margins and has also raised imports from beneficiaries that were already important suppliers before 1976. More specifically, they estimate that by 1979 exports from developing country beneficiaries had increased by 15 percent or $930 million. About 30 percent of this amount represented trade that was diverted from nonbeneficiary exporters to the United States. The U.S. loss in employment from the net export increase is placed at 43,000 jobs.

Given the uncertain energy outlook, the subject studied by Eaton and Eckstein, namely, the desirability of U.S. government oil inventories, is an important issue for U.S. import policy strategy. They first review the history of the government's petroleum reserve and then develop an analytical model for appraising the effects of such a policy. Basically, they conclude from their analysis that the case for government inventories is a limited one. For example, in the absence of externalities, they find no argument for public inventories in competitive markets under either certainty or uncertainty. If oil suppliers are competitive but U.S. imports are large enough to affect price, there is an appropriate optimum tariff but still no welfare-improvement role for inventories. Even in a strategic setting where suppliers and users both possess market power, imposing optimum tariffs is the first-best means for the consuming country to exploit its market power. However, since a threat to impose tariffs may not be credible, adopting a stockpiling policy is a second-best alternative to optimal tariff policy. They note that maintaining a government inventory of oil can also be justified as a means of reducing U.S. vulnerability to the threat of an embargo.

5 Costs and Benefits of Trade Adjustment Assistance

C. Michael Aho and Thomas O. Bayard

5.1 Introduction

The notion of an adjustment assistance program for American workers displaced by import competition dates back to 1945. A proposal for a Trade Adjustment Assistance (TAA) program was first placed on the national agenda in 1954 by David McDonald, head of the steelworkers' union, as a member of the Randall Commission. As part of the package to ensure labor support for the Kennedy Round of the Multilateral Trade Negotiations, the Trade Expansion Act of 1962 established TAA for workers whose layoff could be attributed to a tariff reduction in the industry. The program provided compensation and adjustment services to trade-displaced workers. In 1974 TAA was liberalized to cover all cases where imports "contributed importantly" to worker displacement. This liberalization was an important factor in securing passage of the Trade Act of 1974 which gave the president authority to enter into the Tokyo Round of Multilateral Trade Negotiations.

In the early 1970s TAA was described by advocates of free trade, especially members of the business and academic communities, as "an integral part of U.S. trade policy." But by 1980–81 the TAA program came under intense criticism for being expensive, inefficient, and inequitable.[1] In response to these criticisms, the administration made important legislative changes in the program during the budget reconciliation process in 1981. Recently, amid growing concern that protec-

C. Michael Aho is on the staff of Senator Bill Bradley and Thomas O. Bayard is a program officer at the Ford Foundation.

The authors wish to thank Robert Baldwin, Herbert Blackman, Harry Gilman, Arlene Holen, J. D. Richardson, Brian Turner, and Martin Wolf for comments and helpful discussions. The views expressed are the authors'.

tionist sentiment is rising and that trade policy will become a partisan issue, there has been renewed support for some form of trade adjustment assistance, although not necessarily for the current program (Bergsten and Cline 1982). The TAA program is due to expire in 1983, and Congress will hold hearings and may mandate further revisions then as a condition for maintaining some form of trade adjustment assistance.

In light of the debate surrounding TAA, this paper reexamines the basic and frequently conflicting rationales for a categorical assistance program for trade-displaced workers. It attempts to quantify wherever possible both the costs and benefits of TAA and discusses possible modifications to the current program.

Section 5.2 discusses the equity, efficiency, and political rationales for government involvement in the adjustment process and compares the merits of general and categorical dislocation programs for trade-displaced workers. The section also assesses the goals of adjustment policy—to provide compensation, to facilitate expanded trade, and to promote market adjustment—and the likely trade-offs among these goals. The entire discussion focuses only on the process of worker adjustment to economic dislocation. While firm and community adjustment are important aspects of the problem of economic dislocation, to consider them here would take us too far afield.

Section 5.3 attempts to estimate the costs and benefits of TAA as it was amended in the Trade Act of 1974. As is the case with many social programs with multiple and frequently ill-defined objectives, it is easier to conceptually define the costs and benefits than it is to quantify them. Nonetheless, the section provides up-to-date empirical information which may be useful to policymakers in their evaluation of the program.

The final section summarizes our findings and raises questions which should be addressed in a comprehensive review of the program.

5.2   Rationales for Government Intervention in the Adjustment Process

There are three broad and frequently interrelated reasons for the government to intervene in the process of adjustment to economic change: equity, efficiency, and political efficacy.

5.2.1   Equity

Rarely does an economic change (e.g., a tariff reduction, deregulation, a shift in tastes, a technological innovation, a change in resource endowments, etc.) benefit all members of society. Typically, some individuals gain and others lose in both the long and short run. A change is potentially beneficial to society if the gainers could potentially compensate the losers so that everyone affected is at least no worse off. The decision to actually compensate the losers depends on both equity and political considerations.

In general, the equity basis for compensation is the widely held notion that, when the nation as a whole gains potentially from an economic change, the potential losers should be compensated for at least part of their losses. The magnitude of compensation on equity grounds depends on a socially accepted notion of equity. For some societies, it may depend on the losers' relative position on the income distribution: the relatively poor should have more of their losses compensated than the relatively rich. For other societies, compensation on equity grounds may be strictly proportional to losses.

The equity basis for compensation may speak for the need for a special categorical program like TAA for trade-displaced workers if it can be shown that they differ systematically from other workers who incur adjustment costs from non-trade-related changes. One difference, for example, might be that trade-displaced workers are economically or socially disadvantaged relative to workers who are displaced by technological or other changes. If the government's goal is to improve the income distribution, then a case might be made for a special and more generous form of compensation targeted specifically at workers in import-competing industries.[2]

There is almost no evidence on this point. We do know that workers in import-sensitive industries are generally more economically disadvantaged than workers in manufacturing as a whole (Aho and Orr 1981). There may be some presumption, therefore, that the average trade-displaced worker should have more of his loss compensated than the average manufacturing worker who is displaced for other reasons. However, any displaced worker is likely to be a "marginal" worker and therefore to have different characteristics than the average worker. A priori, it is difficult to argue that a trade-displaced worker is any different than the average, say, technologically displaced worker. The main empirical evidence from a survey done by Mathematica Policy Research (Corson et al. 1979) suggests that the occupational and demographic characteristics of TAA recipients are very similar to those of unemployment insurance (UI) recipients.[3]

A second possible difference between trade-displaced workers and other displaced workers is that, regardless of their current position on the income distribution, workers in import-competing industries tend to have higher adjustment costs and should therefore have more of their losses compensated. This seems to be less an argument for a special categorical program for trade-displaced workers than an argument that any compensation scheme based on equity considerations should provide the same proportional (i.e., to losses) compensation to all workers. The small amount of empirical evidence available suggests that TAA recipients in general do not have higher earnings losses than UI recipients.[4] It could be argued that the true adjustment costs (including nonmonetary costs) are higher for workers in the import-competing sectors. However, it could also be argued that nonmonetary losses are simply proportional to monetary costs. We have no good evidence on the issue of nonmonetary losses.

Another equity argument for a special categorical compensation program for trade-displaced workers is that they have been harmed by a specific historical government policy of promoting expanded trade and are therefore more deserving of compensation than workers who have been displaced for reasons unrelated to government policy. The argument would be stronger if it could be shown that trade-displaced workers have been hurt solely or primarily because of government changes in trade restrictions or because of changes in other trade policies. This was the rationale for the adjustment assistance provisions of the Trade Expansion Act of 1962, which provided compensation for injury incurred as a result of tariff reductions.

The argument has since been extended to suggest that the absence of government intervention to restrict increased imports justifies special compensation for trade-displaced workers. This was an implicit justification for the adjustment assistance provisions of the Trade Act of 1974, which completely severed the connection between tariff reductions and compensation and instead made workers eligible for compensation if it could be shown that imports had "contributed importantly" to worker displacement.

Both of these arguments presuppose the existence of an implicit social contract between the government and workers in import-competing industries implying that the government will compensate them for any losses they incur because of trade changes. But it is very hard to distinguish this from the notion of a more general implicit contract between the government and all workers implying that the government will compensate any worker for losses due to the failure of government to prevent any type of economic change. If the failure of government to prevent a change harmful to some is accepted as a valid criterion for compensation, in principle all workers should be potentially eligible, and there is no equity basis for categorical programs. If specific government action (as opposed to inaction) is accepted as a criterion for compensation, then the equity argument for categorical programs is somewhat stronger.

However, it may simply be the case that voters and policymakers view import-related injury as inherently more "unfair" than losses caused by domestic factors like labor-saving technological change or competition from domestic producers, even if the occupational and demographic characteristics and losses of those affected are identical. Equity considerations might then require a categorical and more generous compensation and assistance program for trade-related injury.

There is one major equity argument against any sort of dislocation program, whether categorical or general. To the extent that displaced workers compete for jobs with new entrants and reentrants (who are frequently women and young people) into the labor force, an effective dislocation program may impose costs on new entrants in the form of longer duration of job search or lower starting wages.

5.2.2 Economic Efficiency

The efficiency argument for government intervention in the adjustment process is that market imperfections or externalities prevent or impede efficient adjustment.

Wage and Price Rigidities

Changes in supply or demand generally cause changes in both output and prices. In markets in which wages and prices are slow to decline in response to long-term shift in supply or demand, more of the required adjustment must come in the form of declines in output and employment. Some of the unemployment resulting from this wage and price rigidity may be involuntary in the sense that workers would be willing to accept work at a lower wage, but are unable to find work at the prevailing (rigid) wage.[5]

The preferred response to wage and price rigidities creating involuntary unemployment might be to attack the problem directly by initiating antitrust action against monopolistic/oligopolistic price-setters. However, this is often infeasible, either politically or because the antitrust mechanism is very slow, so there may be some scope for government intervention to aid workers.

The efficiency argument for government intervention in the case of involuntary unemployment resulting from wage/price rigidities is that the wage inflexibility increases the duration of search and therefore the social cost of unemployment (i.e., output foregone). The government may be able to reduce duration by providing information on alternative employment opportunities as well as retraining and relocation allowances. There is also a strong equity argument for providing income maintenance because the unemployment is involuntary.

Labor Market Congestion

A large-scale permanent layoff may cause some labor market congestion (an externality) if the local labor market is relatively small and workers are relatively immobile. This congestion means that it takes longer for an average displaced worker to find a job than it would in the absence of a mass layoff. One policy response could be to provide job seekers with better information about employment opportunities in other areas or industries and, if need be, to provide training and relocation assistance to speed up the adjustment process.

The literature on labor market congestion also suggests that it may be optimal to slow down the process of adjustment by providing temporary and declining wage subsidies to firms undergoing pressure to adjust their work force when congestion in the "comparable labor market" (defined both in terms of geographic contiguity and comparable skill levels) delays the rate of transfer of workers to other jobs (Lapan 1976, 1978; Cassing and Ochs 1978). Parsons (1980) distinguishes between the congestion effects of an industry's own unemployment rate and the congestion effects of the national unemployment rate. Empirically, he found that the industry unemployment rate seemed positively related to the rate of labor transfer, but that the national unemployment rate was negatively related. Regardless of the type of congestion, an important cause of labor market externality is the slow rate of adjustment of real wages. The optimal dynamic wage subsidy declines as real relative wages in the industry undergoing adjustment decline.

Labor Immobility

Labor immobility per se is not necessarily a market imperfection requiring government intervention on efficiency grounds. If wages were flexible, workers who could not move geographically or across industries because of social or family ties or lack of required skills would have the option of remaining employed at a lower wage. In this case, there is no efficiency rationale for intervention (Magee 1973).

However, if wages are inflexible, immobility may give rise to large-scale and possibly long-term unemployment. The appropriate role of government policy might then be to provide adjustment services such as counseling and training. There may also be an equity and an efficiency rationale for income maintenance because the demographic and occupational characteristics (age, race, sex, marital status, low skills, etc.) giving rise to geographic and occupational immobility also tend to be associated with economically disadvantaged groups, and because immobility causes the duration of job search to increase.

Risk, Uncertainty, and Imperfect Capital Markets

It is frequently argued that investment in human capital is generally more risky than investment in physical capital because owners of human capital do not have access to capital markets allowing them to diversify their assets and otherwise reduce the risk of a decline in demand for their services. It is true, however, that workers may be able to reduce the risk of layoff or income losses through judicious selection of certain skills and by seeking employment in certain industries (Grossman and Shapiro

1981). It is also true that the current tax laws allow workers to depreciate most of the cost of their investment in human capital at the time they make the investment, whereas owners of physical capital must depreciate it over a longer period.[6] Nevertheless, it can be argued that, in the absence of any program to subsidize education and training and in the absence of an unemployment insurance system, workers will tend to underinvest in human capital.

The role of government policy toward capital market imperfections might be to provide loans for training and education (and living expenses while in training). In some cases the government may be able to provide an unemployment insurance scheme more efficiently than either private insurance companies or what would result from bargaining between workers and their employers over unemployment benefits and job security provisions. The argument for government insurance rests on the notion that a very large insurer like the government could pool risk and provide insurance at lower cost. This is not to deny the important role of collective bargaining between management and labor in providing insurance and job security. However, government may be required to supplement this, especially when firms possess monopsony power.

It might also be argued that the government could improve the information available to workers seeking to acquire human capital by providing estimates of the long-term demand for various skills. The Bureau of Labor Statistics and the Employment Service currently provide considerable information of this sort.

None of the preceding discussion about the efficiency rationales for government intervention provides much presumption in favor of a categorical program for trade-displaced workers over a more general program for all dislocated workers. As in the case of the equity arguments for TAA, the efficiency basis for a special program for trade-displaced workers must rest on the fact that they are different from most other workers who lose their jobs. Specifically, it must be shown that the occupational and demographic characteristics of workers in import-competing industries (or the characteristics of import-competing industries) are such that trade-displaced workers require special assistance.

It could be argued that many of the same characteristics of trade-displaced workers that may give rise to an equity basis for special compensation may also give rise to an efficiency rationale for special adjustment services. The same caveat to the discussion of the equity argument applies here: we do not know for certain that the occupational and demographic characteristics of trade-displaced workers are significantly different than those of workers displaced for other reasons. If trade-displaced workers could be shown to have less occupational or geographic mobility or to face more risk or uncertainty of displacement than other displaced workers, then an argument could be made in favor of special adjustment services and unemployment insurance for them. Both Aho and Orr (1981) and Mathematica have shown that the worker populations in import-sensitive industries tend to have slightly higher proportions of women and older workers than the manufacturing average. These are precisely the groups who tend to face sociological or human capital barriers to mobility. However, there is little evidence that TAA recipients on average experience significantly higher earnings losses than UI recipients, so it is difficult to argue for special assistance on either equity or efficiency grounds.

The risk and uncertainty factor has never really been investigated. Shifts in trade are possibly less predictable than shift, for example, in tastes or technology. If so, an argument could be made in favor of special government insurance programs to reduce the adjustment problems of workers in certain traded goods industries if these industries are subsidized abroad or if they are considered important for national security or prestige.

5.2.3   Political Efficacy

The political argument for government intervention is really the best argument for categorical programs to supplement a more general, and less generous, dislocation program. The political argument is that certain interest groups have sufficient political power to block or delay socially beneficial changes unless they are generously compensated and otherwise assisted. The case for a special program like TAA for trade-displaced workers is that the alternative to TAA is increased trade barriers or greater difficulty in reducing existing trade restrictions because of the political power of the potential "losers."

The past and potential political benefits of TAA are substantial. It is generally accepted that the adjustment assistance provisions of both the 1962 and 1974 trade acts were important in obtaining legislative authority for and muting workers' opposition to the Kennedy and Tokyo Rounds of the Multilateral Trade Negotiations (MTN) (Frank 1977). Of course, it is impossible to know whether the MTN would have been approved by Congress in its present form in the absence of TAA. It is also impossible to know how much the current TAA program has reduced the incidence and severity of protectionism.

Nevertheless, it seems likely that the TAA program does serve to reduce protectionism. The amount of political pressure (e.g., campaign contributions and votes) that potential losers are likely to exert on Congress and the executive branch is probably an increasing function of their expected losses. Since studies of the TAA program (Corson et al. 1979; Richardson 1982a; Jacobson 1980) have shown that it provides fairly generous compensation for earnings losses, it is likely that the program has reduced the pressure for trade restrictions by reducing expected losses. Beyond this, the program also serves to provide policy-makers with a more palatable alternative to either increased trade barriers or no response at all to demands by their constituents for assistance. Further, a well-publicized and fairly generous compensation program may reduce public sympathy for protectionist demands. Richardson (1979) cites evidence from political polls suggesting that voters are, in fact, less sympathetic to demands for import protection if there is an alternative way to compensate and assist those injured by import competition. In general, TAA theoretically serves to reduce both the supply and the demand for trade restrictions in the political market for protection.

However, there may be an important exception to the proposition that TAA reduces workers' demands for protection. Ethier (1982) has developed a cyclical model of dumping in which the existence of TAA actually induces foreign dumping and increases domestic employment variability. He suggests that "if the presence of dumping has the political effect of generating protectionist sentiment, the addition of TAA will increase such sentiment—just the opposite of its political intent, and contrary to general belief." This conclusion seems to rest on the assumption that it is the existence per se of dumping that generates demands for protection. Dumping provides a political focal point around which to mobilize workers and the public in support of trade restrictions. If TAA increases the magnitude of dumping and the number of workers affected, it should also stimulate greater protectionist sentiment.

Two factors may tend to offset this. The first is that the level of TAA compensation, while it affects the magnitude of dumping and layoffs, also affects an individual worker's net income loss due to dumping, which is probably also a determinant of the demand for protection. The net effect of TAA on the demand for protection would seem to depend on whether the greater political visibility of dumping, combined with the larger number of workers affected, is offset by the lower, private individual cost of unemployment.

The second possible offsetting factor is the manner in which TAA is financed. In Ethier's model, TAA is not financed by experience-rated taxes on firms (as is UI), but rather out of general revenues. In these circumstances, TAA would tend to encourage layoffs (and dumping). Experience-rated taxes on employers would tend to reduce layoffs and (assuming the tax is not shifted back onto employees) this would reduce workers' (but not employers') support for protectionist policies. In fact, the current TAA program is *not* experience rated, and as we discuss later, there is empirical evidence that TAA encourages temporary layoffs.

Even without the prospect of new multilateral trade negotiations, a strong political case still can be made for continuing a special program for workers in import-sensitive sectors if it is granted that these workers are politically more effective than other workers. There are several characteristics of the import-competing sectors contributing to the political effectiveness of trade-displaced workers. Proponents of trade restrictions have fewer free-rider and organizational problems than opponents both because the benefits of protection are relatively concentrated and the costs are diffuse, and because the industries themselves are more heavily unionized and have higher firm concentration ratios. A large number of states are potentially affected by imports, with a large number of congressional and electoral votes at stake (Bayard and Orr 1982; Baldwin 1982; Wolf 1979). Firms and workers injured by imports may be able to exert more effective political pressure for protection than those harmed by forces identifiable as domestic in origin, such as internal demand shifts or technological changes. This could be the case if voters and policymakers considered foreign competition more unfair than domestic competition, or if there are fewer effective countervailing political pressures when the source of injury is foreign rather than domestic.

The case for a categorical program also rests on the proposition that trade is becoming increasingly important to the United States and that conflicts over trade policy, both among domestic actors and between the United States and its trading partners, are likely to intensify over time (Aho and Bayard 1983).

A number of major sources of potential conflict over trade are on the horizon: the rapid growth of exports of manufactures from the newly industrialized countries; possible negotiations between the developed and developing countries to assure market access and to integrate the developing countries more fully into the trading system; the active industrial policies practiced in many industrial countries to develop specific sectors (particularly high technology industries); and continued conflict with Japan over market access (Blackhurst, Marian, and Tumlir, 1978). In addition, proponents of export promotion should also recognize that one cannot promote exports without also increasing imports, thereby provoking protectionist demands at home.

The medium-term outlook for growth and employment is bleak, and most countries are under significant political pressure to reduce unemployment. The combination of slow growth and painful but necessary adjustments to changes in the structure of comparative advantage is likely to generate protectionist pressures.

The basic political rationale for TAA is to reduce opposition to policies promoting expanded trade and to provide an alternative to protectionism. The demand for programs to promote expanded trade, as well as opposition to these policies, is likely to increase in the future. The political basis for TAA is likely to grow correspondingly stronger over time.

5.2.4 The Goals of an Adjustment Assistance Program

Three major goals of a categorical adjustment assistance program are: to provide compensation, to facilitate expanded trade, and to promote market adjustment. In this section we explore some of the problems involved in determining the appropriate mixture of compensation and adjustment provisions and some of the conflicts and trade-offs between the goals.

Both equity and political considerations may dictate that trade-displaced workers should receive special, and presumably more generous, compensation than workers who are displaced for reasons other than changes in trade. Examined separately, the equity, efficiency, and political criteria may suggest entirely different magnitudes of compensation. The equity rationale for compensation might suggest that the government should calculate the earnings and benefit losses (and, if possible, all the other nonmonetary costs of unemployment) and set the compensation level proportional to these losses. The political basis for compensation does not lend itself to such an easy calculation. If the policy objective is to reduce political pressures that can block or delay socially desirable changes, then the relative political power of the potential losers, rather than their losses per se or their position on the income distribution, determines the magnitude of their compensation. The amount of feasible compensation is clearly somewhere between nothing and the present value of the gains that would accrue to society if the change occurs. Beyond this, it is a political decision to determine whether trade-displaced workers should be compensated for part of, all of, or more than their losses.

In some import-sensitive industries, workers may earn oligopolistic rents or returns from the past structure of protection. On equity grounds, it seems unfair to compensate displaced workers for the loss of these particular rents. However, the same industry characteristics allowing firms and workers to collect these sorts of rents may also be contributing to their political power to influence trade restrictions. On political grounds, therefore, it may be necessary to compensate workers for losses of these returns. The efficiency implications of compensating workers for oligopolistic/oligopsonistic or protectionist rent losses are entirely negative. Compensation could create problems of moral hazard—workers might be induced to enter or to stay in an industry in which the risk of the loss of these rents was reduced by a generous compensation scheme. Compensation of these losses would tend to slow the rate of adjustment to changes in trade and reduce the social gains from adjustment.

The efficiency rationale for compensation is that it allows workers to engage in socially efficient job search. It is generally accepted that if compensation is tied to duration of unemployment, there is an increase in duration which may or may not be socially desirable. On the one hand, increased duration may improve the quality of the match between workers and job opportunities (and hence, increase earnings). On the other hand, compensation reduces the incentives to accept a job quickly and may result in excessive duration. The socially efficient compensation scheme would provide benefits up to the point where the marginal social gain to higher earnings was equal to the marginal social loss due to longer unemployment duration. It is easy to conceive of circumstances in which the socially efficient compensation differs from (i.e., is probably less than) compensation based on equity or political considerations.

There may be several trade-offs between compensation in the form of cash payments and compensation in the form of adjustment services. The workers' losses are caused by the initial spell of unemployment and the subsequent losses in lifetime earnings because of the loss of human capital. But both of these are in part determined by the availability of adjustment services. If government-provided adjustment services are effective in assisting workers to acquire new jobs and skills more rapidly than they would in the absence of the government adjustment services, then the amount of cash compensation required is reduced. To determine the appropriate mix of cash payments and adjustment services, the government needs considerable information about the efficacy and returns to training, relocation, counseling, and other adjustment services for various types of workers.

In all of this, an implicit assumption has been that trade-displaced workers are for the most part likely to be permanently displaced. The results of the Mathematica survey (Corson et al. 1979) suggest that most TAA recipients have been on temporary layoff and have returned to their old industry, and sometimes to their old job with their old firm.[7] Other studies (see table 5.2) found that a higher proportion of displaced workers actually changed jobs or employers. Differences in the incidence of permanent displacement could be the result of a number of factors, including differences in worker eligibility criteria and differences in the stage of the business cycle when layoffs occurred.

In the case of temporary displacements, there is no efficiency basis for either compensation or adjustment services. (Uncertainty over whether displacement is temporary or permanent might provide a basis for some adjustment services and compensation on efficiency grounds.) Both the equity and the political criteria could suggest the need for some compensation for temporary displacements but would not indicate any need for adjustment services.

It could be argued that if firms and workers were fully informed that the industry is periodically subject to temporary trade-related displacements, there would be no equity basis for compensation because the wage-bargaining process would have already compensated workers for the risk of temporary displacement. On the other hand, there may still be a political basis for "compensation" for even temporarily displaced workers in the traded goods sector if these workers could otherwise block the increase in imports. The level of compensation could be fairly small because the intensity of their lobbying effort is likely to be small, given the fact that the wage structure may already reflect the risk of temporary layoff or reduced hours.

The discussion thus far has provided an overview of the rationales for trade adjustment assistance. Given that a TAA program has several potentially conflicting goals—to compensate the "losers" for equity reasons, to buy out those who could impede socially beneficial changes, and to promote efficient labor market adjustment—it is probably not surprising that the current program has attracted so much criticism. Different critics may wish to structure the program to emphasize one specific goal, but any change in program emphasis is likely to evoke criticism for neglecting the other goals. Any attempt to change the current program emphasis must be based on some sort of cost/benefit calculus. In what follows we attempt to make these calculations, although many of the costs and benefits are obviously difficult to quantify.

5.3   Estimating the Costs and Benefits of TAA

5.3.1   Conceptual Overview

As is the case for many social programs with multiple and frequently ill-defined objectives, it is easier to conceptually define the appropriate costs and benefits than it is to quantify them. It is doubtful that the drafters of the TAA legislation in the Trade Act of 1974 were able to make any calculation of the potential costs and benefits of the program. This is not surprising, given the relatively small scope of the 1962 TAA program and the limited empirical research on adjustment assistance available at the time.[8] However, in the last ten years the Labor Department has funded several important studies of both the 1962 and 1974 TAA programs as well as extensive research in the broad area of measuring the costs of worker displacement. In this section we first review the major conceptual problems involved in evaluating the costs and benefits of adjustment assistance, and then we draw on the empirical evidence to assess the TAA program.

Potential Benefits

The political benefits of adjustment assistance are the social gains from liberalized trade, or a reduction in the incidence and severity of protectionism. The potential benefits of freer trade (whether from multilateral trade negotiations, as in the Kennedy and Tokyo Rounds of the MTN; from unilateral reductions in tariff barriers, as in the U.S. generalized system of tariff preferences for developing countries (GSP); or from the avoidance of new trade barriers) are the reduction (or avoidance) of price distortions causing inefficiencies in consumption and in the allocation of resources between the export, import-competing, and nontraded goods sectors of the domestic economy.

As we show later, the annual social (as distinct from private) gains from marginally freer trade are fairly small.[9] It is necessary to emphasize the marginal nature of these calculations because even the most ardent proponents of TAA have never suggested that it can be used to buy once-and-for-all elimination of all trade barriers or to prevent any increase in existing restrictions. However, it is also important to point out that the gains from freer trade are annual ones and that, even when they are heavily discounted, the cumulative social gain can be quite large.

Within the context of the political implications of a TAA program are several other potential benefits, none of which is easily quantified. Goldfarb and Cordes (1979, 1980) have suggested that one potential benefit of any scheme compensating individuals for losses resulting from government action (but not necessarily inaction) is that it fosters the notion that the government is "fair" and unarbitrary in its decision making. The Trade Act of 1962, for example, provided compensation for workers hurt by government action—tariff reductions; the Trade Act of 1974 broadened eligibility for compensation to include injury caused by government inaction—failure to prevent an increase in imports.

An adjustment assistance program, regardless of its domestic equity and efficiency implications, may generate significant foreign policy gains. To the extent that it reduces the use of trade restrictions, TAA promotes expanded trade and a more efficient allocation of resources worldwide. Indeed, the OECD secretariat (1979) has urged the use of "positive adjustment" programs as a substitute for protectionist policies that inhibit the growth of world trade. Maintaining and expanding the liberal world trading system is a major goal of U.S. foreign policy. By demonstrating strong U.S. commitment to adjustment rather than protection, the TAA program may encourage a similar commitment to free trade in other countries.

This demonstration effect may be particularly important for the developing countries. They are acutely aware of the need for adjustment assistance programs in the developed countries as an alternative to protectionism. At the fifth session of the United Nations Conference on Trade and Development (UNCTAD 1979), the Group of 77 argued strongly in favor of adjustment programs. By promoting a reduction in developed country trade barriers, an adjustment assistance program both facilitates a transfer of resources to the developing countries and serves to encourage the developing countries to accept the legitimacy of the principle of free trade.

All of these "political gains" from TAA are based on the assumption that it really buys freer trade by reducing political demands for protection. This is probably unprovable, but we believe that the theoretical arguments presented earlier support the proposition. If TAA is effective in reducing both the demand and the supply of protectionism, there may be additional social gains in the form of reductions in the use of productive resources to lobby for and against trade liberalization and also in the use of resources needed to administer trade restrictions. However, it may be that resources not spent on lobbying or administering trade barriers simply will be diverted to equally unproductive activities elsewhere.

The time dimension is particularly important in any discussion of the potential efficiency gains of adjustment assistance. While the benefits of freer trade occur over an indefinite period of time, the social cost is incurred in the relatively short run. The social cost of trade liberalization is the value of output foregone when resources are involuntarily unemployed during the period of adjustment. The involuntary nature of unemployment is important to emphasize. It is only to the extent that unemployment is the result of market distortions (like wage and price rigidities, labor market congestion, imperfections in the markets for information and capital, etc.) that there is any social gain from government intervention in the adjustment process. Clearly, even if wages and prices were perfectly flexible, there would be some unemployment in the import-competing sector as workers voluntarily become unemployed in order to search for their best alternative employment. This sort of unemployment should not be counted as a social cost because, if search is rational, workers seek alternative employment until the marginal income gains of finding a better job are equal to the marginal income foregone by continuing to search.

The efficiency gain from TAA then is the value of output gained by reducing involuntary unemployment caused by existing market imperfections. Although it seems callous to some, the value of leisure ideally should be subtracted from the output cost of involuntary displacement. In practice (e.g., Bale 1976) the social costs of unemployment, and thus the benefits of reducing it, are usually calculated as the total duration of unemployment times the pretax wage in the next-best employment. These calculations tend to overstate the potential gains from promoting more efficient adjustment by counting all the duration as involuntary and by failing to value leisure.[10]

Richardson (1982b) has suggested that TAA also may facilitate efficient adjustment if it provides workers, firms, and investors in import-competing sectors with an additional "diagnostic signal," both incremental to the usual market indicators and preferable to the perverse signals created by trade distortions. If TAA correctly encourages a leading or anticipatory adjustment to expected changes in firms' competitiveness, it will tend to reduce the duration of unemployment and perhaps also the possibility of labor market congestion which can happen when all of the adjustments occur in a fairly short period. For TAA to play a positive role in promoting adjustment, it must be interpreted as an accurate harbinger of longer-run secular changes. If it is used or viewed as income maintenance to help workers endure relatively short-run or cyclical fluctuations, it is unlikely to serve a useful adjustment function.

The equity gains from TAA are the most difficult to quantify because they rest on a socially accepted definition of equity. Although it may be possible to infer a social welfare function from the government's treatment of various income and social groups and then to compare the actual treatment of TA recipients by income and social class with "predicted treatment," we do not attempt this. Rather, in what follows we simply present data on TAA recipients' characteristics and adjustment experiences and allow readers to draw their own conclusions about the equity of the program.

Potential Costs

Most of the costs of an adjustment assistance program fall under the heading of efficiency losses caused by distorting market incentives to adjust to freer trade. The potential problem with any program attempting to compensate displaced workers is that it will simultaneously serve as a disincentive to adjustment.

Attempting to compensate workers by tying compensation to the duration of unemployment may lead to an increase in unproductive search by lowering the cost of searching. We show below that many of the recent TAA recipients were on temporary layoff. The high benefit levels and extended potential duration of benefits (52–78 weeks for TAA vs. 26–39 weeks for UI recipients) may encourage workers to simply await recall rather than engage in any search. In cases where workers correctly anticipate that layoffs are temporary, it may not be privately or socially productive to engage in job search. However, in cases where layoffs are actually permanent or very long-term and expectations of temporary and short-term displacement are incorrect, high TAA payments and extended availability may impede adjustment.

In contrast to UI payments, which are financed by taxing firms based on their layoff behavior, TAA payments are not experience rated. This leads to several possible implications for firm behavior. On the one hand, TAA may serve as a subsidy if firms and workers incorporate expected TAA payments into their wage bargains. If workers negotiate a wage package including payments in the event of layoff and the existence of TAA allows firms to substitute TAA for firm-financed unemployment benefits or to lower wages, the firm's labor costs are lower by the amount of expected TAA. This in turn allows import-competing firms to produce a higher level of output or earn higher profits and encourages both capital and labor to remain in import-competing firms when they should be transferred to other sectors where the social value of output is higher.

On the other hand, it is possible that TAA benefits are not reflected in either lower wages or benefits. Even if workers captured all of the benefits of TAA and firms were not able to lower wages or benefits directly as a result of TAA, it could still serve to reduce total labor costs and hence raise profits. To the extent that firms hoard labor through the business cycle or in response to short-run shocks, TAA facilitates worker attachment to firms by reducing incentives to look for a new job and therefore reduces the optimal amount of labor hoarding and the firm's labor cost and encourages temporary layoffs. For our purposes, what matters is that, because it is a subsidy, TAA may reduce firms' and workers' incentives to adjust to a long-run change in comparative advantage if it simply allows firms that are otherwise uncompetitive to stay alive longer, or if it simply encourages workers to linger longer waiting for recall.[11]

Although TAA payments are transfers from taxpayers to workers and therefore are not social costs per se, the program's administrative costs and the efficiency costs of using the tax system to raise revenue to fund TAA payments are legitimate social costs.[12] In the next section, we report TAA's administrative costs, but no attempt is made to quantify the disincentive costs of raising funds to finance TAA.

5.3.2   Quantifying Costs and Benefits

To facilitate an evaluation of the TAA program, tables 5.1 and 5.2 present data from the major studies on the occupational and demographic characteristics and adjustment experiences of TAA recipients. The data summarize the results of these studies, but the reader is cautioned not to make explicit comparisons between various studies. In many cases the data are noncomparable because they pertain either to the 1962 or 1974 TAA programs and therefore were based on very different worker eligibility criteria. One major result emerging from these studies is that the adjustment process differs quite dramatically both across industries and occupational and demographic groups and across the stages of the business cycle. One of the major problems, therefore, in designing TAA studies is the selection of appropriate control groups. It is possible to make explicit comparisons between, say, UI and TAA recipients in the Mathematica (Corson et al. 1979) or Neumann and Glyde (1978) studies because attempts were made to select appropriate controls, but it is not appropriate to explicitly compare, say, McCarthy's (1974) results with Neumann and Glyde's since they involve very different populations, drawn at different times, and affected by different phases of the business cycle.

Table 5.1 shows the occupational and demographic characteristics of TAA recipients under both the 1962 act (Bale 1973; McCarthy 1974; and Neumann and Glyde 1978) and the 1974 act (Corson et al. 1979) and also of workers in industries that have lost job opportunities because of imports between 1965 and 1975 (Aho and Orr 1981). Table 5.2 presents data on the adjustment experiences of trade-displaced workers under the two programs.

As discussed briefly in section 5.1, the studies offer very little support for the notion that, in general, trade-displaced workers are very different from other displaced workers. What can be said is that they consistently appear to be somewhat older, have longer firm tenure, and are more heavily unionized. Based on these characteristics, human capital theory would predict somewhat higher earnings losses for trade-displaced workers than for others. However, the fact the TAA recipients also appear to be somewhat less educated and less skilled than other workers would tend to imply lower losses.

The evidence in table 5.2 suggests that permanently displaced TAA recipients may have more adjustment problems than other permanently displaced workers. Neumann and Glyde's sample of TAA recipients under the 1962 act was almost all permanent displacements. They found that they tended to have significantly longer initial unemployment duration and larger initial wage losses than the UI control group. Similar results emerge from the Mathematica survey of TAA recipients under the 1974 act. TAA recipients who changed jobs had an initial spell of almost 42 weeks, compared to 33 weeks for UI recipients. Permanently displaced TAA beneficiaries also tended to have larger initial wage losses than the UI job changers. Overall, Mathematica estimated that the earnings losses for TAA job changers were somewhat higher than for the UI control group, although the difference was not very significant.[13]

However, only a small fraction of TAA recipients (28 percent) in the Mathematica sample actually changed jobs (vs. 42 percent of UI). Moreover, Mathematica found that most TAA recipients expected their layoff to be temporary (81 percent of TAA vs. 73 percent of UI). This may help to account for the relatively small fraction of TAA recipients who received training or counseling. Overall, comparing the entire TAA sample to the UI sample, TAA recipients did not have significantly higher earnings losses than UI recipients.

These results stimulated the press and policymakers to question the overall equity of the TAA program. While the results do tend to support the notion that permanently trade-displaced workers have somewhat greater adjustment costs than job changers in the UI control group, the permanently displaced tend to be a fairly small subset of TAA recipients, at least for the sample period (prior to 1979). (Since 1979 a large number of auto workers have received TAA and a significant fraction of them may be permanently displaced.) Even this generalization is too broad. As table 5.3 shows, the earnings loss estimates in the Mathematica survey vary greatly across industries. For example, permanently displaced auto workers lost $8,000–12,000, while permanently displaced apparel workers lost roughly $6,000. At the same time, temporary displacements in some industries tended to be "overcompensated" for their earnings losses.

Overall the results of the Mathematica survey suggest that TAA recipients, whether permanently or temporarily displaced, tend to have a higher proportion of their losses compensated than the appropriate UI control group. The TAA population does not appear to be very different from the control group in terms of either occupational and demographic characteristics or adjustment costs. It is correspondingly difficult to justify a categorical program for trade-displaced workers solely on equity grounds.

Although it is very difficult to quantify the efficiency implications of the TAA program, the results of the Mathematica survey do not support the notion that TAA has encouraged much labor market adjustment. As table 5.2 shows, only a small fraction of TAA recipients actually changed jobs. Most workers returned to their old employer and frequently to their former job. By the time they were interviewed, Mathematica found that 16 percent of TAA recipients had left their industry and 25 percent had changed occupations (vs. 31 percent and 39 percent of the UI control group). Correspondingly, very few TAA recipients utilized the adjustment provisions of the program. Only 6 percent of TAA recipients received training versus 12 percent of the UI group.[14]

There is evidence from both the Neumann and Glyde and the Mathematica surveys that the higher wage replacement ratio for TAA recipients has lead to longer duration of unemployment. Neumann and Glyde found that a ten percentage point increase in the gross (pretax) wage replacement ratio induced a 3–3.5 week increase in unemployment duration. This estimate is very large relative to studies of UI recipients, where the normal range of estimates is between .5 and 1.0 weeks per ten-point increase in the replacement ratio. Mathematica's estimate of the impact of a ten-point increase in the net (posttax) wage replacement ratio was roughly 1.8 weeks for TAA recipients.

Thus far no one has been able to explain satisfactorily the high estimates of the impact of changes in wage replacement ratios for TAA recipients relative to UI recipients. One possible explanation is that, since the TAA component of the wage replacement ratio is not experience rated, firms may use TAA to finance temporary layoffs. As discussed earlier, TAA may encourage temporary layoffs by reducing the

Table 5.1   Occupational and Demographic Characteristics of Trade-Sensitive Workers

| | 1962 TAA Program | | | | 1974 TAA Program | | | |
| | Bale[a] | McCarthy[b] | Neumann/Glyde[c] | | Mathematica[d] | | Aho/Orr[e] | |
Characteristics	TAA Recipients	TAA Recipients	TAA Recipients	UI Recipients	TAA Recipients	UI Recipients	Import-Sensitive	Manufacturing Average
Sample size	424	191	309	115	590	276	NA	NA
Sample year	1972	1973	1975	1975	1978–79	1978–79	1970	1970
Age (years)								
mean	44	53.7	46.0	38.4	39.9	35.9	NA	NA
median	NA	55.0	NA	NA	38.0	31.0	NA	NA
under 25	NA	2.5	NA	NA	13.3	27.9	15.8	16.4
over 55	NA	54.5	NA	NA	15.5	13.1	28.0	26.5
Race (%)								
white	91	99	86.9	78.2	82.9	80.4	88.5	89.9
nonwhite	9	1	13.1	21.8	17.1	19.7	11.5	10.1
Education								
12th grade or higher (%)	32.8	21.5	NA	NA	NA	NA	37.1	41.7
mean (years)	8–9	9.0	10.3	12.6	10.4	11.4	NA	NA

Married (%)	NA	NA	84.8	67.8	79	68.1	NA	NA
Sex (%)								
male	51	71	57.6	64.3	61.5	64.5	48.9	70.6
female	49	29	42.4	35.7	38.5	35.5	41.1	29.4
Union (%)	NA	NA	78.5	43.5	81.3	65.8	51.3	49.0
Job tenure mean (years)	10.6	13	17.7	5.6	11.8	7.8	NA	NA
Households with income below the poverty level (%)	NA	NA	NA	NA	1.9	3.7	9.8	7.0
Skilled workers (%)	NA	15.1	20.6	35.6	26.7	38.4	38.8	50.0

SOURCES:
[a]Malcolm Bale, "Adjustment to Freer Trade: An Analysis of the Adjustment Assistance Provisions of the Trade Act of 1962," report prepared under contract from the U.S. Department of Labor, 1973.

[b]James McCarthy, "Trade Adjustment Assistance: A Case Study of the Shoe Industry in Massachusetts," report prepared under contract from the U.S. Department of Labor, 1974.

[c]George Neumann and Gerald Glyde, "The Labor Market Consequences of Trade Displacement: Evidence from the Trade Adjustment Assistance Program of 1962," report prepared under contract from the U.S. Department of Labor, 1978.

[d]Walter Corson, et al., "Final Report: Survey of Trade Adjustment Assistance Recipients," report prepared by Mathematica Policy Research, Inc., under contract from the Office of Foreign Economic Research, U.S. Department of Labor, 1979.

[e]C. M. Aho and J. Orr, "Trade Sensitive Employment: Who Are the Affected Workers?" Monthly Labor Review, (Feb. 1981): 29–35.

Table 5.2   Adjustment Experiences of TAA Recipients

| | 1962 TAA Program | | | | 1974 TAA Program — Mathematica | | | | | |
| | Bale | McCarthy | Neumann/Glyde | | TAA | | | UI | | |
	TAA	TAA	TAA	UI	New Job	Old Job	All	New Job	Old Job	All
1. Duration of first spell of unemployment (weeks)	31	18.2	48.7	33.3	41.8	17.4	21.9	32.8	16.3	21.9
2. Workers who changed employers (%)	NA	virtually all	77.9	57.4	—	—	28	—	—	42
3. Average weekly wage before layoff ($)	NA	100.40	140.90	132.80	206	228	223	190	198	195
4. Average weekly wage on first job after layoff ($)	NA	92.64	99.3	109.4	152	249	225	159	219	193
5. Average hourly wage before layoff ($)	3.02	NA	3.40	3.30	NA	NA	NA	NA	NA	NA
6. Average hourly wage on first job after layoff ($)	2.68	NA	2.50	2.86	NA	NA	NA	NA	NA	NA

7. Change in average weekly wage (%)	NA	−7.7	−29.5	−17.6	−26.2	+9.2	+1.0	−16.3	+10.6	−1.0
8. Change in average hourly wage (%)	−11	NA	−26.9	−13.2	NA	NA	NA	NA	NA	NA
9. Average earning loss ($)	3,370– 11,689	NA	NA	NA	(12,200– 12,900)	(1,900– 3,300)	(3,900– 5,200)	(9,800– 11,000)	(1,700– 3,200)	(4,700– 6,100)
10. Total compensation ($)	2,059	2,708	NA	NA	5,400	2,900	3,300	2,600	1,900	2,200
TAA	NA	1,072	NA	NA	2,100	1,100	1,300	—	—	NA
UI	NA	1,636	NA	NA	3,300	1,800	2,000	2,600	1,900	2,200
11. Compensation rate (10/9) (%)	61.1–17.6	NA	NA	NA	(44–42)	152–88	(85–64)	(27–24)	(111–60)	(47–36)
12. Net loss ($) (9–10)	1,300– 9,600	NA	3,300– 26,300	NA	(6,800– 7,500)	(−1,000 to 400)	(600– 900)	(7,200– 8,400)	(−200 to 1,300)	(2,500– 3,900)
13. Ratio of weekly TAA and UI to pre-layoff weekly wage (%)	NA	NA	63.9	51.6	NA	NA	.61	NA	NA	NA
14. Received training (%)	3.8	0	15.2	1.7	7	NA	6.4	NA	NA	12.0
15. Received counseling (%)	31.3	NA	19.1	4.3	39	NA	5.4	NA	NA	12.0

SOURCES: See table 5.1.

Table 5.3   Mean Present Discounted Value of After-Tax Earnings Losses, UI and TAA Benefits, and Net Losses by Industry and Recall Status, TAA Sample (in dollars)

	Automobile			Steel			Other Dutiables			Footwear			Apparel		
	Never Re-called	Ever Re-called	Total	Never Re-called	Ever Re-called	Total	Never Re-called	Ever Re-called	Total	Never Re-called	Ever Re-called	Total	Never Re-called	Ever Re-called	Total
Earnings losses															
Constant real earnings	15,200	2,400	3,600	13,600	2,400	3,100	17,500	0	2,700	10,300	3,700	9,200	10,800	2,100	4,400
Adjusted real earnings[a]	19,100	6,400	7,600	17,600	5,300	6,000	18,500	700	3,400	9,900	3,400	8,800	10,800	2,100	4,400
Benefits															
UI	4,800	2,400	2,600	2,300	2,300	2,300	4,500	1,200	1,700	2,800	2,900	2,800	2,900	800	1,400
TAA	2,400	1,600	1,600	4,100	1,200	1,400	2,400	500	800	1,200	1,000	1,200	2,300	900	1,300
Net loss[b]															
Constant real earnings	8,000	−1,600	−600	7,100	−1,100	−600	10,600	−1,600	200	6,200	−200	5,200	5,600	400	1,800
Adjusted real earnings[a]	12,000	2,400	3,300	11,000	1,700	2,300	11,600	−900	1,000	5,900	−500	4,800	5,600	400	1,800
Sample size	17	160	177	8	132	140	15	84	99	30	6	36	55	149	204

SOURCE: Walter Corson, et al., "First Report: Survey of Trade Adjustment Assistance Recipients," report prepared by Mathematica Policy Research, Inc., under contract from the Office of Foreign Economic Research, U.S. Department of Labor, 1979.

[a]Adjusted by industry for changes in mean weekly earnings and for the effect of increased job experience.

[b]The net loss equals the earnings loss minus UI and TAA benefits. It excludes supplemental unemployment benefits (SUB) received by some workers. These benefits were received by 81 percent of the automobile workers, 65 percent of the steel workers, and 26 percent of workers in others durables. Workers who received SUB received an average of $1,200 and paid back an average of $590 to the SUB funds after receipt of TAA. Workers in the steel industry were not required to return portions of their SUB payments, while most automobile (85 percent) and other durable goods workers (60 percent) did.

firms' need to hoard labor during cyclical and seasonal changes in output because TAA benefits increase worker attachment to the firm. Preliminary results from a study by Utgoff (1982) for the Department of Labor tend to support this hypothesis.

While extended duration in the case of temporary displacement is certainly a social cost, extended duration for permanent layoffs need not be a social loss if it results in higher subsequent earnings or less employment variability. The evidence for TAA recipients is mixed. Neumann and Glyde found a significant positive effect of a higher wage replacement ratio on subsequent wage gains. Mathematica found no statistically significant increase in wages. However, using the Mathematica data, Richardson (1982a) found that the longer duration for TAA recipients may have increased the efficiency of the initial search. His tentative conclusion (based on a relatively small sample of permanently displaced TAA recipients) is that TAA may have reduced the incidence and duration of subsequent spells of unemployment by improving the first match between workers and jobs after receipt of TAA. The evidence from UI research is also mixed. Ehrenberg and Oaxaca (1976) found an earnings gain, while Classen (1977) did not.

Overall, it appears unlikely that the current TAA program has resulted in significant efficiency gains in terms of promoting labor market adjustment to changes in trade. In large part this is because very few TAA beneficiaries were permanently displaced, at least until recently. There is some reason to believe that many of the auto workers currently receiving TAA are on permanent layoff and that they will use more of the adjustment assistance provisions of the program than earlier TAA recipients.

The political rationale for the TAA program is that it is an important element of U.S. commercial policy. In the trade policy context, TAA can be viewed as a "political buy-out"—it both reduces opposition to free trade policies by lowering the adjustment costs of the potential "losers" and provides policymakers with an attractive alternative option, intermediate between protection and no import relief. Admittedly, the evidence to support this proposition is anecdotal: it is very difficult to know what policymakers would have done in the absence of the program. In an earlier paper (Aho and Bayard 1980) we presented some of the evidence for the political gains from TAA, and these are reviewed here.

It is probably not a coincidence that the 1962 and 1974 TAA programs were components of legislation authorizing U.S. participation in the Kennedy and Tokyo Rounds of the MTN. Indeed, in the 1950s and early 1960s labor leaders supported free trade policies and urged adoption of adjustment assistance programs to gain worker support for trade liberalization. By 1970 most labor unions had shifted to a position opposing free trade and in support of legislation like the Burke-Hartke bill which would have rolled back U.S. imports to 1965–69 levels.[15]

Bergsten (1972, 703) has argued that one of the major administration motives for seeking legislative authority for U.S. participation in the Tokyo Round was the desire to preempt legislation like Burke-Hartke. The Trade Act of 1974 provided both the negotiating authority for the Tokyo Round and the provisions of the new TAA program. In large part, the linking of TAA with the trade negotiations may have reflected the recognition that organized labor had the political power to impede, if not thwart, the negotiations. While many labor leaders were skeptical and sometimes hostile to TAA by the 1970s (it was often described as "burial insurance"), by reducing the potential costs of trade liberalization, the expanded TAA program embodied in the 1974 trade act may have served as a "sweetener" (as Robert Strauss, the U.S. Special Trade Representative, used to call concessions to interest groups) to help reduce labor's concerns about the negotiations.

However, the causal linkage of TAA to the MTN does not necessarily imply that it was a quid pro quo for labor's acquiescence to either U.S. participation in the Tokyo Round or the final trade package negotiated.[16] At the time the MTN agreements were presented to Congress for ratification, legislation was also introduced (but never passed) to expand the TAA program. Only at the time did labor insist that TAA was "an important adjunct to the MTN package" and that it represented "a trade-off . . . for government action to further trade liberalization."[17]

It may be that the lack of explicit linkage in 1974 and the introduction of that linkage by 1979 were tactical moves by labor to secure greater influence over both the actual trade negotiations and the scope of the TAA program. Similar considerations may have led Kirkland (1981) to label the subsequent TAA budget cuts as "another broken promise to those who pay the price of trade liberalization."

The strongest evidence that TAA played a role in the MTN is at best circumstantial: the surprising lack of labor opposition to passage of the MTN package. The Trade Agreements Act of 1979 implementing the Tokyo Round agreements was ratified by overwhelming votes of 395 to 7 in the House and 90 to 4 in the Senate. However, the fragility of political support for freer trade, and the linkage between TAA and a liberal trade policy, was noted by Representative Charles Vanik (former chairman of the Subcommittee on Trade) in arguing for an expanded TAA program: "Trade support on the Hill is fragile—there are 100 members of Congress who don't believe in trading with anybody. A majority in opposition to free trade can be achieved if labor is alienated." (*Barrons*, 5 May 1980).

Table 5.4 provides a survey of various estimates of the welfare gains from the MTN. The estimates range from $130 to $900 million annually. These are static estimates. They do not include the potentially large dynamic gains from freer trade. The estimates also pertain only to the effects of the tariff cuts, which were themselves only a small part of the

MTN. Most of the negotiations involved codes of conduct on nontariff measures. If they are fully implemented and enforced, these codes could also result in significant welfare gains. Thus the total welfare gains from the Tokyo Round could be several times the estimates shown in table 5.4, and we would argue that at least some of these gains can be attributed to TAA.

The assumption in all of this is that a liberal adjustment assistance program can be used to gain political support for liberal trade policies and did in fact play an important part in securing congressional support for the Tokyo Round agreements. Moreover, in the absence of a program such as the Tokyo Round negotiations, the United States might have taken two steps backward. Magee's (1972) estimates, adjusted to 1979 dollars, suggest that by 1980 the static welfare loss for the United States of reducing imports to their 1965–69 level, as the Burke-Hartke bill proposed, would have been $6–11 billion annually. Although this probably overstates the case, even trade restrictions in selected industries can have significant consumer and welfare costs when compared with the administrative costs and the benefit levels of the TAA program.

Table 5.5 gives the welfare and consumer cost estimates for four industries where import relief (that is, increased protection) was recommended by the U.S. International Trade Commission or considered by the Carter administration (automobiles). Although the Trade Act of 1974 also includes an escape clause (section 201) for import relief, the existence of TAA provides the president and Congress with an intermediate option between increased import restrictions and no relief. In each of the four cases shown in table 5.5, the president rejected relief and recommended that expedited adjustment assistance be granted instead.

Table 5.5 shows that even in one of the smaller industries, leather wearing apparel, the estimates of the indefinite annual welfare loss of an additional 25 percent tariff ranged from $27 to $60 million, depending on the elasticity assumptions and the degree to which price increases are passed on to the consumer. More significantly for income redistribution, the estimated annual consumer costs were between $61 and $135 million. By comparison, if the entire work force in the leather wearing apparel industry were made redundant and received 70 percent of their former wage (say, 20 percent from TAA for the first 26 weeks and the entire 70 percent for the next 26 weeks) for 52 weeks, benefits paid out under the TAA program would have been only about $21.5 million.

In the more controversial case of automobiles, the annual welfare costs of restricting Japanese imports to 1979 levels (a reduction of some 250,000 units) would range from $43 to $55 million.[18] The estimated consumer costs range from $1–2 billion annually. In announcing his decision not to provide import relief for the automobile industry, President Carter noted that "between this fiscal year and the next, we are

Table 5.4   Rough Orders of Magnitude of the Annual Static Welfare Gains from the Tariff Cuts Agreed to in the Multilateral Trade Negotiations

Study	Estimate	Assumptions	Comments
1. Baldwin/Mutti/Richardson[a]	$129 million	—30% linear cut: —excludes textiles —undiscounted 1979 dollars	Based on tariff line detail. Includes adjustment costs.
2. Cline/Kawanabe/Kronsjo/Williams[b]	$433 million	—30% linear cut; —excludes textiles —undiscounted 1979 dollars	Basically the same as the Baldwin model. Excludes adjustment costs.
3. Magee[c]	$770 million	—30% linear cut; —developing countries included —textiles and certain agricultural products excluded —undiscounted 1979 dollars	Excludes adjustment costs.

4. Stern/Deardorff[d]	$710 million ($905 million in 1979 dollars)	—undiscounted 1976 dollars —uses actual MTN tariff cuts	Based on tariff averages rather than tariff line detail. Excludes adjustment costs.
5. Bayard/Wipf[e]	$200–500 million ($225–638 million in 1979 dollars)	—undiscounted 1976 dollars —lower est. assumes fixed exchange rates; upper estimate assumes flexible rates. —uses actual MTN tariff cuts.	Basically the Baldwin model. Based on tariff line detail. May overestimate gains because it fails to account for lost quota rents when tariffs are reduced. Excludes adjustment costs.

NOTE: None of the estimates takes into account the impact of growing trade volumes on the static annual welfare estimates.

SOURCES:

[a]Baldwin, R. E., J. H. Mutti, and J. D. Richardson, 1980. Welfare effects on the United States of a significant multilateral tariff reduction. *Journal of International Economics* 10: 405–23.

[b]W. R. Cline, N. Kawanabe, T. O. M. Kronsjo, and T. Williams, *Trade Negotiations in the Tokyo Round*, Washington, D.C.: The Brookings Institution, 1978. Figure presented was adjusted by Richardson (1979, pp. II.7–10).

[c]S. P. Magee. "The Welfare Effects of Restrictions on U.S. Trade," *Brookings Papers on Economic Activity*, no. 3 (1972): 645–707. Figure presented was adjusted by Richardson (1979, pp. II.7–10).

[d]R. M. Stern, and A. Deardorff, "An Economic Analysis of the Effects of the Tokyo Round of the MTN," report prepared for the Senate Finance Committee, June 1979, p. 64.

[e]T. Bayard, and L. Wipf, "Trade, Employment, and Welfare Effects of the Tokyo Round Tariff Cuts," paper presented at the American Economic Association meetings, Atlanta, December 1979, p. 8.

Table 5.5   **Recent Cases Where the President Decided to Grant TAA Rather than Import Relief**

Case	Relief Requested	Estimated Annual Consumer Cost	Estimated Annual Welfare Cost	Comments	Workers Certified for TAA	Number of Workers in the Industry[a]
Autos[b] (Spring 1980)	Quota or OMA to restrict Japanese imports to 1979 levels, probably cutting imports by 250,000 units.	$1–2 billion[c]	$43–55 million	(Not an escape clause [201] case) In announcing his decision, the president noted that, "between this fiscal year and the next, we are budgeting over a billion dollars extra to provide trade adjustment assistance to tide the auto workers over until new jobs can be provided for them."	267,236	900,700

Leather wearing apparel[b] (February 1980)	Tariff (25% increase)	$61–135 million	$27–60 million	(201 case)	366	3,328
Copper[b] (August 1978)	Value-bracketed tariff ($.16–.22 specific)	$90–1,600 million	$2–140 million (includes value-bracketed rents)	(201 case) The president noted that a large number of workers in the industry were eligible for and would receive TAA.	69	44,620
Stainless steel flatware[b] (March 1976 and March 1978)	Quota (10,600 thousand dozen units)	$7.6 million	$4.8 million	(201 cases)	222	5,521

[a]U.S. International Trade Commission Reports on Section 201 of the Trade Act of 1974 cases. Employment data for automobiles are from unpublished Bureau of Labor Statistics data for SIC 3711 and 3714.

[b]The consumer and welfare cost estimates for the 201 cases were pulled from interagency staff calculations and involve a variety of methodologies and assumptions. The welfare estimates for autos are based on the Council of Economic Advisors' assumptions and data.

[c]Testimony of George Eads of the Council of Economic Advisors before the House of Representatives, Committee on Ways and Means, Subcommittee on Trade, 18 March 1980.

budgeting over a billion dollars extra to provide trade adjustment assistance to tide the auto workers over until new jobs can be provided for them." To the extent that the existence of the current TAA program makes it easier politically for the president to deny import relief, the program can generate significant welfare gains.

Table 5.6 shows the administrative costs, payments to beneficiaries, and number of beneficiaries in the TAA program since it was liberalized in 1975. In comparing tables 5.4 and 5.6, the sum of administrative costs and payments to workers is clearly far less than the annual static welfare gains from the Tokyo Round tariff cuts alone, at least until 1980. The rise in TAA payments in 1980 was the result of the enormous increase in TAA petitions from automobile workers.[19]

On economic efficiency grounds (as opposed to budgetary considerations), it is not appropriate to compare the welfare gains for the nation as a whole with the sum of administrative costs plus beneficiary payments. It is more appropriate to compare these welfare gains with the administrative costs because they alone represent a net use of social resources. The TAA payments represent a transfer and therefore are not a social cost.

5.4 Summary and Conclusions

Any overall evaluation of the TAA program must necessarily be somewhat subjective. In our opinion the political gains of the TAA program, in the form of the welfare benefits of freer trade, are enormous. Whether these political gains outweigh the sum of the administrative costs, induced labor market inefficiencies, and inequities of the program is more a matter of personal opinion than of professional judgment, given the difficulty of evaluating many of the costs of the program. Until the crisis in the auto industry caused a substantial rise in TAA recipients and

Table 5.6	Trade Adjustment Assistance under the Trade Act of 1974: Administrative Costs and Benefit Payments ($ millions)		
	Administrative Costs[a]	Benefits Payments	Beneficiaries
1975 (April–June)	$2.0	$0.2	NA
1976 FY	9.3	150.3	46,824
1977 FY	11.5	147.9	137,960
1978 FY	19.5	258.2	156,599
1979 FY[2]	18.2	265.0	131,722
1980 FY	29.0	1,630.0	368,265

[a]Source: General Accounting Office, *Restricting Trade Act Benefits Can Save Millions*, 15 January 1980, Washington, D.C.: GPO; and recent budget estimates. Includes federal offices and state employment offices' administrative costs.

expenditures, the annual welfare gains from the MTN alone probably greatly exceeded the sum of TAA administrative costs and beneficiary payments. Taking these beneficiary payments as a maximum estimate of the costs of the program's inequities and inefficiencies, it still appears that there were substantial net benefits from the program, at least until 1980.

The sharp increase in payments in 1980–81 focused the public's and policymakers' attention on the program. Although program costs were expected to fall dramatically by 1982, as the auto industry began to adjust to import competition and higher oil prices, the TAA program was restructured and several modifications were made to attempt to reduce the program's inequities, inefficiencies, and costs. In particular, benefit levels were reduced to UI levels (roughly 50 percent of the average weekly wage) and the combined duration of UI and TAA can not exceed 52 weeks, except for workers receiving training. In addition, the administration proposed a tightening of TAA eligibility requirements so that imports must constitute "a substantial cause" of worker displacement. Substantial cause means a cause that is important and not less important than any other cause. The substantial cause criterion is the same as that used for the escape clause for import relief. Congress initially agreed to tighten eligibility, but later decided to retain the original requirements.

Cumulatively, these changes are likely to both lower TAA expenditures and redress some of the program's inequities and inefficiencies. However, given the trade-offs discussed in this paper, it is likely that these changes also will curtail the program's political effectiveness in reducing the incidence and severity of protectionism.

The program is due to expire on 1 October 1983. In deciding whether to extend, modify, or terminate it, policymakers must weigh the somewhat elusive political benefits of TAA against its more visible (but no less difficult to measure) equity and efficiency costs. It is likely that budgetary considerations also will continue to play a role in policy deliberations. We conclude with two observations that may help to focus the debate over TAA.

The first observation is that, no matter how well-designed the program is, there may always be fundamental trade-offs between the three basic objectives of TAA. Shifts in the program's emphasis toward one objective will often reduce its effectiveness in one or more of its other functions. Much of the evolution of TAA since 1962 can be traced to shifts in policy objectives (Richardson 1982b). The original TAA program was primarily oriented toward equity and (to a lesser extent) efficiency considerations. The relaxation of eligibility criteria (first in 1970 and again in 1974) and the increase in compensation levels reflected growing concern about political opposition to traditional free trade policy. The recent revisions lowering benefits were designed to redress perceived inequities and inefficiencies and to reduce expenditures.

Although our purpose here is not to make detailed suggestions for program reform, three general principles should guide any further changes in the program's emphasis. First, if the program is to be effective in reducing political resistance to U.S. trade policy, and if it is to provide an alternative to protection, the criteria for eligibility should be weaker than those for import relief under the escape clause, and compensation should be somewhat more generous than UI benefits. Second, if equity considerations are to be emphasized, the program should focus on the problems of permanently displaced workers, since they tend to suffer the largest losses. Third, if efficiency considerations dominate, the program should experiment with combinations of cash compensation and services to promote adjustment, and the TAA component of compensation should be at least partly experience rated to reduce disincentive effects.

The second observation is that the program's objectives and desirability should also be evaluated in the context of prospective U.S. trade policy and problems in the 1980s. Earlier it was suggested that trade and trade-related adjustment problems will become increasingly important in this decade. The United States is also considering the possibility of new multilateral trade negotiations to stem the proliferation of trade distortions both here and abroad.

These considerations suggest the need to maintain the domestic political consensus in support of free trade. As Martin Wolf (1979, 7) has noted, "the key aim of any adjustment policy is to make acceptance of the particular change more politically feasible, and all alternatives have to be evaluated in this light." If the alternative to TAA is increased protectionism, the fundamental issue is whether TAA's political contribution to American trade policy will be sufficient to justify its existence.

Notes

1. The TAA program established in the Trade Act of 1974 provided cash payments, training, employment services, and job search and relocation allowances to workers certified by the secretary of labor as having been laid off or forced to work reduced hours because of imports. Cash payments are administered through state unemployment compensation programs and, combined with state unemployment compensation payments, were equal to up to 70 percent of the average wage in manufacturing. Benefits were available for 52 weeks, with an additional 26 weeks available for workers who received training or who were over 60 years old. The Trade Act of 1974 significantly eased the criteria for eligibility established under the Trade Expansion Act of 1962. The 1962 act stipulated that the single most important cause of worker displacement had to be an increase in imports resulting from a tariff reduction. In contrast, under the 1974 act the connection between increased imports and a tariff reduction was completely severed and, in addition, imports need only have "contributed importantly" to worker displacement, where "contributed importantly" is defined as a cause that is important but not necessarily more important than

any other cause. For a detailed discussion of the history of TAA in the United States, see Frank (1977) and Diebold (1972, 151–54). Some of the problems with the program were reported on the front pages of the *Washington Post* (9 April 1980) and the *New York Times* (21 April 1980). Major articles on TAA also appeared in *Barrons* (5 May 1980), the *National Journal* (10 May 1980), and the *Washington Post* (10 February 1981). The program was modified in the Budget Reconciliation Act of 1981. These changes are discussed in section 5.4.

2. Diamond (1982) points out that the government might want to use categorical programs to affect the income distribution because of economic and political limitations associated with progressive income taxation. Akerlof (1978) has shown that categorical programs effecting a desired change in the income distribution may be more efficient than general programs because a categorical program will generally introduce smaller disincentive effects into the economy as a whole.

3. Corson et al. (1979, table II-1, p. 17; table II-2, p. 21). TAA recipients tended to be somewhat older, less educated, and to have longer tenure than UI recipients in the Mathematica survey. These differences are more pronounced when permanently displaced TAA and UI recipients are compared. Of course, this begs the question of whether current TAA recipients are necessarily representative of trade-displaced workers.

4. Corson et al. (1979, table VI-3, p. 143). However, permanently displaced TAA recipients tended to have somewhat greater losses than permanently displaced UI recipients.

5. It should be recognized that some wage/price rigidity is optimal in the sense that the transactions and information costs of continuously adjusting wages and prices exceed the gains. In some cases, workers may be willing to accept some short-run unemployment due to cyclical or seasonal shifts in demand knowing that the probability of recall is high. In these cases, neither firms nor workers may desire to adjust wages or prices in response to short-run fluctuations. In these cases, there is no equity or efficiency basis for either compensation or adjustment services because the existing wage structure presumably already compensates workers for the risk of short-term unemployment.

6. We owe this argument to Harry Gilman who pointed out to us that most of the cost of acquiring human capital is the income foregone while in training. The argument does not apply to expenditures on school tuition, etc., which are not depreciated under the tax laws unless they are used to improve existing skills or are a requirement of the existing job. See also Becker (1975, 22–24) and Boskin (1975).

7. Corson et al. (1979). Many of the TAA recipients in 1979–82 in the automobile industry may be permanently displaced. The Mathematica survey found that 81 percent of TAA recipients expected to be recalled (vs. 73 percent of UI recipients in manufacturing) and that 72 percent were actually recalled (vs. 58 percent for UI recipients in manufacturing). Mathematica also found that the earnings losses of permanently displaced TAA recipients were somewhat higher than the losses of permanently displaced UI recipients (see table VI-3, p. 143 in Corson et al. (1979).

8. Under the 1962 act, no workers were certified eligible for TAA until 1969. Between 1970 and 1974 about 47,000 workers received $69 million in benefits. See Bayard and Orr (1979) for a comparison of the 1962 and 1974 TAA programs. Bale's (1973) study of the 1962 program was completed while the provisions of the new program were under discussion, but it is not clear that his report was considered by the drafters of the 1974 legislation. Bale's study tended to support the notion that trade-displaced workers experienced high adjustment costs. See also Bale (1976).

9. This discussion ignores second-best considerations. Freer trade is assumed to be welfare improving, even though relaxing some distortions in the presence of others that are unchanged is not necessarily socially beneficial. Although some of the calculations presented in the next section are made in a general equilibrium framework, at best they

incorporate only the most readily quantifiable effects, such as terms of trade changes under flexible exchange rates.

10. An exception is Glenday, Jenkins, and Evans (1980) who adjust their calculations both for the value of leisure and for the distortion in wages caused by trade restrictions.

11. Several industries have supplemental unemployment benefits (SUB) as part of their wage package. In some, like the auto industry, TAA payments are deducted from SUB if the layoff is temporary. In others, like the steel industry, TAA is in addition to SUB.

12. The 1974 trade act stipulated that all TAA payments and administrative costs were to be funded out of customs revenues, but this provision was never implemented. Regardless of the source of funding, if TAA payments are incremental to other government expenditures and require a higher deficit or higher taxes, there are efficiency costs of raising the funds.

13. A variety of methodologies are used in the studies reported in table 5.2 to estimate earnings losses. Conceptually, the appropriate concept is "lifetime earnings losses" composed of the loss caused by the initial spell of unemployment, the lifetime losses resulting from a loss of firm-specific human capital and union rents, and losses from the instability of future employment because of the loss of seniority. See Jacobson and Thomason (1979) and Gilman (1979). The Mathematica (Corson et al. 1979) estimates are based on the losses incurred in the first three years after the initial layoff.

14. The training and other adjustment provisions for TAA recipients were never fully funded. Although the Trade Act of 1974 established a trust to be funded from tariff revenues, it has never been implemented. In the past, training has been funded out of miscellaneous funds, including the secretary of labor's discretionary funds under Title III of the Comprehensive Employment and Training Act. With the increased demand for training during the fiscal year 1980, however, the $12 million allocated was exhausted during the first quarter.

15. The criteria for eligibility under the 1962 act were quite stringent and no workers were certified for TAA until 1970. There is no clear connection with the shift in union attitudes, but in 1970 the eligibility criteria for TAA under the 1962 act were relaxed and 47,000 workers eventually received benefits.

16. Bayard and Orr (1982) hypothesized that actual receipt or a high probability of receipt of TAA benefits during the MTN negotiations (1975–79) would have tended to reduce lobbying against tariff cuts. However, their preliminary results suggest no significant relationship between TAA expenditures and the tariff reductions.

17. See Senate Committee of Finance, Subcommittee on International Trade, *Hearings on the Trade Adjustment Assistance Act*, 9 July 1979. 96th Congress, 1st Session. The quotations are from the testimony of John Sheehan, Legislative Director of the United Steelworkers, pp. 84, 166.

18. The welfare estimates do not include the quota rents that might accrue to Japanese exporters. If these were included, the welfare costs could be $1–2 billion annually, given the Council of Economic Advisors' assumptions. In May 1981 the Japanese government announced a cutback of auto exports of 140,000 units. Internal Department of Labor estimates are that the welfare costs could be as high as $220 million (depending on the beneficiaries of the quota rents) in the first year of export restraints.

19. The budget overruns caused by the massive layoffs in the automobile industry gave impetus to a reappraisal of the costs and benefits of the TAA program. In fiscal year 1980 $381 million was budgeted for TAA compared with actual expenditures of $1,630 million. It can be argued that the budget overruns reflect a crisis in the industry rather than a major failure of the program.

References

Aho, C. M., and T. Bayard. 1980. American trade adjustment assistance after five years. *World Economy* 3:359–72.

———. 1982. The 1980s: Twilight of the open trading system? *World Economy* 5:379–406.

Aho, C. M., and J. A. Orr. 1981. Trade sensitive employment: Who are the affected workers? *Monthly Labor Review* (February):29–35.

Akerlof, G. A. 1978. The economics of "tagging." *American Economic Review* 68:8–19.

Baldwin, R. E., J. H. Mutti, and J. D. Richardson. 1980. Welfare effects on the United States of a significant multilateral tariff reduction. *Journal of International Economics* 10:405–23.

Baldwin, R. E. 1982. The political economy of protectionism. In *Import competition and response*, ed. J. Bhagwati. Chicago: University of Chicago Press for the National Bureau of Economic Research.

Bale, Malcolm. 1973. Adjustment to freer trade: An analysis of the adjustment assistance provisions of the Trade Act of 1962. U.S. Department of Labor.

———. 1976. Estimates of trade-displacement costs for U.S. workers. *Journal of International Economics* 6:245–50.

Bayard, T., and J. Orr. 1979. Transitional equity and efficiency: An analysis of U.S. trade adjustment assistance policy. Paper presented at the American Economic Association meetings, Atlanta, December.

———. 1982. Domestic politics and foreign trade policy: U.S. tariff cuts in the Tokyo Round of the MTN. U.S. Department of Labor.

Bayard, T., and L. Wipf. 1979. Trade, employment, and welfare effects of the Tokyo Round tariff cuts. Paper presented at the American Economic Association meetings, Atlanta, December.

Becker, Gary. 1975. *Human capital*. New York: Columbia University Press.

Bergsten, C. F. 1972. Comments. *Brookings Papers on Economic Activity*, no. 3:703.

Bergsten, C. F., and W. R. Cline. 1982. Trade policy in the 1980s. In *Trade policy in the 1980s*, ed. W. R. Cline. Washington, D.C.: Institute for International Economics.

Blackhurst, R., N. Marian, and J. Tumlir. 1978. Adjustment, trade and growth in developed and developing countries. Geneva: GATT Study in International Trade no. 6.

Boskin, M. J. 1975. Notes on the tax treatment of human capital. Paper prepared for a conference on Tax Research at the Office of Tax Analysis, U.S. Department of Treasury.

Cassing, J., and J. Ochs. 1978. Comment. *American Economic Review* 68:950–55.

Classen, K. 1977. The effect of unemployment insurance on the duration of unemployment and subsequent earnings. *Industrial and Labor Relations Review* 30:430–44.

Cline, W. R., and N. Kawanabe, T. O. M. Kronsjo, and T. Williams. 1978. *Trade negotiations in the Tokyo Round.* Washington, D.C.: The Brookings Institution.

Corson, W., W. Nicholson, J. D. Richardson, and A. Vayda. 1979. *Final report: Survey of trade adjustment assistance recipients.* Mathematica Policy Research for the Office of Foreign Economic Research, U.S. Department of Labor.

Diamond, P. A. 1982. Protection, trade adjustment assistance, and income distribution. In *Import competition and response,* ed. J. Bhagwati. Chicago: University of Chicago Press for the National Bureau of Economic Research.

Diebold, W. 1972. *The United States and the industrial world: American foreign economic policies in the 1970s.* New York: Praeger Publishers for the Council on Foreign Relations.

Ehrenberg, R., and R. Oaxaca. 1976. Unemployment insurance, duration of unemployment and subsequent wage gain. *American Economic Review* 66:754–66.

Ethier, Wilfred J. 1982. Dumping. *Journal of Political Economy* 90:487–506.

Frank, C. R. 1977. *Foreign trade and domestic aid.* Washington, D.C.: The Brookings Institution.

General Accounting Office. 1980. *Restricting trade act benefits can save millions.* Washington, D.C.: GPO.

Gilman, H. 1979. The economic costs of worker dislocation. Paper read at a conference on The Economic Costs of Worker Dislocation, National Commission on Employment Policy, Washington, D.C., July.

Glenday, G., G. Jenkins, and J. Evans. 1980. *Worker adjustment to liberalized trade: Costs and assistance policies.* Washington, D.C.: World Bank Working Paper no. 426.

Goldfarb, R. S., and J. J. Cordes. 1979. Alternative rationales for severance pay compensation. Paper presented at the American Economic Association meetings, Atlanta.

———. 1980. Compensating victims of policy change. *Regulation,* (Sept./Oct.): 22–30.

Grossman, G., and C. Shapiro. 1981. A theory of factor mobility. Department of Economics, Princeton University.

Jacobson, L. 1980. Facilitating policy change through compensation: A case study of trade adjustment assistance. Draft report for the Office of Foreign Economic Research, U.S. Department of Labor.

Jacobson, L., and J. Thomason. 1979. Earnings losses due to displacement. Report to the Office of Foreign Economic Research, U.S. Department of Labor.

Kirkland, L. 1981. Statement on U.S. trade policy. Subcommittee on International Trade, Senate Committee on Finance and Subcommittee on International Finance, Senate Committee on Banking, 13 July 1981.

Lapan, H. 1976. International trade, factor market distortions, and the optimal dynamic factor subsidy. *American Economic Review* 66:335–46.

———. 1978. Reply. *American Economic Review* 68:956–59.

Magee, S. P. 1972. The welfare effects of restrictions on U.S. trade. *Brookings Papers on Economic Activity*, no. 3: 645–707.

———. 1973. Factor market distortions, production and trade: A survey. *Oxford Economic Papers* 25:1–43.

McCarthy, J. 1974. Trade adjustment assistance: A case study of the shoe industry in Massachusetts. Washington, D.C.: U.S. Department of Labor.

Neumann, G., and G. Glyde. 1978. The labor market consequences of trade displacement: Evidence from the Trade Adjustment Assistance program of 1962. Washington, D.C.: U.S. Department of Labor.

Organization for Economic Cooperation and Development. 1979. The case for positive adjustment policies. Paris: OECD secretariat.

Office of Foreign Economic Research. U.S. Department of Labor. 1980. *Report of the president on U.S. competitiveness*. Washington, D.C.: GPO.

Parsons, D. O. 1980. Unemployment, the allocation of labor and optimal government intervention. *American Economic Review* 70:626–35.

Richardson, J. D. 1979. *The impact of multilateral trade liberalization on U.S. labor*. MTN Study no. 3. Senate. Committee on Finance, Subcommittee on International Trade. 96th Cong., 1st sess., June.

———. 1982a. Trade Adjustment Assistance under the United States Trade Act of 1974: An analytical examination and worker survey. *Import competition and response*, ed. J. Bhagwati. Chicago: University of Chicago Press for the National Bureau of Economic Research.

———. 1982b. Worker adjustment to U.S. international trade: Programs and prospects. In *Trade policy in the 1980s*, ed. W. R. Cline. Washington, D.C.: Institute for International Economics.

Stern, R. M., and A. Deardorff. 1979. *An economic analysis of the effects of the Tokyo Round of the MTN*. Report prepared for the Senate Finance Committee, June.

United Nations Conference on Trade and Development. 1979. Implications for developing countries of the new protectionism in developed countries. Geneva: UNCTAD secretariat, doc. TD/226.

Utgoff, K. C. 1982. Reduction of adjustment costs associated with trade. Public Research Institute for the U.S. Department of Labor.
Wolf, M. 1979. Adjustment policies and problems in developed countries. Washington, D.C.: World Bank Working Paper no. 349.

Comment   J. David Richardson

This is a fine survey and updating of the U.S. experiment with Trade Adjustment Assistance (TAA) over the past twenty years. It does a great service by tabulating quantitative results from other studies on a comparable basis and by assessing often-neglected administrative costs of the TAA program. Many sensible suggestions are given, some implicit, some explicit, for restructuring TAA to better meet its multiple goals.

I have a few differences in emphasis. One is that I think the authors still sell short the benefits of the TAA experiment. For example, they recognize its political efficacy but do not sufficiently acknowledge its role as catalyst in the congressional passage of the Trade Expansion Act of 1962 and the Trade Act of 1974. Since these laws led to the two deepest and most liberalizing rounds of trade agreements in the postwar period, at least some of the benefits from these agreements should properly be attributed to TAA. Or, while the authors acknowledge that TAA and its 1974 revisions encouraged organized labor to support the Kennedy and Tokyo Rounds, they might have pointed out that it also encouraged "organized capital" to support these initiatives. TAA was viewed by many firms in 1962 as the quid pro quo for escape clause action. Also, while acknowledging TAA's potential as a "diagnostic signal" for workers and firms to adjust, it is worth adding that it did so without itself distorting or weakening any of the natural market signals to adjust (prices, profits, market shares, etc.). Finally, I believe that the authors should give more than just one line to the way TAA encouraged growth in U.S. trade, especially with developing countries, by being a substitute for trade barriers that are all the more tempting to use against those without credible retaliation.

To the authors' suggestions for restructuring TAA, I would add: extension of existing U.S. employment subsidy programs, such as targeted job credits, to workers certified as having been permanently (not temporarily) displaced by trade; self-financing and voluntary loan/insurance programs for the same kind of worker to underwrite retraining and perhaps relocating; and *conditional* extension of unemployment benefits

J. David Richardson is professor of economics at the University of Wisconsin-Madison, and a research associate of the National Bureau of Economic Research.

beyond normal for trade-displaced workers—conditional, for example, on employed workers and firms bearing some sizeable portion of the extra financial burden through negotiated "cost sharing."

Otherwise I take issue with the authors in only one important matter. Most studies of TAA experience find that workers who are permanently displaced by trade suffer more severe adjustment problems and earnings losses than other permanently displaced workers. The authors consign a semblance of that observation to their note 4, while saying in the text that "TAA recipients in general do not have higher earnings losses." Yet the text's conclusion characterizes only the study by Corson et al. (1979) and obviously reflects the high proportion of temporarily displaced TAA recipients in that study. That conclusion does not do justice to earlier studies, nor to the legitimate equity goal of TAA. That goal may indeed have been perverted in the early 1980s, but its usual legitimacy for permanently displaced workers has not been undermined as deeply as the authors suggest.

Reference

Corson, Walter, Walter Nicholson, J. David Richardson, and Andrea Vayda. 1979. *Final report: Survey of Trade Adjustment Assistance Recipients.* Mathematica Policy Research for the Office of Foreign Economic Affairs, Bureau of International Labor Affairs, U.S. Department of Labor.

6   The U.S. Generalized System of Preferences and Its Impacts

André Sapir and Lars Lundberg

6.1 Introduction

In the early sixties, developing countries started to move away from import-substitution strategies. Gradually, these were replaced by outward-looking strategies that emphasized the importance of manufactured exports in the process of industrialization and development. In order to expand their nontraditional exports, the developing nations sought to improve their market access, especially through the reduction of tariff and nontariff barriers in the industrialized countries. At that time, one opportunity to achieve better market access was the GATT-sponsored Kennedy Round of tariff negotiations for which preparatory work was under way. However, the developing countries contested the fundamental GATT principle of most-favored-nation (MFN) treatment whereby a country cannot tax imports of the same item from different countries at different rates. They argued that equal treatment of unequal partners could not constitute an equitable arrangement. The developing nations therefore asked for special and preferential treatment in their favor without reciprocity of concessions on their part.

During the GATT ministerial meeting held in 1963, proposals for special tariff treatment in favor of developing countries were formally

André Sapir is assistant professor of economics at the University of Wisconsin-Madison and is also associated with the Free University of Brussels. Lars Lundberg was a visiting scholar at the University of Wisconsin-Madison and is docent in the Department of Forest Economics, University of Umea, Sweden.

The authors are grateful to Robert Baldwin, Rachel McCulloch, Tracy Murray, and Gordon Streeb for comments and suggestions. They acknowledge their debt to Alan Dickman for extensive computational assistance, and to Steve Parker for both comments and assistance. Financial support was partially provided by the Graduate School Research Committee at the University of Wisconsin-Madison and by a grant from the Ford Foundation to André Sapir.

discussed for the first time. While the developed countries agreed not to require reciprocal tariff cuts by developing countries, they did not accept the proposal that tariffs in developed countries should be cut more on imports from developing nations than on imports from other developed countries. However, the debate on tariff preferences was reopened shortly thereafter at the first meeting of the United Nations Conference on Trade and Development (UNCTAD) in early 1964. Among the principles it adopted, the Conference recommended that developed countries grant preferential concessions to the developing nations without requiring reciprocal concessions. This recommendation was rejected by a group of industrialized countries, among whom the United States was the leading force.[1]

The U.S. opposition to preferences at UNCTAD was supported by both free traders and protectionists in the country. The position of the former group was based on its determination to uphold the MFN principle of nondiscriminatory treatment in trade. On the other hand, the protectionists were against tariff concessions in general because of their fear of additional imports. However, the official U.S. policy toward preferences gradually became untenable as "politically, [it found itself] virtually isolated from all the developing countries and most of the industrialized countries as well."[2] One of the major fears of the United States was the regionalization of world trade resulting from preferential trading arrangements between the European Economic Community (EEC) and the developing countries. Accordingly, in 1967 the United States announced its acceptance of the principle of nondiscriminatory preferences for all developing countries.

The shift of position by the United States paved the way toward preferential tariff treatment in favor of developing nations. This principle was formally accepted at the second session of UNCTAD held in 1968. Under the unanimously agreed upon Generalized System of Preferences (GSP), developing countries would be charged no duty for their exports to the industrialized countries, while each developed country would continue to levy the MFN tariff on products from other industrial countries. The GSP would thus provide the developing countries with a margin of preference equal to the MFN tariff in the industrialized nations.

In 1969 a Special Committee of Preferences was established by UNCTAD to conduct the necessary negotiations for actually establishing the GSP. Despite this effort at international coordination, the work on drawing up GSP schemes proceeded mainly on the national level so that, eventually, each so-called donor country applied a somewhat different scheme and introduced it at a different time. One last problem remained before actually implementing the GSP. The MFN clause of article 1 of the GATT provides that trade be conducted on a nondiscriminatory basis.

Hence, the contracting parties of GATT voted a ten-year waiver from article 1 in June 1971. The next month the EEC was first to introduce its system of preferences. Other countries followed suit soon afterward and, lastly, the United States introduced its GSP program in January 1976.

The delay in the introduction of a GSP scheme by the United States reflects the generally negative attitude toward preferences which has prevailed in this country. The opposition of both free traders and protectionists, as well as the political nature of the U.S. endorsement of the GSP, are reflected in the language of Title V of the 1974 Trade Act which provides the guidelines for the U.S. scheme. Section 501, which grants the president the authority to extend preferences, requires him to do so with due regard to:

(1) their effect on the economic development of developing countries;
(2) their likely impact on U.S. producers; and
(3) the extent of similar preferences being granted by the other major developed countries.

Clearly point (1) is addressed to the free traders who defend the view that a nondiscriminatory reduction in MFN tariff rates would be more beneficial to these countries (and the world) than the GSP. Point (2), on the other hand, is directed at the protectionists who fear the impact of the scheme on U.S. producers. Finally, point (3) makes clear the foreign policy basis for the U.S. acceptance of the GSP.

As we will see in greater detail in section 6.2, the U.S. GSP scheme is subject to a number of restrictions affecting its country coverage, product coverage, and the extent of preferential treatment. Moreover, section 505 of the 1974 Trade Act prescribes that the U.S. scheme will terminate ten years after the date of its enactment (i.e., on 3 January 1985). Although the GSP will probably be renewed for another ten-year period, its future shape remains uncertain at the moment.[3] Some changes to the system were already made following the mandated report on its first five years of operation, and more are expected before Congress approves its renewal.[4] In order to decide on the future of the GSP, a review process was launched in 1983.

The object of this paper is to provide useful input into the decision-making process on the future of GSP. In order to do so, we need to answer the following questions:

(1) What has been the effect of the GSP on the exports by the developing countries to the United States and how has this effect been distributed among individual beneficiaries?
(2) What has been the impact of the GSP on production in different industrial sectors in the United States?
(3) What would be the trade and production effects of the changes in the GSP being considered by policymakers?

The plan of the paper is as follows. In section 6.2, we review the provisions of the U.S. GSP. After discussing methodological questions in section 6.3, an evaluation of the GSP impact on trade and production is undertaken in section 6.4. Finally, section 6.5 summarizes our results and examines the potential effects on trade and production of changes in the GSP scheme.

6.2 Provisions of the U.S. GSP

The GSP schemes introduced by the industrialized countries vary in terms of country coverage, product coverage, and the extent of preferential treatment. In the previous section we outlined the political-economic background of the U.S. decision to grant preferences to the developing countries. Here we will describe the actual provisions of the U.S. GSP and discuss them with reference to that background. As will become apparent, the GSP is a very complex institution. Therefore, it is important to review and understand its functioning before attempting to evaluate its impact and before discussing possible future changes in its operation.

6.2.1 Country Coverage

Section 502 of the 1974 Trade Act deals with the notion of a "beneficiary developing country." However, instead of enumerating the list of developing countries that can benefit from the U.S. GSP, it outlines conditions that should guide the president in determining whether to designate any country a beneficiary developing country. These are as follows: (1) a request by the country to be so designated; (2) the level of economic development of such country; (3) whether or not the other major developed countries extend their GSP scheme to the country; (4) the extent to which the country has assured the United States of equitable and reasonable access to its market and basic commodity resources.

Even if a country meets these four conditions, section 502 specifies that the president shall not designate it as beneficiary in any of the following cases: it is a communist country; it participates in international commodity cartels, such as OPEC; it affords preferences to another developed country causing a significant adverse effect on U.S. commerce; it has expropriated U.S. property without compensation; it refuses to cooperate with the United States to prevent narcotics from entering this country; and it fails to recognize or enforce arbitral awards in favor of U.S. citizens or firms.[5]

In practice, except for those countries that fall within one of the above exclusive categories, all developing countries have been beneficiaries of the U.S. GSP.[6] So far, this has been true regardless of their level of economic development. However, as we will see in greater details in section 6.5, U.S. policymakers are actively discussing the possibility of graduating the most advanced developing countries from GSP eligibility. Indeed, from its inception, there were those in the United States who favored the exclusion of some advanced developing countries from the GSP scheme. However, politically this proved to be a problem in the international arena as the developing countries opposed the idea of discriminatory treatment among themselves. Moreover, the United States had to take into account the fact that both the EEC and Japan had granted beneficiary status to most of the advanced developing nations— even though many restrictions were attached to it.

6.2.2   Product Coverage

Although protectionist groups in the United States were not able to exclude the most competitive developing countries from GSP treatment, they did succeed in restricting the product coverage of the GSP.[7] Section 503 of the 1974 Trade Act, which relates to the eligibility of products, lists the following import-sensitive products as being ineligible for tariff preferences: (1) textile and apparel articles subject to textile agreements; (2) watches; (3) import-sensitive electronic articles; (4) import-sensitive steel items; (5) footwear articles; (6) import-sensitive glass products;[8] and (7) any other articles which the president determines to be import sensitive in the context of the GSP.

The regulations governing the administration of the GSP provide that any interested party may petition to have new articles either removed or added to the GSP list. Decisions are taken by the president based on investigations by the GSP Subcommittee of the Trade Policy Staff Committee. As a result of annual product reviews, 233 products have been added and 27 removed from the original list of 2,729 GSP-eligible items as of 31 March 1982.[9]

6.2.3   Limitations on Preferential Treatment

Rules of Origin

To prevent exports from nonbeneficiary countries from transiting via beneficiary countries for the sole purpose of GSP treatment, donor countries have instituted a set of rules of origin. In the United States, duty-free treatment for GSP-eligible products applies only if (a) a product is imported directly from a beneficiary developing country into the United States; and (b) the sum of the cost or value of materials produced in the beneficiary country plus the direct costs of processing equals at least 35 precent of the value of the product.[10] Although these rules are primarily intended to insure the proper operation of the GSP, in certain instances they also might serve a protectionist purpose. In particular, in some cases they might deter U.S. multinational corporations from responding to GSP margins by transferring production to beneficiary developing countries.[11]

Competitive Need Limitations

Under section 504 of the 1974 Trade Act, a beneficiary developing country loses GSP duty-free treatment for a particular product if its exports to the United States exceeds (1) 50 percent of the value of the total U.S. imports of the product;[12,13] or (2) a certain dollar value adjusted annually in accordance with the growth of the U.S. GNP.[14] The loss of preferences takes effect on 30 March of the following year.[15] Reinstatement to GSP treatment may be considered if U.S. imports of that product from the excluded country fall below the competitive need limitations in subsequent years. Hence, during any given year (from 30 March to the following 29 March), imports of a product from a beneficiary country enter the United States either entirely GSP duty-free or entirely at the MFN rate.[16]

It is often emphasized that competitive need limitations are designed to reserve the benefits of the program for less competitive producers in not-so-advanced developing countries. However, it should also be recognized that these limitations are the result of domestic protectionist pressures.

6.2.4   The Consequence of Exclusions

What is the importance of the various exclusions presently built into the U.S. GSP scheme? A rough answer can be obtained by examining the trade flows presented in table 6.1. For instance, in 1978, U.S. imports from developing countries amounted to $75.9 billion. Out of this sum, $62.0 billion were subject to MFN tariffs and, thus, constitute the potential trade that could benefit from GSP treatment. However, because of restrictive country coverage, only $31.4 billion of dutiable imports from developing nations came from GSP beneficiaries.[17] Moreover, from this amount, only $9.7 billion was eligible for GSP treatment because of product exclusions, most of which covered items with relatively high MFN tariff rates. Finally, the implementation of rules of origin and competitive need limitations further reduced the actual GSP duty-free imports to $5.2 billion. This represents 8 percent of the dutiable imports from all developing countries and 17 percent of the equivalent imports from the beneficiary countries alone. Thus, only a relatively small fraction of the imports from developing countries fall under the GSP program. Moreover, as far as beneficiary countries are concerned, the MFN rate on excluded trade flows tends to be much higher than the preference margin applied to included flows.

Table 6.1   U.S. Imports: Total, MFN Dutiable, and GSP Coverage (billions of
                   dollars)

	1976	1977	1978	1979	1980	1981
From the world						
Total	119.5	145.5	170.7	210.0	245.0	260.0
MFN dutiable	86.2	106.2	125.3	n.a.	n.a.	n.a.
From all developing countries						
Total	55.0	70.2	75.9	96.2	119.1	120.3
MFN dutiable	45.6	58.0	62.0	n.a.	n.a.	n.a.
From all GSP beneficiaries						
Total	28.1	34.7	41.4	51.2	63.5	68.5
MFN dutiable	20.9	25.4	31.4	38.2	53.8	n.a.
GSP eligible trade	6.5	7.7	9.7	11.7	14.3	16.9
Exclusions						
50% limit	(0.7)	(0.8)	(1.0)	n.a.	n.a.	n.a.
dollar limit	(1.2)	(2.0)	(2.2)	n.a.	n.a.	n.a.
rules of origin						
and other[a]	(1.4)	(1.0)	(1.3)	(1.6)	(1.4)	n.a.
GSP duty-free trade	3.2	3.9	5.2	6.2	7.3	8.4

SOURCE: Office of the U.S. Trade Representative.
[a]Including the absence of request for GSP coverage.

6.3 Methodology

Conceptually, a preferential tariff reduction (like the GSP) is similar to
the formation of a customs union. Both give rise to the same static effects,
described often as trade creation (TC) and trade diversion (TD). The TC
effects corresponds to the displacement of domestic production in the
donor country in favor of imports from beneficiary countries. The TD
effect pertains to the substitution by the donor country of imports from
preferred suppliers for imports from nonpreferred countries. If we
assume that U.S. apparent consumption is not affected by the change in
tariffs, one dollar's worth of imports will replace one dollar's worth of
domestic production, and the impact on U.S. output and employment is
then determined only by the trade creation effect. On the other hand, for
beneficiary developing countries more significance is attached to the sum
of the TC and TD effects, which reflects the total impact of preferences
on their exports. This sum is often referred to as gross trade creation
(GTC). According to the theory of customs unions, trade creation increases the welfare of the donor country, since resources are transferred
away from inefficient import-competing sectors. However, trade diversion implies a welfare loss, since imports are diverted from the most
efficient suppliers.

Empirically, several methods have been used to estimate the trade creation and diversion effects of preferential trading arrangements.[18] Among these methods, one can distinguish between ex ante and ex post methods. The former seek to study the effects of preferential tariff reductions in advance of their implementation. In addition to estimates of tariff reduction, ex ante methods require estimates of domestic and foreign supply elasticities as well as of own- and cross-price import demand elasticities. On the other hand, ex post methods seek to isolate the effect of preferential arrangements on actual trade flows from effects of changes in other determinants of trade.

The choice between ex ante and ex post methods obviously depends on the task at hand. In our particular case, the adopted methodology should, ideally, have the following properties: (i) it should provide estimates of the effect of the present U.S. GSP scheme by incorporating information on its actual functioning; and (ii) it should give these estimates for individual countries and individual products in such a way as to enable one to gauge the effects of possible future changes in the GSP.

The ex ante method was first used in the context of the U.S. GSP by Baldwin and Murray (1977). Its primary advantage is that it is particularly well suited for investigating alternative hypothetical policies. However, besides the fact that it relies on rather rough elasticity estimates, this method suffers from another major drawback. In principle, the GSP provides the developing countries a margin of preferential equal to the U.S. MFN tariff which, hereafter, will be referred to as the theoretical preference margin (TPM). By definition, ex ante studies use TPMs to compute the trade effects of the GSP. However, as we have seen earlier, in practice rules of origin and competitive need limitations tend to reduce the amount of imports actually entering duty-free below the total level of imports from GSP beneficiaries.[19] Accordingly, the actual preference margin (APM) will be below the TPM. Hence, for the beneficiary country i and the eligible product j, we can write

(1) $$A_{ij} = p_{ij} T_j,$$

where A and T correspond to AMP and TPM, respectively, and p_{ij} is the proportion of U.S. imports of product j from country i that actually enter GSP duty-free.[20] Thus, because they use theoretical instead of actual preference margins, ex ante evaluations of the GSP system will tend to overestimate its trade effects. This is likely to be true even if the analysis is adjusted by leaving out those trade flows that are a priori excluded from GSP treatment, as in Baldwin and Murray (1977), since this does not account for additional exclusions resulting from the restrictive operation of the GSP rules.

Ex post methods use data for actual trade flows which they compare to an anti-monde (i.e., hypothetical trade flows corresponding to a situation of unchanged tariffs), the difference being the tariff effect. The crucial element here is obviously the construction of the anti-monde. One of the approaches to this problem has been to extrapolate trends in market shares from a period before to a period after the tariff change.[21]

Another approach consists of explicitly introducing a tariff variable in the analysis and statistically estimating the relationship between trade flows and tariff preferences. The main advantage of this method is that it provides a test of the statistical significance of tariff effects. Moreover, it does not require any elasticity estimates nor any nontestable assumption about the anti-monde. On the other hand, the weakness of this and other ex post methods is that in order to give reliable estimates they require a period during which the trade effects of tariff changes are relatively large compared to the effects of other disturbances.

The statistical analysis of the impact of GSP preferences on trade flows requires one to formulate models that are capable of explaining international trade flows by a set of factors that includes tariff preferences. Recently a large number of empirical studies have addressed this issue with the help of cross-section regression models. As Leamer (1974) has pointed out, these models belong to two categories which are the dual of each other. They seek to explain trade flows either for particular products across countries or for particular countries across products.[22]

For the purpose of examining the trade impact of the GSP, the first group of models may be summarized as

(2) $$M_{ij} = F_j(E_i, A_{ij}),$$

where M_{ij} is the U.S. import of product j from country i, E_i is a vector of country i's characteristics, and A_{ij} is the actual preference margin defined earlier. The presence of this vector of country characteristics is a reflection of the theory we adopt to explain comparative advantages: products use certain resources intensively and can be produced more cheaply by countries abundant in these resources. The GSP impact is indicated by the A_{ij} coefficients obtained by estimating equation (2) for each product over a cross-section of countries comprised of both GSP beneficiaries and nonbeneficiaries.[23]

The second group of models may be expressed as

(3) $$M_{ij} = G_i(E_j, A_{ij}),$$

where E_j is a vector of product j's characteristics and the other variables are as previously defined. This vector of product characteristics reflects the dual of the theory of comparative advantages stated earlier: certain resources are abundant in some countries and these countries can produce more cheaply those products that are intensive in the use of these resources. Here the GSP effect may be derived from estimating equation (3) for each exporting country or group of countries over a cross section of products.

If we postulate a simple constant-elasticity form for F_j, we may write equation (2) as

(4) $$m_{ij} = \alpha_j + \beta_j e_i + \gamma_j A_{ij},$$

where $m_{ij} = \log M_{ij}$, and $e_i = \log E_i$. For our purpose, it will be more convenient to formulate the model in terms of market shares, that is:

(5) $$s_{ij} = m_{ij} - c_j = \tilde{\alpha}_j + \beta_j e_i + \gamma_j A_{ij},$$

where $s_{ij} = \log S_{ij}$, $c_j = \log C_j$, $S_{ij} = M_{ij}/C_j$, and C_j is the apparent consumption of product j in the United States, and $\tilde{\alpha}_j = \alpha_j - c_j$. A significantly positive γ_j indicates a GSP effect on U.S. imports of product j. However, because e_i might possibly omit a variable correlated with A_{ij}, γ_j might reflect other factors besides the GSP. To check for this possibility, we will also estimate equation (5) for a year before the GSP scheme was introduced. This gives the opportunity to test the hypothesis that γ_j is significantly positive after, but not before, the tariff change. In case γ_j turns out to be significantly positive in the pre-GSP year, we know that the model omits an additional explanatory variable, the effect of which is captured by A_{ij}. However, if this missing variable cannot be measured, and if we are willing to assume that the bias in the A_{ij} coefficient is constant, the test for a GSP effect will be whether there is a significant increase of γ_j over time. Such a method was applied by Sapir (1981) for evaluating the trade impact of the European Community's GSP.

Another possibility of testing for a GSP effect is to formulate model (2) in terms of changes in market shares from a year before to a year after preferences were introduced:

(6) $$(\Delta S_{ij}) = a_j + b_j(\Delta E_i) + c_j E_i^\circ + d_j A_{ij},$$

where (ΔS_{ij}) and (ΔE_i) refer to changes and the superscript $^\circ$ indicates a year before the GSP. One of the deficiencies with cross-country regressions (5) and (6) is that, although the estimated γ_j and d_j indicate whether the GSP has a significant effect, they do not directly measure either its trade creating or its trade diverting effects. Essentially, this problem is caused by the absence of "normal trade" from those regressions, that is, trade not likely to be affected in any way by the GSP.

As far as model (3) is concerned, in keeping with our previous discussion, it may be written as either

(7) $$s_{ij} = \alpha'_i + \beta'_i e_j + \gamma'_i A_{ij},$$

or

(8) $$(\Delta S_{ij}) = a'_i + b'_i(\Delta E_j) + c'_i E_j^\circ + d'_j A_{ij}.$$

In these cross-product regressions, a significantly positive γ_i' or d_i' indicates gross trade creation due to the GSP if i is a beneficiary country. On the other hand, if i is a nonbeneficiary country, a significantly negative coefficient for A_{ij} indicates trade diversion. The trade creation effect may be obtained either as the difference between GTC and TD, or from the coefficients γ_i' or d_i' when i stands for all exports to the United States.

6.4   Impact of the U.S. GSP on Trade and Production

In this section we will attempt to measure the effects of the GSP on the U.S. economy for 1979, the last year for which all the data required for our study were available. Our analysis will be divided into three parts. First, we present the actual GSP preference margins for 1979 by major beneficiary country. In addition, we briefly review the trend of penetration into the U.S. market by beneficiary developing countries during the seventies. Second, we test whether the performance of beneficiary countries in the U.S. market between 1975 and 1979 may be statistically related to the GSP program. Third, we present estimates of the magnitude of the GSP's impact on U.S. trade and production.

6.4.1   Preference Margins and Market Shares

The possibility for beneficiary developing countries to expand their exports (and market shares) to the United States because of the GSP depends, in the first place, on the amount of trade subject to MFN duties. According to this criterion, the main beneficiary exporters in 1979 were Taiwan, Mexico, Korea, Hong Kong, and Brazil (see table 6.2, col. [2]). Given the amount of dutiable trade, the commodity structure and the GSP product coverage of each beneficiary determine the extent of its GSP eligible trade. Among countries included in table 6.2, these two factors have been relatively favorable for Chile, the Dominican Republic, and Haiti all of which have a high ratio of GSP-eligible to MFN-dutiable trade. The opposite holds for Malaysia, the Philippines, and India.

Besides the level of eligible trade, the potential effect of the GSP also depends on the size of the preference margin. This margin is potentially equal to the MFN duty on eligible products, of which the weighted average is shown in table 6.2, column (4). However as we have seen earlier, in practice due to various exclusions, beneficiary countries continue to pay what might be called "GSP duties" on eligible products. Their weighted average appears in column (5). The difference between the MFN and GSP duties is the actual preference margin which, as the figures displayed in column (6) indicate, varies substantially across beneficiaries. As equation (1) reveals, this margin tends to be higher the larger the MFN duty and the larger the proportion of eligible trade that

Table 6.2   Imports, Duties and Preference Margins for Beneficiary Countries with over $100 Million of GSP-Eligible Imports, 1979

Country	Imports ($ millions)			Duties and Preference on Eligible Trade (%)				Ranking		Preference Margin on Total Dutiable Trade (%)	Tariff Revenue Forgone ($ millions)
	Total (1)	MFN Dutiable (2)	GSP Eligible (3)	MFN Duty (4)	GSP Duty (5)	Preference Margin (6)	(6):(4) (7)	MFN Duty (8)	Preference Margin (9)	(10)	(11)
Mexico	8,980	5,491	1,927	7.50	5.12	2.37	32	7	15	0.83	45
Taiwan	6,426	6,305	2,526	9.22	2.87	6.35	69	3	4	2.54	160
Korea	4,348	3,907	1,151	9.23	2.46	6.77	73	2	2	1.99	78
Hong Kong	4,289	3,566	1,611	10.00	6.06	3.94	39	1	10	1.78	63
Brazil	3,383	1,852	947	3.74	0.89	2.84	76	17	13	1.45	27
Malaysia	2,249	923	184	4.97	3.19	1.78	36	16	17	0.35	3
Philippines	1,648	1,238	305	6.70	2.91	3.79	57	13	11	0.93	12
Singapore	1,532	1,197	372	7.63	2.85	4.77	63	6	8	1.48	18
Peru	1,235	381	187	5.29	1.90	3.39	64	15	12	1.66	6
India	1,148	672	184	6.74	1.43	5.32	80	12	7	1.46	10
Israel	774	652	299	8.34	0.34	7.99	96	5	1	3.66	24
Dominican Rep.	720	329	210	6.66	5.74	0.93	14	14	18	0.59	2
Thailand	646	299	111	7.38	1.91	5.47	74	8	5	2.03	6
Argentina	634	404	177	6.98	2.94	4.04	58	10	9	1.77	7
Chile	468	251	233	3.03	1.08	1.95	64	18	16	1.81	5
Yugoslavia	406	353	179	7.28	0.75	6.53	90	9	3	3.31	12
Portugal	272	259	116	6.88	1.41	5.40	78	11	6	2.42	6
Haiti	234	177	100	8.62	6.14	2.48	29	4	14	1.40	2
All beneficiaries	51,170	38,164	11,725	7.98	3.48	4.50	56	—	—	1.38	528

receives GSP treatment. In turn, this proportion is directly related to the application of rules of origin and competitive need limitations. In general, one should expect rules of origin to affect mostly small and specialized countries exporting highly processed goods with a high ratio of imported intermediate goods to sales value. On the other hand, competitive need limitations should mainly affect large or highly specialized countries. The figures in column (7) indicate that the countries most adversely affected by these rules are the Dominican Republic, Haiti, and Mexico, while those least affected are Israel, Yugoslavia, and India. The actual margin of preference was the highest for Israel, Korea, and Yugoslavia, and the lowest for the Dominican Republic, Malaysia, and Chile.

The product of the actual preference margin and the value of GSP-eligible trade is the tariff revenue foregone by the United States on GSP trade. For a given volume of imports and a given import price, this amount would also indicate the increase in export earnings by beneficiaries as a result of the GSP. If we accept this as a rough estimate of export effects, column (11) in table 6.2 indicates that Taiwan, Korea, and Hong Kong obtained the most benefit in this sense from U.S. preferences. However, this assumes that markets for imported goods are competitive: otherwise, part of this potential benefit for developing countries might be captured by powerful U.S. importers or intermediary traders.[24]

Between 1975 and 1979, the share of imports from GSP beneficiaries in U.S. consumption of manufactures increased from 1.77 to 2.49 percent.[25] Although relatively small on the aggregate level, the loss in market share to GSP countries by U.S. producers is unevenly distributed across products.[26] As indicated in table 6.3, this loss has been substantial for some products. Together, the top twenty products account for more than 40 percent of the total loss of sales for the entire manufacturing sector.

These changes in market shares may reflect the effects of the GSP scheme. However, they are likely to reflect other factors as well. Except for a brief setback in 1975, the market share of GSP countries for total manufactures increased steadily during the seventies. Therefore, the increase of the share since the beginning of the GSP scheme in 1976 is in part a continuation of a previous trend reflecting a long-run change in comparative advantage for certain products in favor of producers in developing countries.

A very rough method of assessing the importance of the GSP is to assume that the trend in market shares reflects long-run changes in international competitiveness, while positive deviations from the trend after 1976 for GSP countries indicate the effects of the GSP. Unfortunately, the period 1972–79 has been subject to economic shocks affecting trade, such as the oil crisis, the 1974 recession, and major currency realignments. Hence, it is difficult to isolate the long-run factors to give a reliable estimate of GSP effects. The trend-adjusted losses reported in

Table 6.3   Loss of Market Share by U.S. Producers to GSP Beneficiaries for
Twenty Products with the Largest Losses

SIC Code	Description	Loss in Market Share, 1975–79 (percentage points)		1979 Market Share (%) GSP Countries
		Actual	Trend-Adjusted	
3021	Rubber and plastic footwear	24.9	9.3	54.3
3151	Leather gloves	16.6	16.6	30.0
3161	Luggage	15.4	10.9	25.1
3674	Semiconductors	11.0	8.7	31.7
3341	Secondary nonferrous metals	9.9	8.1	17.5
3676	Electronic resistors	9.7	5.4	14.0
3171	Women's handbags	9.5	0.0	30.9
3942	Dolls	9.1	9.1	26.7
3944	Games and toys	8.9	8.9	16.1
2435	Hardwood veneer and plywood	8.7	8.7	27.9
3629	Electrical industrial apparatus, nec.	8.7	8.7	15.7
3915	Jewelers' materials	8.7	8.1	48.9
3651	Radios and TVs	8.1	5.7	18.5
3111	Leather tanning	7.6	7.6	12.2
3172	Personal leather goods, nec.	6.8	4.9	12.7
3263	Copper foundries	6.8	4.8	9.1
3269	Nonferrous foundries, nec.	6.7	1.3	16.7
3675	Electronic capacitors	6.7	4.7	12.2
3949	Sporting goods	6.5	4.9	11.8
2499	Wood products, nec.	6.4	6.4	11.7

table 6.3 indicate that, for most of the industries listed, the GSP may have played an important role in accounting for the decline in market shares.[27] However, it is likely that the residuals still contain effects of other factors. Recovery from the 1974 recession has probably tended to increase market shares for imported products in general. In addition, it is possible that the increase in competitiveness for developing countries during the seventies accelerated during 1976–79. In any case, besides being rather crude, trend methods suffer from the fact that they do not permit statistical tests of their results.

6.4.2   Testing for GSP Effects

The Cross-Country Model

In this section, model (2), the cross-country regression, will be used to test for the existence of a GSP effect on the country pattern of U.S. imports for a sample of products. Besides the preference variable A_{ij}, the model should contain the main determinants of trade flows from different countries to the United States. Variables often used in gravity models of international trade are measures of supply capacity, such as GNP or population in the exporting country, and of the distance between trading partners, to reflect transport costs. In this study we have used total exports of manufactures of a country to measure supply capacity. In addition, we have introduced the ratio of the stock of U.S. direct investment in the exporting country to the country's GNP as an indicator of its economic ties with the United States.

Relative factor endowments will influence the country pattern of U.S. imports. For labor-intensive standard products with low-skill requirements, U.S. imports are likely to be large from countries where physical and human capital are relatively scarce. Accordingly, we include in model (2) country measures of the physical capital/labor ratio as well as a measure of human capital.[28] For capital-intensive and technically advanced industries, however, U.S. imports are likely to come from countries where physical and human capital is abundant. The expected signs of the factor endowment variables will thus depend on the type of product.

The equation to be estimated may be written as follows:

$$(5a) \qquad \log S_{ij} = \alpha_j + \beta_{1j}(\log KL_i) + \beta_{2j}(\log HC_i)$$
$$+ \beta_{3j}(\log ME_i) + \beta_{4j}(\log D_i)$$
$$+ \beta_{5j}(\log IN_i) + \gamma_j A_{ij},$$

where S_{ij} is the market share of country i in product j, KL is the physical capital/labor ratio in country i, HC is the human capital intensity, ME is total manufactured exports, D is the distance between country i and the United States, IN is the U.S. direct investment/GNP ratio in country i, and A_{ij} is the actual preference margin on product j for country i. This equation was estimated for a sample of fifteen products defined at the four-digit level of the SIC. These products were selected because they were identified from ex ante calculations by Baldwin and Murray (1977) and Bayard and Moore (1979) of the Department of Labor as having the largest expected GSP effects. For each product, the estimation was made on a sample of thirty-six countries (of which eighteen were GSP beneficiaries) for both 1975 and 1979.[29]

The estimation results indicate that model (5a) performs generally well. As appendix table 6.A.1 shows, the coefficients of the manufacturing exports and direct investment variables have the expected positive sign in all cases, and most are strongly significant. The coefficient for the distance variable is negative, as expected in most cases, but generally not significant. The coefficients for the measures of physical and human capital intensity show varying signs and are in most cases not significant. The explanatory value of the regression varies between .4 and .8.

As far as the preference margin variable is concerned, the results in the left panel of table 6.4 show a positive and significant coefficient in 1979 for

Table 6.4   Coefficient Estimates for the Preference Variables: Cross-Country Model

SIC Code	Description	Equation (5a): Share Levels[a]		Actual Preference Margin[b] (%)	Equation (6a): Share Changes[a] Preference Variables Included		
		1975	1979		A_{ij}	$A_{ij}S_{ij}^{75}$	$A_{ij}S_{ij}^{75}$
2435	Hardwood veneer and plywood	93.4	73.8	.95	−74.3	53.2	51.8
		(1.1)	(.9)		(−.7)	(5.0)	(5.0)
2436	Softwood veneer and plywood	37.0	36.8	13.30	.9	.2	8.3
		(2.0)	(1.9)		(1.3)	(.01)	(.4)
2599	Furniture and fixtures, nec.	48.9	66.6	6.88	−3.1	13.9	13.2
		(3.0)	(3.7)		(−.5)	(3.7)	(3.9)
3079	Misc. plastic products	60.3	55.7	4.47	−1.6	24.2	24.2
		(3.1)	(3.4)		(−.4)	(4.2)	(4.3)
3161	Luggage	139	69.3	.19	−1703	1227	745
		(1.2)	(.7)		(−6.5)	(9.1)	(4.3)
3573	Electronic computing equipment	144	81.3	.79	−21.4	−37.5	−55.1
		(2.8)	(3.1)		(−.3)	(−.4)	(−1.2)
3574	Accounting machines	151	113	2.10	−331	100	69.2
		(2.7)	(3.8)		(−.8)	(1.5)	(1.3)

SIC	Product						
3651	Radios and TVs	146 (2.7)	147 (2.7)	.64	−192 (−3.1)	39.2 (9.2)	33.9 (7.7)
3911	Jewelry, precious metal	16.5 (2.1)	31.4 (2.9)	9.07	−95.5 (−.9)	9.7 (.2)	−10.6 (−.3)
3914	Silverware	9.7 (1.1)	24.7 (2.5)	3.33	−9.3 (−.6)	13.9 (1.1)	13.5 (1.1)
3915	Jewelers' materials	−.87 (−.1)	−14.8 (−1.1)	.81	−99.1 (−1.6)	−2.5 (−.3)	−1.7 (−.2)
3942	Dolls	13.8 (.8)	23.7 (1.8)	7.93	28.2 (1.1)	.6 (.7)	.7 (1.0)
3944	Games and toys	10.8 (1.2)	25.8 (2.6)	8.72	2.8 (.2)	15.7 (6.9)	15.7 (7.0)
3949	Sporting goods, nec.	45.6 (2.1)	55.7 (3.2)	6.11	3.7 (.2)	21.8 (10.2)	21.9 (10.5)
3691	Costume jewelry	1.03 (.2)	12.3 (2.4)	15.66	3.5 (.5)	2.5 (2.2)	2.9 (3.3)

[a]The t-statistics appear in the parentheses.
[b]Average for all beneficiary countries.

twelve out of our fifteen products.[30] However, a closer examination of the estimates shows that only some of these twelve cases reveal a GSP effect, since in some cases the A_{ij} coefficient was also positive in 1975. For four products—silverware (3914), dolls (3942), games and toys (3944), and costume jewelry (3961)—the GSP coefficient increased substantially between 1975 and 1979, was not significantly different from zero in 1975, and became significantly positive in 1979. For furniture and fixtures (2599), jewelry, precious metal (3911), and sporting goods (3949), the coefficient also increased but was already significant in 1975. For those three products, the results indicate that the model omits an explanatory variable, the effect of which gives a bias to the A_{ij} coefficient. If the bias is assumed to be constant, the increase of the coefficient indicates a GSP effect. For the other products there is no indication of any GSP effect, since the γ coefficients did not increase.

The differences in the GSP effect among products seem to be associated with differences in average actual preference margins. The figures in the middle panel of table 6.4 indicate that, except for softwood veneer and plywood (2436), the products for which the preference coefficient has not increased at all were granted very low preference margins (1.42 percent on average). At the other end of the spectrum, the four products with the strongest GSP effects had preference margins averaging 8.91 percent.[31]

An alternative approach for the evaluation of GSP effects with the cross-country model is to estimate equation (6), which relates changes in U.S. market shares to the preference margins for our thirty-six supplying countries. The explanatory variables are different than those in equation (5a). We assume that the change in the market share of a country depends on its rate of increase of production capacity, measured here by the growth rate of GNP (GN_i), and on the rate of change of export prices (PX_i).[32] The higher the GNP growth and the lower the price increase, the more we expect the market share of a country to increase. Finally, as before, we allow for the possibility that changes in competitiveness of countries are linked to their relative endowments of physical and human capital (KL_i and HC_i).

For several reasons, one would not expect the GSP effect on a country's market share to be simply proportional to the preference margin. First, given demand and supply elasticities, the increase of the market share in percentage points will be greater, the higher the initial market share.[33] (There is obviously an upper limit to the possible increase.) Second, there may be a threshold effect; in the short period 1976–79, only the already established exporting countries, with already existing production and distribution capacity, may have been able to take advantage of the preference. Thus, the effect on countries whose initial shares were below a certain critical limit may have been virtually zero. We allow for these possibilities by including the preference variable A_{ij} in the regression, together with an interaction term $A_{ij}S_{ij}^{75}$ equal to the product of the preference margin and the initial share.

The regression equation for the change in market share 1975–79 is:

$$\text{(6a)} \qquad \Delta S_{ij} = a_j + b_{1j}\,\text{GN}_i + b_{2j}\,\text{PX}_i + c_{1j}\,\text{KL}_i$$
$$+ c_{2j}\,\text{HC}_i + d_{1j}A_{ij} + d_{2j}A_{ij}S_{ij}^{75}.$$

If the coefficient of $A_{ij}S_{ij}^{75}$ is zero and that of A_{ij} is positive, there is no threshold effect: whatever its initial share, every country benefits from the GSP. If the coefficient of $A_{ij}S_{ij}^{75}$ is positive and the coefficient of A_{ij} is negative, there is a threshold effect: only when S_{ij}^{75} is larger than $(-d_{1j}/d_{2j})$ does country i benefit from the GSP. A positive coefficient for both $A_{ij}S_{ij}^{75}$ and A_{ij} indicates that every country benefits from the GSP, but the extent of the gain for a particular country depends on its share of the U.S. market in 1975.

As shown in appendix table 6.A.2, model (6a) performs well for some products; for others, the explanatory value is low. In most cases the variables measuring capacity growth and export prices show the expected sign, but coefficients are mostly not significant. This is also true for the factor endowments variables.

The results for the coefficients of the preference margin variables are shown in the right panel of table 6.4 for two sets of regressions, the second of which includes only the interaction terms $A_{ij}S_{ij}^{75}$. Apparently this term captures most of the GSP effect; it is significantly positive for eight out of fifteen products, regardless of whether A_{ij} is present or not. For most of these eight products, the A_{ij} coefficient is not significant. For luggage (3161) and radios and TVs (3651), however, it is significantly negative. The calculated critical share levels for these two products is .14 and .49 percent, respectively.[34] For luggage, this means that only countries with at least .14 percent of the U.S. market in 1975 actually gained from the GSP. These countries were Hong Kong, Korea, Mexico, Philippines, and Taiwan. For radios and TVs, the actual gainers were countries already with at least .49 percent of the market in 1975, that is, Brazil, Hong Kong, Korea, Malyasia, Philippines, and Taiwan. These two products have enjoyed only very small preference margins. Among the other six products with a significant GSP effect on share changes, four also showed signs of a GSP effect based on the estimation of regressions on share levels. These four products (i.e., 2599, 3944, 3949, and 3961) enjoyed large preference margins ranging from 6.1 to 15.7 percent.

The Cross-Product Model

Another way of evaluating the effects of GSP is to use model (3), the cross-product model, to test whether the preference variable A_{ij} helps to explain the product composition of U.S. imports from a particular supplier or group of suppliers, that is, to explain interproduct differences in market shares.

Since physical and human capital can be assumed to be scarce factors in GSP beneficiary countries, we would expect the market share for these countries in a given year to be low for human- and physical-intensive products. Also, we would expect the market share to be high for products with a high preference margin.

The cross-product model could be expressed, alternatively, as determining the levels of market shares in different periods (eq. [7]), or as determining the changes of market shares from a base year to a year after the tariff changes (eq. [8]). In the latter case, the higher the preference granted for a product, the larger we expect the increase in GSP beneficiaries' market share to be. We have estimated both variants, for the market shares of imports from beneficiaries ($i = B$), nonbeneficiaries ($i = N$), and for total imports ($i = T$), for a sample of up to 208 products.[35] However, the regressions on share levels for 1975 and 1979 resulted in negative values for the coefficient of the preference variable for all three groups, including the beneficiaries' share in 1979.[36] The explanation is straightforward. First, MFN tariffs have distorted the composition of U.S. imports against products with high tariffs. Since the period 1975–79 is very short, full adjustment to the GSP has not taken place and this distortion still prevailed for beneficiary imports in 1979. Second, the preference margins (A_{ij}) are positively correlated with the MFN tariffs, that is, in absolute terms the larger the tariff, the larger the preference margin. The combination of these two factors produces the negative "effect."

For changes in market shares, we have estimated the equation:

$$(8a) \qquad \Delta S_{ij} = a_i' + c_{1i}' \, \text{KL}_j + c_{2i}' \, \text{HC}_j + d_{1i}' A_{Bj} + d_{2i}' \, (A_{Bj} S_{Bj}^{75}),$$

where ΔS_{ij} is the change of the market share for product j for country group i, KL_j and HC_j are the physical and human capital intensities of product j, A_{Bj} the weighted average of the individual beneficiaries' A_{ij}'s for product j, and S_{Bj}^{75} the initial market share of beneficiaries. That the factor intensity levels, and not the changes, enter the equations means that the model describes a process of adjustment of the actual trade structure to an equilibrium structure determined by comparative advantage. A change of the structure of U.S. imports from developing countries toward products intensive in unskilled labor would then be expressed in negative coefficients for KL and HC in the equation for beneficiaries' share. The justification for including the preference variable together with the interaction term is analogous to that regarding

Table 6.5   Coefficient Estimates for the Cross-Product Model (8a)

Country Group	Explanatory Variables				
	KL	HC	A_B	$A_B S_B^{75}$	R^2
Beneficiaries	−.38	−.39	−.29	11.08	.59
	(.3)[a]	(1.5)	(3.2)	(15.4)	
Nonbeneficiaries	.15	.60	−.29	2.07	.02
	(.1)	(1.1)	(1.5)	(1.3)	
Total	−.23	.22	−.59	13.15	.16
	(.1)	(.3)	(2.1)	(6.0)	

[a]The t-statistics appear in the parentheses.

equation (6a). The results from the estimation of equation (8a) with a sample of 208 products appear in table 6.5.

The coefficients of KL and HC have the expected signs but are generally not significant. The estimates of the preference coefficients indicate the presence of (net) trade creation as well as gross trade creation, since the increase in the market shares for total imports, as well as for imports from beneficiaries, tend to be higher, the higher the preference is. There is no clear sign of trade diversion, that is, the preference variable is not significant in the equation for nonbeneficiaries. However, the effect of GSP on the market share for these countries can easily be obtained, given the effect on imports from beneficiaries and on total imports. For all these country groups, there seems to exist a strictly positive critical share level. The beneficiaries equation indicates the presence of gross trade creation for all products for which S_B^{75} was greater than 2.6 percent. The equation for total imports indicates that U.S. producers lost market shares as a result of the GSP when S_B^{75} was greater than 4.5 percent.

6.4.3   Calculating the GSP Effect on U.S. Trade and Production

The results of the estimation of our regression equations for both the cross-country and the cross-product models indicate that the GSP appears to have had a statistically significant effect on U.S. trade. Of course, it is difficult to argue that we have managed to isolate entirely the GSP from other factors affecting market shares. Hence, our estimation results must be used with considerable caution. This should be especially the case when using the coefficients of the preference variables to compute the GSP effects.

As we have mentioned earlier, the coefficients from the cross-country equations are not really well suited for the calculation of the GSP effects because of the absence of "normal trade." In addition, a major problem with these equations is that A_{ij} is correlated with the level of economic development and therefore with country characteristics. Accordingly, the coefficient of this variable may tend to capture some of the effects of an increase in competitiveness for beneficiaries unrelated to preferences. In fact, an attempt to compute the GSP effects with the coefficients of equation (6a) gives, for some of our fifteen products, figures that are unreasonably high. Consequently, we limit ourselves to computations based on the cross-product equation (8a) where we have no reason to suspect a correlation between A_{ij} and product characteristics.

Using the results from table 6.5, we have computed the GSP effects reported in table 6.6.[37] Out of the 208 products in the sample, there were thirty-three for which we found a positive GTC effect. The total effect amounted to $930 million, of which 95 percent was accounted for by the top twenty products. Not surprisingly, ten of the fifteen products used in the cross-country regression because of their expected large GSP effects were found to have a positive GTC effect. In general our results indicate that trade creation is about two-and-one-half times larger than trade diversion.

For the sake of comparison, we have supplemented the results in table 6.6 with estimates of the GSP's trade creation effects based on the ex ante methods, using the formula

$$(9) \qquad \Delta M_{ij} = M_{ij} \, \eta_j \, [P_{ij}/(1 + t_j)],$$

where M_{ij} is the imports from beneficiary countries in 1979, η_j is the import demand elasticity, t_j the MFN tariff rate, and P_{ij} the preference margin.[38,39] Expression (9) has been calculated for all GSP beneficiaries and eligible products in two alternative fashions. In the first, we set P_{ij} equal to the MFN tariff t_j (i.e., the theoretical preference margin) as if no limitations affected GSP treatment. In the second alternative, we take into account the actual restrictive effects of the GSP rules by setting P_{ij} equal to the actual preference margin A_{ij} derived from equation (1).

The results of these computations, aggregated by product and by country, are shown in table 6.7 and 6.8, respectively. These figures represent the hypothetical decrease in imports that would have occurred in 1979 if preferences had been eliminated. They are purely indicative and should not be read literally.[40] Essentially, the products emerging here as having the largest effects from the GSP also show up in our ex post computations: games and toys, wood products, jewelry, sporting goods, and pottery products. For all GSP eligible products, expression (9) gives a total TC effect of $2.2 billion when the theoretical preference margin is used. On the other hand, the effect obtained by using the APM is $1.3 billion. The difference between these two figures is an estimate of the impact of GSP limitations on eligible products. As one would have expected, some of the products that have a very high TPM suffer heavily from these limitations. This is especially the case for toys and parts

(73795), sugar (15520), and rubber or plastic household articles (77215). Yet, on the whole, the top twenty products, with a ratio of APM to TPM of 63 percent, are less subject to limitations than the remaining eligible products, for which the equivalent ratio is barely 56 percent.

The figures in table 6.8 indicate a very high concentration of the TC effect in favor of Hong Kong, Korea, and Taiwan, which account for two-thirds of the total effect. Moreover, the top ten countries share 90 percent of this effect. As we have already seen (see table 6.2), GSP limitations affect individual suppliers to rather different degrees. For the leading trio, the average APM/TPM ratio is about 60 percent but with great variations between Hong Kong (36 percent) and Korea (71 percent). For the top ten countries, as well as for all the other beneficiaries, this ratio is roughly the same. Thus, somewhat surprisingly, competitive need limitations do not seem to discriminate against either the big exporters or countries with the largest gains from the GSP.

Given the effects of the GSP on U.S. imports of different products presented in the TC column in table 6.6, the effects on U.S. employment can be computed by assuming that increased imports replace domestic production on a dollar-for-dollar basis. This can be done by multiplying the figures in table 6.6 by the corresponding coefficients for labor requirements per million U.S. dollars of production for 1979. These calculations indicate that the direct effect of the GSP in those twenty industries that account for most of the trade effects amounts to a loss of 24,000 jobs. By using the coefficients of the U.S. input-output table, it is possible to also compute the indirect reduction in employment caused by the fall in demand for intermediate goods as a result of the GSP. The total (direct plus indirect) employment effect of the GSP is estimated to be a loss of 43,000 jobs. The biggest effects occur in the industries producing games and toys, dolls, and artificial flowers. In table 6.9 the employment effects have also been distributed by skill categories. The table shows that the employment of operative personnel is most affected.

The figures in table 6.9 cannot be interpreted as the net increase in unemployment in the United States caused by the GSP, nor the increase in total employment to be expected if the GSP were abolished. We would expect the GSP to result in an increase in employment in other parts of the economy, since increased imports from beneficiaries means an increase in demand for U.S. exports.

6.5 Policy Issues and Conclusions

In the previous section, we have attempted to identify the effects of the GSP on developing country exports to the United States and on U.S. production and employment for 1975–79. This type of exercise is complicated because so many factors influence trade besides tariffs. This has

Table 6.6   Effects of the GSP on Imports from Beneficiary Countries for 1979 ($ million) Estimates Derived from Cross-Product Regressions

TCSIC Code	1972 SIC Code	Description	GTC[a]	TC[b]	TD[c]	Imports from GSP Beneficiaries
3941	3944	Games and toys	90.9	58.8	32.1	416.5
3942	—[d]	Dolls	79.9	79.9	0.0[e]	163.3
3962	—	Feathers and artificial flowers	77.8	77.8	0.0[e]	109.9
3999	—	Manufacturers, nec.	76.0	57.3	18.7	408.2
2499	2492, 2499	Wood products, nec.	75.3	1.3	74.0	364.8
3961	—	Costume jewelry	74.7	54.9	19.8	103.0
3021	—	Rubber footwear	50.7	50.7	0.0[e]	722.1
3949	—	Sporting and athletic goods, nec.	50.4	19.9	30.5	327.0
3913	3915	Lapidary work	48.8	48.8	0.0[e]	711.4
3651	—	Radio and TV receiving sets	47.2	42.9	4.3	1,608.2
3269	—	Pottery products, nec.	40.5	24.5	16.0	89.5
2432	2435, 2436	Veneer and plywood	34.0	25.0	9.0	525.6
2911	—	Petroleum refining	30.1	16.6	13.5	4,536.8

3171	—	Women's handbags and purses	28.9	28.9	0.0[e]	256.2
3339	—	Primary nonferrous metals, nec.	24.8	24.8	0.0	1,038.6
2819	—	Industrial inorganic chemicals	12.7	0.0[f]	12.7	285.9
3662	—	Radio and TV communication equipment	12.0	0.0[f]	12.0	1,005.8
3699	—	Electrical equipment, nec.	11.6	9.3	2.3	102.3
3674	—	Semiconductors	10.4	10.4	0.0[e]	1,852.3
3943	3944	Children's vehicles	10.1	6.5	3.6	46.3
		All above products	886.8	638.3	248.5	
		All manufactured products	928.7	658.3	270.4	

[a]Calculated with equation (8a), for $i = B$.
[b]Calculated with equation (8a), for $i = N$.
[c]Calculated with equation (8a), for $i = T$.
[d]A line means that the SIC and TCSIC codes are identical.
[e]The estimated TD effect was negative and set equal to zero.
[f]The estimated TC effect was negative and set equal to zero.

Table 6.7   Effects of the GSP on Imports from Beneficiaries for 1979
                   ($ millions) Estimates Calculated from Equation (9)

TSUS Code	Description	Trade Creation APM	Trade Creation TPM	Imports from GSP Beneficiaries
53494	Chinaware	46.0	47.5	56.3
74038	Jewelry parts	40.7	57.0	70.1
72733	Wood chairs	33.9	34.5	83.0
73795	Toys and parts	37.7	143.8	256.5
73740	Toy animals	32.4	36.1	64.4
74010	Jewelry	29.6	52.3	131.1
72735	Furniture of wood	29.3	30.8	113.9
77215	Household articles of rubber/plastic	25.5	26.0	55.4
72755	Other furniture nes.	23.7	25.0	45.9
64897	Pipe tools, wrenches, etc.	23.2	23.5	62.3
77460	Articles of rubber/plastic nes.	18.6	62.2	133.4
69440	Airplanes	17.4	18.1	63.4
79115	Fur wearing apparel	17.2	17.5	51.0
67435	Machine tools	16.7	16.9	78.3
73499	Ski equipment	16.2	16.4	52.8
73415	Dice, chessmen, etc.	15.9	16.0	47.0
73454	Baseball gloves	15.6	19.1	38.9
73715	Construction kits	15.0	15.2	27.1
77142	Plastic films	14.9	25.2	44.7
15520	Sugar[a]	14.6	68.3	880.0
All above products		479.1	763.4	—
All GSP eligible products		1,291.3	2,218.2	—

[a]Since sugar is also protected by quotas, this import effect is not likely to be realized.

Table 6.8   Effects of the GSP on the Main Beneficiaries in 1979 ($ millions)
                   Estimates Calculated from Equation (9)

Country	Trade Creation APM	Trade Creation TPM	GSP Eligible Imports
Taiwan	454	655	2,526
Korea	212	299	1,151
Hong Kong	162	455	1,611
Mexico	83	262	1,927
Israel	75	78	299
Brazil	56	87	947
Yugoslavia	41	42	179
Singapore	40	66	372
Philippines	23	36	305
India	19	23	184
All above countries	1,165	2,003	9,501
All beneficiaries	1,291	2,218	11,725

Table 6.9   Effects of the GSP on U.S. Employment

TCSIC Code	Direct Effects — All Skill Groups	Direct Plus Indirect Effects						
		All Skill Groups	Professional, Management	Clerical, Sales	Craftsmen	Operatives	Labor, Service	Farmers
3941	2,181	4,198	683	806	694	1,652	347	12
3942	2,964	5,705	927	1,095	943	2,245	471	16
3962	3,439	6,045	941	1,245	934	2,427	412	93
3999	2,430	4,211	665	796	699	1,690	344	17
2499	52	90	12	11	14	39	14	0
3961	1,795	3,205	505	609	549	1,290	247	5
3021	2,672	3,985	563	624	532	1,891	360	15
3949	702	1,371	221	259	227	529	129	6
3913	1,596	2,851	449	542	488	1,147	220	5
3651	837	2,673	601	489	420	957	202	4
3269	1,864	1,920	230	233	228	1,024	203	2
2432	588	1,389	168	150	218	445	393	15
2911	68	322	78	78	56	66	42	2
3171	1,477	2,430	289	379	309	1,274	147	32
3339	419	915	154	168	186	297	107	3
2819	—	—	—	—	—	—	—	—
3662	—	—	—	—	—	—	—	—
3699	358	596	123	104	86	232	50	1
3674	375	621	138	107	79	250	46	1
3943	241	643	75	89	77	183	38	1
All above products	23,858	42,985	6,822	7,784	6,739	17,638	3,772	230

been especially the case during the seventies, when major disturbances have affected world trade on both the demand and supply sides. In particular, the acquisition of know-how by leading developing countries and their promotion of manufactured exports have resulted in increased international competitiveness, which has coincided with the operation of the GSP. For these reasons, and because it has been rather limited in scope, the effects of the GSP on the performance of developing countries in the U.S. market are difficult to evaluate.

By designing a methodology enabling us to investigate U.S. imports for individual countries and products, we have attempted to isolate the GSP from other determinants of trade. In our cross-country models, we can only claim partial success because our sample design is such that, in some cases, the GSP variable tends to reflect other factors besides tariff preferences. In this respect, we fared better with our cross-product models for which no such problem seems to arise.

Our cross-country regression results clearly indicate that the GSP program has affected trade flows for products enjoying large preference margins. The results of our cross-product regression also indicate the presence of positive GSP effects on imports from beneficiaries, but only in cases where these countries were already major suppliers before 1976. Our regression results indicate that a beneficiary country is more likely to gain from the GSP for a certain eligible product the larger both the preference margin *and* the share in the U.S. market that was already acquired prior to 1976. Obviously, this conclusion to a large extent reflects the fact that the period covered by our investigation is extremely short.

Using the results of our cross-product regressions to estimate the GSP effects, we obtain a gross trade creation effect of nearly $1 billion, which amounts to 15 percent of GSP duty-free imports and 2 percent of total imports from beneficiaries by the United States in 1979. Computations based on the traditional formula of ex ante studies, but using actual instead of theoretical preference margins, gave somewhat larger effects.[41] The trade creation effect, which according to economic theory will lead to an increase in economic welfare in the United States, is more than twice the amount of the trade diversion effect, which is welfare-reducing. Although the overall effects tend to be small, they are large for certain products. Moreover, the effects tend to be concentrated to a few products with high margins and large initial market shares for beneficiaries. Finally, the effects are unevenly distributed among beneficiary countries.

It is likely that the period 1975–79 was too short to allow for the emergence of the full effects of the GSP, in particular with respect to exports of new products by developing countries or new suppliers of more traditional items. In addition, uncertainties related to the functioning of the system have probably also restricted the increase of exports from beneficiaries. Indeed, the way competitive need limitations are designed, it is sometimes difficult to assess whether or when a particular supplier will lose its beneficiary status for a given product. For instance, of the forty-two TSUS items for which India lost this status from January 1976 through March 1983, the average period without preferences was three years, often not consecutive; only for three products did India not receive GSP treatment throughout the entire seven years.

Since March 1981, a system of "discretionary graduation" has added a new source of uncertainty. Under this additional limitation to the GSP scheme, every March the U.S. administration permanently removes certain countries from GSP eligibility on certain products in response to petitions filed by U.S. producers or labor unions. Removal decisions are based on a country's level of development, its competitiveness in a specific product, and the overall economic interests of the United States. So far, the top seven beneficiaries—Taiwan, Korea, Hong Kong, Mexico, Brazil, Singapore, and Israel—have, to varying degrees, been affected by discretionary graduation. For most products, these countries were already affected by competitive need limitations. Some U.S. importers have been complaining that the rules governing discretionary graduation are too vague and give rise to arbitrary decisions by the administration.

This new system is only one of several alternative graduation schemes being considered in the United States for phasing the dominant suppliers out of the GSP program. Other options include: changes in product coverage to eliminate additional import-sensitive products, changes in country coverage to exclude countries above a certain per capita GNP line, or changes in GSP limitations.

The first step in reviewing these alternative options is to specify the different and sometimes conflicting objectives of the U.S. GSP, as reflected in guidelines of the U.S. GSP which specify the need to consider the effect of preferences on the level of economic development of developing countries as well as on U.S. producers.

The GSP should promote exports and economic growth, in particular, for countries at the lowest level of development—measured, for instance, by the per capita income. In addition, an objective for U.S. trade policy in general presumably is to promote an efficient production structure by increased international division of labor. These objectives would call for a GSP designed to result in trade creation. On the other hand, from a protectionist perspective, the ideal GSP, that is, one that helps developing countries without hurting U.S. producers, would be a scheme that generates only trade diversion. The exclusion of certain products from the GSP clearly serves a purely protectionist purpose. These exclusions can be expected to be products with large imports and high comparative costs because of low requirements for human skills and technical knowledge. In this case, countries on the lowest level of development can be expected to suffer greatly from limited product coverage. On the other hand, competitive need limitations might, in principle, favor both U.S. producers and low-income developing countries at the expense of large and established developing country exporters. Whether, indeed, these limitations benefit the poorest developing countries needs to be examined. One measure of the impact of competitive need limitations on beneficiary countries is the ratio between the actual and theoretical preference margins reported in table 6.2, column (7). A system of limitations that benefits the poorest countries would imply a negative correlation between this ratio and an index of the level of development, like per capita GNP. From the figures in table 6.2, this does not seem to be the case.[42] Thus, one suspects that the main effect of competitive need limitations has been to protect U.S. producers rather than redistribute the benefits of the GSP to the least developed countries.

Graduation could be viewed as a new instrument aimed at helping the poorest developing countries benefit from the GSP. However, the targeting of the largest (rather than the richest) beneficiaries seems to indicate that, for the moment, graduation is simply another manifestation of protectionism.[43] Yet it is legitimate for graduation to go hand in hand with the concept of preferences. What is needed is for instruments like competitive need limitations or graduation to be clearly aimed at clearly stated objectives.

Granted that the objectives of the GSP are to promote industrialization in the developing countries (especially the poorest ones) and the international division of labor according to comparative advantage—subject to a relatively smooth adjustment of U.S. producers: How should a desirable GSP program be designed? To our mind, such a program should be comprised of three elements. First, its product coverage should be widened as much as possible to include those products where the least developed countries are likely to be most competitive. Second, competitive need limitations should be connected to the level or the rate of increase of import penetration in general, not to exports from individual countries; also, they could be linked to an injury test. Finally, graduation should become a rule and be based on the stage of development (measured, for instance, by the per capita income) rather than on the size of exports. The innovative aspect of this package is the trade-off between graduation and wider product coverage.

So far only a limited number of products and countries have actually been affected by the GSP. This is the result of both the short time and the limited scope of its operation. The modesty of its success is also related to the complexity of the scheme which has recently increased with the introduction of graduation. The forthcoming review of the GSP by Congress will decide on its future shape and especially on the future of graduation. It is hoped that this paper will contribute to a better understanding of the GSP and help in making future choices.

Appendix

1. Tariff preferences are granted to GSP-eligible products defined at the five-digit level of the tariff schedule of the United States (TSUS). For each of these products a yearly computer tape available from the Office of the U.S. Trade Representative (USTR) provides data on total imports, imports from all nonbeneficiaries, imports from each beneficiary country distinguishing between duty-free and MFN (i.e., GSP-excluded) trade, and the ad valorem MFN tariff rate. These data were used to construct table 6.2.

2. In addition to the above data, the ex ante computation underlying table 6.7 and 6.8 also required estimates of import demand elasticities. These were generously provided by Robert Baldwin for all products defined at the four-digit level of the 1967 Input-Output (I-O) industry classification. Import demand elasticities for five-digit TSUS products were derived by matching the I-O and TSUS classifications.

3. Ex post computations required first the construction of the shares of imports in U.S. apparent consumption, where apparent consumption is defined as the sum of domestic production and imports minus exports. This was done for all products defined at the four-digit level of the 1972 Standard Industrial Classification (SIC).

4. To approximate the GSP product coverage, we restricted ourselves to manufactured products, that is, SIC codes 2011 through 3999, and excluded the following items:
2011–2099, food and kindred products;
2111–2141, tobacco manufactures;
2211–2299, textile mill products;
2311–2399, apparel and other textile products;
3131–3149, footwear and footwear cut stock;
    3211, flat glass; and
    3873, watches.

5. The figures in table 6.3 were computed using four-digit SIC data.

6. In addition to market share data, the cross-country equations of section 6.4.2 required country characteristics. These were obtained as follows:
    a. Data on the physical capital/labor ratio (KL) and human capital (HC) were generously provided by Bela Balassa. The beneficiary

countries (eighteen in all) included in the regressions are: Argentina, Brazil, Hong Kong, India, Israel, Korea, Malaysia, Mexico, Morocco, Pakistan, Philippines, Portugal, Singapore, Taiwan, Thailand, Tunisia, Turkey, and Yugoslavia; the nonbeneficiary

Table 6.A.1 t-Values for the Coefficients of Equation (5a) Estimated for 1979

SIC Code[a]	Explanatory Variables						
	KL	HC	ME	D	IN	A	R^2
2435	−.62	−.34	2.51	.70	2.68	.88	.41
2436	.30	−.70	1.60	−1.57	1.38	1.85	.43
2599	.44	1.06	4.45	−1.27	1.69	3.67	.67
3079	.80	.43	5.62	−.89	3.46	3.41	.76
3161	−2.37	.98	4.14	−1.97	.25	.70	.50
3573	−1.18	.51	6.48	−2.22	3.69	3.09	.81
3574	−.91	−.12	7.13	−2.19	2.68	3.80	.82
3651	.10	−1.94	3.71	−.69	3.83	2.72	.53
3911	.80	−.45	3.83	.58	2.23	2.89	.55
3914	−1.22	.29	5.71	−.83	.95	2.50	.61
3915	−1.58	−.54	3.65	.25	1.13	−1.12	.45
3942	−1.87	1.40	3.84	−1.02	1.59	1.76	.55
3944	−1.33	1.53	5.36	−.49	1.53	2.60	.67
3949	.10	.93	4.84	−.40	1.00	3.16	.68
3961	−.32	−.63	4.45	.41	3.12	2.41	.57

[a]For the description of the products, see table 6.4.

Table 6.A.2 t-Values for the Coefficients of Equation (6a) Estimated for 1975–79

SIC Code[a]	Explanatory Variables					
	GN	PX	KL	HC	AS	R^2
2435	.42	−.16	1.17	−.92	5.04	.50
2436	−1.12	−.87	−.75	1.35	.45	.14
2599	−.08	.77	−.44	−.04	3.88	.45
3079	.60	−.16	1.17	.94	4.26	.47
3161	.98	−.41	.68	−.46	4.34	.54
3573	1.19	−.76	−.33	1.67	−1.16	.16
3574	1.11	−.84	−.27	1.78	1.25	.22
3651	.42	−1.12	−.12	−.09	7.71	.75
3911	−.21	−.14	−.01	−.07	−.25	.01
3914	4.35	−.94	−.72	.86	1.12	.44
3915	−.97	−.37	−.36	−.77	−.17	.10
3942	4.75	−.95	−.36	.76	.96	.55
3944	.64	−.81	−1.26	1.18	7.02	.75
3949	2.43	−.23	1.99	−.65	10.47	.87
3961	3.83	−.85	1.37	−.16	3.31	.66

[a]For the description of the products, see table 6.4.

countries included (also eighteen) are: Australia, Austria, Belgium-Luxemburg, Canada, Denmark, Finland, France, Germany, Greece, Ireland, Italy, Japan, Netherlands, Norway, Spain, Sweden, Switzerland, and United Kingdom.

b. Data on manufactured exports (ME) were derived from International Monetary Fund (IMF), *International Financial Statistics*, and the World Bank, *World Development Report*.

c. The ratio of U.S. investment to GNP (IN) was derived from U.S. Department of Commerce, *Selected Data on U.S. Direct Investment Abroad 1950–76*, 1982.

d. Data on sea distances (*D*) were taken from U.S. Naval Oceanographic Office, *Distance Between Ports*, 1965.

e. The relative price variable (PX) was constructed with data from IMF, *International Financial Statistics* as

$$PX = (WPI^{79}/WPI^{75})/(EX^{79}/EX^{75}),$$

where WPI is the wholesale price index and EX the dollar exchange rate.

7. Actual preference margins (*A*) for each beneficiary country and each product were computed on the basis of duty collected and custom values for seven-digit TSUS products. The aggregation to four-digit SIC products and to countries was made over MFN dutiable trade only.

8. The cross-product equations of section 6.4.2 required industry characteristics. These were taken from the U.S. International Trade Commission's data bank which uses its own industry classification called TCSIC. This classification is closely related to the 1967 SIC. We had to aggregate our four-digit 1972 SIC market share and preference data into the four-digit TCSIC. This was done with a concordance developed in great part by Steve Parker.

9. Most of the trade and production data described in this appendix belong to the data base developed at the University of Wisconsin-Madison with financial support from the U.S. Department of Labor.

Notes

1. For further details about the origin of preferences see UNCTAD (1979, chap. 1) and Murray (1977, chap 1).

2. See U.S. Congress (1967, 79).

3. The EEC GSP which originally was also granted for ten years has already been renewed for another ten years.

4. The operation of the GSP during its first five years is reviewed in U.S. Congress (1980).

5. The last three conditions may be waived if the president determines that doing so is in the national economic interest of the United States.

6. Hence, the developing countries which are nonbeneficiaries of the U.S. GSP are: China and the other communist countries, except Romania and Yugoslavia; the OPEC members, except Ecuador, Indonesia, and Venezuela which were designated as beneficiaries effective 30 March 1980; Greece and Spain which grant preferences to the EEC (Portugal became a beneficiary on 1 October 1976, following its decision to reduce preferences for EEC countries on products of interest to the United States); a few countries which have expropriated U.S.-owned property without compensation (P.D.R. of Yemen, Uganda up to 30 March 1980, and Ethiopia since that date).

7. The GSP schemes of the other major industrialized countries contain similar dispositions.

8. Section 503 does not specify which electonric, steel, and glass articles are import sensitive. The precise determination is made by the president in consultation with various parties on the basis of the probable economic effects of GSP treatment on domestic producers of similar products.

9. See Office of the U.S. Trade Representative (1981, 64–70; 1982, 1).

10. The U.S. GSP contains provisions of cumulative origin for beneficiary countries which are members of designated regional economic associations.

11. This argument is developed by Murray (1977, 89–92).

12. This limitation does not apply to eighty-three products which the Trade Policy Staff Committee considers as not being produced in the United States. For their list, see Office of the U.S. Trade Representative (1981).

13. A de minimis provision effective since 30 March 1980 allows the president to waive this limitation in cases where total U.S. imports of a product does not exceed a certain dollar value to be adjusted annually ($1 million for 1980).

14. This value has grown from $26.6 million for 1976 to $50.9 million for 1982.

15. The date for implementing annual competitive need exclusions and changes in the GSP product list was changed from sixty to ninety days after the end of the calendar year starting in 1980.

16. Obviously the only imports of eligible products actually receiving GSP treatment are those for which preferences are requested and rules of origin are fulfilled. Also, it should be noted that during a calendar year (from January 1 through December 31) some imports would be duty-free and some at the MFN rate if a change in GSP treatment occurred on 30 March.

17. Of the $30.6 billion excluded due to country restrictions, over 90 percent came from OPEC countries. Since the MFN duty on oil is very low, the loss of preferences from these restrictions is not very important.

18. For surveys of methods and results, see Verdoorn and Van Bochove (1974), Sellekaerts (1973), Corden (1975), and Baldwin (1983).

19. For the remaining imports, the preference margin is actually equal to zero.

20. Note that although the TPM for a given product is the same across all GSP beneficiaries, the APM varies across countries.

21. See, for instance, EFTA (1972).

22. Examples of the former category are Leamer (1974) and Sapir and Lutz (1981); examples of the latter are Baldwin (1979) and Branson and Monoyios (1977).

23. Obviously, A_{ij} is equal to zero when either i is a nonbeneficiary country or j is not a GSP-eligible product.

24. This point is made by McCulloch and Pinera (1977).

25. For the definition of manufactures used throughout this section, see the appendix.

26. This is calculated for all four-digit SIC industries as the increase in the share of imports from GSP countries of consumption, minus the loss (if any) of market share of nonbeneficiary countries.

27. The formula used to calculate the trend-adjusted increase in market shares in the period 1975–1979 is

$$dS^* = S_{79} - [4(S_{75} - S_{72})/3 + S_{75}],$$

where S_{79} is the 1979 market share, and the expression in brackets is the projected share in 1979 obtained by extrapolating the 1972–1975 trend. In those cases where dS^* exceeds the actual change dS, the trend-adjusted value is set equal to dS. If dS^* is negative, the adjusted value is set equal to zero.

28. The variables used in the equations are described in greater detail in the appendix.

29. Their list is given in the appendix.

30. The three products with nonsignificant coefficients are 2435 (hardwood veneer and plywood), 3161 (luggage), and 3915 (jewelers' materials).

31. The other three products showing some GSP effects—(2599) furniture and fixtures, (3911) jewelry, precious metal, and (3949) sporting goods—had an average margin of 7.35 percent.

32. To measure growth of supply capacity we used the rate of growth of real GDP instead of growth of manufacturing exports (ME in the previous model), since the latter could not be obtained in constant prices. We assume that a high rate of increase of export prices, PX, results in a fall in the market share. (The definition of PX is given in the appendix). A price index variable would be meaningless for the share level equation.

33. Let η be the import-demand elasticity and ϵ the export-supply elasticity. For a given level of consumption, the market share change is proportional to the product of the preference and the initial share:

$$\Delta S_{ij} = \left(\frac{\epsilon\eta}{\epsilon - \eta}\right) S_{ij}\left(\frac{\Delta t_{ij}}{1 + t_i}\right),$$

where Δt is the preference and t the MFN tariff rate.

34. The critical share value (times 1,000) S_{ij}^{75} is the solution to the equation

$$\hat{a}_{1j} + \hat{a}_{2j}S_{ij}^{75} = 0,$$

where $\hat{a}_{1j}$ and $\hat{a}_{2j}$ are the estimated regression coefficients.

35. As we indicate in the appendix, the products used in these equations are defined at the four-digit level of the TCSIC. The characteristics were not available for all products, hence the sample size varied according to the variables included in the model.

36. The estimation results for equation (7a) are not reported here for lack of space.

37. These were computed as $\hat{a}_{1i}A_{Bj} + \hat{a}_{2i}(A_{Bj}S_{Bj}^{75})$.

38. For the various assumptions underlying the use of this formula see, for instance, Baldwin and Murray (1977).

39. Since we are primarily interested in the effects of the GSP on U.S. production, we disregard the trade diversion. In any event, its computation required data not readily available.

40. This latter problem could have been avoided if we had, instead, based our computations on trade figures for 1975, that is, the last year before the introduction of the GSP. However, we prefer our procedure because it does provide an estimate of the value of the GSP in 1979 which accounts for the autonomous growth of U.S. imports from beneficiary countries between 1975 and 1979.

41. Part of the reason for this is that the ex ante computations cover all products instead of manufactures alone. In addition, as indicated in note 40, they tend to overestimate the effects.

42. A similar finding was made by Weston et al. (1980) for the EEC GSP.

43. For an interesting discussion of the effects of graduation on the least developed countries, see U.S. Department of Labor (1979).

References

Baldwin, R. E. 1979. Determinants of trade and foreign investment: Further evidence. *Review of Economics and Statistics* 61:40–48.

————. 1984. Trade policies in developed countries. In *Handbook of international economics*, vol. 1, ed. R. W. Jones and P. B. Kenen. North-Holland.

Baldwin, R. E., and T. Murray. 1977. MFN tariff reductions and developing country trade benefits under the GSP. *Economic Journal* 87:30–46.

Bayard, T., and M. Moore. 1979. Trade and employment effects of the U.S. Generalized System of Preferences. Office of Foreign Economic Research, U.S. Department of Labor, Washington, D.C. Mimeo.

Branson, W. H., and N. Monoyios. 1977. Factor inputs in U.S. trade. *Journal of International Economics* 7:111–31.

Corden, W. M. 1975. The costs and consequences of protection: A survey of empirical work. In *International trade and finance: Frontiers for research*, ed. P. B. Kenen. Cambridge: Cambridge University Press.

European Free Trade Association. 1972. *The trade effects of EFTA and the EEC 1959–1967*. Geneva: EFTA.

Leamer, E. E. 1974. The commodity composition of international trade in manufactures: An empirical analysis. *Oxford Economic Paper* 26:350–74.

McCulloch, R., and J. Pinera. 1977. Trade as aid: The political economy of tariff preferences for developing countries. *American Economic Review* 67:959–67.

Murray, T. 1977. *Trade preferences for developing countries*. New York: John Wiley.

Office of the U.S. Trade Representative. 1981. *A guide to the U.S. Generalized System of Preferences* (GSP). Washington, D.C.

Office of the U.S. Trade Representative. 1982. Annual GSP changes. Washington, D.C. Mimeo.

Sapir, A. 1981. Trade benefits under the EEC Generalized System of Preferences. *European Economic Review* 15:339–55.

Sapir, A., and E. Lutz. 1981. *Trade in services: Economic determinants and development-related issues*. World Bank Staff Working Paper no. 480. Washington, D.C.

Sellekaerts, W. 1973. How meaningful are empirical studies on trade creation and diversion? *Weltwirtschaftliches Archiv* 109:519–53.

United Nations Conference on Trade and Development. 1979. *Comprehensive review of the Generalized System of Preferences*. Document TD/B/C.5/63. Geneva.

U.S. Congress. 1967. *The future of United States foreign trade policy.* Hearings before the Subcommittee on Foreign Economic Policy of the Joint Economic Committee. 90th Cong., 1st sess., vol. 1. Washington, D.C.: GPO.

————. 1980. *Report to the Congress on the first five years' operation of the U.S. Generalized System of Preferences (GSP).* Committee on Ways and Means, U.S. House of Representatives. 96th Cong., 2d sess. Washington, D.C.: GPO.

U.S. Department of Labor. 1979. LDC graduation: The Generalized System of Preferences (GSP). Washington, D.C. Mimeo.

Verdoorn, P. J., and C. A. Van Bochove. 1972. Measuring integration effects: A survey. *European Economic Review* 3:337–49.

Weston, A., et al. 1980. *The EEC's Generalized System of Preferences.* London: Overseas Development Institute.

Comment   Tracy Murray

The paper by Sapir and Lundberg empirically examines the U.S. program of tariff preferences in favor of developing countries. Their objective is to quantify the effects of the U.S. Generalized System of Preferences (GSP) on (1) developing country exports to the United States and the distribution of such exports across products and across countries, and (2) U.S. production and employment of competing products in total and by sector. Noting that the authorizing legislation for the U.S. GSP automatically terminates the program in January 1985 and that Congress is likely to incorporate a number of modifications in a renewed program, the authors also analyze the effects of selected modifications on developing country exports and U.S. production and employment.

A casual reading of the paper is sufficient to convince any reader that the authors have done a careful and professional job of empirically examining a very complicated trade policy. Though the rigorous critic might be somewhat uncomfortable with their results, I find they meet the very important test of "reasonableness." I find no surprises in their results that (1) U.S. imports under the GSP program were stimulated by roughly 15 percent,[1] (2) that GSP benefits are heavily concentrated by product and by beneficiary developing country, and (3) that the adverse effects on U.S. production and employment are minimal.

Given my general agreement with the empirical results and given that the focus of this conference is on trade policy, I have nothing more to say

Tracy Murray is professor of international economics and business at the University of Arkansas.

about the impact of the GSP as it is currently structured. I am more interested in the alternative modifications that are likely to be incorporated into a renewed GSP, the political process of which is already under way.

The major issues of controversy would include the following:

- the list of beneficiary developing countries and the extent to which reciprocal concessions might be required by the United States;
- the list of eligible products and the extent to which the poorer developing countries can benefit from a GSP program that excludes import-sensitive (generally labor-intensive) products;
- the desire to achieve a more equitable distribution of GSP benefits across the developing countries than currently occurs, given the competitive need criteria and the discretionary graduation policy;
- the desire to safeguard U.S. producers and workers in those isolated cases in which GSP trade might be unduly burdensome; and
- the problem of how to improve the administration of the GSP, especially the annual reviews resulting in modifications in the GSP due to the competitive need criteria and the more ad hoc alterations due to graduation, product review, etc.

The authors examine several of these issues and are able to provide one very important insight. In particular, the competitive need criteria have not operated to promote GSP trade for the poorer beneficiaries at the expense of the more advanced beneficiaries, that is, it has not contributed to a more equitable sharing of GSP benefits across developing countries. Instead the effect of the competitive need system is to benefit U.S. production at the expense of the impacted beneficiaries (more advanced and less advanced). Unfortunately, the empirical results of the paper do not lend themselves to broader application regarding the issues of concern.

Nevertheless, the authors' examinations of the GSP (of the United States and of other donor countries) enable them to suggest answers to some of the questions raised above. They suggest "a desirable GSP program . . . should be comprised of three elements." First, expand the product coverage as much as possible to benefit the poorer beneficiaries. Second, since the competitive need criteria are not a benefit-sharing technique they should become safeguard measures based on import penetration and linked to an injury test: Third, graduation should be based on the stage of development rather than produce-specific export performance. I find these three elements to be inadequate to deal with the political realities surrounding the GSP.

In the first place, a renewal of the GSP is not a foregone conclusion. There is substantial political opposition to any GSP program involving a broad product coverage and a broad beneficiary list. So long as the more advanced developing countries are included in the GSP, the product coverage will be severely limited to the point that the least developed will benefit minimally, if at all. For example, Belize in Central America exports three types of goods—sugar (which is included in the GSP but subject to import quotas), citrus fruit juice, and roughly $5 million in textiles and apparel (mostly men's and boys' garments). Belize cannot and will not benefit from the U.S. GSP unless textiles and apparel are included; this situation is common among a large number of the poorer developing countries. And even if the top ten exporting beneficiaries (such as China-Taiwan, Hong Kong, Korea, Mexico, Brazil, etc.) were "graduated" from the GSP, a number of middle and lower income beneficiaries (such as India) have substantial capacities to export labor-intensive products to the point of displacing domestic production and employment. Thus, there will have to be political compromises if the GSP is to be renewed. And if the U.S. GSP were not renewed, U.S. relations with the third world, to say nothing about the other GSP-granting countries, would deteriorate dramatically. In fact, it should be recognized that the GSP is not really a trade policy at all but instead a policy to promote U.S. relations with developing countries, especially those in Latin America and the Caribbean.

A second point that should be emphasized is that the various aspects of the GSP are highly interdependent. As indicated above, a broad product coverage is inconsistent with a long beneficiary list. It is literally impossible to design a straightforward GSP that equitably benefits all developing countries without adversely affecting U.S. producers and workers. Given this interdependence, I believe that even an "ideal" GSP must be significantly more complicated than the authors suggest and must incorporate political as well as economic considerations.

At the risk of sticking my foot in my mouth, I will venture to suggest that an "ideal" GSP program contains the following elements:

1. To maximize the foreign policy benefits, the beneficiary list should be broad and in line with those of the other GSP-granting countries. The United States should not solicit bilateral reciprocal concessions or attempt to coerce special behavior as a price for beneficiary status. The GSP benefits are not of sufficient importance to obtain large concessions from individual developing countries; small concessions are not worth the ill-will that would be generated.

2. The product list should be as broad as possible, taking into consideration the general beneficiary list and domestic producers and workers interests, that is, roughly as it is today. This, of course, poses a problem for the lower-income beneficiaries that simply cannot produce the manufactured products covered by the current GSP program. There are two approaches to this problem. One is to ignore it and recognize that any

trade policy will benefit some countries more than others; the goal of an equitable distribution of benefits across developing countries is literally an impossible dream.

A second approach would be to include in the authorizing legislation a provision for the selective inclusion of products of export interest to the least developed. Such a provision would be consistent with the international agreement on the desirability of special measures in favor of the least developed among the developing countries. To safeguard the interests of the least developed as well as domestic producers and workers, the more competitive beneficiaries could be immediately denied GSP treatment on these products under a product-graduation provision (see below).

3. As reported by Sapir and Lundberg, the competitive need limitations do not increase the GSP benefits of the poorer beneficiaries (though their *share* may increase by reducing total GSP trade). Also as pointed out, the competitive need limitations are ill-designed to safeguard domestic producers and workers. Thus, the concept should be discontinued.

Politically, however, I suspect that some mechanism to *graduate* the more competitive beneficiaries will be included. The idea of graduation is that as a country develops it becomes more competitive. Eventually the country reaches a point that preferences are no longer justified. Finally, the country progresses to the point that it should join with the other more-developed countries and assist the less-advanced countries. The problem with administering graduation is that economic development is gradual and uneven. A country may be internationally competitive in some sectors and not in others; it may be competitive in the early stages of processing but not in the more advanced stages; it may be competitive in nontechnical standardized products but not in the more sophisticated products. Because of these complications, it would be literally impossible to establish objective criteria for the graduation of countries. Therefore, any attempts to graduate a country from the beneficiary group to the nonbeneficiary group would be arbitrary—and, in all likelihood, political. There would undoubtedly be cases in which a particular beneficiary country would be graduated when other more advanced countries continued to enjoy GSP treatment; some countries would be graduated from one or more of the GSP programs but not from others.

A more logical, fair, and pragmatic approach would be to graduate countries gradually as their economies become more internationally competitive, that is, countries should be graduated product by product, where products are defined by stage of processing as is commonly (though imperfectly) done in the Tariff Schedules of the United States. Establishing general objective graduation criteria is admittedly quite difficult. Some products require a larger scale of operation to be competitive than others. And even more obvious, a predetermined share of the U.S.

import market is irrelevant in determining international competitiveness. The faults of the current competitive need criteria for graduation are obvious; however, I defy anyone to come up with rigorously justifiable criteria that can be made operational.

To establish objective graduation criteria, a pragmatic compromise will have to be the answer. My suggestion is to make the criteria as simple as possible; that is, adopt a single-value limit. Though I do not know what the value should be, to be politically acceptable to the beneficiaries, I suggest that it be set at a level such that initial graduation (in aggregate value) be no larger than the current trade denied GSP treatment because of the competitive need criteria.

Finally, the graduation value limit should be completely separated from any safeguard mechanism designed to protect the interests of domestic producers and workers. It may be desirable to establish a special graduation concept for products that might be selected for inclusion in the GSP to benefit the least-developed countries (see item 2. above).

4. There should be an objective safeguard mechanism to protect the interests of domestic producers and workers. In designing such a provision it must be noted that the elimination of GSP treatment will remedy import injury only in those cases in which GSP duty-free trade has significantly contributed to the injury in the first place. General import injury (i.e., caused by non-GSP imports) cannot be remedied by terminating GSP treatment; general import-relief action is needed. The responsibility for administering such a safeguard could be assigned to the U.S. International Trade Commission (ITC) since the problem is similar to the import-relief provisions of the Trade Act of 1974. To facilitate a prompt remedy when warranted, a temporary termination of GSP treatment could be established on the basis of preliminary findings, as under the countervailing duty provisions of the Trade Agreement Act of 1979.

5. The annual administrative review to add products, delete products, announce the competitive need product-country list, implement discretionary graduation (and nonredesignation of competitive need items), etc., are more trouble than they are worth. Instead simply announce the cases of graduation based on objective criteria and any GSP safeguard actions recommended by the U.S. ITC (which would occur as conditions warrant). Arbitrary modifications in the program should not be made on an annual basis. Periodic reviews of the operation of the U.S. GSP could be made, say, every five years. If warranted, discretionary changes could be made at that time.

Some of these suggestions go beyond the scope of the paper under discussion, especially those involving political considerations. Nevertheless, I believe these suggestions are not drastically different from what the authors would propose, though we might disagree somewhat on individual points. More importantly, however, the results of this paper do provide policymakers with important pieces of information that are relevant to several issues that must be dealt with in establishing a new GSP. Thus, we must conclude that this paper does accomplish much of what the authors set out to do.

Notes

1. Baldwin and Murray (1977) estimated the GSP to stimulate trade by 25 percent using an ex ante technique and pre-GSP trade flows; Murray (1980) found an 18 percent impact during 1974–77 using an ex post method.

References

Baldwin, Robert E., and Tracy Murray. 1977. MFN tariff reductions and developing country trade benefits under the GSP. *Economic Journal* 87 (March):30–46.

Murray, Tracy. 1980. Evaluation of the trade benefits under the United States scheme of generalized preferences. Study published by the United Nations Conference on Trade and Development (UNCTAD) as document TD/B/C.5/66, 20 February.

7 The U.S. Strategic Petroleum Reserve: An Analytic Framework

Jonathan Eaton and Zvi Eckstein

7.1 Introduction

The U.S. government pursues a number of policies affecting imports of oil. An excise tax is imposed on sales of gasoline, and the U.S. government maintains "strategic reserves" of oil in salt domes. There has been discussion of imposing a tariff on oil both to raise revenue and to improve the U.S. terms of trade.

Oil presents U.S. policymakers with a situation that is unusual in three respects. First, in most areas where a protectionist policy has been pursued by the government, the motivation has been primarily domestic, to maintain output and employment levels in different regions and sectors. The second-best nature of tariffs and quotas for these purposes is well known. In contrast, many of the existing and proposed policies toward oil have been justified partly on optimal tariff grounds; the United States is a large importer whose level of imports affects the world price. From a national perspective, restricting imports is a first-best policy. Indeed, the current level of protection may be too low.

Second, oil is an exhaustible resource. Imports in any period affect in an essential way not only the international price today but the world equilibrium in all future periods. The static framework of most trade-theoretic tariff analysis is inappropriate.

Third, the strategic behavior on the part of agents other than the U.S. government is important for the effects of policy. For one thing, the Organization of Petroleum Exporting Countries (OPEC) constitutes a

Jonathan Eaton is professor of economics at the University of Virginia, and a research associate of the National Bureau of Economic Research. Zvi Eckstein is assistant professor of economics at Yale University.

The authors are grateful to Robert Baldwin, Lars Svensson, and Brian Wright for useful comments and discussions on a previous version of this paper.

large supplier. For another, U.S. policies affect the storage and extraction behavior of private agents in the domestic and world economies. The interactions of these groups must be taken into account. Again, a static framework assuming that all agents except the U.S. government are atomistic is inappropriate.

These three considerations make an analysis of optimal commercial policy in terms of traditional trade models difficult. Before an analysis of the welfare effects of the U.S. Strategic Petroleum Reserve (SPR) can be attempted, an analytic framework identifying its effects on U.S. welfare must be specified. Our purpose here is to develop such an analytic framework. The model we develop does not incorporate all aspects of the SPR that we believe to be important. Nevertheless, it suggests a set of considerations that necessarily arise in a strategic setting between a large importing country and a monopolistic supplier.

The remainder of the introduction provides a discussion of the background of the U.S. Strategic Petroleum Reserve and an outline of our analysis.

7.1.1 Background

The current pattern of general public concern about energy supplies is in sharp contrast to the prevailing pattern before 1973. In the early years after World War II, the United States was essentially self-sufficient with respect to crude oil supplies. Concern, largely by members of the petroleum industry, was focused not on problems of shortage but on price effects of abundance. As a result, the U.S. government imposed an oil imports quota in 1959 of 9 percent of the estimated domestic demand. However, imports gradually increased over time and reached approximately 23 percent of total domestic demand by 1972. In May 1973 import quotas were discontinued and a license fee system was substituted. The fee system soon became superfluous, however, with the subsequent quadrupling of world oil prices (Bohi and Russell 1978, 7, 230–35). Despite the quota, considerable excess capacity for crude oil production developed during the sixties, and regulatory federal and state agencies distributed production allocations to the various producers of crude petroleum. The real price of oil was continuously dropping during the sixties until October 1973.

Government storage of oil began in the United States in 1909 with the creation of the Naval Petroleum Reserves which serve exclusively the needs of the U.S. defense forces. As a result of the increase in oil imports to the United States and the Arab oil embargo in 1973–74, there were calls for government storage of petroleum to be held out of ground, available in the short run in relatively large amounts (Glatt 1982, 7–8). In 1973 President Nixon established Project Independence with the purpose of achieving domestic energy self-sufficiency. In the following year the

International Energy Agency (IEA) of oil consuming countries in the OECD established the International Energy Program (IEP). Participants in the program pledged to establish reserves equal to sixty days consumption (to increase to ninety days in 1980). These reserves were to include private storage (which at that time was sufficient to meet the requirements in all the participating countries). The Strategic Petroleum Reserves (SPR) program was established under the Energy Policy and Conservation Act (EPCA) of 1975 as the U.S. component of the IEA program.[1]

The EPCA is a broad piece of legislation designed to "increase domestic energy supplies and availability: to restrain energy demand (and) to prepare for energy emergencies" (Glatt 1982, 9). The act contains a detailed outline for the operation of the SPR. It explicitly claims that "the storage of petroleum products will diminish the vulnerability of the United States to the effects of a severe energy supply interruption and will provide limited protection from the short-term consequences in supplies of petroleum products." A somewhat different purpose of the SPR was suggested by Senator Henry Jackson, who was a strong supporter of the SPR: ". . . with a Strategic Petroleum Reserve, we will have greater credibility, as I see it, in dealing with this problem (oil prices), and we'll help to stabilize the price situation, which otherwise could be one of great havoc."[2]

The EPCA determined that the SPR could contain as many as 1 billion barrels but should have no less than 500 million barrels. It also required the establishment of Industrial Petroleum Reserves by the oil industry and Regional Petroleum Reserves. The Federal Energy Administration (FEA) was given control over the SPR.

Since 1977 oil has been stored at five underground salt domes and salt mine sites in Louisiana and Texas. Purchases of oil proceeded at a rate of 21 thousand barrels per day during 1977 and 162 thousand barrels per day during 1978 (see table 7.1).

In late 1978, however, as a consequence of tight oil market conditions associated with the Iranian crisis, the Carter administration postponed purchases of oil for the stockpile. At that time seven stockpiling nations agreed to curtail stockpiling acquisitions if such acquisition would "result in any pressure on the world oil market" (Glatt 1982, 22–23). Consequently, purchases fell to a daily rate of 67 thousand barrels in 1979 and 44 thousand barrels in 1980. In 1980, however, oil market conditions slackened and purchases resumed. In that year Congress passed the Energy Security Act which required that the president acquire reserves at a minimum rate of 100 thousand barrels per day (Glatt 1982, 11). In fact, during 1981 and 1982 the average acquisition rate has far exceeded that minimum. An issue for the management of the stockpile is whether acquisitions (or drawdowns) should respond to world oil market condi-

Table 7.1   Average Crude Petroleum Production, Petroleum Consumption and End of Year Petroleum Stocks[a]

	Thousands of Barrels per Day							Millions of Barrels (stocks)		
	Total World Production	World Minus USSR and China Production	OPEC Production	US Production	US Con-sumption	IEA[b] Con-sumption (inc. US)	SPR[c]	US (inc. SPR)	SPR	OECD[d] (inc. US)
1973	55748	46193	30989	8208	17308	34150	—	1008	—	NA
1974	55910	45595	30729	8774	16653	32960	—	1074	—	NA
1975	52552	41837	27155	8375	16322	31870	—	1133	—	NA
1976	57405	45592	30738	8132	17461	33770	—	1112	—	NA
1977	59795	47239	31278	8245	18431	34930	21	1312	7	3152
1978	60165	46898	29805	8707	18847	35880	162	1278	67	3089
1979	62698	49116	30928	8552	18513	35900	67	1341	91	3358
1980	59452	45568	26890	8597	17056	33000	44	1392	108	3566
1981	55710	41885	22665	8572	16058	31400	256	1484	230	3537
1982 (March)	51800	37980	18415	8597	15560	31600	182	1401	249	NA

SOURCE: U.S. Department of Energy, *Monthly Energy Review*, September 1982.

[a]Petroleum stocks include crude oil, unfinished oils, natural gas plant liquids, and refined products.

[b]The International Energy Agency includes twenty-one member nations (see details in the *Monthly Energy Review*).

[c]Strategic Petroleum Reserves.

[d]Organization for Economic Cooperation and Development.

tions (as the IEA agreement would suggest) or proceed independently of world market conditions (as implied to some extent by the Energy Security Act of 1980). Our analysis explores this issue.

As of March 1982 the reserves contained 250 million barrels of crude oil, while the current plan is to place 750 million barrels of oil in storage by the end of 1989. Since 1975 several studies have analyzed the ideal size of the SPR. They all try to determine the level of reserves that could maintain the rate of consumption in a period of disruption at the rate in "normal" years. The recommended size varies from 500 to 1000 million barrels (Glatt 1982, 41).

The storage facilities in the salt domes and mines have created several technical problems, including the possibility that the crude petroleum could not be pumped out of storage. It seems, however, that most of these technical issues are now resolved. Since only crude petroleum is stored in the SPR, several different types of crude oil must be stored to provide for different oil by-products.

An important and difficult question for the FEA to consider is the definition of supply interruption that triggers drawdowns from the SPR. An integral issue is the size of the drawdown and the distribution of the reserves in a case of supply interruption. These issues, as well as the decision to establish the SPR in the first place, require an understanding of the rationale and the objectives of the SPR.

The U.S. oil industry requires about 1 billion barrels of crude oil as minimum operating stocks, which equals about sixty days of petroleum consumption. The current goal of the SPR would almost double the days of consumption from the U.S. stock (table 7.1). The United States is a large consumer of oil; it consumes about 36–40 percent of world oil production (excluding the USSR and China). OPEC produces about 50–55 percent of the world production (excluding the USSR and China). As such, we suggest the view that the world oil market consists of one large producer (OPEC) and one large consumer (the United States) is a reasonable first approximation. However, the effect of other (small) producers and consumers as well as the large local production of oil in the United States (about 60 percent of current U.S. consumption) should be considered in extensions of this paper.

7.1.2 Outline and Summary

In section 7.2 we develop a simple two-period model of an oil importing country (the United States) and an oil exporter (OPEC). In section 7.3 we examine the competitive equilibrium of this model. We show that under certainty and in the presence of a full set of contingent commodity markets there is no role for inventories, not to mention government inventories, of any form since there are costs of holding inventories. Introducing a "convenience yield" on inventories, on the basis of their use in facilitating production, provides a justification for holdings of inventories on the part of the private sector. In the absence of production externalities, however, there is no reason for the government to hold inventories. Introducing uncertainty by itself does not provide an argument in favor of U.S. private inventories. Uncertainty combined with the absence of full contingent commodity markets or U.S. property rights in OPEC does imply a role for inventories as a form of portfolio diversification on the part of the United States. Private agents, however, have an incentive to hold inventories at the level that maximizes expected U.S. national welfare. In the absence of externalities, then, we can find no argument in favor of U.S. government inventories when all agents, including the government, behave competitively.

Eckstein and Eichenbaum (1982) show that when oil suppliers are competitive and U.S. imports have an effect on oil prices, an optimal, time consistent tariff policy exists for the United States. However, there is no role for government inventories. Eckstein and Eichenbaum conjectured that if there is a case for government inventories it should stem from strategic considerations arising from the fact that oil prices decrease as U.S. inventories rise.

In section 7.4 we turn to a strategic setting in which the U.S. government and OPEC both have the potential to exercise market power. Imposing the optimal tariff each period (the strategy considered by Eckstein and Eichenbaum 1982) provides the first-best means for the government to exploit its market power. However, unless the government sets its tariffs *before* OPEC establishes its price each period, the government has no incentive to set a tariff at the ex ante optimal level at the time it makes its tariff decision.

In the absence of equity investment by OPEC in the United States the ex post optimal tariff is in fact zero. If OPEC has invested in U.S. equity, however, the optimal ex post tariff is positive as long as oil and capital are complements in production. The tariff acts indirectly as a tax on OPEC's capital income. In anticipation of the tariff, OPEC sets a lower price in the second period. OPEC reduces its price so much that the U.S. price is actually lower despite the tariff. In addition, equity investment by OPEC acts *directly* to reduce OPEC's second period price. The reason is that OPEC takes into account the effect of its pricing decision on the rate of return on its investment in the United States. When capital and oil are substitutes, a higher oil price means a lower return. There are thus two channels whereby a high level of equity investment by OPEC in the United States acts to reduce the second period price of oil. Nevertheless, even when equity holdings are positive, the government would increase U.S. welfare if it could credibly impose the tariff that is optimal from an ex ante perspective.

In this context inventories can act as a second-best substitute for a tariff. The government can reduce the period 2 price by buying inventories in period 1 and selling them in period 2. In section 7.4 we show how, given the period 1 price, the government has an incentive to buy inventories in period 1 and to sell them in period 2 in order to lower the period 2 price. No atomistic private agent has an incentive to pursue this policy since he would take the second period price as given. Whether the government's ex post optimal inventory response actually raises U.S. welfare vis-à-vis the no inventory situation cannot be ascertained in general. In fact it could go either way.

Nichols and Zeckhauser (1977) show how, in the framework we consider here (in the absence of taxes or investment of any form), an inventory policy can raise U.S. welfare as well as OPEC's. An inventory policy reduces the distortion resulting from OPEC's monopoly power. The United States and OPEC share the gain. We present their example in section 7.5. We find, however, that their result is very sensitive to their specification of the problem. We show in another example that if OPEC's utility function is logarithmic rather than linear in each period's consumption, a U.S. inventory policy *lowers* U.S. welfare relative to a no inventory situation. A lower U.S. welfare is also obtained when OPEC and the government set price and inventory simultaneously rather than with OPEC acting as a Stackelberg leader. In each case the positive impact of the anticipation of a U.S. inventory on the first period price more than offsets its negative impact on second period price. When the government chooses inventories, the period 1 price is a bygone so that the government nevertheless has an incentive to set inventories at a positive level. In this case the government's capacity to acquire a stockpile actually reduces U.S. welfare.[3] These results imply that if a government inventory policy is to raise U.S. welfare, inventory purchases must respond to OPEC's prices, that is, OPEC must act as a Stackelberg leader in setting price each period. Another example shows that when the government acts as a Stackelberg leader in setting inventories, the optimal level is zero.

Section 7.6 contains a discussion of some other work that considers the desirability of government inventories. Here we discuss papers by Maskin and Newbery (1978), Wright and Williams (1982), and Tolley and Wilman (1977). Finally, section 7.7 contains some concluding remarks.

7.2   The Model

In this section we describe the main features of the model considered in this paper. Our focus is on bilateral trade in an exhaustible resource, oil, that together with capital enters into production of a single consumed good. There are two nations: the oil consuming country—USA; and the oil supplying country—OPEC. The extraction costs of oil are zero and there is no depreciation of capital. Furthermore, the consumption good is only produced in the USA.

There are two periods of consumption and production in the model. If the consumption good is stored in the first period it serves as capital in the second period. OPEC can invest some of its oil revenues in the first period in the USA and receive the interest payments in the second period.

The definitions of the variables in the model are as follows:

C_i = consumption in the USA in period $i = 1, 2$.

C_i^* = consumption in OPEC in period $i = 1, 2$.

K_i = capital stock in the USA in period $i = 1, 2$, (K_1 is given as an initial condition).

$\Delta K = K_2 - K_1$ = investment in capital in the USA in the first period.

O_i = consumption of oil in the USA in period $i = 1, 2$.

I = inventories of oil in the USA at the end of the first period.

M_i = imports of oil in the USA in period $i = 1, 2$.

θ_i = one plus the import tax rate on oil in the USA in period $i = 1, 2$.

θ_k = one plus the tax rate on foreign investment in the USA in period 2.

P_i = international price of oil in terms of the single consumption good in period $i = 1, 2$.

r = interest payments on capital investment in the USA in the second period.

R^* = stock of oil in OPEC at the beginning of the first period.

$Q_i = F(K_i, O_i)$ = output of the consumption good in the USA in period $i = 1, 2$. $F(\cdot, \cdot)$ is strictly concave in both arguments.

H = OPEC investment in the USA in period one.

$D(I)$ = Units of oil available in the second period given an inventory of I units of oil in the first period. For all $I > 0, 0 \le D(I) \le I, D'(I) > 0$. $I - D(I)$ equals the carrying costs of oil inventories.

Preferences of the representative consumer/producer in the USA and OPEC are given, respectively, by

$$U(C_1, C_2) = U(C_1) + \beta U(C_2), \quad U^*(C_1^*, C_2^*) = U^*(C_1^*) + \beta^* U^*(C_2^*),$$

where $U(\cdot)$ and $U^*(\cdot)$ are strictly concave, and β and β^* are between zero and one. Obviously, one may consider a much more complicated model in which, for example, the total reserves of oil in OPEC, R^*, are uncertain, the USA also has an exhaustible stock of oil, extraction of oil is costly, there are third countries, and the like. We later consider some extensions along these lines, but prefer first to present out model in its simplest form.

While this framework *is* very simple, we believe that it captures the essential relationships between the United States and the oil producing countries. First, it recognizes, although in a simple way, that the supply of oil depends fundamentally on the *intertemporal* allocation of resources. Second, OPEC countries do receive a large share of their consumption goods from the OECD countries. Third, many OPEC countries have substantial investments in OECD countries. Our model allows their oil pricing decisions to affect their return on these investments.

We shall use the model first to consider the competitive allocation of resources in the absence of government intervention. In particular, we wish to determine if there is a case for the government to hold inventories of oil in a competitive, perfect foresight world. The "second-best" arguments in favor of the SPR are not considered, since we do not want here to justify one policy instrument because of the misuse of another policy instrument.

7.3   The Competitive Case

The perfect foresight, optimal allocation can be characterized by solving the "social planning" problem of the above economy. It is straightforward to show that this allocation is identical to the world competitive, perfect foresight equilibrium.[4]

The social planning problem is to maximize

$$(1) \qquad \delta_1[U(C_1) + \beta U(C_2)] + \delta_2[U^*(C_1^*) + \beta^* U^*(C_2^*)],$$

subject to

$$(2) \qquad C_1 + C_1^* + \Delta K \leq F(K_1, O_1),$$

$$(3) \qquad C_2 + C_2^* \leq F(K_1 + \Delta K, O_2),$$

$$(4) \qquad O_1 + O_2 + I - D(I) \leq R^*, \delta_1 \geq 0, \delta_2 \geq 0;$$

by choice of C_1, C_2, C_1^*, C_2^*, ΔK, O_1, O_2, and I. Let λ_1, λ_2, and μ be the Lagrangian multipliers of equations (2), (3), and (4), respectively. Equations (2) and (3) are the world budget constraints each period. Equation (4) states that world oil consumption across the two periods cannot exceed the total supply, $\bar{R}$. Then, the first-order condition with respect to inventories is

$$(5) \qquad -\mu[1 - D'(I)] \leq 0 \qquad (= 0 \text{ if } I > 0).$$

Given that $\mu > 0$, since we assume an economy in which oil is consumed each period, equation (5) implies that $I = 0$ if $0 < D'(I) < 1$. Given our assumption that oil does not appreciate in storage, we conclude that in a perfect foresight equilibrium there will be *no* storage of oil. The reason is that the economy is better off holding the oil in the ground with zero inventory costs than above the ground incurring the cost $I - D(I)$. It is also obvious that the inclusion of linear extraction costs does not affect the above result.

It is of interest to see the characterization of the competitive equilibrium resulting from the above planning solution. Given that P_i is the real price of oil in period $i = 1, 2$, we get that $P_i \equiv (\mu/\lambda_i) = F_2(K_i, O_i), i = 1, 2$, from the first-order conditions with respect to O_i. Then, the equilibrium is characterized by the conditions

$$(6) \qquad \frac{U'(C_1)}{\beta U'(C_2)} = \frac{U^{*\prime}(C_1^*)}{\beta^* U^{*\prime}(C_2^*)} = \frac{P_2}{P_1},$$

and

$$(7) \qquad \frac{P_2}{P_1} = F_1(K_2, O_2) \equiv r.$$

Equation (6) establishes that the marginal rate of substitution is equal to the marginal rate of transformation in both the USA and OPEC, and equation (7) is simply the Hotelling rule for extraction of an exhaustible resource.[5]

7.3.1   Convenience Yield

We next consider the private storage of oil. Private stocks of crude petroleum in the United States are in fact as large as the level of monthly sales (about 300–350 million barrels) and their existence should be explained. These inventories, termed "operating stocks" by the industry, facilitate the process of getting oil to consumers. In economic terms the argument for operating stocks is called the "convenience yield" (see Brennan 1958). It can be modeled analytically using ad hoc functional forms of the costs of holding inventories. These typically yield an inventory rule that is a function of oil consumption or output production (see, e.g., Eckstein and Eichenbaum 1982). Usually it is assumed that for an inventory below some given level, say I^*, there are *negative* marginal costs of inventories where the level I^* is given exogenously. We could introduce a convenience yield into our example by considering a storage technology, $D(I)$, that has the properties $D(I) > I, D''(I) < 0$ over some range $I < \bar{I}$. The competitive solution would then establish

$$(8) \qquad P_2 D'(I) = P_1 r,$$

as the first-order condition for a maximum. Equation (6) and (7) would continue to characterize the optimum. Thus the competitive solution would be fully characterized by the conditions

$$(9) \qquad \frac{U'(C_1)}{\beta U'(C_2)} = \frac{U^{*\prime}(C_1^*)}{\beta^* U^{*\prime}(C_2^*)} = F_1(K_2, O_2)$$

$$= \frac{r}{D'(I)} = \frac{P_2}{P_1}$$

The first three of these conditions would also characterize the planner's solution. If $D(I)$ is increasing and differentiable, the solution establishes $D'(I^*) = 1$ both for the social planner and for the competitive equilibrium. The "convenience yield" argument thus justifies private operating stocks but not any government SPR.

7.3.2 Uncertainty

Another popular reason for private and possibly public inventories is given by the existence of uncertainty about the oil supply or proven oil reserves. The argument is based on precautionary savings to smooth final consumption. In the presence of a full set of contingent commodity markets, this argument seems without merit. Private agents could optimally insure by trading contingent claims. If storage is costly (i.e., if $D(I) < I$), then an allocation (supportable by a competitive equilibrium) without storage exists which is Pareto superior to any allocation with storage. This result would not extend to a situation in which extraction costs are nonlinear, however.

It is possible that a full set of contingent claim markets does not exist. However, a more fundamental problem might be the nonexistence of property rights in an international context. Private agents in the USA cannot obtain property rights over oil that is in the ground in OPEC. Americans may be prohibited from acquiring these rights or else they may not trust OPEC governments' willingness to enforce these rights. In this context an additional argument for storing oil emerges: as a form of insurance.

We illustrate this result in the competitive model by assuming that the total stock of OPEC reserves, R^*, is not known until period 2.[6] We assume there *are* no contingent commodity markets or futures markets. (In fact, there are no formal contingent markets, and futures markets are limited, none covering a period greater than one year.) All oil is sold on spot markets. The second period price, then, is established by equating second period supply, $[R^*(s) - O_1 - I + D(I)]$, where $R^*(s)$ denotes the oil supply in state of nature, s, to second period demand, O_2, determined by the condition

$$(10) \qquad F_2(K_1 + \Delta K, O_2) = P_2.$$

This condition implicitly defines a demand function

$$(11) \qquad O_2 = E(K_1 + \Delta K, P_2),$$

which is increasing in $K_1 + \Delta K$ and decreasing in P_2. Equilibrium price in state s is then established by the condition

(12) $R^*(s) - O_1 - I + D(I) = E[K_1 + \Delta K, P_2(s)]$.

The interest payment on investment is given by

(13) $F_1[K_1 + \Delta K, O_2(s)] = r(s)$.

Consider now the inventory decision of a USA agent in period 1. He chooses ΔK, I, and O_1, taking P_1, H, and $r(s)$ as given, to maximize:

(14) $U[F(K_1, O_1) - \Delta K + H - P_1(O_1 + I)]$
$+ \beta \sum_s \Pi(s) U\{F[K_1 + \Delta K, E(K_1 + \Delta K, P_2(s))] - r(s) H$
$- P_2(s)[E(K_1 + \Delta K, P_2(s)) - D(I)]\}$.

Here $\Pi(s)$ denotes the probability with which $R^* = R(s)$. The first-order conditions for ΔK and I are

(15a) $U'(C_1) \geq \beta \sum_s \Pi(s) U'(C_2) r(s)$ $(= 0 \text{ if } \Delta K > 0)$.

(15b) $P_1 U'(C_1) \leq \beta \sum_s \Pi(s) U'(C_2) P_2(s) D'(I)$ $(= 0 \text{ if } I > 0)$.

If ΔK and I are strictly positive, these conditions imply

(16) $\sum_s \Pi(s) U'(C_2) r(s) = \sum_s \Pi(s) U'(C_2) \dfrac{P_2(s)}{P_1} D'(I)$.

The OPEC first-order conditions with respect to H and M_1 yield that

(17) $\sum_s \Pi(s) U^{*\prime}(C_2^*) r(s) = \sum_s \Pi(s) U^{*\prime}(C_2^*) \dfrac{P_2(s)}{P_1}$,

if H and M_2 are positive. Under certainty, equation (16) is inconsistent with (17), which yields the Hotelling rule, $(P_2/P_1) = r$, since $D'(I) < 1$ (see [9]; and the left-hand side of [16] is greater than the right-hand side). Hence, under certainty, $I = 0$. Under uncertainty, when $U(C_i)$ is concave, then both (16) and (17) can hold as equalities. Hence, there are equilibria in which I is positive. The reason is that under uncertainty $U'(C_2)$ and $P_2(s)$ are positively correlated when $D(I) = 0$. Via Shephard's lemma

(18) $\dfrac{dU'(C_2)}{dP_2} = - U''(C_2) [O_2 - D(I)]$.

The diminishing marginal utility of consumption implies that this expression is positive (assuming that some oil is imported in period 2). Thus when $P_2(s)$ is high, $U'(C_2)$ will also be high: for oil importers, a high price of oil lowers consumption, raising the marginal utility of consumption.

The positive correlation between $U'(C_2)$ and $P_2(s)$ raises the term on the right-hand side of equation (16). The *expected return* on inventories is greater because inventories serve as a hedge. This provides a justification for holding inventories.

Two comments about this result are in order. First, if USA agents could buy oil in the futures market or obtain property rights over oil in the ground in OPEC, inventories would not be desirable as long as $D(I) < I$. Second, this result by itself does not justify the establishment of a *government* reserve unless the government has a superior storage technology (i.e., for the government $D(I)$ is larger).

The simplest competitive case thus yields no justification for inventories at all. A convenience yield, however, or uncertainty with an incomplete set of contingent commodity markets and imperfect cross-national property rights are reasons why oil stocks may benefit the USA. In these cases the private sector holds a level of inventories that maximizes social welfare as well. Therefore, one may still wonder what scope there is for *government* holdings of inventories. Next, we find that once strategic considerations in the relationship between OPEC and the USA are introduced, an argument for a *government* SPR emerges. An argument can also emerge, however, in favor of divesting the government of its capacity to store oil.

7.4 The Bilateral Monopoly Case: A Possible Justification for the SPR

The presence of national market power frequently yields situations in which government intervention can improve national welfare if not world welfare. The nationally optimal tariff is an example.

In fact, in 1978 OPEC provided 65 percent of production in noncommunist countries while the United States accounted for 55 percent of consumption in main consuming countries.[7] There is certainly a presumption of market power on the part of OPEC to the extent that it can maintain its cohesiveness as a cartel. We assume here that it can. There seems to be a presumption of market power on the USA's part as well, although this is less strong. If we were to consider a potential oil-*importing* country cartel consisting of the OECD or the International Energy Agency (IEA), the assumption of a bilateral monopoly situation between sellers and buyers would certainly fit the facts closely. Even in the absence of a cartel arrangement among importers, the assumption of bilateral monopoly seems to capture much of the relationship between OPEC and the USA.

In this section we consider how the presence of a bilateral monopoly situation can create an incentive on the part of the government to establish an SPR. To focus clearly on strategic considerations, we ignore the convenience yield and uncertainty considerations raised earlier. In the next section we show, via example, that by pursuing an inventory policy the government can raise USA welfare. But it can also lower it. Because results are, in general, sensitive to the specification of behavior, we find it useful to discuss alternative "rules of the game" that we can choose among.

7.4.1   Rules of the Game

We now consider alternative rules of behavior in relationships between the USA and OPEC. We identify as OPEC's strategy variables the oil prices (P_1, P_2) and OPEC's level of investment in the USA (H). The USA's strategy variables are the tariff rates on oil in periods 1 and 2 $(\theta_1 - 1$ and $\theta_2 - 1)$, the tax rate on OPEC's investments $(\theta_k - 1)$, and the level of government inventory holdings (I^g). USA private agents, behaving atomistically, choose oil consumption in periods 1 and 2, (O_1, O_2), investment (ΔK), and private inventories (I^p) to maximize discounted utility. We assume that USA private agents correctly anticipate the policies that are actually pursued both by OPEC and by the USA but then take them parametrically.

Open Loop Policies

An open loop policy is one in which values of the strategy variables are set for the current and future periods as of the initial period. Within the class of open loop policies we can identify strategic variables that are chosen by one player prior to the choice of some other strategic variable by the other player (in which case the first player acts as a *Stackelberg leader* with respect to those variables, the first player taking into account the effect of his choice on the response of the second player), or the decisions are made simultaneously by the two players (in which case they act as *noncooperative Nash players* with respect to those variables, each taking the level set by the other player as given in making his choice).

When the game is specified as open loop, the issue of time consistency does not arise. The levels of the strategic variables set in the first period (whether in a Nash or Stackelberg fashion) are the ones actually implemented. A difficulty with this formulation is that the players may not have an incentive, in the second period, to follow the open loop solution. Because of this inconsistency, the open loop policy will not be credible. Open loop solutions therefore may not be able to explain the behavior that we observe. Nevertheless, the open loop solution provides an interesting benchmark against which to compare time-consistent solutions.

Feedback Solutions and Perfect Equilibria

An alternative policy is one that maximizes the objectives of each player as of the period the policy is implemented, taking previous policy as given. The two players thus play a separate game each period. The policies that are pursued each period are the outcome of *that period's* game. Hence, the players' decisions are based on feedback from the previous period. When players correctly take into account the effect of each period's decision on the outcome of subsequent games, then the solution to the set of games is described as "perfect." (See Selten 1975 for a discussion of perfection and Kydland 1977 for a discussion of the distinction between open loop and feedback solutions.) The advantage of a specification of this type is that the emerging solution is based on behavior that is in each player's interest at the time he acts.

Within the class of feedback solutions, we can also distinguish between variables that are chosen in a Nash or Stackelberg fashion. This choice should be dictated by the underlying technology of the problem.

We do not consider all possibilities for structuring the game. We assume the following rules:

R1(a): OPEC acts as a Stackelberg leader each period with respect to price (i.e., OPEC chooses P_1 before USA chooses O_1 and I^g; OPEC chooses P_2 before USA chooses θ_2 and θ_k).

R1(b): OPEC and USA act as Nash players with respect to P_1, θ_1, and I^g in period 1, and with respect to P_2, θ_2, and θ_k in period 2.

R1(c): USA acts as a Stackelberg leader each period (i.e., USA chooses θ_1 and I^g before OPEC chooses P_1, USA chooses θ_2 and θ_k before OPEC chooses P_2).

R2:   USA private agents take the values of USA and OPEC strategic variables as parametric. Subject to these parameters they maximize utility.

R3:   Both OPEC and USA correctly anticipate the effect of their policy on USA private agents' behavior.

R4:   All agents have perfect foresight.

Rule 1(a) best captures the strategy implicit in the IEA's stockpiling procedures: purchases are made contingent upon the oil price that OPEC sets. Rules 1(b) and 1(c) reflect more accurately the stockpiling procedure embodied in the Energy Security Act: purchases proceed independently of OPEC's price.

7.4.2 The Solution

We now attempt to characterize the solution to the game. Since first period decisions affect outcomes in both periods while, in the second period, first period decisions and outcomes are a bygone, it is simplest to consider the second period first.

The Second Period

Profit-maximizing firms in the USA private sector choose O_2 to maximize profits. Given the USA domestic price, $\theta_2 P_2$, this behavior implies the first-order condition

(19) $F_2(K_1 + \Delta K, O_2) \leq \theta_2 P_2$ $(= 0 \text{ if } O_2 > 0)$,

which implicitly defines the second period oil demand function

(20) $O_2 = E(\theta_2 P_2, K_1 + \Delta K)$,

where $E_1 < 0$, $E_2 \lesseqgtr 0$, as oil and capital are substitutes or complements. In the case of constant returns to scale (CRS) in capital and oil this function takes the form:

(20′) $O_2 = e(\theta_2 P_2)(K_1 + \Delta K)$.

Substituting (20) into (19) gives second period output as a function of the capital stock and the second period oil price:

(21) $G(K_1 + \Delta K, \theta_2 P_2)$, $G_1 > 0$, $G_2 < 0$.

In the case of CRS, this function takes the form:[8]

(21′) $g(\theta_2 P_2)(K_1 + \Delta K)$.

OPEC's investment in the USA pays an interest rate r equal, before tax, to the marginal product of capital

$$G_1(K_1 + \Delta K, \theta_2 P_2)[= g\ (\theta_2 P_2) \text{ under CRS}].$$

We assume that USA's objective is to maximize the utility of USA private agents. In period 2, first period consumption is, of course, a bygone, and the policy in period 2 can only affect period 2 consumption. The USA therefore maximizes $U(C_2)$ where

(22) $C_2 = G(K_1 + \Delta K, \theta_2 P_2) - \theta_k G_1 H$
$$- P_2[E(\theta_2 P_2, K_1 + \Delta K) - D(I^g) - D(I^P)].$$

Under rules R1(a) and R1(b), government policy involves choices of θ_2 and θ_k that maximize C_2 taking P_2, as well as ΔK, I^g, and O_1, as given. C_2 is strictly decreasing in θ_k, and a maximum, therefore, involves establishing θ_k at its minimum level (zero), effectively confiscating OPEC investments. When $\theta_k = 0$, the first-order condition for a maximum with respect to θ_2 is given by

(23) $F_2 - P_2 = 0$,

which is satisfied at $\theta_2 = 1$, the zero tariff condition. Since the USA acts taking P_2 as given, the optimal tariff is zero.

An interesting case emerges when USA is constrained to set $\theta_k > 0$, that is, not to confiscate fully OPEC investment. In this case the first-order condition for θ_2 is

(24) $F_2 = P_2 + \theta_k F_{12}\ H$.

Thus, if capital and oil are complements ($F_{12} > 0$) then the tariff on oil should be positive (raising F_2 above P_2), and conversely if they are substitutes ($F_{12} < 0$). Intuitively, the tariff acts as an indirect tax on OPEC investments.[9] If the USA is constrained not to tax these investments fully, then a tariff redistributes income away from OPEC to the USA. In the CRS case, the formula for the optimal tariff is given by

$$(25) \qquad t^* = \frac{\theta_k H}{K + \Delta K - \theta_k H},$$

in which case the tariff is independent of P_2. When there is no OPEC investment in equity or when $\theta_k = 0$ (confiscation of OPEC equity) the optimal tariff is zero.

Consider, now, OPEC's problem. In period 2 OPEC sets P_2 to maximize the utility of OPEC's period 2 consumption. As with the USA, period 1 consumption is at this point a bygone. OPEC therefore sets P_2 to maximize period 2 utility, $U^*(C_2^*)$, where

$$(26) \qquad C_2^* = P_2[O_2 - D(I^g) - D(I^P)] + \theta_k G_1 H.$$

Under rule R1(a), OPEC considers the effect of P_2 on θ_2. The first-order condition with respect to P_2 is given by:

$$(27) \qquad O_2 - D(I^g) - D(I^P) + (P_2 + \theta_k G_{12} H)$$

$$\frac{dO_2}{d(\theta_2 P_2)} (\theta_2 + \frac{d\theta_2}{dP_2} P_2) = 0,$$

subject to the constraint

$$O_2 - D(I^g) - D(I^P) \le R^* - M_1.$$

Dividing (27) by O_2 yields

$$(27') \qquad 1 - \frac{D(I^g) + D(I^P)}{O_2} - \lambda(\theta_2 P_2)(1 + \zeta)$$

$$\left(1 + \frac{\theta_k F_{12} H}{P_2}\right) = 0,$$

where

$$\lambda(\theta_2 P_2) \equiv \frac{dO_2}{d(\theta_2 P_2)} \frac{(\theta_2 P_2)}{O_2},$$

the elasticity of USA oil demand with respect to the USA price ($\theta_2 P_2$), and

$$\zeta = \frac{d\theta_2}{dP_2} \frac{P_2}{\theta_2},$$

the elasticity of the USA tariff with respect to P_2. Note that under CRS, $\zeta = 0$; the USA tariff is independent of P_2.

Condition (27') implicitly defines P_2 as a function of I^g, I^P, θ_2, θ_k, and H. The most important point to note is that the P_2 solving (27') falls as I^g and I^P rise as a share of O_2. In addition, when $H = 0$, P_2 falls as θ_2 rises to maintain a constant domestic price. If $H > 0$ and $G_{12} > 0$ (oil and capital are complements), an increase in θ_2 causes P_2 to fall in greater proportion, lowering not only the world price but the domestic price as well.[10]

This completes the characterization of second-period equilibrium under rule R1(a), with OPEC acting as a Stackelberg leader in setting P_2. When the level of θ_2 implied by equation (24) is independent of P_2, as in the case under CRS, then the solution under rule R1(b), with OPEC and USA acting as Nash players, is exactly the same as under rule R1(a). Under rule R1(c), with the USA acting as a Stackelberg leader in setting θ_2, the USA can impose the traditional optimal tariff. From equation (27'), $\theta_2 P_2$ stays constant or falls as θ_2 rises, if $G_{12} H \geq 0$. In this case the optimal tariff rate is infinite. Introducing extraction costs or other buyers would modify this result, but the point is that the USA can exert its monopsony power via tariffs only if it is able to commit itself to a tariff rate before OPEC sets P_2.

The First Period

Taking the solutions to the second period choice variables, θ_2 and P_2, as given depending on I^P, I^g, $K_1 + \Delta K$, H, and $R^* - M_2$, we now consider how these magnitudes are determined in period 1. Here we assume $\theta_k = 1$ (no taxation of OPEC investment income). The USA private sector takes OPEC and USA government policy variables (P_1, H, θ_1, I_g) as given to maximize

$$(28) \qquad U(C_1) + \beta U(C_2),$$

with respect to O_1, ΔK, and I^P, where

$$(29a) \qquad C_1 = F(K_1, O_1) - \theta_1 P_1 (O_1 + I^P) - \Delta K + H - T_1;$$

$$(29b) \qquad C_2 = G(K_1 + \Delta K, \theta_2 P_2) - \theta_2 P_2 (O_2 - I^P) - G_1 H - T_2.$$

Here T_1 and T_2 denote taxes each period. We assume that they are imposed in a lump-sum fashion. The government constraint implies,

$$(30a) \qquad T_1 = (1 - \theta_1) P_1 (O_1 + I^P) + P_1 I^g;$$

$$(30b) \qquad T_2 = (1 - \theta_2) P_2 [O_2 - D(I^P)] - [P_2 D(I^g)].$$

First-order conditions for a maximum are:

$$(31a) \qquad F_2(K_1, O_1) - \theta_1 P_1 \leq 0 \qquad (= 0 \text{ if } O_1 > 0).$$

$$(31b) \qquad -U'(C_1) + \beta U'(C_2) F_1 (K_1 + \Delta K, O_2)$$
$$\leq 0 \qquad (= 0 \text{ if } \Delta K > 0).$$

(31c) $-U'(C_1)\,O_1P_1 + \beta U'(C_2)\,\theta_2 P_2 D'(I^P)$

$\le 0 \quad (= 0 \text{ if } I^P > 0)$.

These equations implicitly define functions for first period oil demand, investment demand, and private inventory demand.

Consider now the problem facing the USA under rules R1(a) and R1(b). Taking P_1 parametrically, the USA chooses θ_1 and I^g to maximize social welfare, given, as before, by expression (28). The USA correctly anticipates the effect of its decisions this period on this period's private sector behavior (as determined by equations [31]) and on the second period outcome.

Consider the first-order equation for a maximum with respect to I^g:

(32) $-U'(C_1)P_1 + \beta U'(C_2)\left\{ P_2 D'(I^g) \right.$

$+ \dfrac{dP_2}{dI^g}[O_2 - D(I^g)] - D(I^P)\Big\}$

$\le 0 \quad (= 0 \text{ if } I^g > 0)$.

From equation (27) (dP_2/dI^g) is positive. Comparing (32) with (31c), observe that the USA has an incentive to invest in inventories beyond that facing the private sector. The reason is that individuals in the USA private sector, taking both $\theta_1 P_1$ and $\theta_2 P_2$ as given, do not take into account the effect of their own inventory decision on lowering the second period price. The USA internalizes the effect of its own inventory decision on the second period price. The USA then, facing a given *first* period price, has an incentive to accumulate inventories even when the private sector does not.

Subsidizing first period imports, via setting $\theta_1 > 1$, provides an alternative method of lowering P_2 by raising *private* inventories. This approach subsidizes first period oil consumption as well as inventory accumulation, however. A direct government investment in inventories does not suffer this difficulty. The private sector continues to establish $F_2 = P_1$ whether or not I^g is positive. If the government has available a storage technology that is not, at the margin, inferior to that provided by the private sector, then the optimal first period tariff is zero.

Consider now OPEC's decision. OPEC chooses P_1 and H to maximize

$$U^*(C_1^*) + \beta^*(C_2^*),$$

where

$$C_1^* = P_1 M_1 - H;$$
$$C_2^* = P_2 M_2 + F_1 H.$$

Under rule R1(a), OPEC acts anticipating the effect of its choice on I^g and θ_1, as well as on the second period equilibrium. Under rules R1(b) and R1(c), it treats I^g and θ_1 as given. USA inventories augment first period demand. Under rules R1(b) and R1(c), P_1 is necessarily greater when $I^g > 0$. This result does not necessarily emerge when OPEC is a leader. If I^g is very price elastic, it is conceivable that a government inventory purchase could lower P_1. In any event, OPEC will set P_1 at a higher level under rules R1(b) and R1(c), given any level of I^g.

Finally, under rule R1(c), the USA chooses θ_1 and I^g anticipating OPEC's response. Because an increase in I^g now raises P_1, the USA has less incentive to implement a reserve policy. While releasing the inventory lowers the price in period 2, acquiring it raises P_1. Under rules R1(a) and R1(b), USA policy takes the second into account but not the first, P_1 is a bygone when I^g is established. Nevertheless, OPEC, in anticipating (under R1[a]) or observing (under R1[b]) a USA inventory, is likely to establish a higher P_1 as a consequence.

Calculating the overall welfare effects of optimal inventory policy under alternative rules of the game is difficult in a general setting. In the next section we use a simple quadratic case to consider these issues further.

7.5   An Uneasy Case for Government Inventories: A Quadratic Example

We now consider a special case of the game discussed in section 7.4, making specific assumptions about the functional forms that describe technology and preferences. Our first and fourth examples assume that the behavior of the USA and OPEC is described by rule R1(a), OPEC acts as a Stackelberg leader each period. In the second example they act as Nash players, (rule R1[b]). Our third example is one in which the USA acts first (rule R1[c]).

We consider the following production function for Q_i:

$$(33) \qquad Q_i = F(K_i, O_i) = a_0 K_i - \frac{a_1}{2} K_i^2 + a_2 K_i O_i$$

$$+ a_3 O_i - \frac{a_4}{2} O_i^2, \, a_i \geq 0, \, i = 1, 2.$$

Note that this function exhibits *decreasing* returns to scale in capital and oil.

7.5.1   The Second Period

We assume that the return on investment in USA capital is the same for USA citizens and OPEC members and is equal to the marginal product of capital, that is,

(34) $$F_1(K_2, O_2) = a_0 - a_1 K_2 + a_2 O_2.$$

That is, USA sets $\theta_k = 0$. The private sector sets the demand for imports of oil in the second period by equating the marginal product of oil to the market price, that is,

$$F_2(K_2, O_2) = \theta_2 P_2 \text{ and } O_2 = M_2 + D(I),$$

where $I = I^P + I^g$ = private inventories + public inventories. Then we get that

(35) $$M_2 + D(I) = \frac{a_3}{a_4} + \frac{a_2}{a_4}(K_1 + \Delta K) - \frac{\theta_2}{a_4} P_2.$$

We consider only a limited set of instruments for USA intervention. In the second period the only instrument available is the tariff on oil. The objective of the USA is to maximize second period utility by maximizing C_2, that is,

$$\underset{\theta_2}{\text{maximize }} F(K_2, O_2) - F_1 H - P_2 M_2,$$

subject to equations (33)–(35). The first-order condition is:

$$(F_2 - F_{12} H - P_2)\frac{\partial M_2}{\partial \theta_2} = 0,$$

and the optimal tax on imports is

(36) $$\theta_2^* = \frac{a_2 H}{P_2} + 1.$$

Thus the optimal tariff rate is zero in two cases: (i) OPEC does not invest in the first period in the USA ($H = 0$), or (ii) oil and capital are separable in the production of the consumption good ($a_2 = 0$).

Now we turn to OPEC's determination of the second period price by maximizing its second period consumption, that is, it maximizes $P_2 M_2 + F_1 H$ subject to (33)–(36) by choice of P_2. The optimal P_2 turns out to be:

(37) $$P_2 = \frac{a_3}{2} + \frac{a_2}{2}[(K_1 + \Delta K)] - a_2 H - \frac{a_4}{2} D(I).$$

Again we observe that if oil and capital are separable in production ($a_2 = 0$), the capital stock does not affect the determination of oil prices in the second period. Furthermore, P_2 is a linear function of capital, but OPEC has an incentive to decrease oil prices as *its* investment in the USA is larger. This result suggests why different members of OPEC would have different incentives in setting oil prices conditional on their portfolio decisions. Finally, it is important to observe that P_2 decreases as USA inventories go up. This result establishes a possible role for public inventories if the USA in the first period takes into account OPEC supply behavior in the second period, while USA private agents take P_2 parametrically. That P_2 falls as I rises does not depend on the assumption that the USA takes P_2 parametrically in period 2 while OPEC is assumed to act upon (36), that is, OPEC is a Stackelberg leader in setting P_2. Under rule R1(b), in which OPEC takes θ_2^* parametrically so that θ_2 and P_2 are set simultaneously in a noncooperative Nash game, then the optimal P_2 turns out to be:

$$(38) \qquad P_2 = \frac{a_3}{2\theta_2^*} + \frac{a_2}{2\theta_2^*}(K_1 + \Delta K) - \frac{a_2}{2}H - \frac{a_4}{2\theta_2^*}D(I).$$

Note that if $H = 0$ the Nash solution and the solution with OPEC as the Stackelberg leader yield the same price. Otherwise, P_2 may move either way with θ_2. P_2 moves negatively with $D(I)$ as long as θ_2^* is positive. Whichever game is played in the second period, the oil price is not affected by total capital $(K_1 + \Delta K)$ and by H in the same degree. The results in the second period are independent of the utility function since the maximization of welfare is equivalent to the maximization of consumption.

The third logical possibility, of course, obtains when the USA acts as a Stackelberg leader (Rule R1[c]). As we described in section 7.4, in this case the USA can impose the optimal tariff, driving the world price to zero (the marginal extraction cost for oil that we have assumed here).

7.5.2   The First Period and the Complete Solution

Example 1 (Nichols and Zeckhauser)

To solve the first period problem we have to postulate a utility function for both the USA and OPEC. We first assume that utility is linear and that $\beta = \beta^* = 1$. In this case inventories benefit the USA. We then compare the government inventory policy with a tax/subsidy scheme. To do so, we make the following assumptions
A1: $H = \Delta K = 0$, that is, no investment.
A2: $D(I) = I$, that is, no inventory carrying costs for oil.
A1 implies that $\theta_2 = 1$, and as a result we get the following equations for the second period problem:

$$(39) \qquad M_2 = \frac{\tilde{a}_3}{a_4} - \frac{P_2}{a_4} - I.$$

$$(40) \qquad P_2 = \frac{\tilde{a}_3}{2} - \frac{a_4}{2}I,$$

where $\tilde{a}_3 \equiv a_2 K_1 + a_3$. Note that these solutions obtain *either* when the USA and OPEC establish θ_2 and P_2 as the outcome of a noncooperative

Nash game *or* when OPEC acts as a Stackelberg leader. Together (39) and (40) yield

$$(41) \qquad M_2 = \frac{\tilde{a}_3}{2a_4} - \frac{1}{2}I.$$

Since capital is constant, we can write the production of the single good at time i as:

$$(42) \qquad Q_i = F(K_i, O_i) = a + \tilde{a}_3 O_i - \frac{a_4}{2} O_i^2, \qquad i = 1, 2,$$

where $\qquad\qquad a \equiv a_0 - \frac{a_1}{2} K_i^2.$

We consider the economy under alternative USA government policies. *Case (i)*. The USA chooses both M_1 and I in the USA in the first period taking the structure of the period 2 problem as given. Given the linear utility functions, the USA's problem is to maximize

$$F(K_1, M_1 - I) - P_1 M_1 + F(K_1, M_2 + I) - P_2 M_2,$$

subject to (40), (41), and (42) by choice of M_1 and I. The first-order conditions with respect to I and M_1, respectively, are:

$$(43) \qquad \frac{\tilde{a}_3}{2} - a_4\left(\frac{\tilde{a}_3}{2a_4} + \frac{I}{2}\right)\frac{1}{2} + \frac{a_4}{2}\left(\frac{\tilde{a}_3}{2a_4} - \frac{1}{2}I\right)$$

$$+ \frac{1}{2}\left(\frac{\tilde{a}_3}{2} - \frac{a_4}{2}I\right) - \tilde{a}_3 + a_4(M_1 - I) = 0.$$

$$(44) \qquad \tilde{a}_3 - a_4(M_1 - I) - P_1 = 0.$$

Solving for I and M_1 as functions of P_1 we get,

$$(45) \qquad I = \frac{\tilde{a}_3}{a_4} - \frac{4}{3}\frac{P_1}{a_4}.$$

$$(46) \qquad M_1 = 2\frac{\tilde{a}_3}{a_4} - \frac{7}{3}\frac{P_1}{a_4}.$$

Given the above result with respect to USA decision rules, OPEC's problem is to maximize $P_1 M_1 + P_2 M_2$ subject to (40), (41), (42), (45), and (46) by choosing P_1. The result is

$$(47) \qquad P_1 = \frac{9}{17}\tilde{a}_3.$$

Hence, we have the following allocation of resources in the two periods:[11]

$$(48) \quad \begin{cases} O_1 = \dfrac{8}{17}\dfrac{\tilde{a}_3}{a_4}, & O_2 = \dfrac{11}{17}\dfrac{\tilde{a}_3}{a_4}, \\[2ex] P_2 = \dfrac{6}{17}\tilde{a}_3, & I = \dfrac{5}{17}\dfrac{\tilde{a}_3}{a_4}, \end{cases}$$

Utility levels in the USA and OPEC are, respectively,

$$(49a) \qquad U = C_1 + C_2 = 2a_0 K_1 - a_1 K_1^2 + \frac{155}{578}\frac{(\tilde{a}_3)^2}{a_4}.$$

$$(49b) \qquad U^* = C_1^* + C_2^* = \frac{9}{17}\frac{(\tilde{a}_3)^2}{a_4}.$$

Hence, the price of oil falls from period one to period two and inventories are 5/11 of oil consumption at the second period. We now turn to the case where there is no USA government intervention.

Case (ii). USA private agents choose both oil consumption and oil inventories. There is no government intervention. USA private agents maximize profits by setting O_1 such that $F_2(K_1, O_1) = P_1$, and they set $I^P > 0$ if $P_1 < P_2$, otherwise $I^P = 0$. The first-order conditions with respect to O_1 imply that

$$(50) \qquad O_1 = M_1 - I^P = \frac{\tilde{a}_3 - P_1}{a_4}.$$

As a result, we can solve OPEC's problem assuming that $I^P = 0$ then see whether the condition for zero inventories is satisfied. OPEC's problem is to maximize $P_1 M_1 + P_2 M_2$ subject to (40), (41), (49), and $I^P = 0$. Hence, we get $P_1 = P_2 = (1/2)\tilde{a}_3$, and the condition for zero inventories is satisfied. Furthermore, we get $M_1 = M_2 = (1/2)(\tilde{a}_3/2)/a_4) = O_1 = O_2$. Hence, the two periods are completely symmetric, and the model is equivalent to the case in which OPEC is a simple monopoly in both periods separately.

Utility levels in the USA and OPEC are, respectively,

$$(51a) \qquad U = C_1 + C_2 = 2a_0 K_1 - a_1 K_1^2 + \frac{\tilde{a}_3^2}{4a_4};$$

$$(51b) \qquad U^* = C_1^* + C_2^* = \frac{\tilde{a}_3^2}{2a_4}.$$

Case (iii). USA private agents choose O_1 while USA government chooses inventories. The allocation of O_1 is determined by (49) which is identical to (44), the first-order condition with respect to M_1 in case (i). Hence, the solution for USA optimal inventories turns out to be identical to that of case (i): (45), and the final allocation of case (iii) and (i) are identical and given by (37) and (48).

Result. In the above example a monopolistic OPEC behaves as a Stackelberg leader in a time-consistent game, and optimal private inventories are zero. This is equivalent to the result of zero private (optimal) inventories in the case of competition (section 7.3). However, given the fact that the government can exploit the effect of inventories on oil prices in the second period, we find that the optimal USA allocation is to have a positive level of inventories that raises the first period oil price and lowers the second period price.[12] Hence, the USA has a real cost of holding inventories, $(P_1 - P_2)I$, but it creates a welfare gain from changing the terms of trade and reducing the monopoly power of OPEC in the second period.

We present the result in figure 7.1. Moving from no intervention in the USA to a government inventory policy, the demand and marginal revenue curves that OPEC faces are moving from the solid lines to the broken lines. The USA loses the area $P_1^* P B A$ of consumer surplus in the first period, while it gains the area $P P_2^* C B$ of consumer surplus in the second period and here the difference is positive.

Given the sequence of decisions that we assume here, in case (i) we characterize the optimal allocation for the USA. We show in case (ii) that

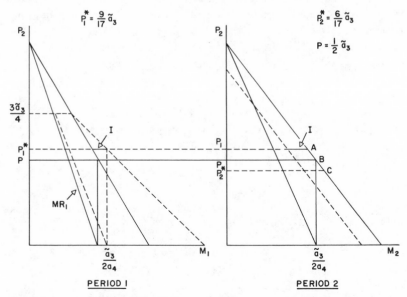

Fig. 7.1   U.S. oil demand with OPEC as a Stackelburg leader.

the private sector does not achieve the same allocation since it cannot exploit the negative effect of inventories on the period 2 oil price. If the only government instrument is a public inventory (case iii), the allocation is the same as in the first case.

Comparing (49) with (51) note that USA welfare is in fact greater when the USA chooses inventories optimally. In addition, OPEC welfare is greater as well. USA inventory policy is reducing a monopoly distortion in a way that benefits both OPEC and the USA. Note that under the inventory policy imports over the two periods together are greater than when the USA does not use inventories.

Could an optimal level of inventories be sustained by other policies? The answer is yes, if the government can impose lump-sum and firm-specific taxes or subsidies to make holding the optimal level of inventories consistent with the firm's profit-maximizing problem. This set of incentives must be specified in the first period. However, once P_2 is determined in the second period there will be no incentive for the government to fulfill its obligations. The previous time-consistency argument applies to the tax incentive program for private inventories. Only by buying the inventories in period 1 itself can the government credibly commit itself to a policy of lowering the second period price through increased inventories.

Example 2

Now assume that rule R1(b) applies, USA and OPEC set I^g and P_1 simultaneously as noncooperative Nash players rather than sequentially, that is, the USA chooses I^g taking P_1 as given, as before, and OPEC sets P_1 taking I^g as given. In the consequent equilibrium we get:

(52)
$$O_1 = \frac{2\tilde{a}_3}{5}, \qquad O_2 = \frac{3\tilde{a}_3}{5},$$
$$P_1^* = \frac{3\tilde{a}_3}{5}, \qquad P_2^* = \frac{2\tilde{a}_3}{5},$$

(53)
$$I^g = \frac{\tilde{a}_3}{5a_4},$$

while

(54a)
$$U = C_1 + C_2 = 2a_0 K_1 - a_1 K_1^2 + \frac{11\tilde{a}_3}{50a_4};$$

(54b)
$$U^* = C_1^* + C_2^* = \frac{13}{25}\frac{\tilde{a}_3}{a_4}.$$

Compared with a situation in which $I^g = 0$, the USA is now worse off while OPEC is again better off.

Moving from a situation in which the USA acts entirely as a Stackelberg follower to one in which the USA and OPEC act as Nash players reduces USA welfare. The reason is that USA inventory demand is price elastic. Given the structure of the problem in period 2, the USA's demand for inventories is given by

$$(55) \qquad I^g = \frac{\tilde{a}_3}{a_4} - \frac{4P_1}{3a_4}.$$

When OPEC incorporates (55) into its decision making, it sets, ceteris paribus, a lower price. Taking I^g as given, it perceives total demand as more inelastic and consequently sets a higher P_1.

This result is illustrated in figure 7.2. While the USA inventory demand shifts OPEC's demand curve rightward in a Nash game, the slope of OPEC's perceived marginal revenue curve is unaffected by a USA inventory policy. When OPEC acts as a leader, the optimal USA inventory policy makes the perceived MR curve flatter. OPEC consequently charges a lower price each period.

Example 3

Consider now the problem posed in example 1 for the case in which the USA acts as a Stackelberg leader, that is, rule R1(c) applies in period 1. We continue to assume that rules R1(a) or R1(b) apply in period 2, so that the structure of the second period game is unchanged. We assume zero tariffs.

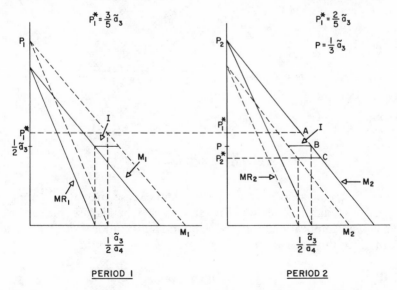

Fig. 7.2   U.S. oil demand with OPEC and the USA as Nash players.

The USA now sets I^g taking the price response of OPEC,

$$(56) \qquad P_1 = \frac{\tilde{a}_3}{2} + \frac{a_4 I^g}{2},$$

as given. It is straightforward to show that in this case the optimal USA policy is to set $I^g = 0$. The same solution as that for example 1, case (ii), that is, the competitive solution without government intervention, obtains here. When the USA must precommit itself to some level of inventories, it chooses a zero level. This result obtains when OPEC has a Bernoulli utility function as well as when OPEC's utility is linear.

Example 4

We now show that a USA inventory policy is not necessarily in the USA's interest even when OPEC acts as a Stackelberg leader. We make the following small modification to example 1. Assume that instead of being linear in consumption (as in equations [49b] and [51b]), OPEC's utility function is Bernoulli:

$$(57) \qquad U^* = \log C_1^* + \log C_2^*.$$

In this case the solution in the presence of a government inventory (cases [i] and [iii]) involves

$$(58) \qquad O_1 = \frac{5\tilde{a}_3}{14 a_4}, \qquad O_2 = \frac{4\tilde{a}_3}{7 a_4},$$

$$P_1 = \frac{9\tilde{a}_3}{14 a_4}, \qquad P_2 = \frac{3\tilde{a}_3}{7 a_4},$$

In addition,

$$(59a) \qquad U = C_1 + C_2 = 2 a_0 K_1 - a_1 K_1^2 + \frac{11}{56} \frac{\tilde{a}_3^2}{a_4}.$$

$$(59b) \qquad U^* = \log C_1^* + \log C_2^* = \log \frac{9}{28}$$

$$+ 2\log \frac{3}{7} + 2\log \frac{\tilde{a}_3}{a_4}.$$

When there is no government inventory (case [ii]), the solution is exactly as that for example 1. The reason is that, in this case, the choice of P_1 has no implications for intertemporal substitution in OPEC. Thus OPEC's utility is given by

$$(60) \qquad U^* = 2\log \frac{1}{4} + 2\log \frac{\tilde{a}_3^2}{a_4},$$

while the USA's welfare continues to be given by (51a).

Again, comparing (59b) and (60), note that OPEC has benefited because the USA has pursued an inventory policy. The USA, however, has lost; (59a) is less than (51a). The reason is that when OPEC has diminishing marginal utility of consumption in period 2, it is less willing to transfer consumption from period 2 to period 1 in response to a USA inventory policy. It sets higher prices in both periods to maintain a higher consumption level in period 2. The USA is consequently worse off. In terms of figure 7.1, when OPEC has a Bernoulli objective function P_1^* and P_2^* are displaced upward relative to P. The loss in period 1 from having an inventory is consequently greater while the gain in period 2 is less. Note also that here total imports over the two periods have *fallen* because of the inventory policy.

Given that the USA is better off without a government inventory, will it in fact set $I^g = 0$? If the USA does set I^g taking P_1 as given it will set $I^g > 0$ for all $P_1 < (3\tilde{a}_3/4)$, given the structure of the remaining problem. As in example 2, once P_1 is set it is too late for the USA to affect P_1 via its inventory policy.

Consider a situation in which the USA announced that it would establish $I^g = 0$. If OPEC believed this announcement it would establish $P_1 = (\tilde{a}_3/2)$. The USA would then have an incentive to establish $I = (\tilde{a}_3/3a_4)$ and drive $P_2 = (\tilde{a}_3/3)$. Anticipating this behavior, OPEC will in fact set P_1 higher. In example 1 the USA nevertheless benefited from having a government inventory when OPEC adjusted P_1 in anticipation of period 1 inventory purchases. An implication of this example and example 2 is that the USA can actually lower USA welfare by developing the capacity to maintain inventories. The absence of such a capacity constitutes a credible commitment not to store oil before OPEC establishes P_1.

7.5.3   Conclusion

These examples suggest that, in a strategic setting, the ability of the USA to pursue an inventory policy can have both desirable and undesirable consequences, depending on both the nature of OPEC's preferences and on the structure of the process whereby OPEC sets prices and the USA sets inventories.

Our results can be interpreted in light of Samuelson's (1972) analysis of the desirability of destabilizing speculation. Like Samuelson, we are considering a situation in which given demand and supply conditions persist for two periods. Samuelson showed that in a competitive setting, that is, one in which buyers and sellers behave as price-takers, a destabilizing speculator would raise the welfare of both buyers and sellers. His own losses would exceed the gain of the other two groups combined, however. Hence, in our example, if the USA faced a competitive OPEC there would be no positive role for a government inventory policy. The government would be acting as a destabilizing speculator. The gain to the rest of the world, not just to USA consumers, would fall short of the capital loss the government would sustain in buying in period 1 to sell in period 2.

In facing a monopolistic seller, however, our examples indicate, first of all, that a government inventory policy can raise not only USA but world welfare. The reason is that the optimal USA inventory rule makes USA demand, on net, more elastic over the two periods. As a consequence the distortion due to monopoly is diminished and both sides can benefit. More oil is consumed overall, so the world is moved closer to the competitive equilibrium.

This result requires that OPEC set prices incorporating the USA's response into its decision. An implication is that to succeed at raising USA welfare the government inventory purchases should respond very closely to actual oil prices; that is, the government should, according to our model, establish purchasing rules that are price contingent.

A second implication of our examples is that, unless the USA acts as a leader in setting I^g before OPEC sets P_1, it may have an incentive to establish a positive inventory even when USA welfare is higher when there is a precommitment to no inventories. The reason is that the loss to the USA from having an inventory is incorporated in the first period price. Once OPEC has established this price it is too late for the USA to avoid the undesirable consequences of having an inventory. From that point on the benefits exceed the costs.

7.6   Other Arguments for Government Inventories

Our analysis has focused on convenience yields, uncertainty, and strategic interactions to explain the existence of petroleum reserves. Only in the third case did we find an argument for government intervention. Other economists have analyzed the case for a strategic reserve and we discuss their results here. Closest in spirit to our own analysis is the paper by Maskin and Newbery (1978) which examines the possible effect of U.S. monopsony power on the optimal tariff response. Wright and Williams (1982) have argued that reserves may be justified as a second-best response to other (suboptimal) government policies, in particular, price controls. Finally, the stockpile has been justified as a means of reducing U.S. vulnerability to the threat of an embargo. Tolley and Wilman (1977) discuss this issue.

7.6.1   U.S. Monopsony Power and Government Inventories

Maskin and Newbery (1978) develop a two-period model in which a monopsonistic United States faces a competitive set of oil producers and other buyers. The optimal open loop policy is for the United States to establish a monopsony price (via an optimal tariff, for instance) that must be equal (in discounted terms) across the two periods to extract positive supplies in the two periods. The two prices must be equal because of Hotelling's formula. In the second period, however, the United States has an incentive to deviate from the period 2 price that is optimal from the open loop perspective. The reason is that the effect of the period 2 price on oil producers' willingness to hold oil in the ground in period 1 is at this point a bygone. The price that is optimal from period 2's perspective can be higher or lower than that which was optimal ex ante. If oil producers and other buyers believe the announced open loop rule in making their period 1 decisions about extraction, the United States can benefit from reneging on the contract. If, however, the rest of the world anticipates the reneging, the United States can lose from its monopsony position. If, say, the government has an incentive to revise the price downward in period 2 and individuals correctly anticipate this revision, the period 1 price will be driven down as well (again via the Hotelling rule). The consequent equilibrium can be worse from the U.S. perspective than one in which the United States has no monopsony power at all. The United States would be best off if it could precommit itself to its optimal open loop policy. If this is not possible it could benefit by somehow divesting itself of its monopsony power in the second period. Otherwise the anticipation that the United States will exercise monopsony power in the second period leads to behavior by other agents in the first period that is detrimental to the United States.

In this context, Maskin and Newbery show that the United States can benefit from government storage in period 1 as a means of precommitting itself to a course of action. By buying stocks of oil the government can establish that it has an interest in maintaining the announced price of oil in the second period when, in the absence of storage, it would want to revise the second period price downward. Maskin and Newbery find that in a rational expectations equilibrium the United States cannot be hurt by a government stockpile while in some circumstances the United States will strictly benefit. The argument here is again in favor of a *government* inventory. Private agents do not have an incentive to invest in inventories as a means of making the government's optimal tariff commitment credible.

7.6.2   Price Controls and Government Inventories

Wright and Williams (1982) develop a model in which agents anticipate that in some periods (e.g., when the price is high) the government will impose price controls on oil. The private rate of return on storing oil into these periods is consequently lower than the social rate of return. The private sector consequently stores too little. There is scope for additional government reserves. Government storage here is a second-best response to other distortionary government policies. The government does not actually have to impose price controls for a justification for inventories to emerge. Private agents simply need to anticipate that controls will be applied with some probability. Wright and Williams do not attempt to model why the government would impose controls and, hence, why it cannot credibly commit itself never to impose controls.

7.6.3 Vulnerability and Government Inventories

The threat of a future embargo by OPEC can provide an additional justification for an inventory. In a competitive setting, of course, this issue does not arise. In the face of a monopolistic exporter, however, the supplier could decide to curtail supplies at some moment. A complete modeling of the embargo issue would require a specification of the supplier's motives in imposing an embargo. A real possibility is that a government inventory is a means of preventing an embargo.

Tolley and Wilman (1977) show that if a country is faced with an exogenous threat of an embargo that a justification for inventories emerges. There is scope for government intervention, however, *only* when the embargo generates external effects. Otherwise, individuals would have an incentive to maintain the socially optimal level of inventories themselves in the face of an embargo threat, as we discussed in section 7.3. They derive the optimal level of the government inventory as a function of the externalities generated by the embargo and the exogenous likelihood and length of a potential embargo.

A more complete analysis would specify (1) the nature of the externalities and (2) the effect of the inventory policy itself on the likelihood and duration of an embargo. An analysis of this sort could be provided in a multiperiod game theoretic framework. It remains an important topic for future research. Aiyagari and Riesman (1982) consider the desirability of the embargo policy to the sellers. They find that only in a very special case can this policy improve the seller's position from a purely *economic* perspective.

The oil price shocks of the last decade have spawned a large literature on policies toward oil. A number of other articles have considered aspects of policies toward oil or optimal stockpile behavior. Examples include Nordhaus (1974), Calvo and Findlay (1978), Gilbert (1978), Wright (1980), Teisberg (1981), Ulph and Folie (1981), Newbery (1981), Ulph and Ulph (1981), and Epple, Hansen, and Roberds (1982).

7.7 Conclusion

This paper investigates the desirability of U.S. government oil inventories in a two-period, two-country model in which the world stock of oil is exhaustible. We show that in competitive markets under certainty or uncertainty there is no welfare improving role for public inventories and, leaving aside operating stocks, a precautionary demand for stocks of oil is the result of the exclusion of international insurance markets or property rights.

We show that only under a limited set of strategic games between the United States and OPEC can one justify public Strategic Petroleum Reserves. Even then their desirability depends on the structure of preferences.

An inventory policy is inferior to imposing optimal tariffs in the two periods. But implementing the optimal tariff may not constitute a *time-consistent* policy (see Kydland and Prescott 1977): while the United States could bring U.S. welfare to a higher level by imposing optimal tariffs in the two periods, the United States may not have an incentive actually to impose the tariff in the period in which it acts. A threat to impose the tariff at the time OPEC sets price may therefore not be credible. An SPR, while not raising U.S. welfare to a level equal to that when optimal tariffs are imposed, may nevertheless raise welfare above that attainable by any other time-consistent policy. An inventory constitutes a second-best, but *credible*, alternative to an optimal tariff policy.

In all our examples the government inventory makes a loss. Consequently, private, atomistic agents, acting as price-takers, have no incentive to hold any inventories at all. Inventories serve the purpose of driving down the price in the second period. The price is driven down for *all* second-period users. Any nonaltruistic individual considering investing in an inventory will not take into account the effect of his own inventory holding on lowering the price for other individuals. The case is one of a classic externality. A government that maximizes welfare will internalize this effect. Hence, in moving to a strategic setting, a justification for a *government* SPR can be made. As its name implies, strategic considerations seem to have motivated the establishment of the U.S. SPR (see Senator Jackson's statement quoted in the introduction.)

Whether or not an inventory enhances welfare depends very much on the structure of decision making in the United States and OPEC, and on the parameters of the system. We find three examples in which the presence of an SPR *reduces* U.S. welfare relative to a situation of zero inventories. Nevertheless, once OPEC has acted, the United States may find it in its interest to pursue an inventory policy. Holding inventories may then constitute a *time-consistent* policy that is inferior to a credible precommitment to hold zero inventories. Merely by developing the capacity to hold inventories the SPR can reduce U.S. welfare.

Another aspect of our analysis is to show that if OPEC invests some of its first-period income in U.S. equities, a credible, welfare-enhancing tariff policy on the part of the United States can emerge. We have not considered the interaction between OPEC investment and government inventories here. We consider this avenue as a promising one for further research on the SPR. One possibility is, since U.S. inventories raise OPEC's first-period income relative to its second-period income, that an inventory policy will increase OPEC's equity investment in the United States. For the reasons we discussed in section 7.3 and 7.4, this investment acts to reduce the second-period price further. There is a second channel, then, whereby a government purchase of inventories in period one can reduce the price of oil in period two.

Notes

1. For a detailed description of the SPR, see Glatt (1982). For a discussion of the quota system that prevailed during 1954–71, see Dam (1971). Dam suggests that in 1969 the tariff equivalent of the quota averaged about $1.25 per barrel.
2. CBS Television Network, *Face The Nation*, Sunday, 18 July 1982.
3. Nichols and Zeckhauser (1977) show that a stockpile can reduce U.S. welfare when the resource constraint is binding. In this context, however, OPEC is not exercising monopoly power by restricting total supply. In fact, even when the resource constraint is *not* binding the inventory can reduce U.S. welfare, as we show.
4. See Varian (1978).
5. Here we assume that capital cannot be consumed and therefore that the interest rate is equal to the marginal product of capital.
6. This uncertainty could arise either from imperfect information about the physical quantity of OPEC's oil or from uncertainty about OPEC's desire to sell oil to the USA. The possibility of an embargo, for example, creates uncertainty about OPEC's supply of oil to the USA. To be consistent with the analysis here, the embargo must be considered as a possibility that is *exogenous* to the USA's behavior. We discuss the issue of an *endogenous* embargo in section 7.6.
7. U.S. imports that year equalled more than one-third of OPEC's production. See table 7.1.
8. Observe that $G_1 = F_1$ and so $G_{12} = F_{12}$.
9. See Marion and Svensson (1981) for a competitive model dealing with the relationship between the oil price and OPEC's investments.
10. This result is reminiscent of the well-known Metzler paradox. Here it arises because of the interaction between the price of oil and the return on capital.
11. Note that it is assumed here that $R^* > (19\bar{a}_3/17a_4)$.
12. This allocation (case [i]) is optimal, subject to the particular rules of the game that we assumed for USA and OPEC.

References

Aiyagari, S. R., and R. Reisman. 1982. Analysis of embargoes and supply shocks in a market with a dominant seller. Mimeo.

Bohi, R. Douglas, and Milton Russell. 1978. *Limiting oil imports: An economic history analysis*. Baltimore: The Johns Hopkins University Press.

Brennan, J. Michael. 1958. The supply of storage. *American Economic Review* 48:49–71.

Calvo, G., and R. Findlay. 1978. On the optimal acquisition of foreign capital through investment of oil export receipts. *Journal of International Economics* 8:513–24.

Dam, K. W. 1971. Implementation of import quotas: The case of oil. *Journal of Law and Economics* 14, no. 1:1–60.

Eckstein, Z., and M. Eichenbaum. 1982. Oil supply disruptions and the optimal tariff in a dynamic stochastic equilibrium model. Mimeo.

Epple, Dennis, Lars P. Hansen, and Will Roberds. 1982. Linear-quadratic games of resource depletion. Mimeo.

Gilbert, R. J. 1978. Dominant firm pricing in a market for an exhaustible resource. *Bell Journal of Economics* 9:385–95.

Glatt, Sandra. 1982. *The Strategic Petroleum Reserves: Progress after seven years*. Discussion Paper D-82E, Energy and National Security Series. Washington, D.C.: Resources for the Future.

Kydland, F. E. 1977. Equilibrium solutions in dynamic dominant-player models. *Journal of Economic Theory* 15, no. 2: 307–24.

Kydland, F. E., and E. C. Prescott. 1977. Rules rather than discretion: The inconsistency of optimal plans. *Journal of Political Economy* 85:473–91.

Marion, N. P., and L. E. O. Svensson. 1981. *World equilibrium with oil price increases: An intertemporal analysis*. Seminar Paper no. 191. Stockholm: Institute for International Studies.

Maskin, E., and D. M. G. Newbery. 1978. Rational expectation with market power—the paradox of the disadvantageous tariff on oil. Warwick Economic Research Paper no. 129.

Newbery, D. M. G. 1981. Oil prices, cartels, and the problem of dynamic inconsistency. *Economic Journal* 91:617–46.

Nichols, Albert L., and Richard J. Zeckhauser. 1977. Stockpiling strategies and cartel prices. *Bell Journal of Economics* 6:66–96.

Nordhaus, W. D. 1974. The 1974 report of the President's Council of Economic Advisers: Energy in the economic report. *American Economic Review* 64:558–65.

Samuelson, P. A. 1972. Feasible price stability. *Quarterly Journal of Economics* 86:476–93.

Selten, R. 1975. Re-examination of the perfect concept for equilibrium points in extensive games. *International Journal of Game Theory* 4:22–55.

Teisberg, T. J. 1981. A dynamic programming model of the U.S. Strategic Petroleum Reserve. *Bell Journal of Economics* 12:526–46.

Tolley, G. S., and J. D. Wilman. 1977. The foreign dependence question. *Journal of Political Economy* 85:323–47.

Ulph, A. M., and G. M. Folie. 1981. Dominant firm models of resource depletion. Mimeo.

Ulph, A. M., and D. T. Ulph. 1981. International monopoly-monopsony power over oil and capital. Mimeo.
Varian, H. 1978. *Microeconomic analysis.* New York: W. W. Norton.
Wright, B. 1980. The cost of tax induced energy conservation. *Bell Journal of Economics* 11:84–107.
Wright, B., and J. Williams. 1982. The role of public and private storage in managing oil import disruptions. *Bell Journal of Economics.*

Comment   John Whalley

This is an extremely well-written and clearly argued paper which presents analytical justifications for the existence of the U.S. Strategic Petroleum Reserve (SPR), primarily on potential terms of trade grounds. What I especially liked about the paper was the helpful introduction which succinctly lists the main points raised in the paper.

The main results presented have strong intuitive appeal to them and I have no basic disagreement with them. It is nonetheless helpful just to briefly summarize them:

(a) In a two period international trade model in which a country is a small open price-taking economy and where there is no foreign ownership of capital, the authors demonstrate that there is no role to be played by a government inventory policy for oil. There is no particular reason for the government to be in the business of accumulating inventories of oil since private markets can meet whatever inventory demands occur. Even in the presence of uncertainty, this result still prevails since with a complete set of Arrow/Debreu contingent commodity markets the free market economy can achieve a Pareto optimal allocation.

(b) If oil prices are affected by import volumes so that we relax the small open price-taking economy assumption, there does exist an optimal tariff for the United States. The authors show that this is a little more complex than the traditional optimal tariff argument which involves a static model. In an intertemporal framework the prices in the two periods have to be taken into account in setting the optimal tariff, but the same basic optimal tariff argument familiar to trade theorists applies.

(c) It is possible to complicate the strategic setting slightly: the authors show that if OPEC owns some U.S. capital, and if capital and energy are complements, then a tariff on energy will reduce the return on OPEC-owned capital, providing a further argument for the use of a tariff on oil.

(d) The authors then go on to argue that an inventory policy such as used in the SPR can provide a second-best substitute for a tariff. The inventories are used to change the time profile of deliveries from OPEC

John Whalley is professor of economics at the University of Western Ontario.

and, in effect, change the structure of demands which OPEC faces in the United States in the two periods. It is worth highlighting that to operate in this way, the inventory policy should ideally be price contingent so that the elasticity of demand for oil in the United States is changed through the operation of the SPR.

(e) The authors dispute an earlier finding of Nichols and Zeckhauser (1977) that it is possible through inventory policy to make both players better off in the implicit two-person game characterizing U.S. and OPEC oil trade. The Nichols/Zeckhauser argument is that OPEC monopoly power leads to a distortion in world energy markets and SPR can offset this distortion in such a way that the United States and OPEC can share the gain. The authors show that this result depends, rather critically, on the utility function specification; if the logarithmic rather than linear utility functions are used, they show that the United States can lose through the SPR.

My main points concerning the paper do not involve the analytics of these results which, as I say, seem to be fairly intuitive and are both clearly and persuasively argued in the paper. I will concern myself with the broader context of their applicability to policy discussion of the SPR.

As the authors hint in much of their discussion, they approach the SPR primarily in terms of attempting to find its rationale as a trading policy rather than as an analysis of its impact as a policy in place. When one goes back to the events surrounding its introduction, however, as the authors state, the SPR is best seen as an outgrowth of the events of 1973. It is thus perhaps better seen primarily as a form of insurance against further embargos and supply disruptions. As such, the insurance approach rather than a deliberate approach to manipulate the terms of trade which the United States faces in oil would seem to be both the rationale for the SPR and the main viewpoint from which to evaluate its impact.

In approaching the SPR from this direction, one immediately begins to think of the potential welfare costs or welfare gains to the United States which might be involved. A very simpleminded approach is to say that the main threat of supply disruptions now appears to have passed, and that if one discounts the insurance significance of the SPR, then the welfare cost to the United States would be dominated by the associated inventory carrying costs. Assuming that oil pumped into SPR remained there to perpetuity, with the SPR accumulating to 750 million barrels by 1989, each priced at approximately $30 a barrel, would yield a welfare cost to the United States in the region of $20 billion. The cost to the United States is simply the foregone resources invested in SPR and left in the ground. This simpleminded approach, while leaving many features remaining to be analyzed, nonetheless provides a ballpark figure from which to evaluate the net benefits by calculating what insurance gains the United States might expect to offset this cost.

A further crucial issue, however, is the possible behavior of firms in response to the existence of SPR. One approach would be to argue that firm behavior totally offsets the existence of the SPR. Firms hold inventories and form their own expectations both of future prices and the probability of supply disruptions, and knowing the existence of the SPR they appropriately modify their own inventory decisions. Under this approach, there is no welfare cost to the United States from the SPR and no terms of trade effect. The only welfare costs are the resource costs of trucking and pumping the oil into the SPR and any administrative costs exceeding the private cost to firms carrying inventory.

An alternative approach would be to make the assumption that firms do not offset the existence of the SPR through their own inventory policies. This could be justified by the assumption that firms face uncertainty about the precise allocations from the SPR they might receive from SPR if there is a supply disruption. Since there are no firm-specific contingent claims on oil in the SPR, firms may well view the government as unable to satisfactorily allocate and organize oil supplies in the event of a supply disruption. In this case the SPR is simply an addition to oil already being held by firms in the United States to cover both normal inventory needs and additional inventory motivated by the probability of a supply disruption. The welfare cost to the United States from SPR is dominated by the inventory carrying costs, and SPR would clearly worsen the terms of trade for the United States, since the SPR constitutes a once and for all addition to the oil demand function for the United States. Oil prices must rise unless the world supply function of oil to the United States is perfectly elastic. These two different approaches of firm offset and no firm offset thus make a substantial difference to the perception of the impacts of the SPR.

In approaching the SPR it would seem that at an intuitive level the probable terms of trade effects are quite small. With current OPEC proven reserves of perhaps 300 billion barrels plus an additional 200 billion barrels non-OPEC reserves, if one accepts optimistic Mexican claims, an SPR of less than 1 billion barrels would seem likely to produce only small terms of trade effects. In addition, it is important to note that the United States is not the only importer of oil, and the terms of trade gains which the authors focus on so heavily in their paper will accrue also to the EEC and Japan. This free-rider aspect of U.S. oil policy is an important complication which should be noted both in evaluating this alternative approach to the SPR and the approach used in the paper.

Two further issues regarding the SPR and an alternative approach to evaluating its effects are also worth raising. First, as soon as one approaches SPR from the insurance viewpoint it would seem important to estimate the potential adjustment costs involved with supply disruptions: how large these are likely to be; which sectors they are concentrated in; and how much labor reallocation costs may be. Indeed the events of 1973 suggest that not only the adjustment costs are at issue, but also the other possible policy regimes associated in the United States with the oil supply disruption. Since the supply disruption by OPEC was accompanied by price controls on oil, this further complicates an evaluation of possible adjustment costs. Some people would argue that the price controls prevented the necessary adjustments taking place as smoothly as perhaps they would have otherwise occurred. Thus, in evaluating the insurance value to the United States of the SPR, one needs to know both the probability of a supply disruption and the potential loss to the United States should that supply disruption occur.

A further point concerns a question raised by the authors in the paper, namely, the possible use of inventories as a second-best policy for tariffs. Little comment is made on the relative efficiency of inventories and tariffs. As the authors state, there is a potential for inventories to act as a second-best substitute for a tariff, but the relative efficiency of the two policies is not fully discussed. At an intuitive level it would seem that an inventory policy is a significantly inferior policy than a tariff since the costs involve unused resources. Resources employed in the inventory policy are idle whereas with a tariff the resource misallocation is the distortion of resources to less desirable uses. While this intuition may not fully apply in this case, given that with a tariff a distortion occurs between domestic and foreign prices, it is nonetheless an important issue to be evaluated in deciding on policy toward the SPR.

Finally, I have some further comments on the paper of a more analytical nature. One point concerns the exclusive use of a two period model rather than an infinite period model. In some areas if finite rather than infinite period models are used, analytical results that apply in the finite case tend to be nonrobust when infinite period models are used. Recent work has analyzed these questions for overlapping generations and infinitely lived consumer models and comes to that conclusion, and it is of some interest whether such nonrobustness might apply in this case.

A further point applies to the introduction of OPEC ownership of capital into the models. The analysis in the paper assumes that OPEC investments in the United States are given, but in a more complete analysis one would perhaps expect to see OPEC investments in the United States as endogenous. Given the endogeneity of these investments, the externality feature associated with a tariff on energy in reducing the return on OPEC-owned capital and providing gains to the United States would seem to disappear since OPEC investments would take that into account. Also in this area there is a substantial amount of recent literature, notably that by Bhagwati and Breacher which the authors might rerfer to.

A further point concerns the third country issue. Most of the analysis is in terms of two countries but, as has already been mentioned, there is a free-rider issue with the terms of trade effects. Europe and Japan in particular free ride on any terms of trade gain from U.S. oil policy.

A final point concerns the convenience yield on oil mentioned in the paper. This is the inventories' yield from their availability to cover potential shocks to the economy either in meeting increased oil demands or covering supply disruptions. What is not made clear in the paper is the extent to which the convenience yield of oil in the SPR is any different than the convenience yield of oil in conventional fields. Some discussion of the technical aspects of this issue in the paper would be helpful.

References

Nichols, Albert L., and Richard J. Zeckhauser. 1977. Stockpiling strategies and cartel prices. *Bell Journal of Economics* 6:66–96.

IV Export-Promoting Policies

Introduction

Like other countries, the U.S. government pursues export-promoting as well as import-restraining policies. The two papers in part IV analyze the two most important of these; namely, the tax incentive policy provided through legislation allowing U.S. firms to create Domestic International Sales Corporations (DISCs), and the policy of providing export credits at below-market rates through the Export-Import Bank.

Utilizing a general equilibrium model, Mutti and Grubert estimate the net export increase from DISCs to be about 3 percent—a figure that is somewhat lower than the increase estimated by the U.S. Treasury Department using a partial equilibrium approach. The distribution impact of the program, according to their calculations, is a wage decline for unskilled workers and a wage increase for skilled workers. Furthermore, they find a net welfare loss for the country of roughly .04 percent of national income.

Fleisig and Hill focus on estimating the amount of the subsidy involved in export credit programs. On the basis of alternative assumptions about whether interest rates are fixed or floating, they estimate that the subsidy element in the U.S. Export-Import Bank's direct loan program was between $213 and $992 million in 1980. The total for all major lending countries ranges from $1.5 billion to $3.5 billion as of 1980, depending on the fixed or floating rate assumption. They conclude that from between half and all of this subsidy is transferred to the foreign borrowers.

8   The Domestic International Sales Corporation and Its Effects

John Mutti and Harry Grubert

8.1   Introduction and Overview

Legislation which allowed U.S. firms to create Domestic International Sales Corporations (DISCs) was enacted in 1971. Under its provisions the tax due on a portion of the export income attributable to a DISC could be deferred, and therefore the program represented a tax incentive to export. The way in which the tax incentive was tied to a reduction in the firm's corporate income tax liability also created an incentive to substitute capital for other factors of production. In 1976 and 1982 the tax benefits from DISC were scaled back by the U.S. Congress. Additionally, the program was criticized by the Europeans as a violation of the General Agreement on Tariffs and Trade (GATT). Nevertheless, DISC was still in place in 1982, its benefits were claimed on 70 percent of all U.S. exports, and a tax saving of roughly $1.5 billion was realized.

Export promotion policies often generate the greatest amount of public attention when the economy is in a business contraction or when the trade deficit is large. In this analysis, these conditions, which imply that disequilibria in labor markets or foreign exchange markets exist, are ignored. Instead, a longer-run general equilibrium approach is taken. In this framework, DISC still might result in a welfare improvement, even though the impact of the subsidy is to worsen the U.S. terms of trade. Such an improvement might occur because of second-best factors, such as

John Mutti is professor of economics at the University of Wyoming. Harry Grubert is with the Office of International Tax Affairs, U.S. Treasury Department, Washington, D.C.

The ideas expressed are solely those of the authors and not the U.S. Treasury Department. Many helpful suggestions from conference participants are gratefully acknowledged, including Alan Deardorff's comments on the appendices. Any remaining errors are our own.

279

the distorting effect of the current corporate income tax or the tax deferral provisions available with respect to income earned abroad by U.S. controlled foreign corporations. In fact, DISC was promoted on the basis that it would give U.S. firms a greater incentive to produce and export from the United States instead of serving foreign markets by locating abroad. A major focus of this paper is to determine the extent to which investment and production at home versus abroad is affected by incentives such as DISC.

In the static, general equilibrium model developed here, two countries are represented, the U.S. and the rest of the world. The model in part is made up of familiar elements, including:

(a) Commodity demand functions in each country describing the choice between imported goods, domestically produced competing goods, home nontraded goods, and exportables.

(b) Factor demand equations in each country in which the demand for each factor depends on the quantity of each good produced and on relative factor prices.

(c) Competitive price equations in which the price of each good is equated to total factor cost.

DISC enters into this framework in several ways. First, it reduces the relative price charged for U.S. exports because it lowers the tax component of export costs. In addition, DISC lowers the cost of capital in export production relative to the cost of other inputs because it lowers the tax only on the return to capital. This tends to increase the demand for capital in the United States. Finally DISC changes the level of real income, which affects U.S. product demands, because the export incentive has to be financed by either an increase in other taxes or lower government expenditures. In other words, the benefit to foreigners in terms of more favorable prices requires a reduction in expenditures by the United States.

This income effect alternatively can be related to the terms of trade change experienced by the United States. If foreigners are able to obtain U.S. goods more cheaply because less U.S. tax is collected on export earnings, the U.S. terms of trade worsen and real income falls. When greater U.S. export output drives up the relative price of exports, this partially offsets the direct tax cost of DISC. Equivalently, the terms of trade loss is reduced.

The model developed here has a few other special features. Production of all goods is assumed to require three factors of production—unskilled labor, skilled labor, and capital—in order that aspects of the controversy over the factor content of trade (see, for example, Baldwin 1971; Branson and Monoyios 1977) be included in the analysis. This situation contrasts to the simpler breakdown of labor and capital alone in two earlier general equilibrium models by Goulder, Shoven, and Whalley (1981) and by Horst (1981) used to analyze international tax policy changes. Also, in the Horst model only a single good was produced abroad, while the Goulder model did not include foreign production, but rather foreign endowments of output. The present model, in which each country produces three goods, allows a more complete representation of the possibilities to reallocate resources across industries in the rest of the world. Such a distinction particularly might be expected to influence the allocation of capital internationally (Jones 1967; Gerking and Mutti 1981).

The effects of DISC on international capital allocation are important in this study for two reasons. First, the potential reduction in U.S. income resulting from the terms of trade loss may be offset if DISC results in more capital being used in the United States, where it will be subject to U.S. rather than foreign taxation. Second, the reallocation of capital may significantly affect the distributional impacts of DISC. The allocation of capital internationally is assumed to depend on relative after-tax rates of return in the United States and the rest of the world. DISC provides an incentive to use more capital in U.S. export production, but U.S. produced capital goods also become cheaper abroad. To include these various and potentially offsetting effects, two alternative treatments of international capital mobility are formulated. A key question addressed is the extent to which after-tax returns across countries or across sectors are equalized. In one formulation of the model, after-tax returns are equalized across sectors within a country, and varying degrees of capital mobility are assumed internationally. This framework, which assumes a very high degree of integration of capital markets domestically, is similar to the work of Goulder et al. and of Horst. An alternative formulation treats the closest substitute for investment in a particular industry not as investment in another sector of the home market, but rather as investment in the same industry abroad. This treatment reflects the perspective of past writings on the operations of multinational corporations by Caves (1971) and Batra and Ramachandran (1980), based on the view that multinational corporations may earn higher than normal returns to specific expertise applicable in their industry alone.

As in previous work, the model is complex enough that analytical solutions do not yield unambiguous signs, and determination of the direction and magnitude of changes in output, prices, and factor rewards must be based on a particular set of parameter values. Empirical projections from these two frameworks are made on the basis of data from the operation of DISCs in 1979. These data provide a useful indication of the relative effects of DISC on outputs and factor rewards, although the absolute size of these changes would be expected to decline if provisions of the 1981 Economic Recovery Tax Act (ERTA) result in sharply reduced corporate tax burdens and a correspondingly smaller differential incentive to export as a result of DISC.

With respect to the two models developed, the simulated results are somewhat similar when a high degree of capital mobility is assumed internationally, but as capital becomes less mobile, substantial differences between them arise. Of particular interest from a policy perspective, the percentage change in the volume of merchandise exports (about 3 percent if all exports were covered by DISC) is roughly 65 percent of the estimate that would be obtained using the same trade elasticities in a partial equilibrium framework. Unskilled labor clearly loses from DISC, while skilled labor benefits if capital can easily be reallocated internationally. From the standpoint of economic efficiency, DISC results in a deterioration of the U.S. terms of trade. The stock of capital used in the United States increases slightly, but the gains from this reallocation are not great enough to offset the terms of trade loss. U.S. welfare falls by roughly half of the tax cost of DISC.

The organization of this paper first is to explain the incentives created by DISC for a single firm. Then the general equilibrium model of the United States and the rest of the world is presented. The major purpose of this model is to show how DISC affects the allocation of resources both nationally and internationally. Values of the appropriate behavioral demand and production parameters are discussed next, followed by the projected changes in outputs and factor rewards attributable to DISC. Consequent welfare effects of DISC on the United States are analyzed, and a concluding section notes other relevant issues for any policy assessment of DISC.

8.2   The Analysis of DISC at the Micro Level

8.2.1   Background and History

Domestic International Sales Corporations, through which exporters can defer (indefinitely) the tax on part of the corporate income earned on exports, were first authorized by the Revenue Act of 1971. There are two basic steps in calculating the portion of export profits that can be tax deferred. The first determines the amount of overall export profits that can be allocated to the DISC, and the second, the percentage of the DISC's income whose taxation can be deferred.

In the first step, a DISC can have profits which do not exceed the greater of:

(1) 4 percent of the gross value of qualified export sales plus 10 percent of related export promotion expenses;

(2) 50 percent of the combined taxable income from exports of the DISC and its parent plus 10 percent of export promotion expenses;

(3) income based on the price actually charged the DISC by the supplier if it can be justified under the normal "arm's-length" rules.

The first two options are departures from normal arm's-length transfer pricing rules and are an important source of DISC benefits. The third pricing or allocation option would ordinarily only be chosen by independent DISCs who export goods purchased from third parties. A corporation producing export goods would choose option (2), the 50 percent rule, if its profit margin were in excess of 8 percent of sales, because it could then defer more income than under the 4 percent rule. If, on the other hand, margins are less than 8 percent of sales, it would choose the 4 percent rule. In fact, DISC exports are split about equally between those using the 4 percent of gross sales rule and those using the 50 percent of combined taxable income rule. However, the 50-50 rule accounts for about 80 percent of the total corporate profits deferred through DISCs. In terms of the capital used in exports, therefore, the 50-50 rule is by far the most significant.

Turning now to the portion of DISC income that can be deferred, a DISC is itself tax-exempt, but its shareholders are taxed on actual or imputed dividends from the DISC. In the original legislation in 1971, a DISC was assumed to distribute 50 percent of its income, whether it actually distributed this large a share of income to the parent or not. This meant that an exporter using the 50-50 rule could defer 25 percent of the overall combined taxable profits from exports. The Tax Reform Act of 1976 limited the 50 percent deferral to DISC profits attributable to exports in excess of 67 percent of average exports in a four-year base period, the last year of which is four years prior to the current tax year. As a result of the incremental rule, the average deferral rate in 1979 was 32.3 percent instead of the earlier 50 percent. In view of the amount of income allocated to the DISC, 18.3 percent of the combined export profits of the DISC and its parent was deferred. DISC therefore represents an 18.3 percent reduction in the corporate tax on export income. This will be regarded simply as a reduction in the tax *rate* on capital income, even though for the small share of benefits derived by users of the 4 percent of sales rule, DISC is more of an ad valorem subsidy on exports unrelated to factor usage. The Tax Equity and Fiscal Responsibility Act of 1982 further reduced DISC benefits by reducing the deferral permitted under previous law by 15 percent, that is, the 50 percent deferral rate now is 42.5 percent.

8.2.2 Economic Incentives Created by DISC

DISC changes the relative cost of exports by lowering the cost of equity capital used in export production relative to the cost of capital elsewhere in the economy. The cost of capital services to a firm reflects the price of the capital good involved in production, the after-tax return that has to be given to investors for them to supply their capital, and any tax liability that results from the capital return. For a given after-tax return at the corporate level, capital must produce a gross return sufficient both to pay investors this after-tax return and to pay the required taxes to the government.

Consider the simple case in which there is only equity capital, that is, no debt, and real capital does not depreciate. (See appendix A for further elaboration.) Assume the price of capital goods used in production is c. Then, for a given required after-tax return of i percent per year, and a tax on the equity return to capital of t, the annual marginal product of capital, m, must be such that $m (1 - t) = ci$. In other words, the annual rental cost of capital input is $ci/(1 - t)$ (Hall and Jorgenson 1967). If the capital tax rate on exports falls from t to t_1, then for the given after-tax return, the marginal cost of capital declines to $(1 - t)/(1 - t_1)$ of its former level. With perfect competition in exports, which is assumed in the paper, export prices fall by the amount of the decline in the marginal cost of output. DISC therefore reduces the price of exports relative to other goods in the same way that a lower payroll tax in a particular activity would lower the activity's price relative to other goods. Workers would be willing to work for a lower gross wage, which is the cost to the employer, because they can get the same after-tax income as in other activities.

DISC also affects factor input usage, because it reduces the extent to which equity capital is discouraged relative to other inputs. Again, taking the case where all capital is financed by equity, and therefore not a deductible cost of doing business, the ratio of the marginal productivities of capital and labor is $ci/[(1 - t)w]$, where w is the wage rate, equal to the marginal productivity of labor. When DISC reduces the corporate tax rate faced, there is an incentive to substitute capital for labor.

8.2.3 The Interaction of DISC and Other Tax Incentives

Looking at the way DISC interacts with other tax incentives, such as the investment tax credit and accelerated depreciation, may help illustrate the way DISC works. The interaction with investment tax credits and depreciation allowances differs. An increased investment tax credit, such as the present 10 percent credit for most equipment, has a limited effect on the *relative* incentive effect of DISC, that is, the cost of exports relative to other goods. An exporter can still continue to enjoy the same DISC benefits and in addition use the additional investment tax credit for any remaining tax liability. On the other hand, increased depreciation allowances, as in ERTA, do erode the DISC benefit. As indicated above, most capital in exports uses the 50-50 pricing rule for DISC income. The amount of tax deferral that can be provided by a DISC therefore depends on the amount of overall *taxable* income on the export sale. Increased depreciation allowances reduce taxable income, which means that the tax saving per dollar of export sales is reduced. In the extreme case where depreciation allowances eliminate taxable income, DISC provides no benefit.

Increased depreciation allowances may also erode the DISC benefits to those using the 4 percent of gross sales rule, because the allocation of income to the DISC cannot result in a loss to the parent. Increased depreciation allowances, as in the Accelerated Cost Recovery System in 1981, will reduce the DISC benefit if they reduce overall *taxable* profit margins below 4 percent.

The interaction between DISC and other tax incentives is clear from the standard Hall-Jorgenson cost of capital formula,

$$\frac{c(1 - k - tZ)}{(1 - t)} (i + \delta),$$

where t is the corporate tax rate, k is the rate of the investment tax credit, i is the required real percentage after-tax return, δ is the annual rate of economic depreciation, and Z is the present value of depreciation allowances (evaluated using the nominal return). DISC is effectively a reduction in the tax rate t. The formula demonstrates that the effect on the cost of capital of a reduction in the tax rate is diluted by an increase in Z, the value of depreciation deductions.

The significance of the effect of the Accelerated Cost Recovery System (ACRS) in ERTA on the incentive effect of DISC can be seen from the changes in the revenue cost of DISC resulting from the enactment of ACRS. The U.S. Treasury Department (1981) estimates that by 1984 the revenue costs of DISC will be 18 percent lower because of ACRS.

8.3   DISC in a General Equilibrium Model

An overview of the general equilibrium approach taken in this study was given in the introduction. Here two different models are developed to be used in evaluating DISC.

8.3.1   The Case of Homogeneous Capital

In this model, two countries are assumed. Each country produces three goods. Also, each country has fixed supplies of unskilled and skilled labor, which are immobile internationally but which can be shifted cost-lessly across industries within a country. Total capital available in the world is fixed. Within a country capital is perfectly mobile among industries, but internationally capital mobility is not sufficient to equalize after-tax returns. This result with respect to international capital flows is somewhat similar to the framework proposed by Kemp and Wan (1974), where international adjustment costs are assumed to exist but the adjustment process also is not modeled explicitly.

In each country perfectly competitive output and factor markets are assumed. Given strictly quasi-concave, linear, homogeneous production functions, full employment of all factors of production is ensured. In country A this condition is represented as

$$(1) \qquad C_{L1}^A X_{1A} + C_{L2}^A X_{2A} + C_{LN}^A X_{NA} = L_A,$$

$$(2) \qquad C_{S1}^A X_{1A} + C_{S2}^A X_{2A} + C_{SN}^A X_{NA} = S_A,$$

$$(3) \qquad C_{K1}^A X_{1A} + C_{K2}^A X_{2A} + C_{KN}^A X_{NA} = K_A,$$

where C_{ij}^k is the amount of input i necessary to produce one unit of output j in country k, X_{iA} represents output of the ith good in country A, and the factor supplies of unskilled labor, skilled labor, and capital are denoted by L_A, S_A, and K_A, respectively. As shown in appendix B, DISC incentives affect the determination of input-output coefficients in industries one and two, and any change in DISC alters optimal factor proportions.

The three aggregate production sectors of the economy represent a composite of industries for which the country is a net importer, X_{1A}, a composite of industries for which the country is a net exporter, X_{2A}, and a nontraded sector, X_{NA}. This characterization of three separate industries is somewhat similar to the trade literature testing the factor content of trade, where regression models are estimated to predict whether an industry is a net exporter or a net importer based on certain industry characteristics. In both that situation and in the present model, factor input requirements are assumed to differ across industries.

However, the definition of a net import or net export industry may suggest another condition not imposed on this analysis. Domestic output in an industry is not assumed to be perfectly substitutable with output from the same industry in the other country. Thus, three similar full-employment equations can be written for country B as follows:

$$(4) \qquad C_{L1}^B X_{1B} + C_{L2}^B X_{2B} + C_{LN}^B X_{NB} = L_B,$$

$$(5) \qquad C_{S1}^B X_{1B} + C_{S2}^B X_{2B} + C_{SN}^B X_{NB} = S_B,$$

$$(6) \qquad C_{K1}^B X_{1B} + C_{K2}^B X_{2B} + C_{KN}^B X_{NB} = K_B,$$

but X_{iA} and X_{iB} are not identical products. Additionally, the assumption that the available supply of capital in the world is fixed, $K_A + K_B = \bar{K}$, allows equation (6) to be rewritten in terms of K_A.

Perfectly competitive output markets, together with the earlier production assumptions, guarantee that producers earn zero profits in equilibrium, so that

(7) $C_{L1}^A \, w_A + C_{S1}^A \, q_A + C_{K1}^A \, r_A/(1 - t_{1A}) = P_{1A}$,

(8) $C_{L2}^A \, w_A + C_{S2}^A \, q_A + C_{K2}^A \, r_A/(1 - t_{2A}) = P_{2A}$,

(9) $C_{LN}^A \, w_A + C_{SN}^A \, q_A + C_{KN}^A \, r_A/(1 - t_{NA}) = P_{NA} = 1$,

(10) $C_{L1}^B \, w_B + C_{S1}^B \, q_B + C_{K1}^B \, r_B/(1 - t_{1B}) = P_{1B}$,

(11) $C_{L2}^B \, w_B + C_{S2}^B \, q_B + C_{K2}^B \, r_B/(1 - t_{2B}) = P_{2B}$,

(12) $C_{LN}^B \, w_B + C_{SN}^B \, q_B + C_{KN}^B \, r_B/(1 - t_{NB}) = P_{NB}$,

where w_i is the wage paid to unskilled labor in country i, q_i is the wage paid to skilled labor in country i, r_i is the after-tax return to capital paid in country i, and t_{ij} is an ad valorem tax levied on capital income in industry i of country j. Also, P_{ij} is the price of X_{ij} received by the producer. Again, because goods produced in the same industry but in different countries are not assumed to be identical, five relative price terms must be included, with the price of the nontraded good in A being the numéraire. Since capital is perfectly mobile within a country, the same after-tax return to capital is earned in all industries, but clearly the before-tax returns will differ when tax rates across industries differ.

Consumers in each country choose among five different goods, X_{1A}, X_{2A}, X_{1B}, X_{2B}, and the relevant nontraded good, X_{NA} or X_{NB}. That is, country A exports some of its net import goods and country B exports some of its net import goods. Quantities demanded will depend on income and the relative prices of these goods, inclusive of any tariffs. Because this formulation is quite standard, the relevant equations are presented in appendix B, which shows the way DISC affects import prices seen by foreigners. One aspect which does deserve special attention is the relevant income expression, which depends on four types of terms: (1) the value of production within a country; (2) net earnings from foreign investment after payment of foreign taxes; (3) tariff revenues; and (4) the value of subsidies paid to foreigners through DISC export promotion.

(13) $Y_A = P_{1A}X_{1A} + P_{2A}X_{2A} + X_{NA} + r_B(\tilde{K}_A - K_A)$
$+ \text{TAR}_{1A}P_{1BA}X_{1BA} + \text{TAR}_{2A}P_{2BA}X_{2BA}$
$- \text{DISCP} \cdot P_{1A}X_{1AB} - \text{DISCP} \cdot P_{2A}X_{2AB}$.

(14) $Y_B = P_{1B}X_{1B} + P_{2B}X_{2B} + P_{NB}X_{NB} + r_B(\tilde{K}_B - K_B)$
$+ \text{TAR}_{1B}P_{1AB}X_{1AB} + \text{TAR}_{2B}P_{2AB}X_{2AB}$.

Y_i is the value of nominal income in country i. $\tilde{K}_i$ indicates country i's ownership of capital, while K_i is the amount of worldwide capital used in country i. The amount of capital used in a country can change in response to economic incentives. When capital is reallocated from country A to country B, then K_A declines and K_B increases. The United States is a net creditor to the rest of the world, so that $(\tilde{K}_A - K_A) > 0$, while the rest of the world is a net debtor, where $(\tilde{K}_B - K_B) = -(\tilde{K}_A - K_A) < 0$. TAR_{ij} represents ad valorem tariff rates levied in country j on imports of i goods, P_{ijk} are the prices charged to consumers in country k for good i produced in country j, and the X_{ijk} are interpreted similarly in the case of sales. The DISCP terms represent the cost to the United States of the tax benefit offered to exporters. It is the difference between the tax exporters would have paid without DISC and their tax payments inclusive of DISC benefits. The additional tax that exporters would pay without DISC reflects *both* the higher tax rate *and* the higher pretax income that would have to be earned to end up with the same after-tax income.

To more fully understand the representation of capital in this model, recognize that the production functions are based on a flow of capital services. The income equations also include terms that represent payments to foreigners for a flow of capital services. However, the capital services available in a country will be proportional to the stock of capital located in it, and this stock will change when the location of capital internationally shifts. The relocation of capital represents a stock adjustment which could be written in terms of the actual capital stocks. To simplify notation, though, separate terms are not introduced to represent them. Rather, because available capital stocks always are assumed to be proportional to the physical flows of capital services (e.g., machine hours per year), both the stock of capital in country i and the flow of capital services available in country i are assumed to be represented by K_i.

It is assumed that capital goods in A are identical to those in B. However, they are not transported physically from one country to another. Therefore, any capital reallocation implicitly is based on the situation where capital depreciates in the country losing capital, while new capital is produced in the country gaining it. In each country, capital is assumed to be manufactured from the five available goods in the same proportions as consumers demand them. Capital goods are therefore equivalent to the average consumption good in each country. Actual depreciation rates and gross investment decisions are not included in the model, which gives net outputs and the new reallocation of capital.

The new equilibrium allocation of the world capital stock depends on relative after-tax rates of return and is represented by

(15)
$$\frac{K_A}{\bar{K}} = g_0 \left[\frac{r_A}{\text{CPI}_A} \Big/ \frac{r_B}{\text{CPI}_B} \right]^{g_1}$$

The CPI terms represent a price index for each country. The rate of return in a country depends on the value of the marginal product of physical capital, r, and its price of capital, CPI. Because DISC results in lower prices of capital goods abroad, CPI_B, the percentage rate of return abroad does not fall in the same proportion as the fall in the value of the marginal product of capital abroad, r_B. Ignoring this price of capital effect would result in a larger projected shift of capital into the United States than would actually occur. The model would yield the same results if it were expressed in terms of the percentage rate of return, i, and the cost of capital goods, c, presented earlier in the Hall-Jorgenson framework.

Of the ten demand equations referred to above, only nine are considered explicitly in order to set quantity demanded equal to quantity supplied in five markets and thereby close the model. Thus, this model consists of twenty-seven equations (six full-employment equations, six zero-profit equations, nine commodity-demand equations, one international capital flow equation, and five market balance equations) to determine changes in six industry outputs, six factor rewards, nine quantities demanded, five relative prices, and the flow of capital internationally. All equations are expressed in percentage rates of change, as shown in appendix B, which is the form in which the model is applied to predict percentage changes in outputs, factor rewards, and capital flows as a result of DISC. This method of analysis differs from the approach of Goulder et al., which works from *levels* of outputs and factor rewards to predict final levels of these variables. The changes in these variables predicted here would be expected to give a close approximation to any solution based on the more general technique of Goulder et al., since the effects of DISC are quite small in relation to the U.S. economy. Thus, any interaction terms ignored in the process of differentiating the model should be insignificant.

8.3.2 The Case of Industry-Specific Capital

The alternative case of industry-specific capital requires no modification of the demand side of the model. With respect to supply conditions, if the capital currently employed in each industry is regarded as specific to that industry, then in each country three full-employment equations for the three categories of capital replace the single previous equation. Thus, equation (3) is replaced by

$$(16) \qquad C_{K1}^A X_{1A} = K_{1A},$$

$$(17) \qquad C_{K2}^A X_{2A} = K_{2A},$$

$$(18) \qquad C_{KN}^A X_{NA} = K_{NA};$$

and equation (6) becomes

$$(19) \qquad C_{K1}^B X_{1B} = K_{1B},$$

$$(20) \qquad C_{K2}^B X_{2B} = K_{2B},$$

$$(21) \qquad C_{KN}^B X_{NB} = K_{NB}.$$

Allowing for industry-specific capital means that six different returns to capital must be determined. Therefore, the zero-profit equations (7) to (12) must be rewritten in terms of these separate variables.

Also, the reallocation of capital no longer is summarized in terms of perfect mobility domestically and some degree of mobility internationally. Rather, if capital employed in a single sector is to expand, it must be attracted from other sectors, but in no case is this transfer costless. An example of the framework considered is as follows:

$$(22) \quad K_{1A} = g_{1A0} \left[\frac{r_{1A}}{\text{CPI}_A} \middle/ \frac{r_{1B}}{\text{CPI}_B} \right]^{g_{1A1B}} \cdot \left[\frac{r_{1A}}{r_{2A}} \right]^{g_{1A2A}}$$

$$\cdot \left[\frac{r_{1A}}{r_{NA}} \right]^{g_{1ANA}} \cdot \left[\frac{r_{1A}}{\text{CPI}_A} \middle/ \frac{r_{2B}}{\text{CPI}_B} \right]^{g_{1A2B}}$$

$$\cdot \left[\frac{r_{1A}}{\text{CPI}_A} \middle/ \frac{r_{NB}}{\text{CPI}_B} \right]^{g_{1ANB}} .$$

Capital is assumed to be more mobile from one country to another in the same industry than it is between different industries in the same country, because owners of capital have specialized knowledge about their present industry. Thus, g_{1A2A} is assumed to be smaller than g_{1A1B}, for example. Costs of transferring capital from outside the industry and outside the country are assumed to be even higher, so that g_{1ANB} is smaller than g_{1A2A}. Also, since

$$(23) \quad \frac{\partial K_{1A}}{\partial (r_{1A}/r_{2A})} = \frac{-\partial K_{2A}}{\partial (r_{1A}/r_{2A})},$$

for example, the values of the g_{ij} across the different capital-flow equations are not independent. Similar equations are introduced for K_{2A}, K_{NA}, K_{1B}, and K_{2B}.

The four additional capital-flow equations plus the four additional full-employment conditions represent the modifications to be included in the model with industry-specific capital. This thirty-five equation system determines changes attributable to DISC in six industry outputs, ten factor rewards, nine commodity demands, five relative output prices, and five capital flows. Again, the differentiated form of the complete model is presented in appendix B.

8.4   Empirical Implementation of the Model

As stated in the introduction, few unambiguous results can be deduced a priori in this model, and any conclusions drawn will depend on the set of parameter values considered to be most appropriate. The three aggregate goods were created on the basis of industry information reported in the

1972, eighty-five-sector, input-output table of the United States. Non-traded goods and services, X_{NA}, basically were considered to be utilities, construction, transportation and communication, wholesale and retail trade, social and personal services, finance, banking and real estate, and government. Net export goods, X_{2A}, where an export surplus was reported in 1972, essentially were grains, chemicals, and machinery. Net import goods, X_{1A}, where imports exceeded exports in 1972, included many consumer durables and nondurables.

Factor intensities of production are based on the value-added figures from the input-output table. Direct and indirect capital and labor requirements for each of the three aggregate sectors are calculated from the direct value-added shares and the matrix of direct and indirect intermediate input requirements reported at the eighty-five-sector level. These data alone only allow the breakdown of factor requirements to distinguish between capital and labor, and therefore additional information is necessary to decompose the labor requirements into skilled and unskilled components. The basis for that distinction is information on industry employment made available by Professor Robert Baldwin. This employment figure is multiplied by the annualized minimum wage to indicate the return to unskilled labor in an industry, and the remainder of labor value-added is attributed to skilled labor. By assuming that wage rates across industries are identical, these value-added figures also can be used to infer the physical allocation of resources implicit in the full-employment equations.

With respect to general statements characterizing U.S. industry, the nontraded sector has above average capital requirements, unskilled labor requirements well above average, and skilled labor requirements well below average. The export sector has skilled labor requirements well above average, and unskilled labor requirements well below average, while the import sector is slightly less skill intensive and slightly more unskilled labor intensive than exports. These findings are roughly consistent with studies of the factor content of trade (Branson and Monoyios 1977; Bowen 1980) concerning the skill intensity of exports versus imports. However, much larger factor requirement differences exist between both tradable sectors and the nontradable sector.

Partial elasticities of substitution between capital and unskilled labor, unskilled labor and skilled labor, and capital and skilled labor do not appear to be well established. A survey piece on this subject by Hamermesh and Grant (1980) indicates that most studies deal only with the breakdown of production workers versus nonproduction workers, which cannot be easily related to differential amounts of human capital in each category of workers. Grant's dissertation (1979) provides estimates based on data where years of educational attainment could be distinguished, although his survey work notes the possible downward bias of cross-sectional estimates relative to those based on time series. His figures are adapted to give the following set of figures applied to all industries in the study: $\sigma_{KL} = \sigma_{LS} = .60$, and $\sigma_{KS} = .05$. In other words, a very low degree of substitution between capital and skilled labor is assumed relative to the other trade-offs in factor usage.

Demand elasticities are generated from the assumption of utility tree functions of the following form:

(24) $U_A = U_A[(X_{1A}, X_{1B})\ (X_{2A}, X_{2B}), X_{NA}]$.

(25) $U_B = U_B[(X_{1A}, X_{1B}), (X_{2A}, X_{2B}), X_{NB}]$.

If this nested utility function is CES in form, then as shown by Armington (1969), own and cross-price elasticities of demand can be derived directly from information regarding expenditure shares and elasticities of substitution at different levels of the utility tree. For example, the own and cross-price elasticities of demand for X_{1A} sold in country A will be

(26) $N_{1A,1A} = (1 - S_{1A})\ \sigma_1 + S_{1A}N_1$,

(27) $N_{1A,1B} = (1 - S_{1A})\ (\sigma_1 - N_1)$,

where S_{1A} is the share of the budget spent on X_1 which is allocated to X_{1A}, σ_1 is the elasticity of substitution between X_{1A} and X_{1B}, and N_1 is the elasticity of demand for the aggregate commodity X_1. To form a consistent aggregate such as X_1 requires that the income elasticity of demand for X_{1A} and X_{1B} be identical, and in this study all income elasticities are set equal to one. The elasticity of substitution between the two traded goods in the same utility tree is assumed to be 3, the corresponding elasticity between the three general categories X_1, X_2, and X_N is assumed to be 1.25, and the elasticity of demand for all current consumption as an aggregate is -1. As examples of what these values imply with respect to more commonly estimated parameters, the import elasticity of demand in the United States for X_{1B} equals -2.69, and the elasticity of demand for U.S. exports of X_{2A} to the rest of the world equals -2.79.

Information regarding flows of capital internationally is quite limited, as is information with respect to the initial division of capital across countries. Bowen (1980) estimates that in 1975 the United States accounted for roughly one-third of the world's capital stock. The mobility of capital internationally represents one of the weakest links empirically in the present model, and therefore different values of capital responsiveness are simulated to test the sensitivity of the results to the somewhat arbitrary assignment of values.

Although the general degree of capital mobility is varied in simulations for both specifications of the model, in the case of industry-specific capital a single set of values is used to represent differences in the cost of reallocating capital from one sector to another. Capital flowing across countries in the same traded good industry is assumed to be twice as responsive to rate of return differentials as capital flowing from other industries in the same country, and ten times as responsive as capital flowing from other industries in the opposite country. For example, from equation (23) the following relationship among coefficients holds: $g_{1A1B} = 2g_{1A2A} = 10g_{1ANB}$.

To estimate the direct effect of DISC on export prices, start with the tax saving per dollar of export sales, which was .94 percent in 1979. If DISC were eliminated and exporters increased their prices to maintain after-tax returns, their *taxable* income would increase. For example, if they increased prices by 1 percent, their after-tax income would only go up by .54 percent of sales and tax liability by .46 percent, with a 46 percent tax rate. Therefore, to regain the full .94 percent loss in tax benefits, exporters would have to raise their prices by .94/.54 or 1.74 percent. This is the estimated DISC impact on export prices.

DISC resulted in a reduction in the cost of capital in export production of 11.4 percent in 1979. We assume that the change in the marginal cost of capital is equal to the change in the average cost. The marginal cost is not estimated directly because of the difficulty in implementing the Hall-Jorgenson formula on a comprehensive scale. The estimate of the change in the average cost of capital is based in part on the various components of the net cost of capital in the corporate sector computed by Ballard, Fullerton, Shoven, and Whalley (1982). These include the after-tax corporate profits, federal and local corporate income taxes, property taxes, and interest paid. A federal corporate tax rate is computed after adding back investment tax credits to corporate liabilities because, as noted above, DISC represents an approximately 18.3 percent reduction in corporate taxes *before* credits. This 18.3 percent reduction in taxes is used to compute a new post-DISC level of corporate taxes, holding the amount of after-tax profits constant. This is then used to compute a new aggregate cost of capital which reflects the lower tax attributable to DISC. The incentive to substitute capital for labor in the production of X_{1A} and X_{2A} depends on this cost reduction and the share of industry output which is exported. Because the share of X_{2A} output which is exported is five times greater than the share of X_{1A} output which is exported, DISC has a much greater effect on factor proportions in X_{2A} than in X_{1A} production.

The estimated effects of DISC on the cost of capital and on export prices are based on the *average* tax saving by exporters per dollar of sales and investment income. One reason why the marginal incentive may differ from the average in this context is the incremental provisions introduced in 1976. For an additional dollar worth of exports, the DISC would in 1979 obtain a full deferral rate of 50 percent, but there would be some loss in later years because the base for computing incremental exports in future years increases. It turns out that in 1979 the marginal deferral rate would have been equal to the average observed rate if firms used a 12 percent discount rate.

The estimated effects of DISC on prices and on the cost of capital assume that any deferral of tax through the use of a DISC is the equivalent to the exemption of tax, that is, the deferral can be indefinite. The retained earnings of a DISC have to be invested in certain specified "qualified" export assets, but this limitation does not seem to be significant. This is suggested by the fact that *actual* dividends by DISCs to their parents in 1979 were only 73 percent of the distributions assumed under the DISC rules. Furthermore, total DISC assets grew much faster than they would have simply from retained earnings. All of this means that DISCs could profitably use assets substantially in excess of those they had to hold to prevent the taxation of previously deferred income.

8.5   Empirical Results: A Positive Analysis

Projected changes in output and the allocation of capital internationally are reported in table 8.1. The corresponding changes in factor rewards and output prices are reported in table 8.2. For each of the two different model specifications (homogeneous versus industry-specific capital), three sets of values are reported to demonstrate how sensitive the results of the model are to the extent of capital mobility internationally. The polar case of no international capital mobility, $g = 0$, is included to demonstrate what limiting values will be reached as mobility declines.

Table 8.1   Projected Impacts on Output and Capital Utilization from DISC (all figures represent percentage changes)

Vari-able	Case of Homogeneous Capital			Case of Industry-Specific Capital		
	$g = 100$	$g = 1$	$g = 0$	$g = 100$	$g = 1$	$g = 0$
X_{1A}	$-.067$	$-.069$	$-.078$	$-.068$	$-.011$	.401
X_{2A}	.802	.800	.791	.800	.447	$-.326$
X_{NA}	$-.063$	$-.064$	$-.068$	$-.062$	$-.036$	$-.150$
X_{1B}	.091	.092	.097	.091	.072	.031
X_{2B}	$-.057$	$-.056$	$-.052$	$-.056$	$-.014$	.052
X_{NB}	$-.038$	$-.037$	$-.036$	$-.038$	$-.030$	$-.015$
K_A	.038	.031	.000	—	—	—
K_{1A}	.042	.036	.010	.038	$-.056$	.000
K_{2A}	1.256	1.252	1.227	1.250	.908	.000
K_{NA}	$-.085$	$-.092$	$-.126$	$-.083$	$-.049$	.000
K_{1B}	—	—	—	.085	.063	.000
K_{2B}	—	—	—	$-.061$	$-.022$	.000

Table 8.2   **Projected Impacts on Prices and Factor Rewards from DISC (all figures represent percentage changes)**

Vari-able	Case of Homogeneous Capital			Case of Industry-Specific Capital		
	$g = 100$	$g = 1$	$g = 0$	$g = 100$	$g = 1$	$g = 0$
wA	−.099	−.101	−.110	−.098	−.065	−.221
qA	.100	.092	.054	.099	.079	−.175
rA	.003	.024	.130	—	—	—
$r1A$	—	—	—	.003	−.003	−.804
$r2A$	—	—	—	.018	1.138	3.547
rNA	—	—	—	.001	−.028	.888
wB	−.661	−.664	−.680	−.661	−.620	−.802
qB	−.607	−.620	−.614	−.611	−.576	−.778
rB	−.611	−.612	−.686	—	—	—
$r1B$	—	—	—	−.607	−.543	−.574
$r2B$	—	—	—	−.607	−.548	−.372
rNB	—	—	—	−.608	−.610	−.861
$P1A$	.045	.045	.043	.045	.037	−.327
$P2A$	.054	.052	.046	.056	.271	.558
$P1B$	−.633	−.636	−.655	−.633	−.589	−.754
$P2B$	−.634	−.637	−.654	−.634	−.592	−.721
PNB	−.601	−.604	−.623	−.601	−.572	−.765
$CPIA$	−.022	−.023	−.025	−.022	−.010	−.084
$CPIB$	−.635	−.638	−.656	−.635	−.599	−.781

Projections obtained from parameter values greater than $g = 100$ are not very different from those reported, and consequently the values obtained at $g = 100$ represent an alternative extreme.

8.5.1   The Case of Homogeneous Capital

The outcome from the model based on homogeneous national capital will be discussed first. In the case of the United States, output of the net export good, X_{2A}, rises, while output of the net import good and the nontraded good both fall. The decline in output in the nontraded sector is not surprising, since the DISC incentives draw resources into export production and out of other sectors of the economy. X_{1A} output declines as a consequence of the balance-of-payments constraint imposed. If the value of U.S. exports rises, then the rest of the world must export more to the United States, a result that is achieved by a fall in the price of country B's output relative to country A's domestic prices. The net import sector is most affected by this reaction, and its output falls. The greatest increase in X_{2A} output occurs when capital is most mobile internationally, since additional resources can be attracted without driving up input costs as much. The greatest declines in X_{1A} and X_{NA} output occur when capital is least mobile, since the greater incentive to substitute capital for other factors of production in X_{2A} output now can be satisfied only by attracting it out of the other domestic sectors, X_{1A} and X_{NA}.

Within country B, output of X_{1B} rises while output of the other two composite goods falls. When capital is not as mobile internationally, domestic output in country B does not fall as much, since more capital is available to use in production within the country. The reallocation of capital to the United States occurs because U.S. after-tax returns rise. This result cannot be guaranteed a priori, since expansion of U.S. export production may require other factors more intensively than capital and thereby offset the factor price incentive which increases demand for capital. However, that situation does not arise given the relevant set of parameter values in each economy.

The impact effect of the DISC incentive represents a reduction of .46 percent in the U.S. economy-wide gross capital return required to maintain given after-tax returns, but even in the case where near-perfect capital mobility is assumed, the U.S. capital stock increased by only .038 percent. This capital reallocation is not as large as Horst (1981) projects. Possible explanations for this difference are the attention paid to real versus nominal capital returns in the United States and abroad, and the allowance for more than one producing sector in the rest of the world. When foreign capital prices fall relative to U.S. prices, then less new investment is likely to be made in the United States in comparison with the case of constant foreign prices. When more than one producing sector exists in the foreign economy, the elasticity of the foreign demand for capital schedule is likely to increase. The fact that the U.S. capital stock increases only slightly does not mean that capital mobility is unimportant, though, because changes in income distribution depend quite strongly on it.

Wages of unskilled labor are most adversely affected by DISC. Because the export sector requires little unskilled labor, that labor can remain fully employed only by accepting a large cut in wages. Skilled labor is used intensively in the export sector, and when capital is highly mobile internationally, this factor gains the most in relative terms from DISC. However, as capital mobility declines internationally, so does the benefit to skilled labor from DISC. A smaller capital inflow into country A means a smaller increase in demand for output from A producers, or equivalently, less demand for the fixed factors, unskilled labor and skilled labor. While returns to unskilled labor fall for this reason, the effect on skilled labor is even more pronounced because of the extremely low elasticity of substitution between skilled labor and capital. When demand for skilled labor falls, a large decline in its relative price is necessary to maintain full employment. Finally, a related result implied above is that returns to capital rise, and this increase is greatest when U.S. capitalists need not contend with the reallocation of capital from the rest of the world.

Prices of U.S. traded goods rise slightly, but the U.S. terms of trade still fall by approximately two-thirds of the initial DISC price effect. That is, the price of imported foreign goods falls by roughly one-third of the 1.74 percent DISC price effect. The U.S. output shift toward traded goods forces a similar change in the rest of the world, as the nontraded sector declines in both countries.

8.5.2   The Case of Industry-Specific Capital

When the capital is industry specific, but nevertheless highly mobile internationally, projected effects of DISC are very similar to those already described: U.S. output of net exports, X_{2A}, rises at the expense of X_{1A} and X_{NA}, while foreign output of net exports, X_{1B}, rises and output of X_{2B} and X_{NB} falls; capital is reallocated toward X_{2A} production from elsewhere in the U.S. economy and from abroad; wages of unskilled labor fall, and skilled labor gains.

As capital mobility declines, capital initially in X_{2A} becomes the specific factor most likely to benefit from increased demand for X_{2A} or from the incentive to use K_{2A} rather than other inputs. In the polar case where $g = 0$, capital is immobile both internationally and across sectors within each economy. In that situation any resource reallocation across sectors is limited to skilled and unskilled labor, a situation differing considerably from the case of $g = 0$ in the homogeneous capital model, where capital reallocation within the U.S. economy still was possible. Consequently, in the more restrictive situation depicted by the figures in the last column of tables 8.1 and 8.2, significant differences appear in comparison with any of the other results. Some of these projections appear counterintuitive. For example, why does DISC result in a decline in the output of X_{2A} but an increase in the output of X_{1A}? Exports of both goods still rise, but domestic demand for X_{2A} falls because of the relatively large increase in its prices. The contraction in the supply of X_{2A} seems best explained in terms of a Rybczinski-like effect. Contraction of output of X_{NA} results in the release of skilled and unskilled labor, but since the nontraded sector is highly intensive in unskilled labor, that factor is released in relatively greater amounts than skilled labor. The net import sector, X_{1A}, requires slightly more unskilled labor than the net export sector, X_{2A}. Therefore, the additional unskilled labor available would be absorbed by greater X_{1A} output and reduced X_{2A} output, with skilled labor being released from X_{2A} to use with the additional unskilled labor in X_{1A}. Perhaps this situation is of limited relevance in policy analysis, but if capital immobility is identified with shorter-run policy impacts, these short-run effects suggest counterintuitive output incentives and a large windfall to owners of capital in the export sector.

An additional distinction that arises in the case of industry-specific capital is the relatively smaller terms of trade deterioration, but a larger decline in the value of foreign investment income. These somewhat offsetting effects still leave a decline in U.S. income and its consequent demand implications, which were explained above.

8.5.3 Comparison of Partial and General Equilibrium Analysis

One question of interest in a policy context has been the projected effect of DISC on U.S. exports and employment in those industries. The DISC report of the U.S. Treasury Department (1981) estimates the change in the value of U.S. exports on the basis of a partial equilibrium framework, where the label "partial equilibrium" is applied because of the lack of attention to balance-of-payments constraints. In other words, U.S. exports are assumed to increase, and the balance-of-payments position of foreign countries is allowed to worsen with no pressure for adjustments on their part. Such a situation would represent an equilibrium result only if the United States were willing to continually increase its lending to foreign borrowers irrespective of rates of return.

The general equilibrium model developed here projects an increase in exports of 3.1 percent. The increase in exports derived from a simple partial-equilibrium analysis for the same export demand elasticities assumed here would yield a 4.9 percent increase in exports. In contrast, a Marshall-Lerner type of analysis, which attempts to go one step further than the simple partial analysis by computing the appreciation of the dollar resulting from the initial "partial" expansion in exports and then recomputing the change in exports, results in an export expansion of 2.9 percent.

Why is the increase in exports in the general equilibrium model somewhat larger than in the standard Marshall-Lerner framework? One reason is that the initial loss in U.S. income associated with the DISC subsidy is not introduced into the usual Marshall-Lerner analysis. This loss in income results from the necessity to finance the DISC incentive, that is, lowering export prices cannot be costless to the United States. Because U.S. consumption is strongly oriented to U.S.-produced goods, a loss in U.S. income tends to create an excess supply of U.S. production, limiting the appreciation of the dollar necessary in the Marshall-Lerner analysis.

8.6 Normative Analysis of DISC

The welfare or economic efficiency effects of DISC must be evaluated in a second-best setting, where the existence of other distorting policies is recognized. The focus of the present study on internationally mobile capital suggests an important set of distortions to include: the set of international taxes on capital income. A basic condition for DISC to improve world efficiency is fairly stringent—DISC must result in the reallocation of capital away from low-tax uses toward high-tax uses. This situation may arise if current foreign tax rates are lower than in the United States, since U.S. tax code provisions allow the income of U.S.-controlled foreign corporations to avoid U.S. taxation until the income is repatriated to the United States. If DISC causes U.S.-based multinational corporations (MNCs) to choose domestic over foreign locations, world efficiency may be enhanced because capital would move to where it has a higher pre-tax return, even inclusive of DISC benefits.

The main problem with this second-best argument is that the United States is not now, at the corporate level, a high-tax country. The Commerce Department benchmark survey, *U.S. Direct Investment Abroad, 1977*, indicates that in 1977 foreign manufacturing affiliates of U.S. companies paid an average income tax rate of 42.0 percent. The comparable U.S. rate, including federal, state, and local taxes, on their parents was 45.8 percent. In addition, the U.S. rate on new investment has been reduced substantially since 1977 because of ACRS and the other provisions of the Economic Recovery Tax Act of 1981 (ERTA), even after the cutbacks in 1982 are considered. For example, the effective tax rate on new investment in equipment in manufacturing as a whole is now about what it was before ERTA for equipment used in exports. To the extent that DISC draws capital from abroad, it will come, *on the average*, from countries in which the corporate tax rate is at least as high as in the United States.

Of course, from the standpoint of national welfare, the United States still can gain from the inflow of capital even when the world as a whole loses. Traditional analysis of international capital flows suggests some of the relevant factors to consider: the terms of trade loss to the United States from subsidizing exports may be offset by the gain to the United States as a net creditor to the rest of the world, if real returns to capital rise internationally as a result of DISC. Furthermore, since the United States collects little tax from U.S.-based multinational investments in high-tax countries, as a result of the foreign tax credit allowed up to the value of the U.S. tax liability, the United States will gain from the reallocation of capital into jurisdictions where U.S. rather than foreign taxes on capital are collected. Finally, if capital is reallocated within the U.S. economy from low-tax to high-tax sectors, a welfare gain will result.

As shown in appendix C, the change in U.S. potential welfare as a result of DISC can be approximated by the following expression:

$$(28) \qquad U^* = \frac{P_{1A} X_{1AB}}{Y_A} \cdot P_{1A}^* + \frac{P_{2A} X_{2AB}}{Y_A} \cdot P_{2A}^*$$

$$- \frac{P_{1B} D_{1BA}}{Y_A} \cdot P_{1B}^* - \frac{P_{2B} D_{2BA}}{Y_A} \cdot P_{2B}^*$$

$$- \text{DISCREV} + \frac{r_A K_{1A}}{(1 - t_{1A}) Y_A} \cdot K_{1A}^* + \frac{r_A K_{2A}}{(1 - t_{2A})} \cdot K_{2A}^*$$

$$+ \frac{r_A K_{NA}}{(1 - t_{NA}) Y_A} \cdot K_{NA}^* - \frac{r_B K_A}{\text{CPI}_B Y_A} \cdot K_A$$

$$+ \frac{r_B (\tilde{K}_A - K_A)}{\text{CPI}_B Y_A} \cdot (r_B^* - \text{CPI}_B^*)$$

$$+ \frac{\text{TAR}_{1A} \cdot P_{1B} D_{1BA}}{Y_A} \cdot (P_{1B}^* + D_{1BA}^*)$$

$$+ \frac{\text{TAR}_{2A} \cdot P_{2B} D_{2BA}}{Y_A} \cdot (P_{2B}^* + D_{2BA}^*).$$

The first five terms represent the terms of trade effect attributable to DISC, which is expected to be negative since the loss in U.S. export receipts from the tax subsidy is not completely offset by cheaper imports. The next four terms represent the potential gain to the United States from the reallocation of capital both within the United States from low-tax to high-tax sectors and also from abroad. If there were no taxes levied at home or abroad, and capital could be moved across borders costlessly, these four terms would sum to zero. The r_B^* term shows the U.S. gain as a net creditor to the rest of the world if the real return to capital rises abroad, and the final two terms are the gain in U.S. tariff revenue collected if the value of imports rises.

This expression is evaluated for the three sets of simulated values reported from the model based on homogeneous capital. The corresponding expression for the case of industry-specific capital requires modifying the capital flow terms to include industry-specific rates of return and allowing for the U.S. net creditor position with respect to the three different types of capital used in country B. In all cases the United States experiences a welfare loss as a result of DISC. In the case of homogeneous capital this loss is smaller when capital mobility is larger, but in the case of heterogeneous capital just the opposite result holds. Assuming DISC applies to all U.S. exports, the estimated annual losses in the case of homogeneous capital are .037 percent of national income when capital is highly mobile ($g = 100$), .037 percent of income when capital is moderately mobile ($g = 1$), and .040 percent when capital is completely immobile ($g = 0$). For the case of heterogeneous capital, the welfare loss estimates are .041, .039, and .030 percent of income for the three cases analyzed, as reported in descending order of capital mobility. These net efficiency effects equal approximately half of the revenue cost of DISC, a percentage much higher than generally is obtained in the analysis of domestic tax policies. While the DISC-induced welfare loss appears small as a percentage of national income, in absolute value this estimate is more than three times the projected gain to the United States from a 50 percent pre–Tokyo Round multilateral tariff reduction (Baldwin, Mutti, and Richardson 1980). Furthermore, the tariff reduction policy results in an increase in exports nearly twice that of DISC. The primary reason that the DISC welfare effects are so large relative to the volume of trade affected is that DISC results in a substantial terms of trade loss to the United States, and reallocation of capital into the United States is not sufficient to offset that loss.

8.7 Qualifications

The results discussed above clearly are dependent on the parameter values chosen as well as the way each model is formulated. The theoretical framework and the empirical basis for the parameter values used were discussed previously, but additional points are raised here.

One possibility ignored is the incentive for greater capital formation from the increase in the after-tax return to capital. The greater the responsiveness of savings to this rate of return, the larger the increase in U.S. output which eventually will be realized, and the larger the tax base from which to make up the DISC revenue loss. Goulder, Shoven, and Whalley (1981) simulate such a scenario in five-year intervals, to illustrate the path of adjustment followed by the economy, while Horst (1981) considers the new steady-state solution and an intermediate position in which one-fifth of the eventual adjustments have been made. The projected effect of DISC on total savings is not unambiguous on a priori grounds. The higher real rate of return does give a price incentive for additional saving, but the loss in real income may reduce saving.

Also, the quantitative analysis in this paper has assumed that export markets are competitive. If the model were expanded to include noncompetitive behavior and added elements, such as variable advertising intensity, the results may differ in various ways. One change would involve the calculated reduction in the marginal cost of capital attributable to DISC. In the estimates described earlier, we assumed that all of the marginal after-tax return to capital in exports was made up of the competitive, required real rate of return. If, on the contrary, some of the return reflects monopoly rents, the decline in the *marginal* cost of capital because of DISC would be smaller than we have estimated it to be. The effect of DISC on export price and the increase in exports would therefore be somewhat overstated in our estimates, while the gain to monopoly producers at the expense of the other factor inputs would be ignored.

It is also conceivable that, if exporters have the opportunity to increase advertising and marketing efforts, the decline in export prices may be less than indicated in a simple model. The welfare loss because of the decline in the terms of trade may for that reason also be overstated, but with a somewhat larger, but not necessarily compensating, loss because of overinvestment in marketing. However, it is not clear why a decline in capital costs should lead to disproportionate increases in advertising. Furthermore, the statement by some market observers that DISC does not lower an exporter's prices may simply reflect the fact that export markets *are* competitive, and that a single exporter cannot affect market prices. In that case, the market supply shifts assumed in our model would be appropriate.

8.8   Related Policy Concerns

The main purpose of this paper has been to explain the incentives created by the DISC program and to project how they might alter the location of production internationally and the factor rewards in the United States and abroad. Several other policy aspects of the DISC program have not been addressed in this analysis, and these issues are discussed briefly to conclude the paper.

One issue not considered is the effect of alternative tax policies on production and factor rewards. If the United States were to adopt a corporate tax cut resulting in the same revenue loss as DISC, would returns to capital rise to a greater extent and attract a greater inflow of capital into the United States? Would the changes in income distribution be similar to those created by DISC? These questions of differential incidence actually were implicit in the 1978 tax proposals of the Carter administration. A similar framework in which to consider these trade-offs would be to impose a balanced budget constraint, and to consider any disincentives that would arise from tax increases necessary to make up for the tax expenditures on DISC. The present study does not obtain Horst's (1981) result that the DISC revenue loss is largely made up by additional taxes collected from the reallocated capital, primarily because he assumes a much larger differential in taxes on capital income across different sectors of the U.S. economy than the figures reported by Ballard, Fullerton, Shoven, and Whalley (1982).

Another issue that frequently arises is the relationship between the DISC provisions and border tax adjustments in the form of rebates on value-added and other "indirect" taxes on exports. It is sometimes claimed that DISC is simply the equivalent of these border tax adjustments and that the United States is at a disadvantage relative to its trading partners in having a greater portion of its tax revenue in the form of "direct" taxes, such as the corporate income tax.

While the GATT distinction between rebates on direct and indirect taxes lacks a sound theoretical basis, previous analysis consistent with the model in this paper makes it clear that DISC is not the equivalent of border tax adjustments on indirect taxes (Johnson and Krauss 1970). The reason is that border tax adjustment practices involve not only a rebate of taxes on exports but also the imposition of the indirect tax (such as the value-added tax) on similar imports. This imposition of taxes on imports prevents the allocational and terms of trade effects that have been the subject of this paper. Resources do not flow out of import-competing goods because the tax on imports restores the relative competitiveness of domestically produced goods. The imposition of taxes on imports at the same time as the rebate on exports means that the terms of trade do not tend to fall for the exporting country, unlike the case of DISC, because *in real terms* the export supply schedule is not shifted in the same way. This is not to say that border tax adjustments as implemented by EEC countries are completely neutral. Because value-added taxes are typically of the consumption type, that is, they exempt capital goods, they are not uniform, and border tax adjustments do have an effect. However, they do not necessarily give any trade advantage to the countries using them.

A related observation is that if the main justification for DISC rests on its foreign trade impacts, rather than its ability to increase capital formation or to raise U.S. national income, then a complete analysis of DISC should compare it to alternative ways of meeting export goals. The other major U.S. export incentive program is the Export-Import Bank, which provides various kinds of credit-financing assistance to exporters. The Export-Import Bank would appear to have some advantages over DISC in terms of *relative* effectiveness. For one thing, it can target on exports whose demand is most elastic. Apart from any mercantilistic considerations, targeting on highly elastic demands may be beneficial in reducing the terms of trade loss that results from an export incentive. In some extreme cases, subsidizing the highly elastic exports may improve overall terms of trade. However, the first-best policy would be simply to impose taxes on the exports with lower elasticities.

Nevertheless, it is not entirely clear that the Export-Import Bank is successful in focusing on highly elastic imports, even though its procedures explicitly attempt to do so. The main problem is that, by its nature, the Export-Import Bank is limited to assisting large, durable equipment exports such as commercial aircraft and electrical generating equipment. It can offer few benefits to the wide range of industrial materials, such as chemicals and semiconductors, whose demand may be highly elastic. The limited scope of the Export-Import Bank can be seen from the fact that all Export-Import Bank programs, including credit guarantees and insurance, assisted $18.1 billion of exports in fiscal year 1980. The comparable figure for DISC exports is above $130 billion, including almost $100 billion of manufactured exports.

The Export-Import Bank may have one advantage in that it may be an effective threat against foreign subsidies. Its financing can be targeted to exports competing against products receiving subsidies from other governments, and it can be withdrawn when foreign subsidies are eliminated. But, here again, the Export-Import Bank's scope is relatively narrow because it is directed only against foreign *credit* subsidies and not the whole range of foreign intervention.

Finally, Export-Import Bank programs have an effect on capital flows which differs from DISC and is undesirable from the U.S. point of view. In contrast to DISC, which lowers the cost of capital in the U.S. export sector, the Export-Import Bank's primary effect is to lower the cost of capital to foreign users of U.S.-made equipment. Export-Import Bank programs would be expected to cause a capital outflow from the United States.

In addition to these economic issues, there is the significant legal issue regarding the consistency of DISC with U.S. obligations to the GATT. In July 1972, soon after the enactment of the DISC legislation, the European Economic Community (EEC) filed a complaint in GATT that the DISC provisions constituted an export subsidy under article XVI:4 of the General Agreement on Tariffs and Trade, which states that contracting parties shall cease to grant subsidies on the export of any product (other than a primary product) which results in the price of the export being lower than the comparable price in domestic markets. The remission or exemption of direct (income) taxes on exports was also specifically included in a 1960 GATT illustrative list of prohibited subsidy measures. After the EEC filed its complaint, the United States in turn filed complaints against Belgium, France, and the Netherlands on the grounds that their territorial tax systems, which exempt foreign income, resulted in export subsidies because the income of foreign sales affiliates in low-tax countries did not reflect arm's-length prices on sales from the parent.

In November 1976, the GATT panels which reviewed the DISC and related cases found that DISC as well as the challenged tax practices of the three EEC countries violated article XVI. In December 1981, the GATT Council, which is an assembly of all members, accepted the panel report subject to the qualification that: (a) economic processes located outside a country, including those involving exported goods, need not be taxed by the exporting country; (b) transactions between exporting enterprises and foreign buyers must adhere to arm's-length principles; and (c) article XVI:4 does not prohibit the adoption of measures to relieve double taxation of foreign-source income. The United States agreed to the adoption of the reports as modified by the qualifying statement but did not accept the conclusion of the panel report that DISC was a violation of article XVI:4. It interpreted the qualifying statement as an exoneration of DISC.

Even though the United States refused to acknowledge that DISC violated the GATT, it recognized that the unresolved DISC issue greatly inhibited its ability to bring claims on other issues to the GATT. Therefore the United States announced at a GATT Council meeting in October 1982 that, while not conceding the issue, it would present a legislative proposal to the Congress which would address the concerns of its trading partners. However, as of the end of 1982, it was not clear whether these legislative proposals would involve the simple elimination of the DISC incentive or the transformation of DISC into some GATT legal form with the same tax benefits to exporters.

Appendix A

The following model demonstrates the incentives which DISC creates for a typical firm. The firm is assumed to maximize after-tax profits from its sales in the United States and abroad. Production can be sold domestically or in the export market, and deductible production costs are pro-rated on the basis of output shares in each market. The expression to maximize is:

$$£ = (1 - t_{1A})[p_{1AA}X_{1AA} - \frac{X_{1AA}}{X_{1A}}(rBK + wL)] - r(1 - B) K$$

$$+ [1 - t_{1A}(1 - D)][p_{1AB}X_{1AB} - \frac{X_{1AB}}{X_{1A}}(rBK + wL)]$$

$$+ \lambda[X_{1A}(K, L) - X_{1AA} - X_{1AB}],$$

where p_{1AA} is the price charged for sales of X_{1A} in country A, X_{1AA} is the volume of sales of X_{1A} in country A, B is the share of capital financed by bonds or debt, r is the after-tax return to capital received by lenders, t_{1A} is the tax rate on corporate income, and D is the tax saving from DISC.

Differentiating this expression with respect to X_{1AA} and X_{1AB} yields two first-order conditions which can be set equal to each other and manipulated to give

$$\frac{p_{1AB}}{p_{1AA}} = \frac{(1 - t_{1A})}{1 - t_{1A}(1 - D)}\left[1 - \frac{rBK + wL}{p_{1AA}X_{1A}}\right] + \frac{rBK + wL}{p_{1AA}X_{1A}}.$$

Let $[(rBK + wL)/p_{1AA}X_{1A}]$ equal $\emptyset$, and recognize that $\emptyset$ is the share of receipts accounted for by deductible production costs. Correspondingly,

$(1 - \emptyset)$ represents the return to equity capital as a share of sales. Therefore,

$$\frac{p_{1AB}}{p_{1AA}} = \frac{1 - t_{1A}}{1 - t_{1A}(1 - D)}[1 - \emptyset] + \emptyset,$$

which shows that if there is no return to equity capital, then $\emptyset = 1$ and DISC provides no incentive to charge a lower price in export markets. The smaller $\emptyset$ is, the more significant DISC is in encouraging a price gap in favor of exports.

DISC also leads to an incentive to substitute capital for labor, since it reduces the penalty on equity capital because of the corporate income tax. Differentiating the profit expression with respect to K and L yields two first-order expressions from which the ratio of marginal productiveness can be formed:

$$\frac{\text{MP}L}{\text{MP}K} = \frac{(1 - t_{1A})\,\psi_{1AA}\,w + [1 - t_{1A}(1 - D)]\,\psi_{1AB}\,w}{(1 - t_{1A})\psi_{1AA}\,Br + rB + [1 - t_{1A}(1 - D)]\,\psi_{1AB}\,Br},$$

where ψ_{1AA} is the share of output sold in country A. This expression can be written in terms of percentage rates of change in a quite compact form if it is assumed that the initial position is one of no DISC incentive:

$$\hat{\text{MP}}L - \hat{\text{MP}}K = \hat{w} - \hat{r} + \frac{\psi_{1AB}(1 - B)t_{1A}}{(1 - t_{1A}B)(1 - t_{1A})}\,dD$$

$$- \frac{(1 - B)}{(1 - t_{1A}B)}\frac{dt_{1A}}{1 - t_{1A}}.$$

The terms on the right-hand side demonstrate how tax policy changes alter the relative cost of using capital and labor.

Appendix B

In this appendix the two general equilibrium models are expressed in terms of percentage rates of change of all variables. The model based on homogeneous (H) capital nationally is presented first.

Full-Employment Equations

(H1) Unskilled labor in country A:

$$C_{L1}^A X_{1A} + C_{L2}^A X_{2A} + C_{LN}^A X_{NA} = L_A.$$
$$\lambda_{L1}^A X_{1A}^* + \lambda_{L2}^A X_{2A}^* + \lambda_{LN}^A X_{NA}^* - (\lambda_{L1}^A \theta_{S1}^A \sigma_{LS}^{A1} + \lambda_{L2}^A \theta_{S2}^A \sigma_{LS}^{A2}$$
$$+ \lambda_{LN}^A \theta_{SN}^A \sigma_{LS}^{AN})(w_A^* - q_A^*) - (\lambda_{L1}^A \theta_{K1}^A \sigma_{LK}^{A1} + \lambda_{L2}^A \theta_{K2}^A \sigma_{LK}^{A2}$$
$$+ \lambda_{LN}^A \theta_{KN}^A \sigma_{LK}^{AN})(w_A^* - r_A^*) = L_A^* + \lambda_{L1}^A \theta_{K1}^A \sigma_{LK}^{A1} \phi_{1AB}\text{DISC1}A$$
$$+ \lambda_{L2}^A \theta_{K2}^A \sigma_{LK}^{A2} \phi_{2AB}\text{DISC2}A.$$

Where λ_{ij}^{k} is the share of the total stock of factor i used in the production of good j in country k; θ_{ij}^{k} is the share of the value of output of good j attributable to factor i in country k; σ_{ij}^{km} is the partial elasticity of substitution between factors i and j in the production of good m in country k; and ϕ_{ijk} is the percentage of output of good i produced in country j which is sold in country k. DISC is the percentage reduction in the cost of capital used in the production of goods for export. The use of an asterisk signifies the percentage change in a variable.

(H2) Skilled labor in country A:

$$C_{S1}X_{1A} + C_{S2}X_{2A} + C_{SN}X_{NA} = S_A.$$

$$\lambda_{S1}^{A}X_{1A}^{*} + \lambda_{S2}^{A}X_{2A}^{*} + \lambda_{SN}^{A}X_{NA}^{*} - (\lambda_{S1}^{A}\theta_{L1}^{A}\sigma_{LS}^{A1} + \lambda_{S2}^{A}\theta_{L2}^{A}\sigma_{LS}^{A2}$$
$$+ \lambda_{SN}^{A}\theta_{LN}^{A}\sigma_{LS}^{AN})(q_{A}^{*} - w_{A}^{*}) - (\lambda_{S1}^{A}\theta_{K1}^{A}\sigma_{SK}^{A1} + \lambda_{S2}^{A}\theta_{K2}^{A}\sigma_{SK}^{A2}$$
$$+ \lambda_{SN}^{A}\theta_{KN}^{A}\sigma_{SK}^{AN})(q_{A}^{*} - r_{A}^{*}) = S_{A}^{*} + \lambda_{S1}^{A}\theta_{K1}^{A}\sigma_{KS}^{A1}\phi_{1AB}\text{DISC1}A$$
$$+ \lambda_{S2}^{A}\theta_{K2}^{A}\sigma_{KS}^{A2}\phi_{2AB}\text{DISC2}A.$$

(H3) Capital in country A:

$$C_{K1}^{A}X_{1A} + C_{K2}^{A}X_{2A} + C_{KN}^{A}X_{NA} = K_A.$$

$$\lambda_{K1}^{A}X_{1A}^{*} + \lambda_{K2}^{A}X_{2A}^{*} + \lambda_{KN}^{A}X_{NA}^{*} - (\lambda_{K1}^{A}\theta_{L1}^{A}\sigma_{LK}^{A1} + \lambda_{K2}^{A}\theta_{L2}^{A}\sigma_{LK}^{A2}$$
$$+ \lambda_{KN}^{A}\theta_{LN}^{A}\sigma_{LK}^{A})(r_{A}^{*} - w_{A}^{*}) - (\lambda_{K1}^{A}\theta_{S1}^{A}\sigma_{KS}^{A1} + \lambda_{K2}^{A}\theta_{S2}^{A}\sigma_{KS}^{A2}$$
$$+ \lambda_{KN}^{A}\theta_{SN}^{A}\sigma_{KS}^{AN})(r_{A}^{*} - q_{A}^{*}) = K_{A}^{*} - (\lambda_{K1}^{A}\theta_{L1}^{A}\sigma_{LK}^{A1}$$
$$+ \lambda_{K1}^{A}\theta_{S1}^{A}\sigma_{KS}^{A1})\phi_{1AB}\text{DISC1}A - (\lambda_{K2}^{A}\theta_{L2}^{A}\sigma_{LK}^{A2}$$
$$+ \lambda_{K2}^{A}\theta_{S2}^{A}\sigma_{KS}^{A2})\phi_{2AB}\text{DISC2}A.$$

(H4) Unskilled labor in country B:

$$C_{L1}^{B}X_{1B} + C_{L2}^{B}X_{2B} + C_{LN}^{B}X_{NB} = L_B.$$

$$\lambda_{L1}^{B}X_{1B}^{*} + \lambda_{L2}^{B}X_{2B}^{*} + \lambda_{LN}^{B}X_{NB}^{*} - (\lambda_{L1}^{B}\theta_{S1}^{B}\sigma_{LS}^{B1} + \lambda_{L2}^{B}\theta_{S2}^{B}\sigma_{LS}^{B2}$$
$$+ \lambda_{LN}^{B}\theta_{SN}^{B}\sigma_{LS}^{BN})(w_{B}^{*} - q_{B}^{*}) - (\lambda_{L1}^{B}\theta_{K1}^{B}\sigma_{LK}^{B1} + \lambda_{L2}^{B}\theta_{K2}^{B}\sigma_{LK}^{B2}$$
$$+ \lambda_{LN}^{B}\theta_{KN}^{B}\sigma_{LK}^{BN})(w_{B}^{*} - r_{B}^{*}) = L_{B}^{*}.$$

(H5) Skilled labor in country B:

$$C_{S1}^{B}X_{1B} + C_{S2}^{B}X_{2B} + C_{SN}^{B}X_{NB} = S_B.$$

$$\lambda_{S1}^{B}X_{1B}^{*} + \lambda_{S2}^{B}X_{2B}^{*} + \lambda_{SN}^{B}X_{NB} - (\lambda_{S1}^{B}\theta_{L1}^{B}\sigma_{LS}^{B1} + \lambda_{S2}^{B}\theta_{L2}^{B}\sigma_{LS}^{B2}$$
$$+ \lambda_{SN}^{B}\theta_{LN}^{B}\sigma_{LS}^{BN})(q_{B}^{*} - w_{B}^{*}) - (\lambda_{S1}^{B}\theta_{K1}^{B}\sigma_{KS}^{B1} + \lambda_{S2}^{B}\theta_{K2}^{B}\sigma_{KS}^{B2}$$
$$+ \lambda_{SN}^{B}\theta_{KN}^{B}\sigma_{KS}^{BN})(q_{B}^{*} - r_{B}^{*}) = S_{B}^{*}.$$

(H6) Capital in country B:

$$C_{K1}^B X_{1B} + C_{K2}^B X_{2B} + C_{KN}^B X_{NB} = K_B.$$

$$\lambda_{K1}^B X_{1B}^* + \lambda_{K2}^B X_{2B}^* + \lambda_{KN}^B X_{NB}^* - (\lambda_{K1}^B \theta_{L1}^B \sigma_{LK}^{B1} + \lambda_{K2}^B \theta_{L2}^B \sigma_{LK}^{B2}$$
$$+ \lambda_{KN}^B \theta_{LN}^B \sigma_{LK}^{BN})(r_B^* - w_B^*) - (\lambda_{K1}^B \theta_{S1}^B \sigma_{KS}^{B1} + \lambda_{K2}^B \theta_{S2}^B \sigma_{KS}^{B2}$$
$$+ \lambda_{KN}^B \theta_{SN}^B \sigma_{KS}^{BN})(r_B^* - q_B^*)$$

$$= K_B^* = - \frac{K_A}{K_B} K_A^*.$$

Zero-Profit Equations

(H7) Production of X_{1A} in country A:

$$C_{L1}^A w_A + C_{S1}^A q_A + C_{K1}^A r_A/(1 - t_{1A}) = P_{1A}.$$
$$\theta_{L1}^A w_A^* + \theta_{S1}^A q_A^* + \theta_{K1}^A r_A^* = P_{1A}^*.$$

(H8) Production of X_{2A} in country A:

$$C_{L2}^A w_A + C_{S2}^A q_A + C_{K2}^A r_A/(1 - t_{2A}) = P_{2A}.$$
$$\theta_{L2}^A w_A^* + \theta_{S2}^A q_A^* + \theta_{K2}^A r_A^* = P_{2A}^*.$$

(H9) Production of X_{NA} in country A:

$$C_{LN}^A w_A + C_{SN}^A q_A + C_{KN}^A r_A/(1 - t_{NA}) = P_{NA} = 1.$$
$$\theta_{LN}^A w_A^* + \theta_{SN}^A q_A^* + \theta_{KN}^A r_A^* = 0.$$

(H10) Production of X_{1B} in country B:

$$C_{L1}^B w_B + C_{S1}^B q_B + C_{K1}^B r_B = P_{1B}.$$
$$\theta_{L1}^B w_B^* + \theta_{S1}^B q_B^* + \theta_{K1}^B r_B^* = P_{1B}^*.$$

(H11) Production of X_{2B} in country B:

$$C_{L2}^B w_B + C_{S2}^B q_B + C_{K2}^B r_B = P_{2B}.$$
$$\theta_{L2}^B w_B^* + \theta_{S2}^B q_B^* + \theta_{K2}^B r_B^* = P_{2B}^*.$$

(H12) Production of X_{NB} in country B:

$$C_{LN}^B w_B + C_{SN}^B q_B + C_{KN}^B r_B = P_{NB}.$$
$$\theta_{LN}^B w_B^* + \theta_{SN}^B q_B^* + \theta_{KN}^B r_B^* = P_{NB}^*.$$

Demand Equations in country A

(H13) Demand for X_{1A} in country A:

$$D_{1AA} = f_1(P_{1A}, P_{1B}, P_{2A}, P_{2B}, Y_A).$$
$$D_{1AA}^* = E_{1A1A}^A P_{1A}^* + E_{1A1B}^A P_{1B}^* + E_{1A2A}^A P_{2A}^*$$
$$+ E_{1A2B}^A P_{2B}^* + E_{Y1A}^A Y_A^*.$$

(H14) Demand for X_{1B} in country A:

$$D_{1BA} = f_2(P_{1A}, P_{1B}, P_{2A}, P_{2B}, Y_A).$$

$$D^*_{1BA} = E^A_{1B1A} P^*_{1A} + E^A_{1B1B} P^*_{1B} + E^A_{1B2A} P^*_{2A}$$
$$+ E^A_{1B2B} P^*_{2B} + E^A_{Y1B} Y^*_A.$$

(H15) Demand for X_{2A} in country A:

$$D_{2AA} = f_3(P_{1A}, P_{1B}, P_{2A}, P_{2B}, Y_A).$$

$$D^*_{2AA} = E^A_{2A1A} P^*_{1A} + E^A_{2A1B} P^*_{1B} + E^A_{2A2A} P^*_{2A}$$
$$+ E^A_{2A2B} P^*_{2B} + E^A_{Y2A} Y^*_A.$$

(H16) Demand for X_{2B} in country A:

$$D_{2BA} = f_4(P_{1A}, P_{1B}, P_{2A}, P_{2B}, Y_A).$$

$$D^*_{2BA} = E^A_{2B1A} P^*_{1A} + E^A_{2B1B} P^*_{1B} + E^A_{2B2A} P^*_{2A}$$
$$+ E^A_{2B2B} P^*_{2B} + E^A_{Y2B} Y^*_A.$$

(H17) Demand for X_{NA} in country A:

$$D_{NA} = f_5(P_{1A}, P_{1B}, P_{2A}, P_{2B}, Y_A).$$

$$D^*_{NA} = E^A_{NA1A} P^*_{1A} + E^A_{NA1B} P^*_{1B} + E^A_{NA2A} P^*_{2A}$$
$$+ E^A_{NA2B} P^*_{2B} + E^A_{YNA} Y^*_A.$$

Where D_{ijk} represents the quantity of good i produced in country j that is demanded in country k; E^m_{ijkl} is the elasticity of demand of purchasers in country m for good i produced in country j with respect to a change in the price of good k produced in country l; and E^m_{yij} is the income elasticity of demand of purchasers in country m for good i produced in country j. The percentage change in income is:

$$Y^*_A = \Pi_{1A} P^*_{1A} + \Pi_{2A} P^*_{2A} + \frac{r_A K_{1A}}{(1 - t_{1A})Y_A} K^*_{1A}$$

$$+ \frac{r_A K_{2A}}{(1 - t_{2A})Y_A} K^*_{2A} + \frac{r_A K_{NA}}{(1 - t_{NA})Y_A} K^*_{NA} - \frac{r_B K_A}{Y_A} K^*_A$$

$$+ \frac{r_B(\widetilde{K}_A - K_A)}{Y_A} r^*_B + \text{TAR1A} (P^*_{1B} + D^*_{1BA})$$

$$+ \text{TAR2A} (P^*_{2B} + D^*_{2BA}) - \text{DISC REV}.$$

Where Π_{iA} is the share of GNP accounted for by output of good i, TAR_{iA} represents the share of GNP in country A accounted for by tariff revenue collected from imports of good i, and DISC REV is the grossed up value of the tax saving to exporters due to DISC.

Demand Equations in country B

(H18) Demand for X_{1A} in country B:

$$D_{1AB} = g_1(P_{1A}, P_{1B}, P_{2A}, P_{2B}, P_{NB}, Y_B, \text{DISC}).$$

$$D^*_{1AB} = E^B_{1A1A} P^*_{1AB} + E^B_{1A1B} P^*_{1B} + E^B_{1A2A} P^*_{2AB}$$
$$+ E^B_{1A2B} P^*_{2B} + E^B_{1ANB} P^*_{NB} + E^B_{Y1A} Y^*_B.$$

(H19) Demand for X_{1B} in country B:

$$D_{1BB} = g_2(P_{1A}, P_{1B}, P_{2A}, P_{2B}, P_{NB}, Y_B, \text{DISC}).$$

$$D^*_{1BB} = E^B_{1B1A} P^*_{1AB} + E^B_{1B1B} P^*_{1B} + E^B_{1B2A} P^*_{2AB}$$
$$+ E^B_{1B2B} P^*_{2B} + E^B_{1BNB} P^*_{NB} + E^B_{Y1B} Y^*_B.$$

(H20) Demand for X_{2A} in country B:

$$D_{2AB} = g_3(P_{1A}, P_{1B}, P_{2A}, P_{2B}, P_{NB}, Y_B, \text{DISC}).$$

$$D^*_{2AB} = E^B_{2A1A} P^*_{1AB} + E^B_{2A1B} P^*_{1B} + E^B_{2A2A} P^*_{2AB}$$
$$+ E^B_{2A2B} P^*_{2B} + E^B_{2ANB} P^*_{NB} + E^B_{Y2A} Y^*_B.$$

(H21) Demand for X_{2B} in country B:

$$D_{2BB} = g_4(P_{1A}, P_{1B}, P_{2A}, P_{2B}, P_{NB}, Y_B, \text{DISC}).$$

$$D^*_{2BB} = E^B_{2B1A} P^*_{1AB} + E^B_{2B1B} P^*_{1B} + E^B_{2B2A} P^*_{2AB}$$
$$+ E^B_{2B2B} P^*_{2B} + E^B_{2BNB} P^*_{NB} + E^B_{Y2B} Y^*_B.$$

Where the change in income is

$$Y^*_B = \Pi_{1B}(P^*_{1B} + X^*_{1B}) + \Pi_{2B}(P^*_{2B} + X^*_{2B})$$
$$+ \Pi_{NB}(P^*_{NB} + X^*_{NB}) + \text{TAR}1B(D^*_{1AB} + P^*_{1AB})$$
$$+ \text{TAR}2B(D^*_{2AB} + P^*_{2AB}) + \frac{r_B(\widetilde{K}_B - K_B)}{Y_B} r^*_B - \frac{r_B K_B}{Y_B} K^*_B.$$

Also, $P^*_{1AB} = P^*_{1A} - \text{DISC } P,$

and $P^*_{2AB} = P^*_{2A} - \text{DISC } P.$

Where DISC P is the price incentive explained in appendix A.

Capital-Flow Equation

(H22) $K_A = g_0 \left[\dfrac{r_A}{\text{CPI}_A} \Big/ \dfrac{r_B}{\text{CPI}_B} \right]^{g_1}.$

$$K^*_A = g_1(r^*_A - \text{CPI}^*_A - r^*_B + \text{CPI}^*_B).$$

Market Equilibrium Conditions

(H23) $X_{1A} = D_{1AB} + D_{1AA}.$

$$X^*_{1A} = \phi_{1AB} D^*_{1AB} + \phi_{1AA} D^*_{1AA}.$$

(H24) $X_{2A} = D_{2AB} + D_{2AA}$.

$X_{2A}^* = \phi_{2AB} D_{2AB}^* + \phi_{2AA} D_{2AA}^*$.

(H25) $X_{NA} = D_{NA}$.

$X_{NA}^* = D_{NA}^*$.

(H26) $X_{1B} = D_{1BA} + D_{1BB}$.

$X_{1B}^* = \phi_{1BA} D_{1BA}^* + \phi_{1BB} D_{1BB}^*$.

(H27) $X_{2B} = D_{2BA} + D_{2BB}$.

$X_{2B}^* = \phi_{2BA} D_{2BA}^* + \phi_{2BB} D_{2BA}^*$.

The modifications necessary for the model with industry-specific capital are presented next.

Full Employment of Factors of Production

(S1) Unskilled labor in country A:

$$C_{L1}^A X_{1A} + C_{L2}^A X_{2A} + C_{LN}^A X_{NA} = L_A.$$

$$\lambda_{L1}^A X_{1A}^* + \lambda_{L2}^A X_{2A}^* + \lambda_{LN}^A X_{NA}^* + (\lambda_{L1}^A \theta_{S1}^A \sigma_{LS}^{A1} + \lambda_{L2}^A \theta_{S2}^A \sigma_{LS}^{A2}$$
$$+ \lambda_{LN}^A \theta_{SN}^A \sigma_{LS}^{AN})(q_A^* - w_A^*) + \lambda_{L1}^A \theta_{K1}^A \sigma_{LK}^{A1}(r_{1A}^* - w_A^*)$$
$$+ \lambda_{L2}^A \theta_{K2}^A \sigma_{LK}^{A2}(r_{2A}^* - w_A^*) + \lambda_{LN}^A \theta_{KN}^A \sigma_{LK}^{AN}(r_{NA}^* - w_A^*) = L_A^*$$
$$+ \lambda_{L1}^A \theta_{K1}^A \sigma_{LK}^{A1} \phi_{1AB} \text{DISC}1A + \lambda_{L2}^A \theta_{K2}^A \sigma_{LK}^{A2} \phi_{2AB} \text{DISC}2A.$$

Where the after-tax returns to capital in each industry no longer must change by the same percentage.

(S2) Skilled labor in country A:

$$C_{S1}^A X_{1A} + C_{S2}^A X_{2A} + C_{SN}^A X_{NA} = S_A.$$

$$\lambda_{S1}^A X_{1A}^* + X_{S2}^A X_{2A}^* + \lambda_{SN}^A X_{NA}^* + (\lambda_{S1}^A \theta_{L1}^A \sigma_{LS}^{A1} + \lambda_{S2}^A \theta_{L2}^A \sigma_{LS}^{A2}$$
$$+ \lambda_{SN}^A \theta_{LN}^A \sigma_{LS}^{AN})(w_A^* - q_A^*) + \lambda_{S1}^A \theta_{K1}^A \sigma_{KS}^{A1}(r_{1A}^* - q_A^*)$$
$$+ \lambda_{S2}^A \theta_{K2}^A \sigma_{KS}^{A2}(r_{2A}^* - q_A^*) + \lambda_{SN}^A \theta_{KN}^A \sigma_{KS}^{AN}(r_{NA}^* - q_A^*) = S_A^*$$
$$+ \lambda_{S1}^A \theta_{K1}^A \sigma_{KS}^{A1} \phi_{1AB} \text{DISC}1A + \lambda_{S2}^A \theta_{K2}^A \sigma_{KS}^{A2} \phi_{2AB} \text{DISC}2A.$$

(S3) Industry 1 capital in country A:

$$C_{K1}^A X_{1A} = K_{1A}.$$

$$X_{1A}^* + \theta_{L1}^A \sigma_{LK}^{A1}(w_A^* - r_{1A}^*) + \theta_{S1}^A \sigma_{KS}^{A1}(q_A^* - r_{1A}^*) = K_{1A}^*$$
$$- \theta_{L1}^A \sigma_{LK}^{A1} \phi_{1AB} \text{DISC}1A - \theta_{S1}^A \sigma_{KS}^{A2} \phi_{1AB} \text{DISC}1A.$$

(S4) Industry 2 capital in country A:

$$C_{K2}^A X_{2A} = K_{2A}.$$

$$X_{2A}^* + \theta_{L2}^A \sigma_{LK}^{A2}(w_A^* - r_{2A}^*) + \theta_{S2}^A \sigma_{KS}^{A2}(q_A^* - r_{2A}^*) = K_{2A}^*$$
$$- \theta_{L2}^A \sigma_{LK}^{A2} \phi_{2AB} \text{DISC}2A - \theta_{S2}^A \sigma_{KS}^{A2} \phi_{2AB} \text{DISC}2A.$$

(S5) Industry N capital in country A:

$$C_{KN}^{A} X_{NA} = K_{NA}.$$

$$X_{NA}^{*} + \theta_{LN}^{A} \sigma_{LK}^{AN}(w_{A}^{*} - r_{NA}^{*}) + \theta_{SN}^{A} \sigma_{KS}^{AN}(q_{A}^{*} - r_{NA}^{*}) = K_{NA}^{*}.$$

(S6) Unskilled labor in country B:

$$C_{L1}^{B} X_{1B} + C_{L2}^{B} X_{2B} + C_{LN}^{B} X_{NB} = L_{B}.$$

$$\lambda_{L1}^{B} X_{1B}^{*} + \lambda_{L2}^{B} X_{2B}^{*} + \lambda_{LN}^{B} X_{NB}^{*} + (\lambda_{L1}^{B} \theta_{S1}^{B} \sigma_{LS}^{B1} + \lambda_{L2}^{B} \theta_{S2}^{B} \sigma_{LS}^{B2}$$
$$+ \lambda_{LN}^{B} \theta_{SN}^{B} \sigma_{LS}^{BN})(q_{B}^{*} - w_{B}^{*}) + \lambda_{L1}^{B} \theta_{K1}^{B} \sigma_{LK}^{B1}(r_{1B}^{*} - w_{B}^{*})$$
$$+ \lambda_{L2}^{B} \theta_{K2}^{B} \sigma_{LK}^{B2}(r_{2A}^{*} - w_{B}^{*}) + \lambda_{LN}^{B} \theta_{KN}^{B} \sigma_{LK}^{BN}(r_{NB}^{*} - w_{B}^{*})$$
$$= L_{B}^{*} = 0.$$

(S7) Skilled labor in country B:

$$C_{S1}^{B} X_{1B} + C_{S2}^{B} X_{2B} + C_{SN}^{B} X_{NB} = S_{B}.$$

$$\lambda_{S1}^{B} X_{1B}^{*} + \lambda_{S2}^{B} X_{2B}^{*} + \lambda_{SN}^{B} X_{NB}^{*} + (\lambda_{S1}^{B} \theta_{L1}^{B} \sigma_{LS}^{B1} + \lambda_{S2}^{B} \theta_{L2}^{B} \sigma_{LS}^{B2}$$
$$+ \lambda_{SN}^{B} \theta_{LN}^{B} \sigma_{LS}^{BN})(w_{B}^{*} - q_{B}^{*}) + \lambda_{S1}^{B} \theta_{K1}^{B} \sigma_{KS}^{B1}(r_{1B}^{*} - q_{B}^{*})$$
$$+ \lambda_{S2}^{B} \theta_{K2}^{B} \sigma_{KS}^{B2}(r_{2B}^{*} - q_{B}^{*}) + \lambda_{SN}^{B} \theta_{KN}^{B} \sigma_{KS}^{BN}(r_{NB}^{*} - q_{B}^{*}) = S_{B}^{*} = 0.$$

(S8) Industry 1 capital in country B:

$$C_{K1}^{B} X_{1B} = K_{1B}.$$

$$X_{1B}^{*} + \theta_{L1}^{B} \sigma_{LK}^{B1}(w_{B}^{*} - r_{1B}^{*}) + \theta_{S1}^{B} \sigma_{KS}^{B1}(q_{B}^{*} - r_{1B}^{*}) = K_{1B}^{*}.$$

(S9) Industry 2 capital in country B:

$$C_{K2}^{B} X_{2B} = K_{2B}.$$

$$X_{2B}^{*} + \theta_{L2}^{B} \sigma_{LK}^{B2}(w_{B}^{*} - r_{2B}^{*}) + \theta_{S2}^{B} \sigma_{KS}^{B2}(q_{B}^{*} - r_{2B}^{*}) = K_{2B}^{*}.$$

(S10) Industry N capital in country B:

$$C_{KN}^{B} X_{NB} = K_{NB}.$$

$$X_{NB}^{*} + \theta_{LN}^{B} \sigma_{LK}^{BN}(w_{B}^{*} - r_{NB}^{*}) + \theta_{SN}^{B} \sigma_{KS}^{BN}(q_{B}^{*} - r_{NB}^{*}) = K_{NB}^{*}.$$

And since the world stock of capital is given:

$$K_{1A} + K_{2A} + K_{NA} + K_{1B} + K_{2B}$$
$$+ K_{NB} = \bar{K},$$

then

$$K_{NB}^{*} = - (\lambda_{K1}^{A} k_{AB}/\lambda_{KN}^{B}) K_{1A}^{*} - (\lambda_{K2}^{A} k_{AB}/\lambda_{KN}^{B}) K_{2A}^{*}$$
$$- (\lambda_{KN}^{A} k_{AB}/\lambda_{KN}^{B}) K_{NA}^{*} - (\lambda_{K1}^{B}/\lambda_{KN}^{B}) K_{1B}^{*}$$
$$- (\lambda_{K2}^{B}/\lambda_{KN}^{B}) K_{2B}^{*},$$

where $k_{AB} = K_{A}/K_{B}$.

Zero-Profit Equations in Production

(S11) Production of X_{1A} in country A:

$$C_{L1}^A w_A + C_{S1}^A q_A + C_{K1}^A r_{1A}/(1 - t_{1A}) = P_{1A}.$$
$$\theta_{L1}^A w_A^* + \theta_{S1}^A q_A^* + \theta_{K1}^A r_{1A}^* = P_{1A}^*.$$

(S12) Production of X_{2A} in country A:

$$C_{L2}^A w_A + C_{S2}^A q_A + C_{K2}^A r_{2A}/(1 - t_{2A}) = P_{2A}.$$
$$\theta_{L2}^A w_A^* + \theta_{S2}^A q_A^* + \theta_{K2}^A r_{2A}^* = P_{2A}^*.$$

(S13) Production of X_{NA} in country A:

$$C_{LN}^A w_A + C_{SN}^A q_A + C_{KN}^A r_{NA}/(1 - t_{NA}) = P_{NA} = 1.$$
$$\theta_{LN}^A w_A^* + \theta_{SN}^A q_A^* + \theta_{KN}^A r_{NA}^* = 0.$$

(S14) Production of X_{1B} in country B:

$$C_{L1}^B w_B + C_{S1}^B q_B + C_{K1}^B r_{1B} = P_{1B}.$$
$$\theta_{L1}^B w_B^* + \theta_{S1}^B q_B^* + \theta_{K1}^B r_{1B}^* = P_{1B}^*.$$

(S15) Production of X_{2B} in country B:

$$C_{L2}^B w_B + C_{S2}^B q_B + C_{K2}^B r_{2B} = P_{2B}.$$
$$\theta_{L2}^B w_B^* + \theta_{S2}^B q_B^* + \theta_{K2}^B r_{2B}^* = P_{2B}^*.$$

(S16) Production of X_{NB} in country B:

$$C_{LN}^B w_B + C_{SN}^B q_B + C_{KN}^B r_{NB} = P_{NB}.$$
$$\theta_{LN}^B w_B^* + \theta_{SN}^B q_B^* + \theta_{KN}^B r_{NB}^* = P_{NB}^*.$$

The nine demand equations are identical to those presented in the model with homogeneous capital, equations (H13) through (H21), and they are not repeated here. Also, the market equilibrium conditions (H23) through (H27) are unchanged. However, because several types of capital exist in the present model, there are four additional international capital flow equations, and each involves more pairwise comparisons than in the simpler model.

Capital Flow Equations

(S31) $K_{1A} = h_{1A}(r_{1A}, r_{1B}, r_{2A}, r_{NA}, r_{2B}, r_{NB}, \text{CPI}_A, \text{CPI}_B).$
$K_{1A}^* = g_{1A1B}(r_{1A}^* - \text{CPI}_A^* - r_B^* + \text{CPI}_B^*) + g_{1A2A}(r_{1A}^* - r_{2A}^*)$
$\quad + g_{1ANA}(r_{1A}^* - r_{NA}^*) + g_{1A2B}(r_{1A}^* - \text{CPI}_A^* - r_{2B}^* + \text{CPI}_B^*)$
$\quad + g_{1ANB}(r_{1A}^* - \text{CPI}_A^* - r_{NB}^* + \text{CPI}_B^*).$

(S32) $K_{2A} = h_{2A}(r_{1A}, r_{1B}, r_{2A}, r_{2B}, r_{NA}, r_{NB}, \text{CPI}_A, \text{CPI}_B).$
$K_{2A}^* = g_{2A2B}(r_{2A}^* - \text{CPI}_A^* - r_{2B}^* + \text{CPI}_B^*) + g_{2A1A}(r_{2A}^* - r_{1A}^*)$
$\quad + g_{2ANA}(r_{2A}^* - r_{NA}^*) + g_{2A1B}(r_{2A}^* - \text{CPI}_A^* - r_{1B}^* + \text{CPI}_B^*)$
$\quad + g_{2ANB}(r_{2A}^* - \text{CPI}_A^* - r_{NB}^* + \text{CPI}_B^*).$

(S33) $K_{NA} = h_{na}(r_{1A}, r_{1B}, r_{2A}, r_{2B}, r_{NA}, r_{NB}, \text{CPI}_A, \text{PCI}_B)$.

$K_{NA}^* = g_{NA1A}(r_{NA}^* - r_{1A}^*) + g_{NA2A}(r_{NA}^* - r_{2A}^*)$
$+ g_{NA1B}(r_{NA}^* - \text{CPI}_A^* - r_{1B}^* + \text{CPI}_B^*)$
$+ g_{NA2B}(r_{NA}^* - \text{CPI}_A^* - r_{2B}^* + \text{CPI}_B^*)$
$+ g_{NANB}(r_{NA}^* - \text{CPI}_A^* - r_{NB}^* + \text{CPI}_B^*)$.

(S34) $K_{1B} = h_{1B}(r_{1A}, r_{1B}, r_{2A}, r_{2B}, r_{NA}, r_{NB}, \text{CPI}_A, \text{CPI}_B)$.

$K_{1B}^* = g_{1B1A}(r_{1B}^* - \text{CPI}_B^* - r_{1A}^* + \text{CPI}_A^*) + g_{1B2B}(r_{1B}^* - r_{2B}^*)$
$+ g_{1BNB}(r_{1B}^* - r_{NB}^*) + g_{1B2A}(r_{1B}^* - \text{CPI}_B^* - r_{2A}^* + \text{CPI}_A^*)$
$+ g_{1BNA}(r_{1B}^* - \text{CPI}_B^* - r_{NA}^* + \text{CPI}_A^*)$.

(S35) $K_{2B} = h_{2B}(r_{1A}, r_{1B}, r_{2A}, r_{2B}, r_{NA}, r_{NB}, \text{CPI}_A, \text{CPI}_B)$.

$K_{2B}^* = g_{2B2A}(r_{2B}^* - \text{CPI}_B^* - r_{2A}^* + \text{CPI}_A^*) + g_{2B1B}(r_{2B}^* - r_{1B}^*)$
$+ g_{2BNB}(r_{2B}^* - r_{NB}^*) + g_{2B1A}(r_{2B}^* - \text{CPI}_B^* - r_{1A}^* + \text{CPI}_A^*)$
$+ g_{2BNA}(r_{2B}^* - \text{CPI}_B^* - r_{NK}^* + \text{CPI}_A^*)$.

Where the elasticity values within equations are restricted in accord with the pattern described in equation (28) of the text, and values across equations fulfill the following types of constraints:

$$\frac{\partial K_{1A}}{\partial(r_{1A}/r_{1B})} = -\frac{\partial K_{1B}}{\partial(r_{1A}/r_{1B})}.$$

$$K_{1A}\frac{(r_{1A}/r_{1B})}{K_{1A}} \cdot \frac{\partial K_{1A}}{\partial(r_{1A}/r_{1B})} = -\frac{(r_{1A}/r_{1B})}{K_{1B}}$$

$$\frac{\partial K_{1B}}{\partial(r_{1A}/r_{1B})} \cdot K_{1B}.$$

$$\frac{K_A}{K_B} \cdot \frac{K_{1A}}{K_A} \cdot g_{1A1B} = -\frac{K_{1B}}{K_B} g_{1B1A}.$$

$$k_{AB} \cdot \lambda_{K1}^A \cdot g_{1A1B} = -\lambda_{K1}^B g_{1B1A}.$$

Appendix C

In this appendix the net efficiency or welfare effects of adopting DISC are explained. An initial assumption is that a community welfare function exists, and its value depends on aggregate consumption of the five goods available within a country. More accurately, then, potential welfare is measured, since no attention is paid to the redistributive policies within the country determining actual welfare. This welfare function is represented as

(A1) $\qquad U_A = U(D_{1AA}, D_{1BA}, D_{2AA}, D_{2BA}, D_{NA})$.

Given that a price ratio equals the corresponding ratio of marginal utilities in equilibrium, a change in utility can be expressed as

(A2) $\qquad \dfrac{dU_A}{U_{NA}} = P_{1A}dD_{1AA} + P_{1B}dD_{1AB} + P_{2A}dD_{2AA}$

$$+ P_{2B}dD_{2AB} + dD_{NA},$$

where U_{NA} is the marginal utility of consuming an additional unit of X_{NA}. Since there is no net saving in this model, a change in the value of consumption must equal a change in the value of income, which allows equation (A2) to be rewritten as:

(A3) $\qquad \dfrac{dU_A}{U_{NA}} = dY_A - D_{1AA}dP_{1A} - D_{1BA}dP_{1B}$

$$- D_{2AA}dP_{2A} - D_{2BA}dP_{2B}.$$

Although income was expressed in terms of output in the text, to analyze welfare changes it is more useful to work from the comparable definition in terms of factor income:

(A4) $\quad Y_A = w_A L_A + q_A S_A \dfrac{(r_A)}{1 - t_{1A}} K_{1A} + \dfrac{(r_A)}{1 - t_{2A}} K_{2A}$

$$+ \dfrac{(r_A)}{1 - t_{NA}} K_{NA} + r_B (\tilde{K}_A - K_A)$$

$$+ \text{TAR}_{1A} \cdot P_{1B}D_{1BA} + \text{TAR}_{2A} \cdot P_{2B}D_{2BA} - \text{DISCREV}.$$

Differentiating this equation results in an expression to use in equation (A3) for dY_A. Based on the zero-profit conditions in the production of X_{1A}, X_{2A}, and X_{NA}, the factor reward terms dw_A, dg_A, and dr_A can be eliminated, giving

(A5) $\quad \dfrac{dU_A}{U_{NA}} = (X_{1A} - D_{1AA})dP_{1A} + (X_{2A} - D_{2AA})dP_{2A}$

$$- D_{1BA} \, dP_{1B} - D_{2BA} \, DP_{2B} - \text{DISCREV}$$

$$+ \dfrac{(r_A)}{1 - t_{1A}} dK_{1A} + \dfrac{(r_A)}{1 - t_{2A}} dK_{2A} + \dfrac{(r_A)}{1 - t_{NA}} dK_{NA}$$

$$- r_B \, dK_A + (\tilde{K}_A - K_A)(dr_B/\text{CPI}_B - r_B d\text{CPI}_B)$$

$$+ \text{TAR}_{1A} \cdot d(P_{1B}D_{1BA}) + \text{TAR}_{2A} \cdot d(P_{2B}D_{2BA}).$$

The r_B and CPI_B terms require some explanation. They reflect the possibility that as capital abroad depreciates, it can be replaced by spending less than the initial allowance for depreciation because the real prices of capital goods have declined. Dividing both sides of the equation by Y_A gives the percentage change in welfare as:

(C-6)
$$\frac{dU_A}{U_{NA}}\frac{1}{Y_A} = U^* = \frac{P_{1A}X_{1AB}}{Y_A}P_{1A}^* + \frac{P_{2A}X_{2AB}}{Y_A}P_{2A}^*$$

$$- \frac{P_{1B}D_{1BA}}{Y_A}P_{1B}^* - \frac{P_{2B}D_{2BA}}{Y_A}P_{2B}^* - \text{DISCREV}$$

$$+ \frac{r_A K_{1A}}{(1-t_{1A})Y_A}K_{1A}^* + \frac{r_A K_{2A}}{(1-t_{2A})Y_A}K_{2A}^*$$

$$+ \frac{r_A K_{NA}}{(1-t_{NA})Y_A}K_{NA}^* - \frac{r_B K_A}{\text{CPI}_B Y_A}K_A^*$$

$$+ \frac{r_B(\tilde{K}_A - K_A)}{\text{CPI}_B Y_A}(r_B^* - \text{CPI}_B^*)$$

$$+ \frac{\text{TAR}_{1A} \cdot P_{1B}D_{1BA}}{Y_A}(P_{1B}^* + D_{1BA}^*)$$

$$+ \frac{\text{TAR}_{2A} \cdot P_{2B}D_{2BA}}{Y_A}(P_{2B}^* + D_{2BA}^*).$$

References

Armington, P. 1969. A theory of demand for products distinguished by place of origin. *International Monetary Fund Staff Papers* 16:159–77.

Baldwin, R. 1971. Determinants of the commodity structure of U.S. trade. *American Economic Review* 61:126–46.

Baldwin, R., J. Mutti, and D. Richardson. 1980. Welfare effects on the United States of a signficant multilateral tariff reduction. *Journal of International Economics* 10:405–23.

Ballard, C., D. Fullerton, J. Shoven, and J. Whalley. 1982. Complete documentation of the U.S. general equilibrium model. Prepared for the Office of Tax Analysis, U.S. Treasury Department.

Batra, R., and R. Ramachandran. 1980. Multinational firms and the theory of international trade and investment. *American Economic Review* 70:278–90.

Bowen, H. 1980. *Changes in the international pattern of factor abundance and the composition of trade.* Economic Discussion Paper no. 8, U.S. Department of Labor, Bureau of International Labor Affairs.

Branson, W., and N. Monoyios. 1977. Factor inputs in U.S. trade. *Journal of International Economics* 71:111–32.

Caves, R. 1971. International corporations: The industrial economics of foreign investment. *Economica* 38:1–27.

Gerking, S., and J. Mutti. 1981. Possibilities for the exportation of production taxes. *Journal of Public Economics* 16:233–52.

Goulder, L., J. Shoven, and J. Whalley. 1981. Domestic tax policy and the foreign sector. January. Mimeo.

Grant, J. 1979. Labor substitution in U.S. manufacturing. Ph.D. diss., Michigan State University.

Grossman, G. 1981. Partially mobile capital: A general approach to two-sector trade theory. Mimeo.

Hall, Robert E., and Dale W. Jorgenson. 1967. Tax policy and investment behavior. *American Economic Review* 57:391–414.

Hamermesh, D., and J. Grant. 1980. Econometric studies of labor-labor substitution and their implication. *Journal of Human Resources* 16:518–42.

Horst, T. 1981. An economic analysis of the foreign international sales corporation proposal. *Tax Notes*, 7 December, pp. 1347–51.

Horst, T., and T. Pugel. 1977. The impact of DISC on the prices and profitability of U.S. exports. *Journal of Public Economics* 7:73–87.

Johnson, H., and M. Krauss. 1970. Border taxes, border tax adjustments, comparative advantage, and the balance of payments. *Canadian Journal of Economics* 3:595–602.

Jones, R. 1967. International capital movements and the theory of tariffs and trade. *Quarterly Journal of Economics* 81:1–38.

Kemp, M., and H. Wan. 1974. Hysteresis for long-run equilibrium from realistic adjustment costs. In *Trade, stability and macroeconomics*, ed. G. Horwich and P. Samuelson. New York: Academic Press.

U.S. Department of Treasury. 1981. *The operation and effect of the Domestic International Sales Corporation legislation, 1979 annual report*. Washington, D.C.: GPO.

Comment   Stephen P. Magee

This is a very comprehensive and, I think, quite competent paper on both theoretical and empirical considerations related to the DISC. I have only two brief comments. The first is that there is no necessary reason why we might expect an increase in the DISC to also be associated with an expansion of U.S. exports. If the DISC were obtained in an endogenous policy model in which resources are removed from export production in order to effect the adoption of DISC, then the increase in rent seeking

Stephen P. Magee is professor of finance at the School of Business of the University of Texas at Austin.

could cause a decline in exports at the very time when the DISC is adopted. Of course, this does not mean that the welfare of exporting interests is harmed. The favorable tax benefits could easily offset the reduction in the quantity of exports in such a way that the exporter's welfare would improve.

A second and related point is that in an endogenous policy model, causation does not run from the change in the policy to the change in exports. Rather, both exports and the policy itself are caused by other underlying determinants.

Both of these points are outside the scope of the current model and should not be interpreted as a direct criticism of an obviously fine paper.

Comment   William R. Cline

John Mutti and Harry Grubert have provided an impressive analysis of the DISC. Their model brings out important effects that would be missed in a partial equilibrium approach. As a major example, it is only with a general equilibrium analysis that they are able to identify adverse effects of the DISC on unskilled labor, arising primarily from the reduction of output and employment in nontraded goods caused by reallocation of resources to exportables.

Certain elements of the model do raise questions. The basic price equations are composed only of factor costs; there is no treatment of costs of intermediate inputs. Even considering that the model is aggregative and therefore that intermediates tend to disappear, there should nonetheless be inputs from even the three broad aggregate sectors into each other. Similarly, it is not apparent how the model takes into account imported intermediate inputs.

It is noteworthy that the welfare effects cited are small while the transfer effects are large; in this regard, the analysis of DISC shows results symmetrical to those of trade protection.

The model results are driven crucially by the balance-of-payments constraint. This constraint is the main cause of a reduction of output in the sector of import substitutes (sector $1A$). That is, with the balance of payments constrained to be unchanged, import substitutes at home must be partially replaced by imported goods to compensate for the DISC-induced rise in exports.

Other specifics warrant mention. The parameter 1.25 as an elasticity of substitution would seem high for categories as broad as the three economy-wide categories used. (Can education services, good 3, readily be substituted in demand for grain, good 2, or oil, good 1?) The results for

William R. Cline is a senior fellow of the Institute for International Economics, Washington, D.C.

rate of return to capital in the partner country are puzzling: as the stock of capital in country B declines because of a reallocation of capital away from B to country A, it might have been expected that the rate of return to capital rises in response to greater scarcity; instead, it declines (table 8.2).

Despite these assorted questions about the model itself, it would appear to provide a useful representation of the economic effects of DISC. My remaining comments therefore focus on the political economy of DISC. In terms of the paper itself, the analysis brings out a powerful and heretofore unrecognized argument against DISC: this tax mechanism *reduces* jobs and output in import-competing industries. If labor and management in steel, automobiles, and textiles were aware of this analytical conclusion and agreed with it, DISC's days would be numbered. Even more significant politically, the main effect of DISC identified by Mutti and Grubert is not that it increases U.S. exports, but instead that it reduces the wage of unskilled labor. This finding, a result of the reduced output of (labor-intensive) nontradables as resources shift to exports, should be a politically sensitive strike against DISC if past experience in the field of import protection (where impact on unskilled labor is a significant consideration) is any guide.

It must be noted, however, that these key results turn on the assumption of unchanged balance of payments. Country B's exports must increase to offset the rise in country A's exports. Yet the implicit assumption of the creators of DISC is just the opposite. DISC exists to increase the net trade balance of the United States, not to reshuffle workers and resources from import substitutes to export products. In theoretical terms, that underlying political-economic premise cannot be justified except perhaps in periods of obvious overvaluation of the exchange rate. As it happens, however, the United States is currently in just such a period; the dollar is perhaps 20 percent above an equilibrium level, while the trade deficit for 1983 could reach $70 billion or more and the current account deficit correspondingly would also be large. In this context, especially if the dollar is to remain overvalued as the consequence of mismatch between tight monetary and loose fiscal policy (because of inability to act in reducing budget deficits), second-best instruments that do raise the trade balance (rather than leaving it unchanged, as in the Mutti-Grubert analysis) may be appropriate. If DISC, the Export-Import Bank, and other export-stimulating devices are ever justified, it is in periods such as the present.

Even in terms of the goals of the legislators who created DISC, however, it seems to be ineffective, judged by the Mutti-Grubert analysis. It increases exports only by 2 percent. This finding is not a great surprise, considering that its subsidy equivalent amounts to only 1.7 percent of the export price, which in turn reflects the fact that DISC reduces capital costs only by 11 percent, and capital costs themselves are only one-fifth of product price.

The paper's implicit policy recommendation is to use the Export-Import Bank as the preferred vehicle for stimulating U.S. exports (if that objective is taken as given), and more specifically, the Export-Import Bank's support should be focused on those U.S. exports that are price-elastic in foreign demand. That is, the United States should be a price-discriminating monopolist.

Other major issues arise in a broader policy context than that directly addressed by the Mutti-Grubert study. Perhaps the most important is that DISC is the Achilles' heel of U.S. policy on trade subsidies. Subsidies are certain to be a key area of trade conflict in the 1980s and beyond. Other countries are emphasizing industrial policies, and that strategy inevitably means subsidies. In some cases the results of these subsidies are and will be trade distorting. But the United States will not be in a credible position to insist on greater adherence of the EEC, Japan, and others to GATT principles on subsidies as long as the DISC stands in flagrant violation of those principles. It is important for U.S. ability to negotiate that DISC be abolished or at least reformed.

If DISC is eliminated, some substitute will be needed in practical political terms. The Export-Import Bank is the best substitute. Unfortunately, it is not trusted as a permanent alternative because administrations have found it too easy to cut its funding in the past. Moreover, the Export-Import Bank is viewed to some extent as narrowly concentrated in favor of large firms, such as aircraft producers, while DISC is an across-the-board instrument.

For its part, the Reagan administration is committed to the elimination of DISC and its replacement by something that is compatible with the GATT. Just what that might be remains unclear.

One proposed alternative would be the FISC—a Foreign International Sales Corporation. This strategy would essentially move all DISCs to post boxes in offshore locations that do not tax, following the lead of the Belgians and French, whose export tax subsidies they justify on grounds that they occur offshore. Nontaxation of foreign operations is accepted by GATT practice. The risk of the FISC is that it will be considered to be an artificial device, equivalent to a tax haven, designed to circumvent DISC's violations of GATT; major foreign countries would seem unlikely to judge such a vehicle as truly GATT-compatible.

The best policy strategy would be to eliminate DISC entirely. To this end, it would be necessary to reshape political alliances by highlighting the small export effects of DISC and, more importantly, its adverse effect on output and employment in import-competing industries and on wages of unskilled labor. As a complement to this strategy it would also be appropriate to enlarge the Export-Import Bank's activity as long as the United States maintains a substantially overvalued exchange rate.

9 The Benefits and Costs of Official Export Credit Programs

Heywood Fleisig and Catharine Hill

9.1 Introduction

Governments support export credits in, broadly, two ways: through direct loan and subsidy programs and through insurance and guarantee programs. Under direct loan programs, government institutions extend export credits directly, often in association with private financing. Under subsidy programs, governments operate indirectly on export credits by extending preferential refinancing and interest subsidies to private lenders. In the United States, Canada, and Japan, official export institutions lend directly to both domestic exporters and foreign importers at fixed subsidized rates. In Germany, France, the United Kingdom, and Italy, official institutions combine direct lending, refinancing of private export credits at preferential rates, and interest rate subsidies to achieve similar results.[1]

The subsidy in officially supported export credits arises in several ways: loans are made at fixed rates to borrowers who would normally qualify only for variable rate loans, at maturities generally longer than available in the private market for comparable loans to such borrowers, and at lower rates than these borrowers would otherwise pay. Governments also subsidize exports through loan insurance and guarantee programs when

Heywood Fleisig and Catharine Hill are with the World Bank, Washington, D.C.

The authors are obliged to J. Michael Finger, Ben Crain, and David Dod for numerous helpful comments, encouragement, and support during this project. Nicholas Hope, Jeffrey Katz, and Thomas Klein of the World Bank, and Bevan Stein of the Organization for Economic Cooperation and Development, provided comments and invaluable guidance through the data. Mark Connell provided excellent research assistance. Any errors of fact or logic remain the authors' responsibility, as do the views expressed in this paper, which are not necessarily those of the World Bank.

they sell insurance and guarantees at prices below their true market value.

When a government guarantees or insures a loan made to finance an export, it creates a financial instrument against which the lending institution, either a bank or an exporter, can borrow at rates close to the government borrowing rate. The potential profit on a guaranteed or insured loan to the lender equals the rate at which the importer could have borrowed in the private market without insurance or a guarantee, and the rate at which the lender can borrow against the guaranteed loan, minus any insurance or guarantee fees.

All of the countries considered have institutions that extend export credit insurance or guarantees. Through these institutions the government assumes a large proportion of the credit risk on loans to foreign buyers. Although the subsidy element on an insured or guaranteed loan is generally smaller than on a directly supported export credit, there are about three times more insured or guaranteed export credits outstanding than direct loans. Therefore, the total subsidy on such programs may still be substantial.

This paper analyzes the costs and benefits of the direct loan and subsidy programs. Section 9.2 considers various methods of determining the subsidy element in official export credits and presents estimates of the export credit subsidies provided by the major lending countries. It estimates that the subsidy in the direct loan and subsidy programs for these countries ranged from $1.5 billion to $3.5 billion in 1980. Of this amount, after export price changes, it is estimated that developing countries received between $500 million and $2.4 billion.

This paper then analyzes the market factors that determine the subsidy's effect on export prices and volumes and, thereby, the ultimate division of the subsidy between borrowers and lenders. Borrowers are found to receive between 50 and 100 percent of the subsidy, depending on the supply, demand, and market structure of the export industries receiving subsidized credit. Section 9.3 raises a variety of issues relevant in assessing the social costs and benefits to borrowers and lenders resulting from the subsidy and the ensuing changes in export prices and volumes. This paper concludes by describing the various international efforts that have been made to limit official export credit subsidies.

9.2 Measuring the Subsidy on Official Export Credit Programs

Outstanding direct and subsidized export credits of the major lending countries (Canada, France, Germany, Italy, Japan, the United Kingdom, and the United States) amounted to nearly $55 billion at the end of 1978. These lenders offered substantial subsidies, charging interest rates between 7 and 8 percent, at the same time that private lenders charged rates between 5 and 15 percent.

9.2.1 Methods of Calculating the Subsidy on Official Export Credits

Calculating the subsidy on official export credits requires first making a judgment about the private rate that the borrower would have paid. This rate will always exceed the government borrowing rate, but beyond that will depend on the characteristics of both the borrower and the loan. The subsidy element may be calculated as an annual interest differential or as the present value of future interest differentials over the life of the loan.

The subsidy a borrower receives equals the difference between the official export credit institution's rate and the rate charged in the private market for the same type of loan and borrower. Some estimates compute the subsidy by comparing the government borrowing rate with the official export credit rate. Such computations underestimate the subsidy, however, because importers will always pay a higher interest rate on their loans, given currency denomination and maturity, than will the government of the country issuing the currency. The reasons are, first, that privately granted export credit is tailored to the individual transaction—a retail transaction—with a low volume and a high overhead. In contrast, government debt is marketed in large volumes and in standardized units and maturities. Second, privately granted export credit, because of this individual tailoring, is harder to resell; by contrast, liquid markets exist at most maturities for government debt. Finally, only the government of the currency-issuing country can absolutely guarantee the payment of bonds denominated in its own currency because only that government can legally create that currency at will. Since no private or foreign government borrower can make the same guarantee about his debt, lenders will always require additional compensation for this added risk. The market interest rate measures the cost to society of granting export credit when its productive resources are fully employed (see Appendices A and B). The government interest rate, at full employment, will always fall short of the private market rate for the same maturities, for the reasons discussed above. At full employment, the social cost is the difference between the export credit agency's rate and the market rate. The difference between the export credit agency's rate and the government interest rate provides only some peripheral information relating to the budgeted cost—not the social cost—of the export credit granting agency.

Fixed-Rate and Floating-Rate Estimates

Borrowers can pay interest on their loans at interest rates fixed over the life of the loan, or at interest rates that float above the wholesale bank rate. Typically, good credit risks can borrow at either rate, while riskier borrowers must take floating rate loans.

This paper computes the subsidy under both of these assumptions about the riskiness of the borrower. It estimates the subsidy for borrowers who otherwise would have borrowed at fixed rates by multiplying the loans granted in each year by the difference between the bond rate at which they could have borrowed and the interest rate charged on the direct export credit. It derives the total subsidy on the loan portfolio by adding the subsidies on all loans still outstanding. It estimates the subsidy for borrowers who would otherwise have financed their imports with a floating rate loan by multiplying the outstanding portfolio of officially supported export credits by the interest rate differential between the lending country's short-term market rate and the average interest rate actually received on the portfolio.

These methods produce an ex post measure of the subsidy that represents the savings in debt service in any given year under different assumptions about the alternative borrowing possibilities available to the borrowing country. The two measures of the subsidy may differ from ex ante expectations of the subsidy. In the fixed-rate calculation, the savings in interest payments in future years are set at the time the loan is committed and, if the borrower does not refinance, the expected and actual future interest subsidy are equal. In the floating rate case, the subsidy in any year will change with movements in the short-term interest rate. The expected subsidy and the actual subsidy will, therefore, only be equal if borrowers realize their expectations of movements in the floating rate.

The procedures followed under these two methods can be illustrated with the export financing activities for one year, 1980, of the Export-Import Bank of the United States (Eximbank).

Only the best of Eximbank's borrowers could have borrowed at the U.S. Aaa corporate bond rate. Assuming that all borrowers from Eximbank could have obtained loans at the Aaa corporate bond rate results in the fixed-rate estimate of the value of the subsidy. Given detailed information on the loans in the outstanding portfolio, the fixed-rate subsidy can be calculated as

$$(1) \qquad \sum_{t=T}^{1980} A_t (r_t^{AA} - r_t).$$

A_t = authorizations made in t still outstanding in 1980.

r_t^{AA} = corporate Aaa bond rate in t.

r_t = average interest rate on loans authorized in t.

T = year during which oldest outstanding loans were authorized.

Table 9.1 shows the amount of direct loans authorized and the weighted-average interest rate charged. The Aaa corporate bond is also shown,

Table 9.1   Estimation of the Eximbank Loan Subsidies

	Weighted-Average Interest Rate on Direct Loans	New Direct Loan Authorizations (millions of dollars)	Aaa Corporate Bond Yield	Estimated Subsidy (millions of dollars)
1971	6.00	2,300	7.39	32.0
1972	6.00	2,200	7.21	26.6
1973	6.00	2,900	7.44	41.8
1974	6.38	4,300	8.57	94.2
1975	7.90	2,300	8.83	21.4
1976	8.42	2,100	8.43	0.2
1977	8.50	800	8.02	-3.8
1978	8.38	2,900	8.73	10.2
1979	8.28	4,300	9.63	58.1
1980	8.44	3,600	11.94	126.0

SOURCES: Weighted-average interest rates were supplied by Eximbank staff. The Aaa corporate bond yield was taken from the *Federal Reserve Board, Annual Statistical Digest*, and *Federal Reserve Bulletin*, various issues.

as is the amount saved annually by Eximbank borrowers—the subsidy. The total subsidy on Eximbank's loan portfolio in any year is the sum of the subsidies on the debt still outstanding from earlier years.

If the data on the percent of past authorizations still outstanding are not available, these estimates assume that all loans authorized in a given year have a maturity equal to the average and that t/T percent (where T = average maturity and t ranges from 1 to T) of loans authorized ($T + 1 - t$) years in the past are still outstanding. For example, one-ninth of loans authorized nine years ago would still be outstanding, given $T = 9$. These estimates weight the resulting subsidy so that the weighted average of loan authorizations made in the past equals the total outstanding export credits. Using this procedure for Eximbank yields a fixed-rate estimate of the subsidy equal to $213.5 million for 1980.

If the data on past authorizations are not available, these estimates assume that authorizations have remained constant over time. Since authorizations have generally been increasing for the countries considered, this assumption will yield a lower bound for the fixed-rate estimate. For example, using this procedure for Eximbank yields an estimate of the subsidy of $171.2 million for 1980.

The floating-rate comparison is appropriate in cases where the borrowers are not creditworthy enough to secure fixed-interest loans by selling bonds. Instead, they borrow at rates that follow the Eurocurrency rates. In 1980, on a portfolio of $13.8 billion, Eximbank earned a return of 7.31 percent. Comparable floating rate on Eurodollar loans for that year bore an average rate of 14.5 percent, so the subsidy was 7.19 percent on $13.8 billion, or $992 million. The floating-rate subsidy in 1980 is calculated as

(2) $\bar{A}_{1980}(r^E_{1980} - \bar{r}_{1980})$.

$\bar{A}_{1980}$ = total outstanding official export credits in 1980.

r^E_{1980} = Eurocurrency loan rate in 1980.

$\bar{r}_{1980}$ = average interest rate on total outstanding official export credits in 1980.

Computing the subsidy requires knowing the weighted-average interest rate on the entire portfolio. Sometimes the lending agency supplies that information, but in other cases the lending agency supplies only the average interest rate for each year's authorizations. In the latter case, computing the average interest rate on the entire portfolio requires knowing the volume of each year's authorizations still outstanding. When the lending agency does not supply that information either, we estimate the authorizations still outstanding, by year, as we did for the fixed-rate estimate of the subsidy (see above).

The above estimates assume that borrowers faced, as an alternative, the market rate on loans denominated in the same currency as the subsidized export credit. Recently, countries have begun providing officially supported export credits in foreign currencies. In such cases, the subsidy for any one country is the difference between the subsidized rate and the market rates for loans in the currencies in which the subsidized export credits are made. This procedure was used for the calculation of the subsidy for Canada, where a large proportion of loans are denominated in U.S. dollars. Although several other countries have started to provide official export credits in foreign currencies, inadequate data prevented our taking this into account in the subsidy calculations. The error introduced is probably small, however, both because foreign currency authorizations have only become important in the last few years and because authorizations are not immediately reflected in outstanding loans.

An alternative method for calculating the subsidy would be to express it as the discounted present value of the fixed-rate subsidy on loans authorized in any one year. The subsidy would equal the difference between the face value of the subsidized loan and the present value of the repayment stream computed at the market rate of interest.[2] Computing the present discounted value of the subsidy permits representing and analyzing the interest subsidy in a price-equivalent form: borrowers should be indifferent between receiving the interest subsidy and receiving a decrease in the price of the good equal to the present discounted value of the interest subsidy. However, official institutions lend only a portion of the purchase price of an export; since that portion differs both between countries and within countries among different goods, and since some important countries do not report these data, computing the price-equivalent subsidy still does not permit comparing its size to export prices or unit values.

The present value of the subsidy, moreover, is difficult to compute because its calculation requires information on people's beliefs about the future course of interest rates (for a floating-rate loan) or about their refinancing plans (for a fixed-rate loan). By contrast, the method presented in section 9.2.1 avoids this problem by calculating the interest subsidy for one year on all loans outstanding in that year.

9.2.2   Empirical Findings

Following the methods illustrated above with U.S. data, this paper estimates that the total subsidy of the major lending countries amounted to about $1.5 billion in 1980 if the borrower's alternative was, in actuality, a fixed-rate loan (see table 9.2). A negative entry in this table implies that a borrower took an official loan at a rate in excess of the market bond rate. Since a sensible borrower would not willingly do that, negative entries rather indicate that the typical recipient of official export credits, contrary to assumption, could not borrow at the fixed bond rate assumed and that the estimate of $1.5 billion is too low.

If the typical recipient of official export credit would have borrowed at floating rates in the absence of official lending, the estimated subsidy rises to about $3.5 billion in 1980 (see table 9.3). Negative subsidies, as shown in the table, can arise either where borrowers are unable or unwilling to refinance their fixed-rate official loans at lower floating rates. Borrowers

Table 9.2   Estimate of the Subsidy When Borrowers' Alternative Is a Fixed-Rate Loan ($ million)[a]

	1976	1977	1978	1979	1980
Canada	14.6	13.7	24.6	(27.3)[b]	(46.9)
France	n.a.	n.a.	420.5	(464.8)	(552.4)
Germany	23.9	6.3	(−5.4)	(−16.2)	(−17.5)
Italy	53.3	74.0	94.2	(110.9)	(128.8)
Japan	36.7	31.7	21.2	15.4	(55.6)
United Kingdom	289.7	358.7	423.9	(499.9)	(543.1)
United States	108.3	81.6	57.5	85.2	213.5
Total	526.5	566.0	1,036.5	1,187.3	1,522.8

[a]The estimates are based on data obtained from the Export-Import Bank of the United States. For a detailed discussion of the data, see appendix C.

[b]The numbers in parentheses were calculated assuming outstanding loans remained constant over the previous year. This was done when data were not available for recent years. Since most programs have been growing, this should provide a lower bound on the estimate of the subsidy.

might be unable to refinance at the spreads assumed in table 9.3 (50 basis points over the three-month interbank rate in the country where the loan is made). In that case, table 9.3 underestimates the subsidy.[3] On the other hand, borrowers might be unwilling to refinance longer-term fixed rate commitments at lower, floating short-term rates if they foresaw a pattern of short-term rates over the life of the longer-term loan that would make it unprofitable for them to refinance; it is difficult to imagine an operational test of this explanation.

Lacking direct information on the regional distribution of the subsidy by type of borrower, this paper estimates it by assuming that lenders subsidize all borrowers by approximately the same amount. Then the distribution of the loans by type of borrower would be the same as the distribution of the subsidy by type of borrower. Table 9.4 shows the distribution of loans by type of borrower: 69 percent of the loans went to developing countries, 24 percent to Eastern Europe and China, and the remainder to other developed countries.[4]

The entire subsidy is not transferred to foreign borrowers, however, because domestic exporters in the lending country can raise prices and recapture part of the subsidy's benefits. Section 9.3.1 discusses why recapture probably ranges between zero and one-half in most typical markets. Applying these recapture rates to the estimated range of total subsidy granted by the export credit—$1.5–$3.5 billion—yields an estimate of subsidy actually transferred of $.75–$3.5 billion.

Assuming that the transferred subsidy is distributed by type of borrower in the same proportion as the pattern of lending implies that developing countries would have received about 70 percent of the transferred subsidy, or $.5–$2.4 billion. Because the Arrangement on Guide-

Table 9.3   Estimate of the Subsidy When Borrowers' Alternative Is a Floating-Rate Loan ($ million)[a]

	1976	1977	1978	1979	1980
Canada	−14.8	−23.6	91.0	(151.2)[b]	(288.4)
France	n.a.	n.a.	152.2	(336.4)	(725.1)
Germany	−76.2	−44.4	(−113,1)	(−40.3)	(39.5)
Italy	169.5	134.4	81.4	(92.8)	(222.0)
Japan	95.4	−35.2	−253.7	−107.9	(471.5)
United Kingdom	243.0	37.4	118.4	(533.0)	(855.9)
United States	−86.4	−44.6	189.8	546.3	992.2
Total	330.5	24.0	266.3	1,511.5	3,524.6

[a]The estimates are based on data obtained from the Export-Import Bank of the United States. For a discussion of the data, see appendix C.

[b]The numbers in parentheses were calculated assuming outstanding loans remained constant over the previous year. This was done when data were not available for recent years. Since most programs have been growing, this should provide a lower bound on the estimate of the subsidy.

Table 9.4   Geographic Distribution of Subsidized Export Credits

Lender	Borrower	1978 (percentage)	1979 (percentage)
France	Developed countries	19	5
	Eastern Europe and China	18	33
	Less developed countries	63	62
	Total	100	100
Germany	Developed countries	7	5
	Eastern Europe and China	28	26
	Less developed countries	66	69
	Total	100	100
Italy[a]	Developed countries	—	—
	Eastern Europe[b]	52	30
	Less developed countries	48	70
	Total	100	100
Japan	Developed countries	4	2
	Eastern Europe and China	26	43
	Less developed countries	70	55
	Total	100	100
United Kingdom	Developed countries	13	15
	Eastern Europe and China	34	19
	Less developed countries	53	66
	Total	100	100
United States	Developed countries	16	11
	Eastern Europe and China	1	2
	Less developed countries	83	87
	Total	100	100
Total	Developed countries	12	7
	Eastern Europe and China	22	24
	Less developed countries	66	69
	Total	100	100

SOURCE: *Trends in Export Credits among Major Competitors.* Export-Import Bank of the United States. Policy Analysis Staff. Washington, D.C., 6 March 1981.
[a]The figures for Italy only include credits with a repayment term over five years.
[b]Figures for Italy do not include loans to China.

lines for Officially Supported Export Credits (see section 9.4) permits lower interest rates and longer maturities for low-income countries, 70 percent is a conservative estimate of the proportion of the subsidy going to developing countries.

9.3   The Benefits and Costs of Export Credit Subsidy Programs

In both competitive and most monopolistic export markets, recipients of subsidized export credits cannot lose while, symmetrically, providers of subsidized export credits cannot gain, so long as there are not external costs or benefits. This section first analyzes how the market reaction of export prices and volumes to the subsidy determines the final distribution of the subsidy between lending country exporters, lending country citizens who provide the subsidy, and the borrowing country importers. In view of the modest size of these programs relative to the output of the lending countries, we have used a partial equilibrium approach for this analysis. The section concludes by considering a variety of external costs and benefits that affect the social costs and benefits arising from various redistributive and efficiency aspects of the program.

9.3.1 The Distribution of the Subsidy between Borrowers and Exporters

The distribution of the subsidy will depend on supply, demand, and market organization in the markets receiving subsidized export credit. In a competitive market, when officially supported export credits increase demand for a good whose supply is totally inelastic, subsidized buyers bid up the price above its previous level. Since the quantity sold remains constant, by assumption, buyers can only be satisfied when the price has risen by enough to extinguish the extra demand created by the subsidy. The export price must rise then by the full amount of the subsidy. The domestic exporting industry, therefore, recaptures the entire subsidy through higher prices, and the borrowing country gains nothing. If the price of the export is fixed on world markets, whatever the supply conditions, the entire subsidy is also transferred to the domestic exporting industry. The existence of many perfect substitutes for the subsidizing country's exports means that only a slight price advantage suffices to capture much of the market. Subsidy recipients will bid up the price of the subsidizing country's exports by nearly the full amount of the subsidy and still willingly buy the same or greater amounts than before.

If supply is less than totally inelastic and the price of the export is not given on world markets, however, some of the subsidy must be transferred to the borrowing country to induce them to purchase more. When supply curves are infinitely elastic over the range of the subsidy, all of the subsidy is transferred to the borrowing country importers.

If the exporter in the lending country is a monopolist, some of the subsidy must be transferred to the borrowing country importer. The monopolist always operates in the elastic portion of his demand curve and can always increase profits by expanding sales volume when his demand curve shifts out.

Given available information on supply, demand, and market organization in the markets receiving subsidized export credit, this paper estimates that borrowers receive between 50 and 100 percent of the subsidy (see appendix A). In competitive markets, existing estimates of elasticities of supply and demand (Stern, Francis, and Schumacher 1976) suggest that almost all of the subsidy is transferred to the borrower. If the exporters in lending countries are monopolists, this paper estimates that borrowers get half of the subsidy,[5] though this finding rests on assumed values for the second derivatives of demand and marginal cost functions.

9.3.2   Distributional Effects within Lending Countries

If official export credit lending does not solve a market failure within the lending country, and markets are competitive, then overall efficiency or output cannot rise. If the subsidy eliminates no market failure but, at the same time, makes borrowing country importers and lending country exporters better off, then it must make other citizens of lending countries worse off. If borrowing country importers receive any of the subsidy, as is likely, the lending country as a whole must lose. Depending on whether the price or volume of exports rises, nonsubsidized citizens in lending countries bear the cost in different ways.

In a fully employed economy, real net exports can rise only by reducing real domestic investment, consumption, or government expenditure (see appendix B for further discussion). If the rise in net exports forces a decline in domestic investment projects, the lending country citizens lose the market rate of interest on the foregone investment,[6] while the lending country government receives the lower, subsidized interest rate on the same quantity of exports. The loss to the lending country government and its nonsubsidized citizens amounts to the difference between the market rate and the lower subsidized rate. These losses may, however, be partly offset by terms of trade gains that increase exporters' profits when the subsidized loan increases demand. As discussed above, however, the lending country typically will not recover part of this subsidy; that part will be transferred to the borrowing country and lost through the inefficient use of resources.

When the economy is fully employed, but where an increase in imports offsets the rise in exports so that net exports remain unchanged, the net cost to the subsidizing country is the same as before. Purchasers of imported goods pay the higher world market interest rate to finance their additional imports, while their government receives the lower, subsidized interest rate on the additional exports it financed. As before, gains to exporters partly offset this loss, but the rest of the subsidy is retained by borrowing country importers or absorbed by the higher cost of less efficient production.

9.3.3   Other Benefits and Costs to Borrowing Countries

While borrowing countries generally gain from the subsidy on export credits even after prices adjust, other costs, difficult to quantify, may offset the gain. Restrictions on the currency denomination of the export credit may distort the currency denomination of the borrowing country's debt and, thereby, offset part of the gain from the subsidy to the borrowing country. The subsidy calculation may also overstate the gain to borrowing countries if they compete in third markets against exports from industrialized countries that receive subsidized credit.

Portfolio Effects

Just as a country will choose a portfolio of international reserve currencies that, by various accounts, produces some optimal risk-return combination in the light of that country's future consumption and investment plans, so a country will desire a portfolio of international debt denominated in different currencies that achieves the same end.

If the borrowing country's acceptance of the export credit leads to denominating additional debt at market rates in a currency that moves the borrowing country away from its optimal debt portfolio, then the above estimate of the interest subsidy overestimates the gain to the borrower. The gain to the borrower cannot be negative, however, since the subsidy expands the choices available to the borrower, and the borrower need not accept the subsidized credit to purchase the export.

Terms of Trade Effects

The gain to borrowing countries from subsidized export credit may be offset if the borrowing countries also export goods to third markets which compete with exports from industrial countries that receive subsidies. When a developing country's exports compete with goods which receive subsidies from industrial countries, its terms of trade deteriorate. The fact that many developing countries have instituted official export credit programs to match industrial country subsidies suggests that these countries do export goods competitive with subsidized industrial country exports. In particular, some evidence exists that developing countries have become increasingly competitive at producing customized capital goods.

When developing countries compete against industrial country exports to other developing countries that receive subsidized credit, the distribution of the subsidy among individual developing countries changes, but the estimate of the transfer to all developing countries does not. Subsidies granted or price reductions on developing country exports to industrial countries could, however, reduce the estimates of the transfer presented here. Developing country exports competing against industrial country exports that receive most subsidized export credits (SITC category 7), however, amounted to only $14 billion in 1980, while industrial country export credits go primarily to developing countries. Given this, terms of trade for developing country exports would have to deteriorate far beyond those ever experienced to reverse the estimates of the flows given above. At most, even assuming that all developing country exports of such goods to industrial countries compete against goods receiving subsidized credits, the subsidy estimate would be reduced by about 25 percent.[7]

9.3.4   Other Benefits and Costs to Lending Countries

The exporter generally recaptures only part of the export credit subsidy through higher prices. Whether the lending country as a whole gains from the subsidy, therefore, depends on whether the official export credit solves a market failure within the lending country. A variety of externalities on which export credit subsidies could act have been advanced by proponents of officially supported credits. Even where these arguments have merit, however, in few cases are export credit subsidies the best means of achieving a given goal.

The Effects of Officially Supported Export Credits on Employment

Export subsidies can increase employment in export industries. However, when the economy is already at full employment, employment in the subsidized export industry rises at the expense of employment elsewhere. Since total employment cannot increase beyond full employment, and the resulting resource shift may temporarily aggravate inflation, employment gains in export industries provide no net social gain for the subsidizing country.

In the face of general unemployment, an export subsidy can increase total employment. However, so can monetary and fiscal policies. Moreover, as general tools to regulate the economy, monetary and fiscal policies may be superior to export subsidies. The export credit subsidy normally increases the production of exports relative to other domestically produced goods, increasing the relative cost of the export goods to domestic consumers. Unless considerations other than a general increase in employment prompt the use of subsidies, other policies—such as monetary and fiscal policies—could increase employment and output without these side effects on relative prices and sectoral outputs. No reason exists, moreover, to believe that an export subsidy will provide a stronger or less inflationary stimulus to employment than other forms of budgetary spending or tax reductions.

In addition, if export credits do not vary over the business cycle, their beneficial effects in reducing unemployment in recessions will bear a cost later when they contribute to overheating the economy during booms. Since export credits are often committed far in advance of actual transactions and are usually extended over periods that are longer than any one stage of the cycle, and since future cycles cannot be perfectly foreseen, great difficulties beset the use of export credits for stabilization purposes.[8] These rigidities enhance the desirability of alternative policies to deal with unemployment and inflation.

Export subsidies could be used to support employment in chronically depressed industries or regions. The subsidy could serve as an alternative to unemployment payments if it were clear that, in the absence of the subsidy, the unemployed labor in a particular industry or region would not be employed elsewhere. However, pursuing such a policy for a long time would result in increasing losses to the country by extending the period of time during which resources were used inefficiently.

Official Export Credits and Capital Market Imperfections

Sometimes the absence of private market credit may indicate a market imperfection that prevents the gains from trade from being fully realized. In such a case, the government can correct the market deficiency by providing credit, making society's use of resources more efficient.

The original impetus for the formation of the Eximbank arose in such a situation. The Eximbank was set up during President Franklin D. Roosevelt's administration to finance trade with the Soviet Union. The administration viewed opening diplomatic relations with the Soviet Union as an important political objective. At the same time, it wished to alleviate the constricting effects that the 1930 Hawley-Smoot Tariff had on trade and to promote exports as a means of increasing domestic employment. Since the economy was in a depression, these were all important policy objectives. The Soviet Union, unlike many other countries, was agreeable to increasing imports at that point.

At the same time, the private market was unlikely to finance trade with the Soviets. The lack of diplomatic recognition had slowed the development of commercial ties, and unofficial State Department policy, together with the Johnson Debt Default Act, operated to block loans to countries that had defaulted on war debts. Unlike the present situation, there was much evidence then to support the view that the private market would not have lent sufficiently to secure the side effects that were considered desirable on political and economic grounds.

Similarly, after World War II, when the U.S. government viewed the level of private lending to Europe as insufficient to prevent economic difficulties and consequent political disorder that could have seriously compromised the NATO alliance, the Eximbank was one of the institutions used to channel government loans to Europe.

The absence of private market loans, however, does not prove that the market is imperfect. Some less-developed countries, for example, cannot float bonds in the bond market. Many reasons exist for this, all relating to the absence of the kind of creditworthiness and volume of credit demand that makes floating a bond issue worthwhile. Likewise, many corporations cannot raise funds by selling bonds. Instead, they and smaller partnerships and individuals must ordinarily finance their business loans by borrowing from a retail bank at higher rates of interest than bond issuers pay.

Most less-developed countries raise funds by borrowing from banks in the Eurodollar market or in national banking markets. Their loans typically have interest rates that float at a predetermined number of basis points (hundredths of a percentage point) over a benchmark interest rate, such as the prime rate or the London Interbank Offer Rate (LIBOR). When an official export credit institution lends to such a borrower at, for example, a rate comparable to a lower corporate bond rate, it grants that country a subsidy equal to the difference between the retail rate it would have been charged because of the greater risk, and the rate charged by the official institution.

When a bank refuses credit to a foreign borrower at market rates because of the condition of the country or of the borrower within the country, then the risk attached to the loans exceeds that represented by the retail rates that banks typically charge these countries. The subsidy granted by the official institution is greater than the difference between the rate it charges and the market rate because it is taking a risk larger than the one reflected in the market rate.

When the private sector responds to risky loans by charging higher rates or by refusing to make them at all, this does not, as noted, necessarily mean that a market imperfection exists. When such imperfections are absent, official loans at below-market rates cannot raise total income or increase efficiency. Without solving a market imperfection, such practices can only redistribute income away from nonsubsidized citizens and toward domestic exporters or citizens of a borrowing country.

Matching Foreign Subsidized Credit Programs

If a foreign government permanently subsidizes an export product, the policy that would yield the largest income for another country's citizens as a group would permit the foreign producer to supply the good. In this way, the country that does not match the foreign subsidy can earn larger quantities of foreign exchange and import more goods by reallocating domestic resources from the production of the foreign-subsidized good to the next most productive sector. The receipts from the sales of these next-best exports will be only marginally lower, and the subsidy to foreigners will no longer be necessary. Although neither workers nor equipment can be reallocated without costs, reallocation involves a one-time cost whereas matching subsidies involves a permanent stream of costs. For that reason, the reallocation of resources may be cheaper when the foreign subsidy program is expected to last a long time.

If it is known, however, that the foreign country's subsidy is only temporary, then the lending country may gain by competing with a matching subsidy. Whether a country will benefit from matching subsidies depends on whether the costs of competing in the short run are outwieghed by the benefits of not having to shift productive resources first out of and then back into the affected export sector.

Any one lending country might use subsidized export credits to bring pressure on other countries that refuse to curb their own subsidized lending through an international agreement. Whether this would produce a benefit for any one country would depend on the cost to the country of continued subsidization of exports by other countries.

Common views of fairness may also dictate matching foreign subsidies. When one government subsidizes export credits, it injures the producers in other countries who are competing directly with those subsidized products in both the foreign and domestic markets. Because neither workers nor equipment can be reallocated without cost, citizens in the nonsubsidizing country as a whole may temporarily lose income and wealth. The workers and capital owners in the industry will typically bear these costs, but costs will be spread to other citizens through programs such as unemployment insurance. These risks are quite similar to those borne by other groups of industrialists and workers who face weather changes, technical changes in foreign countries, demand changes, input price changes, and changes in local governments' subsidies and tax exemptions. Nonetheless, when one government makes a conscious decision aimed largely and necessarily at damaging exporters in other countries, the fellow citizens of damaged exporters may believe this commercial misfortune is more inequitable than the others described above. In this case, a country may be willing to sacrifice some efficiency to attain an outcome it sees as more equitable. The total costs of the subsidy must be weighed against the equity considerations.

The Effect of Officially Supported Export Credits on the Exchange Rate

Increased exports can produce exchange rate appreciation. Where small interest rate subsidies produce a large increase in the total value of exports, an export credit subsidy program may result in exchange rate appreciation. However, where comparatively large interest rate subsidies fail to produce a much larger increase in exports, any appreciation may be quickly reversed.

After the merchandise sale, however, the receipt of interest payments on the subsidized loan will fall short of the payments on foreign loans made by citizens who were originally crowded out of the national capital market. This net drain on interest payments will reduce the current account. Therefore, after the initial, temporary rise in export receipts, the subsidized loan may produce a current account deficit and exchange rate depreciation that counteracts the initial trade surplus and exchange rate appreciation.

The Benefits of an Increase in Exports

A rise in exports can reflect a socially desirable increase in productivity or in savings, but subsidizing exports does not force this relation to operate in reverse. For example, exports may increase because productivity rises in the export industries. If the exchange rate does not change, exporters will either supply more exports at the old price, undersell their competitors, or deliver a higher quality product at the same price. The rise in productivity would be a clear benefit to the country, with more output resulting from a given quantity of inputs. However, the rise in exports would only reflect these gains; it would not produce them.

Similarly, higher saving rates can increase net exports, but subsidizing exports need not raise total national saving. A rise in saving will reduce the consumption of imported goods and free up more domestic goods to be exported, thus increasing the current account surplus. Such an increase in the current account surplus means citizens are accumulating capital in foreign countries. Accumulation of foreign assets passes on a larger total capital stock to future generations of citizens. Although the future generation's consumption gain is partly offset by the current generation's loss, so long as both generations fully undertake this shift, no external cost warrants using public policy to undo the savings decision.

In economies at full employment, however, a subsidized rise in exports can occur only at the expense of some domestic activity—consumption, investment, or government expenditure—or when offset by a corresponding rise in imports. If imports rise to provide the goods absorbed by the increase in exports, then the subsidy has produced no rise in net exports. If the subsidy does increase net exports at the expense of domestic consumption or government spending, then the subsidy may ultimately raise the total of domestic and foreign investment. However, the domestic expenditure most likely to fall as a consequence of subsidy-induced rises in borrowing rates is domestic investment. In this case, there will be no net increase in capital passed on to future generations, although future generations will get more capital located in foreign countries. Citizens as a group will gain no obvious advantage from such a shift.

A Foreign Policy or National Security Role for Official Export Credits

Official export credits are sometimes justified as a way of protecting industries that are important for national defense, and as a way of transferring resources to foreign countries that need economic aid. It is doubtful, however, that export credit subsidies are an efficient way of achieving either of these ends.

If a country wished to preserve an industrial activity within its borders on national security grounds, it could achieve that by subsidizing the exports of that industry.[9] Secondary national defense benefits may also accrue from having a larger pool of skilled workers in a given industry. It must be shown, however, that an export credit subsidy is a relatively inexpensive way to achieve this end. For example, if maintaining a core of trained technicans and a manufacturing capacity in naval nuclear generating units is an important national defense objective, then a standing annual order for such devices might be cheaper than subsidizing the export of entire nuclear power plants, which include mostly goods and services that are unrelated to defense preparedness.

Official export credits may also serve a foreign aid function. This does not, however, appear to have been their primary purpose. In the United States, for example, official export credits have been more concentrated in Europe than is foreign aid, and do not bear much relation to the pattern of foreign aid disbursement in areas outside Europe (see table 9.5). If official export credits are distributed differently from other foreign assistance, it is unclear how to evaluate them as effective foreign aid instruments. It might be that an addition to foreign aid would be voted by lending countries' governments in exactly the way it is spent by official export credit institutions; but, on the other hand, it might not be. Official export credits are also an inefficient form of foreign aid since they are tied to the export of particular goods. As discussed above, part of the subsidy is absorbed in the inefficient use of resources, lost to both domestic citizens and foreigners alike.

On occasion, the granting of export credits might also be valuable as a foreign policy device if it enabled a government to take quicker action. This was the case in the United States in the past, when the Eximbank was set up to finance trade with the Soviet Union in the 1930s and later used to assist in European recovery after World War II.

Other Externalities

A variety of other purposes for subsidized export credits could be advanced. In all cases, however, not only does the existence of an externality justifying government involvement need to be proved, but the use of export credit subsidies rather than other policies must be shown to be optimal. For example, subsidized export credits might be part of a successful industrial policy program. The case for adopting an industrial policy would first have to be made, however, and only then could the relative efficacy of subsidized export credit relative to other policies be evaluated. The different economic performances of intensive users of

Table 9.5   Distribution of U.S. Economic Assistance and Eximbank Loans, by Region, Fiscal Years 1962–79 (percentages of annual totals)

	1962–76		1977		1978		1979	
	Economic Assistance	Eximbank Loans	Economic Assistance	Eximbank Loans	Economic Assistance	Eximbank Loans	Economic Assistance	Eximbank Loans
Near East and South Asia	38.2	11.4	63.5	2.8	59.5	2.3	63.8	8.9
Latin America	19.4	22.0	9.3	21.1	8.9	32.9	11.1	15.0
East Asia	28.7	20.6	9.0	33.2	8.7	38.8	8.7	40.1
Africa	10.3	5.6	11.1	19.8	13.9	19.1	14.8	16.2
Europe	2.1	32.6	4.1	21.5	9.0	5.9	1.5	18.7
Canada	0.0	1.8	0.0	0.1	0.0	0.8	0.0	0.3
Oceania	1.3	6.0	3.0	1.4	0.1	0.3	0.2	0.8
Total[a]	100.0	100.0	100.0	100.0	100.0	100.0	100.0	100.0

SOURCE: Agency for International Development, *U.S. Overseas Loans and Grants and Assistance from International Organizations, Obligations, and Loan Authorizations, 1 July 1945–30 September 1979*, Washington, D.C.

[a]Columns may not add to totals because of rounding.

official export credit—the United Kingdom and Japan, for example—suggest caution in adopting easy generalities.

9.4 International Controls of Officially Supported Export Credits

Countries have attempted to control subsidized export credit terms since the 1930s. The Berne Union (the International Union of Credit and Investment Insurers) was formed in 1934 to provide a forum for the discussion and exchange of information among member export credit insurance agencies, now numbering thirty-five member agencies from twenty-seven countries. Over the years, the Berne Union has made nonbinding recommendations on the regulation of export credit policies. For example, in 1953 the member nations agreed to limit maturities to five years on export credit for heavy capital goods, and to three years on all other export credit. Beginning in the late 1960s, members increasingly disregarded these guidelines.

In 1963 the Organization for Economic Cooperation and Development (OECD) Trade Committee established a Group on Export Credits and Credit Guarantees. The Export Credit Group, as it is known, organized an information exchange system in 1972, which provided for prior consultation on credit of longer than five years. At the same time, the OECD reached agreement on credit terms for ships and aircraft.

Negotiations continued for a more comprehensive agreement on export credits. On 27 October 1974 the Export Credit Group concluded an informal agreement which has come to be known as the "Gentlemen's Agreement." It stipulated a minimum interest rate of 7½ percent on credits of over five years, and a maximum repayment period of three years on credits granted to wealthy nations.

Jurisdictional confusion slowed the negotiations in 1975, when both the European Commission and the individual governments claimed the right to negotiate on commercial policy for European Economic Community (EEC) members. Because the European Court of Justice awarded this authority to the European Commission, the export credit agreement concluded on 1 July 1976 was enacted as a series of unilateral declarations by the nations involved in its negotiation rather than as a formal agreement. These nations—Canada, France, Germany, Italy, Japan, the United Kingdom, and the United States—agreed to a matrix of minimum interest rates and maximum repayment terms for officially supported credit of two years or more for three different income categories of recipient nations (see table 9.6). This 1976 agreement, known as the "Consensus," was accepted by thirteen additional OECD members during the succeeding year.

The dispute with the European Commission was resolved by 1977, and on 1 April 1978 the "Arrangement on Guidelines for Officially Supported

Table 9.6   **Initial Consensus Minimum Interest Rates**

Category of Country (per capita income)	Repayment Term	
	2–5 Years	Over 5 Years
Relatively poor (under $1,000)	7.25	7.50
Intermediate ($1,000–$3,000)	7.25	7.75
Relatively rich (above $3,000)	7.75	8.00

Export Credit" was concluded, superseding the Consensus. The members of the EEC participated as a single unit. The Arrangement reiterated the conditions specified in the Consensus and continued as a voluntary set of guidelines.

Because the Arrangement specifies the same minimum interest rates for credit denominated in all currencies, it permits actual credit subsidization to vary both over time and across countries. As market rates increased over time, the fixed minimum interest rates permitted a greater subsidy. The same fixed minimum rates permitted countries with high market interest rates to offer larger subsidies than could countries with low market rates.

At the request of participants in the OECD Arrangement, Mr. Axel Wallen, former chairman of the OECD Export Credit Group, examined alternatives to the existing Arrangement. This study (OECD 1980) discussed two alternatives to the fixed matrix: a "uniform moving matrix" and a "differentiated rate system." The uniform moving matrix would link the Arrangement minimum rates to a basket of market interest rates of participant countries. The minimum interest rate would be identical for all currencies, but the level would be tied to some average of market rates. If market interest rates increased, therefore, the minimum rate of officially supported export credits would also increase, preventing the subsidy on officially supported export credits from automatically increasing. As with the existing Arrangement, however, subsidization rates would vary considerably from currency to currency, depending on the individual currency's market interest rates relative to the Arrangement minima.

The differentiated rate system would specify different minimum interest rates for each currency. Rather than equalize nominal interest rates, this system would attempt to equalize interest rate subsidization. If minimum interest rates were defined to equal comparable market rates for each currency, subsidies would be eliminated. Alternatively, minimum rates could be specified to allow for an agreed absolute or proportional rate of subsidization.

Despite a great deal of pressure, principally from the United States, little progress has been made in reforming the Arrangement according to either of the alternatives suggested in the Wallen Report (OECD 1980). In the summer of 1980 at the Venice Summit, the United States supported the differentiated rate system but was unable to reach agreement with the EEC. Instead, Arrangement signatories modestly increased the minimum interest rates and stated their intention to pursue a better solution.

Additional increases in the Arrangement minimum interest rates were negotiated in November 1981 and July 1982. The next round of negotiations was scheduled for May 1983, but because of the recent easing of interest rates, a further increase in the Arrangement rates appears unlikely.

The principle features of the present Arrangement are:

Cash payment. A minimum 15 percent cash payment is required on all contracts, no part of which may be provided by the donor agency.

Interest rates. Recipient countries are divided into three categories— category 1 contains those with per capita GNP over U.S.$4,000; category 2 contains those with per capita GNP under $4,000 but not eligible for International Development Association (IDA) assistance; and category 3 contains those eligible for IDA assistance. Minimum interest rates vary according to the category of country and term of the loan (table 9.7).

Maturity terms. Category 3 countries must repay loans within 10 years; all others must repay within 8½ years.

Exceptions. The Arrangement exempts agricultural commodities, military equipment, commercial jet aircraft, and nuclear power plants.

Table 9.7   Current Arrangement Minimum Interest Rates (as of 1 January 1983)

Category of Country	Repayment Term		
	2–5 Years	5–10 Years	5–8½ Years
Category 3 (relatively poor)	10.00	10.00	—
Category 2[a] (intermediate)	10.85	—	11.35
Category 1	12.15	—	12.40

[a]Countries recently graduated to Category 2 (e.g., Algeria, Colombia, Malaysia, Nigeria) are eligible for export credit at 11.35 percent with repayment terms up to 10 years, rather than 8½ years.

Partial exceptions allow extended repayment terms for satellite ground stations, conventional power plants, and cryogenic (liquified natural gas) tankers.

Local-cost support. The Arrangement pertains to financing the foreign exchange cost of export goods from the lending country, not to local costs incurred in installing equipment in the borrowing country. The Arrangement prohibits local-cost financing in relatively rich countries, but permits local-cost insurance and guarantees.

Mixed Credit. Export credits generally involve less than a 5 percent grant element. All credits with a grant element below 15 percent require prior notification of other Arrangement signatories. Credits involving a 15–25 percent grant element require prompt notification, while those with more than a 25 percent grant element are considered Official Development Assistance and are exempted from notification requirements.

Appendix A   *Efficiency Losses and Income Redistribution Arising from Export Credit Subsidization*

For both competitive and most common monopolistic export markets, where external gains and losses are absent, a lending country cannot make itself better off by providing export credits at subsidized rates; nor can a borrowing country make itself worse off by accepting them.[10] Under typical supply, demand, and cost conditions, subsidizing export credit produces a combination of some loss in efficiency together with redistribution of income away from citizens providing the subsidy and toward domestic exporters and foreign importers. These effects become extreme at the limit: a lending country offering exports in perfectly price-inelastic supply or facing perfectly price-elastic excess demand will transfer nothing to the borrowing country; on the other hand, a lending country offering exports in perfectly price-elastic supply will transfer nothing to its home exporters from the subsidy program.

This analysis examines equilibrium reached in the market for the export good as prices and quantities adjust to a change in the export credit subsidy. We have not used a more general eqilibrium framework for two reasons. First, the smallness of these programs relative to the economies providing the loans would make the computation of the effects econometrically nonoperational. Second, proper expansion to more general effects would require a major escalation in complexity, since analyzing export credits perforce requires dropping the assumption that trade is balanced and introducing instead a framework that optimizes over time.

The subsidy, s, is the present value of the interest rate subsidy expressed per unit of quantity demanded. The demand curve is entirely a foreign demand curve, so only the export market is shown. In equilibrium, the demand price and supply price will differ by the amount of the subsidy, so

(A1) $$P_S(Q_S) = P_D(Q_D) + s.$$

In a competitive market, the social gain to the lending country, GL, from subsidizing the export credit equals the producers' surplus less the cost of the subsidy. For inverse supply curves whose integral is defined over the closed interval $[0, Q^*]$, social gain, GL, will be

(A2) $$GL = P_S Q^* - {}_0\!\int^{Q^*} P_S(Q)dQ - sQ^*.$$

Totally differentiating expression (A2), the change in the gain with respect to the subsidy will be

(A3) $$\frac{dGL}{ds} = Q^* \frac{dP_S}{ds} - \frac{sdQ^*}{ds} - Q^* = Q^* \left(\frac{dP_S}{ds} - 1\right) - \frac{sdQ^*}{ds}.$$

The social gain to the borrowing country, GB, equals the consumers' surplus plus the subsidy. For inverse demand curves whose integral is defined over the closed interval $[0, Q^*]$, the social gain, GB, will be

(A4) $$GB = {}_0\!\int^{Q^*} P_D(Q)dQ - P_S Q^* + sQ^*.$$

Totally differentiating expression (A4), the change in gain to the borrowing country with respect to the subsidy will be

(A5) $$\frac{dGB}{ds} = - Q^* \left(\frac{dP_S}{ds} - 1\right).$$

Endogenous Price, Upward-Sloping Supply Curve, Downward-Sloping Demand Curve

Where prices are endogenous, the changes in the quantities of exports supplied equal those demanded in equilibrium, so that $dQ_S = dQ_D = dQ^*$. The change in the equilibrium quantity of exports (Q^*) with respect to the subsidy (s) can be derived from (A1) and will be

(A6) $$\frac{dQ^*}{ds} = \frac{1}{\dfrac{\partial P_S}{\partial Q_S} - \dfrac{\partial P_D}{\partial Q_D}} \geqslant 0.$$

Given that $Q_S(P_S) = Q_D(P_D)$, and $P_S = P_D + s$, the change in the equilibrium supply price will fall between zero and one:

$$\text{(A7)} \qquad \frac{dP_S}{ds} = \frac{-\dfrac{\partial Q_D}{\partial P_D}}{\dfrac{\partial Q_S}{\partial P_S} - \dfrac{\partial Q_D}{\partial P_D}}, \ 0 \leqslant \frac{dP_S}{ds} \leqslant 1.$$

Evaluating (A3) by expressions (A6) and (A7) indicates that the leanding country cannot gain from the credit subsidy ($[dGL/ds] \leqslant 0$), while similarly evaluating (A5) indicates that the borrowing country cannot lose from the credit subsidy ($[dGB/ds]) \geqslant 0$).

Endogenous Price, Horizontal Supply Curve

If the supply curve is horizontal ($P_S[Q_S] = k$), substitution of $\partial P_S/\partial Q_S = 0$ in (A6) implies

$$\text{(A8)} \qquad \frac{dQ^*}{ds} = \frac{1}{-\dfrac{\partial P_D}{\partial Q_D}} > 0,$$

while, by assumption,

$$\text{(A9)} \qquad \frac{dP_S}{ds} = 0.$$

Evaluating expression (A3) with the values shown in (A8) and (A9) indicates that the lender must lose ($[dGL/ds] < 0$), while similarly evaluating expression (A5) indicates that the borrower must gain the entire subsidy ($dGB = Q^*ds$).

Endogenous Price, Vertical Supply Curve

Since $dQ_S = dQ_D$ when the price is endogenous, a vertical supply curve implies that $dQ_S = dQ_D = dQ^* = 0$. Totally differentiating the inverse demand curve shown in (A1), given that $dP_D = 0$ because $dQ_D = 0$, indicates that

$$\text{(A10)} \qquad \frac{dP_S}{ds} = 1.$$

Evaluating expression (A3) given $dQ^* = 0$ and $dP_S = ds$ indicates that the lending country on net loses nothing ($[dGL/ds] = 0$); rather, inelastic supply forces the transfer of the subsidy from domestic taxpayers to domestic producers of the subsidized export product. Similarly, evaluating expression (A5) with those values indicates that the borrowing country gains nothing ($[dGB/ds] = 0$), but rather returns the entire subsidy to the lending country by paying a higher price for the product.

Exogenous Price, or Horizontal Demand Curve

If a country is a relatively small supplier in the international market, it can take the world market price as given. In this case, $P_S = P_W + s$, for a constant P_W. Recalling that domestic purchasers are not eligible for the loan subsidy,

(A11)
$$\frac{dP_S}{ds} = 1,$$

while

(A12)
$$\frac{dQ^*}{ds} = \frac{1}{\frac{\partial P_S}{\partial Q_S}} > 0.$$

Substituting the values of expressions (A11) and (A12) into expression (A3), the subsidizing country must lose because of the inefficiency resulting from the increase in production ($[d\text{GL}/ds]) < 0$). Substitution in (A5), however, indicates that the borrowing country does not gain because the export price rises by the amount necessary to absorb the subsidy ($[d\text{GB}/ds] = 0$).

Monopolist Exporter

If a country's export market is monopolistic, the monopolist will set the market price at a level that maximizes profit. The monopolist's total cost curve is assumed to be $C = C(Q)$. In the presence of a subsidy, the price charged by the monopolist will be

(A13)
$$P_M = P_D(Q) + s.$$

Assuming the monopolist sells only in the export market, monopolist profits will be

(A14)
$$\pi = QP_M - C(Q) = QP_D(Q) + sQ - C(Q).$$

If the monopolist maximizes profits,

(A15)
$$\frac{\partial \pi}{\partial Q} = \frac{Q\partial P_D}{\partial Q} + P_D - \frac{\partial C}{\partial Q} = 0.$$

The second-order condition will be

(A16)
$$\frac{\partial^2 \pi}{\partial Q^2} = Q\frac{\partial^2 P_D}{\partial Q^2} + 2\frac{\partial P_D}{\partial Q} - \frac{\partial^2 C}{\partial Q^2} < 0.$$

The change in the quantity of exports (Q^*) with respect to the subsidy (s) can be derived by totally differentiating (A15) and will be

(A17) $\qquad \dfrac{dQ^*}{ds} = \dfrac{-1}{Q\dfrac{\partial^2 P_D}{\partial Q^2} + 2\dfrac{\partial P_D}{\partial Q_D} - \dfrac{\partial^2 C}{\partial Q^2}} > 0.$

This is greater than zero by the second-order condition, expression (A16). From (A13) and (A17)

(A18) $\qquad \dfrac{dP_M}{ds} = \dfrac{-\dfrac{\partial P_D}{\partial Q}}{Q\dfrac{\partial^2 P_D}{\partial Q^2} + 2\dfrac{\partial P_D}{\partial Q} - \dfrac{\partial^2 C}{\partial Q^2}} + 1,$

or, by the second-order condition and $(\partial P_D/\partial Q) < 0$:

(A19) $\qquad \dfrac{dP_M}{ds} = \dfrac{Q\dfrac{\partial^2 P_D}{\partial Q^2} + \dfrac{\partial P_D}{\partial Q} - \dfrac{\partial^2 C}{\partial Q^2}}{Q\dfrac{\partial^2 P_D}{\partial Q^2} + 2\dfrac{\partial P_D}{\partial Q} - \dfrac{\partial^2 C}{\partial Q^2}} < 1.$

Note that dP_M/ds is not necessarily positive. If the numerator in (A19) is greater than zero, then dP_M/ds will be negative.

Assuming that the monopolist sells only in the foreign market, the social gain to the lending country, GL, will equal the producer's surplus less the cost of the subsidy. For monopolist cost curves whose integral is defined over the closed interval $[0, Q^*]$, social gain will be

(A20) $\quad \mathrm{GL}_M = P_M Q^* - {}_0\!\int^{Q^*} MC(Q)dQ - sQ^*, \qquad \dfrac{\partial c}{\partial Q} = MC(Q).$

Totally differentiating expression (A20), the change in the gain with respect to the subsidy will be

(A21) $\quad \dfrac{d\mathrm{GL}_M}{ds} = Q^*\dfrac{dP_M}{ds} + P_M\dfrac{dQ}{ds} - MC(Q)\dfrac{dQ}{ds} - Q^* - s\dfrac{dQ}{ds}$

$\qquad\qquad = Q^*\left(\dfrac{dP_M}{ds} - 1\right) + (P_M - s - MC(Q))\dfrac{dQ}{ds}$

$\qquad\qquad = Q^*\left(\dfrac{dP_M}{ds} - 1\right) + (P_D - MC(Q))\dfrac{dQ}{ds}.$

Using (A15), (A17), and (A18) and noting the second-order condition,

(A22) $\qquad \dfrac{d\mathrm{GL}_M}{ds} = \dfrac{s}{Q\dfrac{\partial^2 P_D}{\partial Q^2} + 2\dfrac{\partial P_D}{\partial Q} - \dfrac{\partial^2 C}{\partial Q^2}} < 0.$

Therefore, the lending country loses from the credit subsidy ($[d\text{GL}/ds]$) < 0).

The expression for the gain to the borrower facing a monopolistic exporter is the same as in the competitive case (expression [A4]). Evaluating the change in the gain to the borrowing country, expression (A5) with expression (A19) indicates that the borrowing country gains from the credit subsidy ($[d\text{GB}/ds]$) > 0).

Empirical Estimates of the Distribution of the Subsidy between Borrowers and Exporters

In the competitive case, expression (A5) shows the gain to the borrower resulting from the subsidy. Representing the gain in relation to the total subsidy yields

(A23)
$$\frac{d\text{GB}}{Qds} = 1 - \frac{dP_S}{ds}.$$

Substituting for dP_S/ds from expression (A7) yields

(A24)
$$\frac{d\text{GB}}{Qds} = \frac{\dfrac{\partial Q_S}{\partial P_S}}{\dfrac{\partial Q_S}{\partial P_S} - \dfrac{\partial Q_D}{\partial P_D}}.$$

Using $Q_S = Q_D$ and assuming that $P_S = P_D$ before the subsidy is introduced, $d\text{GB}/Qds$ can be written as

(A25)
$$\frac{d\text{GB}}{Qds} = \frac{\epsilon}{\epsilon - \eta}, \qquad \epsilon > 0 \text{ and } \eta < 0,$$

where ϵ and η are the elasticities of supply and demand for exports, respectively.

Using previously estimated supply and demand elasticities (Stern, Francis, and Schumacher 1976), $d\text{GB}/Qds$ ranges approximately between three-quarters and one and, therefore, most of the subsidy is transferred to the borrower.

In the monopolist case, the gain to the borrower as a result of the subsidy as a proportion of the total subsidy is

(A26)
$$\frac{d\text{GB}}{Qds} = 1 - \frac{dP_M}{ds}.$$

Substituting for dP_M/ds from expression (A19) yields

(A27)
$$\frac{d\text{GB}}{Qds} = 1 - \frac{Q\dfrac{\partial^2 P_D}{\partial Q^2} + \dfrac{\partial P_D}{\partial Q} - \dfrac{\partial^2 C}{\partial Q^2}}{Q\dfrac{\partial^2 P_D}{\partial Q^2} + 2\dfrac{\partial P_D}{\partial Q} - \dfrac{\partial^2 C}{\partial Q^2}}.$$

Evaluation of the sign or the magnitude of this expression is impossible without estimates of the second derivatives of the demand and cost curves. If we assume the demand and marginal cost curves are linear, as the intermediate case between the convex and concave alternatives, then $d\text{GB}/Qds = 1/2$, and the borrower receives half of the subsidy.

Therefore, admittedly in the presence of some potentially large gaps, present knowledge about competitive and monopolistic market structure of industries receiving subsidized export credits suggests that borrowers receive between half and all of the subsidy on official export credits.

Appendix B *The Macroeconomics of the Size and Distribution of the Cost of Export Credit Subsidies*

Appendix A analyzed the distribution of costs and benefits of the export subsidy program in a microeconomic framework. Since, at full employment, domestic exporters and foreign importers must gain from subsidized credit, while total domestic output cannot rise, the subsidizing taxpayers must lose from the program. This appendix shows this outcome in terms of the GNP accounts; the results are similar.

Case 1: Export Subsidies That Result in Additional
Export Volumes at Full Employment

Suppose that when the export subsidy increases foreign demand for exports, the export price remains unchanged but the volume of exports rises. Rearranging the national income identity produces:

(A28) $\bar{Y} - C - I - G + M = X.$

If the economy is at full employment, so that Y is at its maximum ($Y = \bar{Y}$), the rise in exports cannot occur out of additional production; instead consumption, investment, or government expenditure must fall, or imports must rise.

If the rise in exports is achieved by increasing imports, no change occurs initially in the trade balance. The lending country gains an asset—the export credit that bears interest at the lower, subsidized rate; at the same time, lending country citizens incur an identical liability to finance additional imports, but they pay interest at the unsubsidized world interest rate. The lending country net debt position does not change, but the lending country loses the difference between the subsidized and the unsubsidized interest rates. Exporters sell a larger volume of their products, but total lending country national output remains unchanged. Foreign importers pay the lower, subsidized interest rate to the lending country, while lending country importers pay the higher market interest rate and a larger total interest bill to foreigners.

Suppose now that imports remain unchanged, so that exports and the trade balance increase by reducing domestic investment. At the margin, domestic investment earns the domestic, unsubsidized rate of interest. By giving up the domestic investment project, lending country investors lose the unsubsidized rate of interest on the foregone domestic investment project now devoted to exports; in exchange, the lending country receives the lower, subsidized rate of interest on the rise in exports. If consumers require the same marginal return on a unit of consumption that they require on a unit of investment, then a rise in exports at the expense of domestic consumption produces the same net loss for society. If the government requires the same marginal return on government expenditure that its private citizens receive on private investment, then a rise in exports at the expense of government expenditure produces the same net loss for society.

Case 2: Export Credit Subsidies That Increase Export Values
        and Unit Values but Leave Export Volumes Unchanged

If the volume of exports does not change, export promotion incurs no real cost to the economy as a whole. The preceding discussion rests on the assumption that there is such a real cost, and that it is borne by investors, consumers, or the government. This section establishes that, even in the absence of such a real cost, the loss to the nonsubsidized sector will exactly equal the gain to the subsidized sector.

With constant real exports, resulting from a vertical export supply curve, the export price (P_X) will rise by the change in the present value of the interest subsidy per unit of sales (appendix A, expression A10):

$$(A29) \qquad dP_X = ds\,.$$

Assume, for simplicity, that there are two types of goods—those produced for home consumption, H, and those produced for export, X. The geometrically weighted GNP deflator would then be

$$(A30) \qquad P_Y = P_H^{\,a} P_X^{\,(1-a)}.$$

Assume now that the central bank pursues credit policies that prevent the GNP deflator from rising despite the credit subsidy's initial upward impact on export prices, so that the rate of change of the GNP deflator is

$$(A31) \qquad \dot{P}_Y = a\dot{P}_H + (1-a)\dot{P}_X = 0\,.$$

The real value of exporters' output measured in terms of GNP is

$$(A32) \qquad V_1 = \frac{X P_X}{P_Y}\,.$$

The change in that value as a result of the subsidy is

(A33) $$dV_1 = \frac{XdP_X}{P_Y} = \frac{Xds}{P_Y}.$$

The real value of products produced for home consumption measured in terms of GNP is

(A34) $$V_2 = \frac{HP_H}{P_Y},$$

and this will fall by the same amount as the rise in the real value of exports

(A35) $$dV_2 = \frac{-Xds}{P_Y}.$$

Appendix C *Data on Official Export Credits*

Organization for Economic Cooperation and Development

The Development Assistance Committee (DAC) of the OECD collects information on transfers of long-term financial resources from DAC member countries to developing countries. DAC reports data for officially supported export credits comprising directly extended official export credits and officially insured or guaranteed private export credits. Guaranteed private export credits, in turn, include financial credits and supplier credits. Supplier credits are private export credits extended by an exporter. Financial credits refer to credits by a bank or other financial institution extended to a foreign buyer. Included under guaranteed private export credits are credits on which an export creditor receives official support, including discounting of an export credit at preferential terms by an official agency or provision of a subsidy to an export creditor to reduce the interest rate charged by him to the borrower.

Data reporting procedures raise problems in calculating the subsidy. When official support for export credits takes forms other than direct credits (e.g., the United Kingdom's interest make-up scheme or France's rediscounting facilities), program activities show up in data for guaranteed private export credits. As a result, while OECD data permit deriving figures on total officially supported export credits, they do not permit isolating those programs equivalent to the direct loan program of the U.S. Eximbank.

The OECD Trade Committee's Group on Export Credits and Credit Guarantees also collects data on officially supported export credits. These data do not, however, differentiate among types of systems used to support export credits and, therefore, do not permit breaking out the equivalent of direct loan programs only.

World Bank

Under the Debtor Reporting System (DRS), the World Bank collects information on the external debt of developing economies that have received either World Bank or International Development Association (IDA) loans. Countries report changes in their long-term external public and publicly guaranteed debt to the DRS. For the *World Debt Tables*, several other sources supplement these data, including the OECD's Creditor Reporting System (CRS) and the World Bank's Capital Markets System (CMS). Available data on private debt without public guarantees are also included. The data are broken down by official and private creditors. Officially extended buyer export credits can be identified for the United States, Germany, Japan, and Canada. As with the OECD data, however, credits receiving support through refinancing at preferential rates or interest rate make-up schemes are included in private-source loans and cannot be distinguished from other private credits.

Berne Union

The Berne Union (the International Union of Credit and Investment Insurers) collects data on export credit insurance and guarantees issued by thirty-five export credit and insurance agencies from twenty-seven countries.

Berne Union data cover commitments and offers. Commitments are export credits for which insurance or guarantees have been issued by Berne Union member agencies. They are reported on an outstanding basis, net of repayments, and include undisbursed amounts. Commitments are broken into short-term credits and payments due on an annual basis. Offers, reported separately, are potential export credits which have not yet reached the contract stage and for which insurance and guarantees have not been issued. The Berne Union presents data organized by recipient country and by Berne Union member agency, updated on a quarterly basis.

Commitments include supplier credits extended directly by the exporter (which are said to be "insured") and buyer credits or financial credits extended by private banks (which are said to be "guaranteed"). Commitments also include export credits extended directly by two member agencies, the U.S. Eximbank and Canada's Export Development Corporation (EDC). Berne Union data also indirectly include official export credit support supplied by the remaining five countries discussed in the paper (Germany, France, Italy, Japan, and the United Kingdom), since each country requires insurance or guarantees for official support. The Berne Union data as reported cannot, however, be used to calculate the subsidy element on direct official export credits; although they include such credits, they are aggregated with other export credits for which insurance and guarantees have been issued by Berne Union member agencies.

Export-Import Bank of the United States

The Export-Import Bank of the United States submits a semiannual report to Congress on competition in the provision of officially supported export credit and financing (*Report to the U.S. Congress on Export Credit Competition and the Export-Import Bank of the United States*). Until recently, data on official export credit financing programs were reported for the seven countries considered in this paper. Financing programs include both direct credits, such as those extended by the U.S. Eximbank and Canada's EDC, and refinancing facilities and interest rate subsidy programs (programs comparable to direct export credits).

Notes

1. The export credit programs of these countries are discussed in detail in Organization for Economic Cooperation and Development (1982) and Midland Bank (1980).

2. Boyd (1982) defines the subsidy in this way, and Feinberg (1982) reviews three studies that use this concept of the subsidy.

3. A 50-basis point spread probably underestimates the cost of export credit, particularly to developing countries. If the spread is increased to 200 basis points, the estimate of the subsidy increases from $3.5 billion to $4.5 billion, and most of the entries in the table turn positive.

We might calculate the subsidy more accurately by using available data on the actual risk premiums that borrowers receiving official subsidized export credit pay in the private market. If most borrowers pay a higher spread than we have assumed, or if some borrowers receiving subsidized export credits are not creditworthy enough to borrow in the private market, then we have underestimated the actual subsidy.

4. Currently we do not have data on the geographic distribution of direct and subsidized loan programs. We assumed, therefore, that such programs were distributed geographically in the same pattern as the sum of direct and subsidized loan programs and guarantee programs. In addition, no information was available on the geographic distribution of Canadian official export credits. We assumed, therefore, that it equaled the average of the other lending countries.

5. See appendix A for an analysis of the competitive and monopolistic situations.

6. If private citizens and the government choose additional consumption and investment expenditures so that the returns on those expenditures equaled those on additional investment projects, the cost of additional exports to society would be the same whether investment, consumption, or government expenditure is displaced.

7. We thank Helen Hughes for bringing this point to our attention and Ernst Lutz for providing the trade data.

8. In the United States, the evidence suggests that export credits have not been used countercyclically. Instead, direct loan authorizations have been high when unemployment has been low.

9. Aircraft producers receive one of the largest shares of official export lending. Military considerations do not generally govern such loans, though. Subsidized loans are made for civilian aircraft that are generally not used by the military. In the United States, for example, most military airframes are made by other companies, and when the government finance sales of those planes, it does so with loans from other programs. Indeed, Appendix II, section 5 of the Export-Import Bank Act of 1945, as amended through 10 November 1978, states that the "Bank shall not extend loans, guarantees, or insurance under this Act in connection with the sale of defense articles or defense services."

10. In several special cases paying an export subsidy, as compared to levying a tariff or doing nothing, may increase domestic welfare. When domestic product markets are imperfectly competitive, and producers sell in both the home and foreign markets, an export subsidy rather than a tariff may increase domestic welfare. For example, if a domestic monopolist has a decreasing marginal cost curve, an export subsidy will lead to increased output and lower average costs. If the monopolist can discriminate between the domestic and foreign markets, the falling marginal cost of total output will lead the monopolist to reduce prices in the domestic market and increase the welfare of domestic consumers. The optimal export subsidy will balance the cost of the subsidy against the increased consumer surplus. Even if the monopolist cannot discriminate between the two markets, an export subsidy may increase welfare under certain elasticities of demand in the home and foreign markets (Auquier and Caves 1979).

These results do raise the possibility that policymakers, in structuring an export credit subsidy program, could identify industries with increasing returns or could base subsidies on different home and foreign demand conditions.

However, two serious problems greatly weaken this case for export subsidization: first, the argument artifically restricts policymakers' choices, thereby neglecting the even superior welfare outcome that the subsidizing government could achieve by simply regulating the home monopolist's home market price; and second, the rise in the monopolist's real output that contributes to the rise in home welfare must, under full employment, incur costs that reduce other output whose loss is not accounted for in the calculation.

References

Auquier, A. A., and Caves, R. E. 1979. Monopolistic export industries, trade taxes, and optimal competition policy. *Economic Journal* 89:559–81.

Bank for International Settlements. 1969. *Export credit insurance and export credit*, vol. 1, *Country studies*. Basle: Bank for International Settlements.

Basevi, G. 1970. Domestic demand and ability to export. *Journal of Political Economy* 78:330–37.

Boyd, J. H. 1982. Eximbank lending: A federal program that costs too much. *Federal Reserve Bank of Minneapolis Quarterly Review* (Winter), pp. 1–17.

Cizauskas, Albert C. 1980. *The changing nature of export credit finance and its implications for the developing countries*. World Bank Staff Working Paper no. 409. Washington, D.C.: The World Bank.

Export-Import Bank of the United States. Various years. *Report to the U.S. Congress on export credit competition and the Export-Import Bank of the United States.* Washington, D.C.: Export-Import Bank of the United States.

————. Various years. *Annual report of the Export-Import Bank of the United States.* Washington, D.C.: Export-Import Bank of the United States.

————. 1981. *Trends in export credits among major competitors.* Policy Analysis Staff Report. Mimeo.

Feinberg, R. E. 1982. *Subsidizing success, the Export-Import Bank in the U.S. economy.* Cambridge: Cambridge University Press.

Fry, Richard. Various years. *Export finance service.* The Banker Reserch Unit Annual Report. London: The Banker Research Unit.

————. 1979. Competition in export credit terms. *The Banker* (August):65–71.

Hovarth, J. 1975. Are Eximbank credits subsidized?: Toward an empirical analysis. *U.S. financing of East-West trade*, ed. Paul Marer. Indiana University.

Midland Bank. 1980. Export credit facilities: An international comparison. *Midland Bank Review* (Autumn):20–29.

Organization for Economic Cooperation and Development. Various years. *OECD financial statistics*, vol. 1, tables. Paris: OECD.

————. 1980. *Arrangement on guidelines for officially supported export credits—interest rate study.* Report by Axel Wallen to the OECD Trade Directorate. Paris: OECD.

————. 1982. *The export credit financing systems in OECD member countries.* Paris: Director of Information, OECD.

Stern, Robert M., Jonathan Francis, and Bruce Schumacher. 1976. *Price elasticities in international trade.* London: Macmillan.

United States. Congress. House of Representatives. Subcommittee on International Trade, Investment and Monetary Policy of the Committee on Banking Finance and Urban Affairs. 1981. *The benefits and costs of the Export-Import Bank loan subsidy program.* 97 Cong., 1st sess., 5, 12, 17, 18 March and 28 April 1981.

U.S. Federal Reserve System. 1980. *Annual statistical digest, 1974–78.* Washington, D.C.: Publications Services of the Federal Reserve System.

————. 1982. *Federal Reserve Bulletin* 68 (1):A68. Washington, D.C.: Publications Services of the Federal Reserve System.

Comment   Rachel McCulloch

With export performance in general and the role of subsidized export credit in particular currently subjects of intense policy debate, a thorough reexamination of the rationale for and likely effects of export credit programs is indeed timely. Fleisig and Hill, in evaluating the costs and benefits of these programs, stress several important points often obscured or neglected in policy discussions.

The first, a major theme of the paper, concerns the cost of direct loan and subsidy programs. As the authors indicate, the appropriate cost measure reflects the difference between actual credit terms obtained and the best terms otherwise available to a given borrower.[1] While actual terms are usually a matter of public record, the alternative must be inferred from market rates at the time the loan was made, a process that in turn requires an ex post assessment of the borrower's creditworthiness at that time.

To estimate the subsidy element in credit obtained through the Export-Import Bank of the United States (Eximbank) and similar agencies of six other industrialized nations, Fleisig and Hill use two proxies for borrowers' market alternatives. The first is the Aaa corporate bond yield, the rate available to the best corporate borrowers. This is used to generate a lower limit of the amount of the subsidy. Less creditworthy borrowers would be unable to secure such loans, however. Instead, they would have to borrow at floating rates determined in the Eurocurrency market. Eurocurrency rates are therefore used to estimate an upper limit of the amount of the subsidy. In both cases, the authors calculate the total subsidy in a given year for all loans outstanding in that year. Because new loan authorizations have been increasing over time, this procedure yields a figure less than the value of the *current* subsidy to exports implied by the programs.

In several instances, the subsidy calculated by this method is negative, that is, the actual rate was above the hypothetical market alternative. As the authors note, such negative values probably mean that, contrary to assumption, recipients of official export credits could not borrow at the rate assumed. In such cases, however, the estimated subsidy should be set at zero. This would yield higher values for both the lower and upper limits than those reported in the paper.

A second major theme of the paper is the potential benefit to the exporting country from subsidized export credit (most of the same arguments would apply also to a wide range of other export incentives). Fleisig and Hill strongly question the common justifications of export credit programs on efficiency grounds. In the absence of market failure,

Rachel McCulloch is professor of economics at the University of Wisconsin-Madison.

efficiency is necessarily reduced by such programs, while the presence of market failure neither ensures that intervention will improve the situation nor that export credit subsidization is the most efficient type of intervention.

As the authors note, when resources are fully employed any increase in exports must entail increased imports or reduced domestic absorption. Another possibility, not explored by the authors, is that the effect on total exports is minor. If other nations offer similar terms, it is unlikely that subsidized credit has an important effect on total exports even for the industries directly affected, and it is quite possible that any increase for these industries is offset by reduced sales for the nation's other exporters. Even when resources are idle, a case for subsidized export credit on macroeconomic grounds is weak. Fleisig and Hill note that monetary and fiscal stimulus could achieve the same effect without distorting the allocation of resources between industries. More important but never mentioned is that, like import restrictions, successful export incentives merely shift employment in beggar-your-neighbor fashion to other nations competing in the same foreign markets. Arguments for subsidized export credit to maintain the viability of a domestic industry are similarly second-best.[2] If a given production level is required (e.g., for national security reasons), a direct production subsidy is the most efficient way of ensuring this.

With respect to the distributive impact of subsidized export credit, the authors seem to be on firm ground in asserting that exporters and foreign borrowers typically share the gain; the precise division depends on conditions of supply and demand. Fleisig and Hill work out the details for two cases, perfect competition and simple monopoly. Here the analysis seems curiously devoid of institutional content, especially in a paper prepared for a conference on U.S. trade policies. Surely it is relevant that the lion's share of U.S. export credit supports the sales efforts of just a tiny number of large oligopolistic firms. In 1980, loans supporting sales of aircraft alone accounted for nearly one-half the total, with the successful U.S. exporter usually facing at most two rival suppliers worldwide. Apart from aircraft, the purchases most frequently financed through Eximbank are of major capital equipment, including such specially tailored items as turnkey industrial facilities, nuclear power plants, and communications satellites. On the demand side, purchasers obtaining credit are almost always national governments or enterprises owned by them.

Thus, at least for U.S. export credit programs, the model of perfect competition is largely irrelevant. Sellers are monopolists or oligopolists, and since the nature of the products facilitates price discrimination, Fleisig and Hill's assertion that the buyer necessarily shares in the benefits need not hold. On the other hand, these buyers are hardly likely to be price-takers, so the final bargain struck is likely to include some gains to both parties. Unfortunately, the potential for corruption is obviously present; there is a clear danger that any benefits to the importing nation will be captured by government officials responsible for awarding the contract.[3]

The authors' discussion of costs and benefits focuses exclusively on the exporting and importing nations. Yet, as already indicated, this is inappropriate. If competing exporters do nothing in response, their share of lucrative export markets will be invaded. More typically, all suppliers offer comparable credit terms. In fact, the Eximbank justifies its operations as merely allowing U.S. exporters—in selected industries—to compete on "equal" terms with their foreign rivals. Obviously the effect on total exports from all suppliers is likely to be small, which explains the ongoing efforts, described by Fleisig and Hill without comment as to motivation, to negotiate international controls on this type of trade intervention.

Notes

1. As the authors' analysis implies, neither the profits and losses of the credit agency nor the delinquency and default experience on loans is directly relevant in calculating the amount of the subsidy. Until recently, Eximbank operations yielded a positive net income, and its annual report highlighted dividends paid by the agency to the U.S. Treasury. This net income was generated by borrowing at essentially government rates and relending at higher ones still well below the market alternative available to borrowers. Such "profits" are not a measure of national benefit or cost of Eximbank activities, but only of budgetary impact.

2. The FY 1980 report of the Eximbank indicates continued support for the "essential aircraft sector" and explains that although this financing absorbs a "substantial portion of the Bank's resources, official support is necessary to ensure that U.S. manufacturers maintain their competitive position in export markets."

3. Recognizing the extent to which sales of aircraft dominate the Eximbank credit totals leads to still other questions concerning ultimate gains and losses. Even if the actual cost per plane is lower to the purchaser than in the absence of such programs, are developing countries well served by incentives to expand the operations of their money-losing national airlines? And what of U.S. commercial airlines, which must compete on some international routes with foreign carriers benefiting from Eximbank credit subsidies?

V Levels of Protection in the Developed Countries

Introduction

The two papers in part V adopt a broader viewpoint than those in the other sections by appraising protection levels in the developed countries from both tariffs and nontariff measures. Deardorff and Stern utilize their computable general equilibrium model, which covers thirty-four countries and divides production into twenty-two tradable and seven nontradable sectors, to estimate protection in value-added terms. The most notable feature of their results is that their estimates of protection are considerably lower than either nominal tariffs or simple effective rates calculated in the usual manner. They attribute most of this outcome to their assumption that imports and domestic production are imperfect substitutes. In addition to these absolute differences in levels of protection, they also find that the rank order of protective rates among industries given by their calculations differs significantly from those resulting from the usual method of calculating effective rates of protection. Still another of their conclusions is that sectors with the greatest export interests will benefit most from the Tokyo Round cuts in protection.

Hughes and Krueger also find the incidence of import protection, specifically the nontariff protection against imports of manufactured goods from the developing countries, to be less than is generally believed. They arrive at this conclusion by first reviewing the highly visible nontariff barriers imposed against developing country manufacturing exports, then examining the rates at which these countries were able to increase their import shares in industrial country markets during the 1970s, and finally by considering the evidence on geographical shifts in the origin of imports from developing nations. In their view, the rate of increase of the market shares of the developing countries during the 1970s was sufficiently great to make it difficult to imagine that these rates would have been significantly higher in the absence of any protectionist measures.

10 The Effects of the Tokyo Round on the Structure of Protection

Alan V. Deardorff and Robert M. Stern

In this paper, we use the Michigan Model of World Production and Trade to analyze the structure of protection in the United States and abroad as it was altered by reductions in tariffs and selected nontariff barriers (NTBs) negotiated in the Tokyo Round. We employ a methodology developed in Deardorff and Stern (1983b) which accounts for the protective effects of trade barriers in many countries simultaneously, both directly and indirectly through the exchange rate changes that these barriers may induce. In addition to calculating the effects of the Tokyo Round on the structure of protection, we also examine how our measures of protection correspond to alternative specifications of our data inputs and assumed technology, and to a number of economic variables and other characteristics of our model, including the resource flows that are calculated directly by the model.

The paper is organized as follows. We describe the Michigan Model briefly in section 10.1, our methodology in section 10.2, and data and results in sections 10.3 and 10.4. Some concluding remarks are given in section 10.5.

10.1 Description of the Model

The Michigan Model is a disaggregated, microeconomic model that we have developed in the past several years to analyze the effects of changes

Alan V. Deardorff and Robert M. Stern are associated with the Department of Economics and the Institute of Public Policy Studies, the University of Michigan.

The authors would especially like to thank Robert Baldwin for his valuable comments on various versions of this paper. Useful comments were also received from other participants in the NBER conference and in seminars at the University of Michigan, Georgetown University, and the University of Colorado.

in tariffs and NTBs and a variety of other important variables.[1] The equations of the model are listed in the appendix. While a full description of the model is given in Deardorff and Stern (1981), some brief comments describing the model may nonetheless be useful here for those not familiar with our previous work.

The model incorporates supply and demand functions and market-clearing conditions for twenty-two tradable and seven nontradable industries in thirty-four countries.[2] There is also an aggregated sector representing the rest of the world. Exchange rates are assumed to be flexible in all the industrialized countries except New Zealand and pegged in most developing countries.

Supply and demand functions interact on both national and world markets to determine equilibrium prices, quantities traded and produced, plus the flexible exchange rates. Labor demand functions also determine employment in each industry and country. We abstract from such macroeconomic determinants of aggregate employment as levels of government spending, taxes, and the money stock. Instead, aggregate expenditure is adjusted endogenously to hold aggregate employment constant in each country.

Supply and demand functions were derived from maximization of profit and utility functions. These in turn were selected to permit a rich variety of behavior, but also to have parameters that could be either readily observed from available data or inferred from published econometric estimates. The current version of the model uses a base of 1976 data on trade, production, and employment for all thirty-four countries, plus tariffs in the industrialized countries. To describe technology, we use the 1972 input-output table for the United States and the 1970 national tables for the individual EEC-member countries and for Japan. The U.S. table is applied to the remaining industrialized countries. We use the 1970 input-output table for Brazil and apply this table to the other developing countries. Estimates of import demand elasticities and elasticities of substitution between capital and labor were obtained from the literature.

For want of a better measure, we represent existing NTBs in developed countries in terms of the fractions of 1976 trade that were covered by any kind of NTB in particular sectors and countries. We then model these sectors as less sensitive to tariff changes than would otherwise be the case. Specifically, the model includes, for each industry and country, an endogenous tariff-equivalent variable that reduces changes in imports to a fraction of what they would be without NTBs. That fraction is taken to be the fraction of trade not covered by NTBs in 1976. In addition, the model also includes several shift parameters in supply and demand functions that can be used to represent aggregate negotiated changes in NTBs as described below.

For developing countries, we have data on trade, production, and employment but no data on tariffs and NTBs. This is not serious since they will make few, if any, changes in policies as a result of the Tokyo Round. We do, however, capture elements of their existing NTBs by modeling a system of import licensing in most of these countries.

10.2 Conceptual Framework

Our conceptual framework[3] derives from the theory of effective protection, which is defined by Corden (1966, 22) as "the percentage increase in value added made possible by the tariff structure." Since our model treats prices as endogenous, it is well suited to the measurement of value added. But, more importantly, our model incorporates general equilibrium relations and takes into account the rather moderate degree of substitution between imports and home-produced goods that characterizes behavior in international trade.[4] We can thus provide a more realistic indication of the degree to which industries are protected than is possible using the simple partial equilibrium formula that was so popular in early studies of effective protection. Further, because of the multilateral and flexible exchange rate features of the model, we can capture the protective effects of both domestic and foreign tariffs, as well as the effects of changes in exchange rates.

To proceed more formally, let us define the value added per unit of an activity which produces a good j as:

$$(1) \qquad v_j = p_j^O - \sum_{i=1}^{n} a_{ij} p_i^I,$$

where v_j is value added per unit in production of good j, p_j^O is the price that producers receive for their output of good j, p_i^I is the price they must pay for intermediate inputs of good i, and a_{ij} is the number of units of good i used in producing one unit of good j. Our objective is to calculate the "change in per unit value added" (CPVA) that will result from the implementation or change of some measure of protection. From equation (1), in proportional terms, this is

$$(2) \qquad \text{CPVA}_j \equiv \frac{\Delta v_j}{v_j} = \left(\frac{1}{1 - \sum\limits_{i=1}^{n} b_{ij}} \right) \left[\frac{\Delta p_j^O}{p_j^O} - \sum_{i=1}^{n} b_{ij} \frac{\Delta p_i^I}{p_i^I} \right],$$

where

$$(3) \qquad b_{ij} = \frac{p_i^I a_{ij}}{p_j^O}$$

is the share of input i in the value of production of a unit of good j. The changes (Δs) in equation (2) can refer to the results of any protective policy one wishes to examine. Most often, they refer to the results of implementing an entire structure of tariffs, starting from a base of free trade. But they could just as easily be used to measure the effects of changing particular tariffs or groups of tariffs, or installing or removing a system of nontariff barriers.

Calculation of all of the price changes that appear on the right-hand side of equation (2) would normally be very difficult, though, of course, that is what our computational model is designed to do. In most previous studies of the structure of protection, however, the problem has been considerably simplified by assuming that all traded goods are infinitely elastically supplied at given world prices p_i^W. It follows, for imported goods, that the domestic prices p_i^D of both outputs and inputs are given by the world price plus the tariff. For ad valorem tariffs t_i, this gives us

$$(4) \qquad p_i^D = (1 + t_i)p_i^W.$$

The price changes that result when these tariffs are levied, starting from tariffs of zero, are just the tariffs themselves, since the world prices are constant. Equation (2) then provides the following simpler measure of protection:

$$(5) \qquad ERP_j \equiv \frac{\Delta v_j}{v_j} = \frac{t_j - \sum_{i=1}^{n} b_{ij} t_i}{1 - \sum_{i=1}^{n} b_{ij}}.$$

This is the formula used by Corden (1966) and many others to measure the protection due to a tariff structure. For convenience, we shall use the term, "effective rate of protection," to refer only to this simple calculation, and reserve the term "change in per unit value added," or CPVA, for the more accurate measure of protection defined in equation (2).[5]

As our derivation of (5) indicates, and as Corden himself acknowledges, the validity and usefulness of (5) depend on a number of assumptions, of which the following three will be of particular interest to us here:[6]

1. Goods are infinitely elastically supplied or demanded on world markets, so that tariff-exclusive prices are independent of the tariffs themselves.
2. Exchange rates are held constant.
3. Foreign tariffs are either constant or irrelevant.

Each of these assumptions plays in identifiable role in causing differences between ERP and CPVA. These differences were explained and verified using our model in Deardorff and Stern (1983b). Since they are important for interpreting the results in this paper, we shall review them here as well.

10.2.1 Exogeneity of Tariff-Exclusive Prices

For this to be true, two further assumptions are necessary. First, the country must be sufficiently small, as a participant in world markets, so that its changes in supply and demand do not affect world prices. For some countries this may be approximately true, but for the United States it most certainly is not. Thus, if the United States were to levy tariffs and consequently reduce its demand for imports, the world prices in affected sectors would fall and the U.S. domestic price would not rise by the full amount of the tariff. The precise implication of this phenomenon for calculation of protection in equation (2) depends on how the country's importance to world markets is distributed among outputs and inputs. But we would expect, in general, that by dampening the domestic price changes that occur, country size would tend to reduce somewhat the levels of protection.

The second assumption needed for price exogeneity is that domestic and foreign goods are perfect substitutes. If they are not, then even if the price of an import rises by the full amount of the tariff, the price of a corresponding domestic good will not. Thus imperfect substitutability will further dampen the price changes in equation (2) and reduce levels of protection below what would be calculated by the ERP.

Imperfect substitutability is also what warrants the distinction we made in equations (1) and (2) between input and output prices. Outputs are, by definition, domestically produced, while inputs will in general come from both imported and domestic sources. If the two are imperfect substitutes, with the prices of domestic goods varying by less than the price of imports as just suggested, then the prices of outputs will also vary by less than the prices of inputs. When, as we impose a structure of tariffs, all are tending to rise, this means that the positive term in (2) is dampened by more than the negative terms, and the level of effective protection is reduced algebraically compared to (5).

All prices are endogenous in our computational model. World prices are determined simultaneously by the interaction of all countries together, and no country is assumed ex ante to be small. Further, domestic and traded goods are distinct, with finite elasticities of substitution between them based on empirically estimated import elasticities. Thus from what we have said so far, we would expect our calculations of CPVA based on equation (2) to be both smaller in absolute value and more often negative than the effective rate of protection based on the Corden formula (5). This was confirmed by our numerical results in Deardorff and Stern (1983b).

10.2.2   Exogeneity of Exchange Rates

While Corden defined effective protection under the assumption of a fixed exchange rate, he recognized the inevitability of an eventual exchange rate change in response to the imposition or elimination of a complete structure of tariffs. He thus suggested a simple adjustment of all effective rates to take this into account. Such an ad hoc procedure is not necessary for us here, since our computational model can be solved for endogenous exchange rates along with everything else. Nor need the effect of the exchange rate change be quite so trivial as it was for Corden, since different sectors can be affected differently by exchange rates in our model.[7]

In general terms, both we and Corden expect exchange rate adjustment to alter the protection calculation as follows. When a country imposes tariffs in most industries, its trade balance is expected to improve. If the exchange rate is flexible, its currency will appreciate to restore equilibrium, and this will reduce the domestic prices of both imports and exports, leading to negative protection in those sectors which were least protected by the tariffs themselves. Thus, exchange rate flexibility reduces and makes more negative our measures of CPVA based on equation (2) as compared to analogous rates based on fixed currency values. Naturally, the opposite is true of the CPVA due to a general tariff reduction rather than an increase.

10.2.3   Exogeneity of Foreign Tariffs

Nothing in the concept of effective protection limits it to a country's own tariffs, though these are obviously the only policies that can be taken into account in the simplified formula (5). Industries also experience protective and antiprotective effects from the tariffs levied by other countries, and one might want to include them with a country's own tariffs in a complete analysis of the structure of protection worldwide. Whether to do so is largely a matter of choice, depending less on economic reasoning than on the question one wishes to answer. For our purpose here of analyzing the effects of the Tokyo Round of multilateral trade negotiations, the world view is clearly the most appropriate.

Presumably a country's own tariffs tend to protect its industries and foreign tariffs tend to play the opposite role. Therefore, we expect levels of protection to be even smaller and more negative when allowance is made for foreign tariffs. It thus appears that the modifications of the simple analysis that we have discussed here—endogenizing prices and exchange rates and allowing for foreign tariffs—all tend to reduce, either absolutely or algebraically, the levels of protection that we should expect.

10.2.4   Traded versus Nontraded Goods

The treatment of nontraded goods has always been a source of difficulty in calculations of effective protection. The problem is that the prices of nontraded goods are not pegged to any world prices as in equation (4). Corden (1966) describes two alternative procedures for handling them, neither of which is wholly satisfactory. One alternative is to include them with the traded inputs in both summations of equation (5), letting their tariffs in the numerator be zero. This would be valid only if the nontraded goods were themselves infinitely elastically supplied, so that their prices would be unaffected by the tariffs on traded goods. Since this is manifestly implausible, especially if the nontraded goods are themselves produced with traded inputs, Corden prefers the second alternative of including nontraded goods with value added, and thus excluding them from both summations in (5). This second alternative, which differs from the first only in the denominator, leaves us with no clear idea of which sectors are actually being protected by the levels of effective protection that we measure.

An important advantage of using our computational model to estimate protection via equation (2) instead of (5) is that none of this difficulty arises. From the model we have estimates of how all prices are affected by tariffs, and these include the prices of nontraded goods. Thus, we can include nontraded with traded goods in calculating (2), and the results refer clearly to the protection of value added actually employed directly in each sector. Protection of value added in nontraded sectors is handled in the same way.

Using the simple formula (5) to estimate effective protection of nontraded sectors, one would of course find their levels of protection to be negative. This results from the rise in the prices of traded inputs that are used in the nontraded sectors. In a general equilibrium context, however, this can be reversed. Tariffs on most tradable goods, especially if levied by all countries at once, tend to act like a consumption tax on tradables, raising their prices relative to nontradables. As demanders substitute toward nontradables their prices also tend to rise, and since the output price in (2) gets a larger weight than even the combined prices of the inputs, the nontradables in general may be protected positively. This phenomenon, that tariffs may afford positive protection to nontradable industries, is an important implication of a general equilibrium model that deserves to be studied further.

10.3 Data

The Tokyo Round of Multilateral Trade Negotiations (MTN) was concluded in April 1979. It marked the seventh round of multilateral reductions in trade barriers negotiated under the auspices of the General Agreement on Tariffs and Trade (GATT) since World War II. Tariffs on industrial products had last been reduced on a major scale in the Kennedy Round, which was concluded in 1967 and implemented over the subsequent five years. The Tokyo Round tariff reductions began in 1980 and will be phased in over a seven-year period. An even more noteworthy accomplishment of the Tokyo Round is the negotiation of a series of codes covering such NTBs as customs valuation, government procurement, import-licensing procedures, subsidies and countervailing duties, and product standards.

In Deardorff and Stern (1983a), we used our model to analyze the effects of the Tokyo Round negotiations on trade, employment, economic welfare, exchange rates, and domestic prices for the thirty-four countries and twenty-nine sectors covered by the model. To obtain the tariffs for use in the model, we began at the line-item level of the Brussels Tariff Nomenclature and aggregated by ISIC sector in each country, using own-country imports as weights for each of the twenty-two tradable sectors. This was done for both the pre-Tokyo Round tariff rates and the offer rates that were negotiated. The differences between these rates thus represent the negotiated changes in tariffs.

As mentioned above, because of the lack of information, we were unable to represent most existing NTBs in our model in an explicit manner to capture their protective effects. What we did was to calculate the fraction of trade covered by any kind of NTB in particular sectors and countries and to model these sectors as less sensitive to tariff changes than would otherwise be the case. This may not be too great a drawback for present purposes. Except for certain bilateral agricultural concessions and the liberalization of government procurement, whose effects we did model explicitly together with the tariff reductions,[8] the NTB codes that were negotiated do not lend themselves readily to quantification. Moreover, most of the existing NTBs affecting trade in agricultural products, textiles and clothing, footwear, iron and steel products, consumer electronic products, automobiles, and shipbuilding were exempted from the negotiations.

10.4 Results

The weighted average nominal tariffs by sector for pre- and post-Tokyo Round are shown in columns (1) and (4) of tables 10.1–10.3 for the United States, EEC, and Japan.[9] The rank order by sector is shown in parentheses. Thus, the sectors with the highest nominal tariffs in the United States were wearing apparel, textiles, leather products, nonmetallic mineral products, and glass and glass products. In the EEC, the highest nominal tariffs were in wearing apparel, food products, footwear, chemicals, and transport equipment. In Japan, the highest nominal tariffs were in food products, agriculture, footwear, wearing apparel, and nonelectric machinery.

Levels of the effective rate of protection based on formula (5) for pre- and post-Tokyo Round are shown in columns (2) and (5) of tables 10.1–10.3, together with the sector rankings.[10] We used here the first of Corden's alternatives for handling nontraded goods mentioned above. That is, they are included in both summations in (5) but with zero tariffs. These simplified effective rates are noticeably higher than the nominal rates, especially in the United States and the EEC, although in Japan several of the effective rates were negative. Further, the nontraded sectors all have negative effective rates.

In columns (3) and (6) of tables 10.1–10.3, we report the "change in per unit value added" (CPVA) for pre- and post-Tokyo Round based on our model, using equation (2) above. These calculations were obtained by reducing the tariffs from their given levels to zero and then using the negative of the resulting price changes in equation (2) to calculate the CPVAs by sector. The calculations in column (6) reflect as well the agricultural concessions and liberalization of government procurement. Since the results in columns (3) and (6) are based on a full model solution, they take into account all of the interactions both within and among all thirty-four countries in the model.

The most noticeable feature of these results, which was also noted in Deardorff and Stern (1983b), is that our model calculations of CPVA are an order of magnitude smaller than the nominal tariffs and the simple effective tariffs based on the Corden formula. Also, there are many more sectors with negative protection in our calculations. We discussed earlier several reasons why we expect smaller and more negative values for our measure of protection than have traditionally been calculated. The most important of these reasons, based on our model, appears to be the imperfect substitutability between domestic and foreign goods.[11]

Given the importance of imperfect substitutability, some further explanation of how it works may be useful. When tariffs are increased, they raise the prices of imports. If domestic goods were perfect substitutes for imports, their prices also would rise by the same amount. But if substitution is imperfect, an equal rise in domestic prices would leave demand unchanged while increasing supply. Equilibrium requires instead that domestic prices rise by less than import prices to stimulate both supply and demand by equal amounts. This smaller rise in domestic prices means that protection, as calculated from equation (2), is reduced from what it would be if substitution were perfect.

Note further that domestic prices are only part of what appears in the numerator of (2). Import prices also enter, but negatively, to the extent that imports are used as inputs. Thus, imperfect substitution reduces substantially the protective effect of tariffs on output prices, but does not reduce by nearly as much the antiprotective effect of tariffs on input prices. Together these two mechanisms can account for much of the reduction in measures of protection going from columns (2) to (3) and (5) to (6) in the tables.

A related phenomenon, not mentioned so far, is the effect of tariffs on exports. If domestic and foreign goods were perfect substitutes, then a given industry could not both export and import. But with imperfect substitution such two-way trade can and does take place. Now, producers for export enjoy no increase at all in their output price when tariffs are

Table 10.1   Protection Measures in the United States (Percent levels and changes in protection. Numbers in parentheses are column ranks.)

		Pre-Tokyo Round			Post-Tokyo Round			Change due to Tokyo Round		
	ISIC	Nominal Tariffs (1)	Effective Rate of Protection (Corden) (2)	CPVA (Change Per Unit Value Added) (3)	Nominal Tariffs (4)	Effective Rate of Protection (Corden) (5)	CPVA (Change Per Unit Value Added) (6)	Nominal Tariffs (7)	Effective Rate of Protection (Corden) (8)	CPVA (Change Per Unit Value Added) (9)
Traded goods:										
Agr., for., & fish.	(1)	2.20(18)	2.09(18)	−1.96(29)	1.80(17)	1.91(18)	−0.21(27)	−0.40(4)	−0.18(12)	1.74(1)
Food., bev., & tob.	(310)	6.30(10)	13.41(5)	−0.01(20)	4.70(7)	10.16(4)	−0.05(24)	−1.60(12)	−3.26(22)	−0.04(23)
Textiles	(321)	14.40(2)	28.33(2)	0.12(5)	9.20(2)	18.02(2)	0.16(3)	−5.20(22)	−10.31(29)	0.04(7)
Wearing apparel	(322)	27.80(1)	50.63(1)	0.14(4)	22.70(1)	43.30(1)	0.12(5)	−5.10(21)	−7.33(28)	−0.02(21)
Leather products	(323)	5.60(11)	5.62(14)	0.11(6)	4.20(9)	4.95(12)	0.30(1)	−1.40(10)	−0.67(16)	0.19(2)
Footwear	(324)	8.80(5)	13.14(6)	0.06(9)	8.80(3)	15.37(3)	0.07(7)	0.0(1)	2.23(1)	0.01(13)
Wood products	(331)	3.60(16)	4.58(15)	0.10(7)	1.70(18)	1.72(19)	0.05(9)	−1.90(14)	−2.86(20)	−0.05(26)
Furniture & fixt.	(332)	8.10(6)	12.33(8)	0.02(14)	4.10(11)	5.52(11)	−0.01(22)	−4.00(19)	−6.81(26)	−0.04(22)
Paper & paper prod.	(341)	0.50(22)	−1.14(28)	−0.02(23)	0.20(22)	−0.86(28)	0.00(14)	−0.30(3)	0.27(4)	0.03(9)
Printing & publ.	(342)	1.10(21)	1.32(20)	−0.00(18)	0.70(21)	0.90(20)	0.00(15)	−0.40(5)	−0.43(14)	0.00(15)
Chemicals	(35A)	3.80(14)	5.76(13)	−0.24(26)	2.40(16)	3.66(15)	−0.12(26)	−1.40(11)	−2.11(18)	0.12(4)

Pet. & rel. prod.	(35B)	1.40(19)	4.27(16)	-0.02(22)	1.40(19)	4.69(13)	-0.00(20)	0.0(2)	0.42(3)	0.02(11)
Rubber products	(355)	3.60(15)	2.37(17)	0.15(3)	2.50(14)	1.95(16)	0.15(4)	-1.10(9)	-0.42(13)	0.00(16)
Nonmet. min. prod.	(36A)	9.10(4)	15.93(4)	0.31(2)	5.30(5)	9.23(6)	0.18(2)	-3.80(18)	-6.70(25)	-0.13(28)
Glass & glass prod.	(362)	10.70(3)	16.87(3)	0.08(8)	6.20(4)	9.77(5)	0.03(11)	-4.50(20)	-7.10(27)	-0.04(24)
Iron & steel	(371)	4.70(13)	7.81(11)	0.04(12)	3.60(12)	6.18(9)	0.05(10)	-1.10(8)	-1.63(17)	0.01(14)
Nonferrous metals	(372)	1.20(20)	1.03(21)	0.03(13)	0.70(20)	0.50(21)	0.05(8)	-0.50(6)	-0.53(15)	0.02(10)
Metal products	(381)	7.50(8)	12.70(7)	-0.02(21)	4.80(6)	7.86(7)	-0.01(21)	-2.70(16)	-4.84(23)	0.01(12)
Nonelec. machinery	(382)	5.00(12)	6.25(12)	-0.16(25)	3.30(13)	4.06(14)	-0.08(25)	-1.70(13)	-2.20(19)	0.08(6)
Elec. machinery	(383)	6.60(9)	9.38(10)	-0.26(27)	4.40(8)	6.34(8)	-0.22(28)	-2.20(15)	-3.04(21)	0.03(8)
Transport equip.	(384)	3.30(17)	1.80(19)	-0.43(28)	2.50(15)	1.94(17)	-0.28(29)	-0.80(7)	0.14(8)	0.15(3)
Misc. manufact.	(38A)	7.80(7)	11.11(9)	0.34(1)	4.20(10)	5.79(10)	0.11(6)	-3.60(17)	-5.32(24)	-0.23(29)
Nontraded goods:										
Mining & Quarrying	(2)		-0.70(26)	-0.09(24)		-0.47(26)	0.02(12)		0.23(5)	0.10(5)
Elec., gas, & water	(4)		-0.20(23)	0.05(10)		-0.16(23)	0.01(13)		0.04(11)	-0.05(25)
Construction	(5)		-4.69(29)	-0.01(19)		-2.88(29)	-0.02(23)		1.81(2)	-0.01(17)
Wh. & ret. trade	(6)		-0.77(27)	0.02(15)		-0.55(27)	0.00(16)		0.21(6)	-0.02(20)
Transp., stor., & comm.	(7)		-0.52(25)	0.01(16)		-0.35(25)	-0.00(18)		0.17(7)	-0.02(19)
Fin., ins., & real est.	(8)		-0.14(22)	0.05(11)		-0.09(22)	-0.00(19)		0.05(10)	-0.05(27)
Com., soc., pers. serv.	(9)		-0.41(24)	0.01(17)		-0.28(24)	-0.00(17)		0.13(9)	-0.01(18)

Table 10.2   Protection Measures in the European Community (Percent levels and changes in protection. Numbers in parentheses are column ranks.)

		Pre-Tokyo Round			Post-Tokyo Round			Change due to Tokyo Round		
	ISIC	Nominal Tariffs (1)	Effective Rate of Protection (Corden) (2)	CPVA (Change Per Unit Value Added) (3)	Nominal Tariffs (4)	Effective Rate of Protection (Corden) (5)	CPVA (Change Per Unit Value Added) (6)	Nominal Tariffs (7)	Effective Rate of Protection (Corden) (8)	CPVA (Change Per Unit Value Added) (9)
Traded goods:										
Agr., for., & fish.	(1)	7.10(13)	6.18(17)	-0.44(18)	4.86(12)	4.10(17)	-0.53(22)	-2.24(14)	-2.08(14)	-0.09(23)
Food, bev., & tob.	(310)	12.44(2)	20.96(2)	-0.20(14)	10.06(3)	17.83(3)	-0.07(13)	-2.38(16)	-3.13(21)	0.13(8)
Textiles	(321)	9.78(8)	11.42(11)	-1.52(28)	7.17(8)	8.79(10)	-1.14(29)	-2.62(18)	-2.63(17)	0.38(3)
Wearing apparel	(322)	16.77(1)	23.49(1)	-0.50(19)	13.37(1)	19.26(2)	-0.41(19)	-3.40(21)	-4.23(26)	0.09(11)
Leather products	(323)	3.65(18)	1.35(21)	-0.70(22)	2.01(21)	-2.19(28)	-1.07(28)	-1.63(8)	-3.54(23)	-0.37(28)
Footwear	(324)	11.67(3)	17.90(4)	-0.74(23)	11.63(2)	20.08(1)	-0.64(24)	-0.04(2)	2.17(1)	0.10(10)
Wood products	(331)	3.31(19)	2.00(20)	0.38(3)	2.51(18)	1.68(20)	0.11(6)	-0.79(4)	-0.32(10)	-0.27(27)
Furniture & fixt.	(332)	8.50(9)	18.20(3)	-0.83(24)	5.60(9)	11.30(8)	-0.52(21)	-2.90(19)	-6.90(29)	0.31(5)
Paper & paper prod.	(341)	7.32(12)	11.13(12)	0.54(1)	5.37(11)	8.29(12)	0.11(7)	-1.95(10)	-2.85(20)	-0.43(29)
Printing & publ.	(342)	3.23(20)	-0.64(22)	0.07(11)	2.06(20)	-1.03(26)	0.09(10)	-1.17(5)	-0.39(11)	0.02(15)
Chemicals	(35A)	11.49(4)	17.00(5)	-0.88(25)	7.95(5)	11.71(6)	-0.67(25)	-3.55(22)	-5.29(27)	0.20(7)

Industry		C1	C2	C3	C4	C5	C6	C7	C8	C9
Pet. & rel. prod.	(35B)	1.16(22)	3.11(19)	0.37(4)	1.16(22)	3.39(18)	0.11(8)	0.0 (1)	0.28(4)	-0.26(26)
Rubber products	(355)	5.28(16)	3.76(18)	-0.63(20)	3.54(17)	2.29(19)	-0.52(20)	-1.74(9)	-1.47(12)	0.10(9)
Nonmet. min. prod.	(36A)	5.19(17)	8.95(15)	0.03(12)	3.66(16)	6.52(15)	0.02(11)	-1.53(6)	-2.43(16)	-0.01(16)
Glass & glass prod.	(362)	9.89(7)	15.30(7)	-0.29(17)	7.70(7)	12.16(5)	-0.20(17)	-2.19(13)	-3.14(22)	0.09(12)
Iron & steel	(371)	6.21(15)	15.43(6)	-0.25(15)	4.67(14)	11.59(7)	-0.18(15)	-1.54(7)	-3.84(25)	0.08(13)
Nonferrous metals	(372)	2.56(21)	9.92(14)	0.07(10)	2.13(19)	8.29(11)	-0.04(12)	-0.43(3)	-1.63(13)	-0.11(24)
Metal products	(381)	7.88(10)	10.75(13)	-0.26(16)	5.46(10)	7.07(13)	-0.19(16)	-2.42(17)	-3.68(24)	0.07(14)
Nonelec. machinery	(382)	6.45(14)	7.35(16)	-0.88(26)	4.37(15)	4.71(16)	-0.57(23)	-2.07(12)	-2.64(18)	0.31(4)
Elec. machinery	(383)	9.92(6)	13.51(9)	-0.66(21)	7.89(6)	10.79(9)	-0.40(18)	-2.03(11)	-2.72(19)	0.26(6)
Transport equip.	(384)	10.23(5)	14.65(8)	-1.38(27)	7.95(4)	12.31(4)	-0.99(26)	-2.27(15)	-2.34(15)	0.39(2)
Misc. manufact.	(38A)	7.70(11)	12.13(10)	-1.88(29)	4.67(13)	6.55(14)	-1.02(27)	-3.03(20)	-5.58(28)	0.86(1)
Nontraded goods:										
Mining & quarrying	(2)		-0.72(24)	-0.10(13)		-0.51(22)	-0.14(14)		0.22(5)	-0.04(18)
Elec., gas, & water	(4)		-0.80(25)	0.20(7)		-0.61(23)	0.14(4)		0.19(9)	-0.05(21)
Construction	(5)		-4.10(29)	0.21(6)		-2.96(29)	0.17(3)		1.14(2)	-0.04(20)
Wh. & ret. trade	(6)		-1.76(28)	0.26(5)		-1.37(27)	0.20(2)		0.39(3)	-0.06(22)
Transp., stor., & comm.	(7)		-0.94(27)	0.12(9)		-0.74(25)	0.09(9)		0.20(7)	-0.03(17)
Fin., ins., & real est.	(8)		-0.66(23)	0.45(2)		-0.46(21)	0.34(1)		0.19(8)	-0.11(25)
Comm., soc., pers. serv.	(9)		-0.83(26)	0.18(8)		-0.61(24)	0.13(5)		0.21(6)	-0.04(19)

Table 10.3   Protection Measures in Japan (Percent levels and changes in protection. Numbers in parentheses are column ranks.)

	ISIC	Pre-Tokyo Round			Post-Tokyo Round			Change due to Tokyo Round		
		Nominal Tariffs (1)	Effective Rate of Protection (Corden) (2)	CPVA (Change Per Unit Value Added) (3)	Nominal Tariffs (4)	Effective Rate of Protection (Corden) (5)	CPVA (Change Per Unit Value Added) (6)	Nominal Tariffs (7)	Effective Rate of Protection (Corden) (8)	CPVA (Change Per Unit Value Added) (9)
Traded goods:										
Agr., for., & fish.	(1)	18.40(2)	21.17(4)	0.86(1)	18.40(2)	21.40(4)	0.77(1)	0.0 (1)	0.23(14)	−0.08(26)
Food, bev., & tob.	(310)	25.40(1)	49.80(2)	−0.18(20)	25.40(1)	50.31(1)	−0.14(20)	0.0 (2)	0.51(7)	0.03(10)
Textiles	(321)	3.30(14)	−3.55(24)	−0.37(24)	3.30(12)	−2.41(24)	−0.39(24)	0.0 (3)	1.14(2)	−0.02(18)
Wearing apparel	(322)	13.80(4)	41.62(3)	−0.13(18)	13.80(4)	42.20(3)	−0.09(16)	0.0 (4)	0.58(4)	0.04(9)
Leather products	(323)	3.00(15)	−15.56(28)	−0.05(16)	3.00(13)	−14.75(28)	−0.12(19)	0.0 (5)	0.81(3)	−0.07(24)
Footwear	(324)	16.40(3)	51.99(1)	0.06(4)	15.70(3)	50.02(2)	−0.02(13)	−0.70(14)	−1.98(21)	−0.08(27)
Wood products	(331)	0.30(21)	−30.94(29)	−0.32(22)	0.30(21)	−30.59(29)	−0.27(22)	0.0 (6)	0.35(11)	0.05(8)
Furniture & fixt.	(332)	7.80(6)	16.45(5)	0.03(8)	5.10(7)	10.26(5)	0.00(10)	−2.70(19)	−6.18(27)	−0.02(20)
Paper & paper prod.	(341)	2.10(17)	1.22(15)	−0.04(14)	2.10(16)	1.75(14)	−0.05(14)	0.0 (7)	0.53(6)	−0.00(14)
Printing & publ.	(342)	0.20(22)	−1.58(23)	−0.01(12)	0.10(22)	−1.51(23)	−0.01(12)	−0.10(9)	0.07(17)	0.01(11)
Chemicals	(35A)	6.20(10)	8.69(11)	−0.04(13)	4.80(8)	6.39(11)	−0.11(17)	−1.40(15)	−2.31(22)	−0.07(25)

Pet. & rel. prod.	(35B)	2.80(16)	5.21(13)	0.51(2)	2.20(15)	4.14(13)	0.17(2)	−0.60(13)	−1.08(20)	−0.34(29)
Rubber products	(355)	1.50(18)	−5.17(27)	−0.78(26)	1.10(18)	−4.99(27)	−0.60(25)	−0.40(11)	0.18(16)	0.18(3)
Nonmet. min. prod.	(36A)	0.60(20)	−0.92(19)	−0.16(19)	0.50(20)	−0.54(19)	−0.11(18)	−0.10(10)	0.38(10)	0.05(7)
Glass & glass prod.	(362)	7.50(7)	12.02(9)	−0.05(15)	5.10(6)	8.10(7)	−0.07(15)	−2.40(18)	−3.92(25)	−0.02(19)
Iron & steel	(371)	3.30(13)	4.77(14)	−0.48(25)	2.80(14)	4.34(12)	−0.65(27)	−0.50(12)	−0.43(19)	−0.17(28)
Nonferrous metals	(372)	1.10(19)	1.18(16)	−0.08(17)	1.10(19)	1.73(15)	0.09(4)	0.0 (8)	0.55(5)	0.17(4)
Metal products	(381)	6.90(9)	12.52(7)	−0.33(23)	5.20(5)	9.23(6)	−0.23(21)	−1.70(17)	−3.29(24)	0.10(6)
Nonelec. machinery	(382)	9.10(5)	15.57(6)	−0.23(21)	4.40(10)	6.74(9)	−0.27(23)	−4.70(22)	−8.83(29)	−0.04(22)
Elec. machinery	(383)	7.40(8)	12.49(8)	−1.10(28)	4.30(11)	6.73(10)	−0.86(28)	−3.10(20)	−5.76(26)	0.24(2)
Transport equip.	(384)	6.00(12)	8.42(12)	−1.73(29)	1.50(17)	0.03(16)	−1.58(29)	−4.50(21)	−8.39(28)	0.15(5)
Misc. manufact.	(38A)	6.00(11)	10.00(10)	−0.87(27)	4.60(9)	7.30(8)	−0.62(26)	−1.40(16)	−2.70(23)	0.25(1)
Nontraded goods:										
Mining & quarrying	(2)	−1.49(22)		0.06(5)		−0.99(22)	0.01(9)		0.50(9)	−0.05(23)
Elec., gas, & water	(4)	−1.11(21)		−0.00(11)		−0.79(21)	−0.00(11)		0.33(12)	−0.00(15)
Construction	(5)	−5.07(26)		0.06(6)		−3.64(25)	0.06(5)		1.43(1)	0.00(12)
Wh. & ret. trade	(6)	−0.59(18)		0.04(7)		−0.39(18)	0.03(6)		0.21(15)	−0.00(17)
Transp., stor., & comm.	(7)	−1.04(20)		0.02(10)		−0.54(20)	0.02(7)		0.50(8)	0.00(13)
Fin., ins., & real est.	(8)	−0.21(17)		0.16(3)		−0.16(17)	0.14(3)		0.05(18)	−0.03(21)
Com., soc., pers. serv.	(9)	−3.96(25)		0.02(9)		−3.69(26)	0.02(8)		0.27(13)	−0.00(16)

raised and, if anything, suffer a fall in price if world markets weaken. Thus, producers for export experience only antiprotective effects of tariffs. When they are averaged in with producers for domestic markets, as they are in the calculations we report, they account still further for the smallness of our measures of CPVA.

Regarding nontraded goods, we find that in most cases they are protected positively rather than negatively in a general equilibrium model.

Finally, in columns (7) to (9) of tables 10.1–10.3, we report the *changes* due to the Tokyo Round in nominal tariffs, simple effective tariffs based on equation (5), and our model calculations of CPVA based on equation (2). The calculations in column (9) are of most immediate interest since they provide an indication of which sectors will tend to expand or contract relatively in response to the tariff reductions and NTB concessions that were negotiated among the major industrialized countries.

Thus, in the United States, the largest percentage increases in value added due to the Tokyo Round were recorded in agriculture, leather products, transport equipment, chemicals, and mining and quarrying; while the largest percentage declines were in miscellaneous manufactures, nonmetallic minerals, finance, insurance, and real estate, wood products, and electricity, gas, and water. For the EEC, the largest percentage increases in value added due to the Tokyo Round were in miscellaneous manufactures, transport equipment, textiles, nonelectric machinery, and furniture and fixtures; and the largest declines were in paper and paper products, leather products, wood products, petroleum and related products, and finance, insurance, and real estate. For Japan, the largest increases were in miscellaneous manufactures, electrical machinery, rubber products, nonferrous metals, and transport equipment; and the largest declines were in petroleum and related products, iron and steel, footwear, agriculture, and chemicals.

To make comparisons involving the columns in these tables, we calculated both simple and rank correlations for each pair of columns in each table. Based on these correlations (which are not reported here but are available on request), it does not seem to matter very much whether one uses nominal tariffs or effective tariffs to measure protection. The two are highly correlated for each group of columns. On the other hand, our measure of CPVA is generally not significantly correlated with either of the other two measures of protection. Thus, one needs something like the approach based on our model to evaluate correctly the positions of individual sectors due to protection or changes therein. Otherwise, the effects of general equilibrium and imperfect substitution are not taken into account. Corden's simple formula does not even provide a poor approximation for this purpose.

The similarity of pre- and post-Tokyo Round structures of protection also is apparent from the correlations, regardless of how protection is measured. This can be seen by comparing columns (1) and (4), (2) and (5), and (3) and (6). Likewise, the change in protection due to the Tokyo Round is for the most part strongly negatively correlated with the levels of protection, again regardless of how both are measured. This is evident by comparing columns (1) and (4) with (7), (2) and (5) with (8), and (3) and (6) with (9). Thus, the effects of the Tokyo Round were in the direction of undoing the protection that previously existed, but were not strong enough to cause the overall pattern of protection to change significantly.

Besides calculating the effects of the Tokyo Round as just noted, we made several additional calculations of interest. These involved alternative measures of CPVA, correlation analysis designed to explain the nature of tariff reductions in the Tokyo Round, evaluation of indicators of resource pull, some further comparisons of the structures of protection in pre- and post-Tokyo Round, and the effects of the Tokyo Round on the developing countries. Let us consider each of these in turn.

10.4.1   Alternative Measures of CPVA

Our basic measure of the CPVA due to the Tokyo Round is calculated from our model assuming simultaneous changes in both tariffs and quantifiable NTBs in all (developed) countries at once. Also, our basic solution assumes a technology of fixed coefficients among intermediate inputs. To investigate the importance of these assumptions, we conducted alternative runs of the model in which we calculated CPVA for tariff changes only, for own-country tariff and NTB changes only, and for a version of the model with a Cobb-Douglas technology. The results were as follows.

For most developed countries, it made little difference whether the tariff and NTB changes for all countries were accounted for or only the own-country effects were calculated. This may be a surprise, since one might expect the effects of foreign tariff reductions to be quite different from one's own. The reason that this is not the case is that the patterns of tariff reduction were quite similar in most countries. This means that foreign tariff reductions do tend to offset the effects of domestic ones, but in the same industries, thus merely dampening their effects and not changing their pattern very much.[12] This pattern of correlated tariff reductions may bear out earlier observations of previous negotiations, namely, that trade liberalization has usually been balanced, presumably to avoid major industry dislocation.

Further, it does not seem to matter very much for the structure of protection whether negotiated changes in NTBs are or are not included in calculating the effects of the Tokyo Round. All correlations between the two sets of results are large and quite significant except for Norway and Sweden, where correlations are negative, and to a lesser extent Finland,

Switzerland, and Mexico. These are all countries where NTB concessions were substantial, especially compared to country size.

Finally, the introduction of a Cobb-Douglas technology into the model in place of fixed coefficients made virtually no difference for the results, especially in the major industrialized countries.[13] Both simple and rank correlations were above 0.90 and highly significant for CPVA measures from the two runs, except in a few developing countries.

10.4.2 Explanations of the Pattern of Changes in Tariffs and Protection

We correlated both nominal tariff changes and CPVA with a number of variables that we thought might help to explain *why* tariffs were reduced as they were in the Tokyo Round. The ideas here stem from the recent interest in the political economy of protection. Ideally, policymakers and their constituents understand the economy well enough so that it is the actual *effects* of protection that guide their lobbying and policy choices. These effects are what we try to capture in our CPVA measure. However, if either our measure is inaccurate or, more likely, if policymakers are unable to perceive where true economic interest lies, then they may view nominal tariffs as the more appropriate indicator of protection, and it is this that will be correlated with the variables explaining protection.

One problem here is that the variables we look at are likely to influence both the level of protection and its change. Thus, for example, import penetration seems a likely source of protectionist pressure, and this could show up as small Tokyo Round tariff reductions and hence a large protective effect of the Tokyo Round. On the other hand, this same import penetration would also account for high pre-Tokyo Round tariffs and, if in general tariffs are reduced by some across-the-board proportion, it would also show up as large tariff reductions and a small or negative protective effect. Therefore, we do not know a priori whether a determinant of protection will show up in our results as a large or as a small protective effect due to the Tokyo Round. Our results are important in indicating the pattern of changes that are likely to have occurred, but they do not tell us anything about the validity or otherwise of various political theories of protection.

A final problem with the interpretation of these correlations concerns the mechanism of causation. The CPVA is calculated endogenously in our model and depends on everything in it. It is not at all an exogenous indicator of the results of the Tokyo Round negotiations. Thus it may be, as we have found before, that virtually *any* pattern of tariff reductions will tend to benefit traded sectors at the expense of nontraded ones, and thus give us a positive correlation between CPVA and import or export shares independently of whether the negotiations in fact favored sectors with large trade shares. Again, our results telling who has benefited are valid.

But whether this benefit was the deliberate outcome of the political process or instead a built-in economic effect of the way an economy responds to trade liberalization, we cannot say.

With these remarks as caveats, let us turn now to our findings. The patterns we report are based on correlations that were run between pairs of variables, both for individual countries and industries, across groups of countries and industries, and overall.

Initial Tariffs. As just explained, an across-the-board tariff reduction would reduce large tariffs the most, and a harmonization formula (e.g., the Swiss formula) should have this effect to an even greater extent. When we correlated nominal tariff changes with initial (pre-Tokyo Round) nominal tariff levels, this was confirmed. That is, the correlation between the two was negative and significant, although not terribly large. Thus, tariffs in the Tokyo Round were in fact reduced the most in those sectors where they were initially highest.[14] Interestingly, this relationship does *not* carry over to the estimated effects of the Tokyo Round as measured by the CPVA. Here the only significant correlations are positive, but these are few enough to be not particularly meaningful. Thus, it appears that initial tariffs are a poor guide to the protective effects that actually occurred as the general equilibrium implications of the Tokyo Round worked themselves out.

Initial Protection. When we correlated CPVA due to the Tokyo Round with the CPVA due to initial tariffs, we did find a strong relationship. The simple correlation is negative and significant (-0.61). Previously protected sectors appear therefore to be the greatest losers from the Tokyo Round. It may well be that this result is the automatic bias in favor of traded goods that we normally observe for trade liberalization. Presumably those sectors that were initially the most protected were also rather lightly involved with trade as a result.

Trade Shares. We correlated both tariff changes and CPVA due to the Tokyo Round with various import and export shares. Since trade shares are zero for nontraded sectors, and since tariff changes were zero for the developing countries, the only meaningful correlations here are those for the traded sectors of the developed countries. We looked first at each sector's share of its country's imports and exports. We found nothing significant for import shares, yet small but significant correlations with export shares. The latter were negative for tariff changes, but positive for CPVA. This indicates that tariffs tended to be reduced in most sectors with large export shares, but that these sectors were also the most likely to benefit from reductions overall. This suggests that it is not really the country's own tariff reductions that are providing the benefit here, but rather those of its trading partners. We have already seen how the tariff changes tend to be correlated across countries, so this makes some sense. The failure of the import shares to show a significant correlation is somewhat surprising, given our expectation of benefits from relying on trade. Indeed, when nontraded sectors are included, the correlation does become positive and significant, making it clear that traded sectors benefit more than nontraded ones, but within the traded sector group we find no such relationship.

Looking at countries' shares of *world* exports and imports by sector, similar results were found. No significant correlations appeared for import shares, but significant correlations were noted for export shares of world markets. Again though, they are small and of opposite sign for tariff changes and CPVA. These indicate that tariff reductions were largest where they were also presumably the least meaningful, that is, in those sectors and countries with the most dominant export positions in world markets. Furthermore, since the benefits of general trade liberalization go substantially to exporters, it is the dominant export sectors and countries that benefit the most.

Net Exports. We also looked for correlations with net export positions and found results that parallel those for exports above.

Final Demand Shares. In light of the observation that tariffs are highest on final goods and lowest on primary and semiprocessed goods, we might then expect some relationship between our results and the shares of final demand in total demand by industry. However, we did not find anything significant here either, except for a slight tendency for tariffs to be reduced most in sectors with large final demand shares. Thus, we find no evidence that protection has become any more or less cascaded against imports of final goods as the result of the Tokyo Round.

Labor Shares. To see whether the Tokyo Round favored labor-intensive industries, we correlated tariff changes and CPVA with shares of labor in both value added and gross output. Nothing meaningful was found.

Employment. As another check on the connection between protection and labor, we correlated our results with employment, both levels and shares. While nothing much significant was found, the results had one odd feature. Simple correlations were not significant, but in several instances rank correlations, though small, were. These rank correlations show some evidence, admittedly weak, that tariffs were reduced most in those sectors where both employment levels and shares were large, while at the same time the Tokyo Round had its most beneficial effects, measured by CPVA, in these same sectors.

NTBs. We correlated CPVA with our data on quantitative restrictions on trade and found nothing significant.

10.4.3 Indicators of Resource Pull Effects of Protection

Corden's formula in equation (5) for the effective rate of protection was intended to provide a better indicator of the effect of protection on resource allocation than was provided by nominal tariffs. Our measure of CPVA is intended to be even better. To check that the various measures do in fact perform this way, we correlated them with estimates calculated from the model of changes in employment, changes in outputs, and changes in the returns to capital by sector and country. The results of these correlations demonstrate clearly the superiority of our measure of CPVA over both nominal and effective tariffs in determining resource flows.[15]

Looking first at employment changes, in percentage terms, we found a strong positive relationship between these and our CPVA measure. The rank correlation across developed country traded sectors was 0.97 and was almost as high when developing countries and nontraded goods were included. Simple correlations were smaller, but still significant at the 99 percent level. Corden's effective tariff changes showed no significant correlation with employment changes in developed country traded sectors. Nominal tariff changes did even worse, since they showed a small but significant *negative* correlation with employment changes, even for developed country traded goods. The reason, again, is the similarity of tariff reductions among the developed countries, which leads employment to expand in precisely those sectors where tariffs are being reduced the most. Here, presumably, it is the fact that our measure of protection captures worldwide tariff changes that makes it work so well.

Output changes, again in percentage terms by sector and country, were similarly well explained by our CPVA measure and not at all by nominal and effective tariff changes. The only difference in comparison with the employment change results just noted is that nominal tariffs no longer showed any significant correlation of any sign.

Finally, we calculated the change in the return to capital by sector and country due to the Tokyo Round as an indicator of the incentives for long-run resource movement. This was calculated as the change in value added net of wages, as a percent of the (fixed) value of the capital stock. From this definition it may not be surprising that the CPVA will be related to it, since their definitions overlap. However, the relationship is not at all trivial, since changes in employment change the wage bill in a direction that could conceivably cancel out improvements in the return to capital. Nonetheless, our correlations showed the strongest connection yet between CPVA and changes in the return to capital, both simple and rank correlations being close to unity wherever we measured them. Once again, both nominal and effective tariffs failed to show any significant correlations with this variable worth noting.

We conclude therefore that our measure provides a vastly superior indicator of resource flows than the alternatives. Given that our basis for comparison is the pattern of resource flows calculated by our own model, the success of our measure may not be surprising. But the failure of even the Corden measure to correspond at all with these calculated flows is surprising indeed, since the Corden formula is intended to yield an approximation to the same economic magnitude of the change in per unit value added. Nonetheless, the Corden measure seems to provide no guidance at all, and nominal tariffs are actually misleading as to the pattern of resource flows as we have calculated them.

10.4.4 Further Comparison of the Pre- and Post-Tokyo Round Structure of Protection

We have already noted that changes in protection were negatively correlated with their levels prior to the Tokyo Round. This was also true for the structure of protection remaining after completion of the Tokyo Round. Both of these results are consistent with the view that the Tokyo Round tended to reduce tariffs across the board, without much effect on the cross-industry and cross-country pattern of protection. This was verified even more strongly when we correlated the structures of protection for the pre- and post-Tokyo Round with each other. Here both simple and rank correlations were in the 90 percent range throughout and highly significant.

It was also of interest to examine whether the efforts to "harmonize" the tariff reductions using the Swiss formula had the desired effect of making structures of protection more uniform. To check this we calculated coefficients of variation of our CPVA measures of pre- and post-Tokyo Round protection across industries, across countries, and overall. These turned out to have remained roughly the same before and after the Tokyo Round, suggesting that if levels of protection are indeed more uniform, it is only because they are closer to zero. This is in marked contrast, incidentally, to the pattern of nominal tariffs. The coefficients of variation for these fell consistently due to the Tokyo Round for all countries, almost all industries, and overall. Thus, while the general adherence to the Swiss formula resulted in some harmonization of nominal tariffs, this may not be particularly meaningful in terms of harmonizing levels of protection.[16]

10.4.5 The Terms of Trade of the Major Developing Countries

Our final concern was to investigate whether the structure of changes in tariffs and NTBs in the Tokyo Round was biased in favor of, or against, the major developing countries. As an indicator of this, we correlated the changes in world prices that our model ascribes to the Tokyo Round with various measures of trade performance of the developing countries. These measures were import shares, export shares, and trade balances. None of the results was significant, with some minor exceptions. This suggests that the effects of the Tokyo Round were *not* significantly biased either for or against the major developing countries as far as changes in world prices are concerned.[17]

10.5 Conclusion

In this paper we have analyzed the protective effects of the changes in tariffs and NTBs that were negotiated in the Tokyo Round, using the Michigan Model of World Production and Trade. Since prices are endogenous in the model, we are able to calculate the changes in value added by sector for all the major industrialized and developing countries that participated in the Tokyo Round negotiations. We take into account the direct effects of changes in both domestic and foreign tariffs and NTBs, as well as the direct effects of exchange rate changes that may result from trade liberalization.

Clearly a general equilibrium model like ours is needed to analyze how individual sectors may be affected by trade liberalization. It will not be very helpful in this regard to look at changes in nominal tariffs or even effective rates of protection calculated under simplified conditions. As our results show, calculations from the model of changes in value added by sector are very good indicators of the sectoral resource shifts that tend to take place within a general equilibrium model.

Among the many findings noted in the paper, the following are especially noteworthy:

1. As just mentioned, the change in per unit value added (CPVA) as calculated using our model, provided substantially different information about the structure of protection than is available from either nominal or effective tariffs. This information is also superior in that it is closely related to the flows of resources that changes in protection bring about, while other measures are not very useful in this respect.

2. The Tokyo Round reduced protection most in those sectors that were previously most protected. Nonetheless, the pattern of protection remains substantially unaltered from what it was before.

3. The greatest benefits of the Tokyo Round will tend to be felt in those sectors with the greatest export interests. This is true even though these are also the sectors in which nominal tariffs tended to be reduced the most, and this reflects the fact that the pattern of tariff reductions was quite similar across most countries.

4. We found no evidence that levels of protection have become more uniform as a result of the Tokyo Round. Nor did we find, within the constraints of our model and the level of aggregation of our data, any significant evidence that protection is becoming any more or less cascaded against imports of final goods, or that the Tokyo Round has been biased against the exports of the major developing countries.

Appendix *Equations of the Model*

Country System Equations

Supply functions for export (X) and home (H) markets:

(A1) $S_{ij}^I = S_{ij}^I(p_{ij}^I, p_{i1}^H, \ldots, p_{in'}^H, p_{i1}^M, \ldots, p_{in'}^M, \bar{w}_i, \bar{K}_{ij}^I); I = X, H;$

$i = 1, \ldots, m; j = 1, \ldots, n$ or n'.

Demand functions for imported (M) and home-produced (H) goods;

(A2) $D_{ij}^I = D_{ij}^I(p_{ij}^J, [p_{ij}^I], E_i, S_{i1}^H, \ldots, S_{in'}^H, S_{i1}^X, \ldots, S_{in}^X, \bar{G}_{ij}); I,$

$J = M, H; i = 1, \ldots, m; j = 1, \ldots, n$ or n'; $[]$ if $j \leq n$.

Export and import prices:

(A3) $p_{ij}^I = [t_{ij}^{Meq}]R_i p_j^W; I = X, M; i = 1, \ldots, m; j = 1, \ldots, n;$ $[]$

if $I = M$.

Consumer expenditure and tariff revenue:

(A4) $E_i = \bar{E}_i^0 + \sum\limits_{j=1}^{n} (t_{ij}^{Meq} - 1)R_i p_j^W D_{ij}^M;$

$i = 1, \ldots, m.$

Market equilibrium for home goods:

(A5) $S_{ij}^H = D_{ij}^H;$

$i = 1, \ldots, m; j = 1, \ldots, n'.$

Tariff equivalents (a: quotas; or b: import licensing):

(A6a) $t_{ij}^{Meq} = t_{ij}^{Meq}(\bar{t}_{ij}^M, D_{ij}^M, \bar{Q}_{ij}^M);$

$i = 1, \ldots, m; j = 1, \ldots, n.$

(A6b) $D_{ij}^M = L_{ij}\left(\sum\limits_{k=1}^{n} p_k^W S_{ik}^X + \bar{B}_i^K \right);$

$i = 1, \ldots, m; j = 1, \ldots, n.$

Employment by industry:

(A7) $D_{ij}^L = D_{ij}^L([S_{ij}^X], S_{ij}^H, [\bar{K}_{ij}^X], \bar{K}_{ij}^H);$

$i = 1, \ldots, m; j = 1, \ldots, n$ or n'; $[]$ if $j \leq n$.

Net exports:

(A8) $N_{ij}^X = S_{ij}^X - D_{ij}^M;$

$i = 1, \ldots, m; j = 1, \ldots, n.$

World System Equations

Market equilibrium for traded goods:

(A9) $\sum_{i=1}^{m} N_{ij}^{X} + N_{j}^{row}(p_{1}^{W}, \ldots, p_{n}^{W}, R_{1}, \ldots, R_{m}) = 0;$

$j = 1, \ldots, n.$

Trade balances:

(A10) $B_{i}^{T} = \sum_{j=1}^{n} p_{j}^{W} N_{ij}^{X};$

$i = 1, \ldots, m.$

Exchange rates (a: fixed; or b: flexible):

(A11a) $R_{i} = \prod_{j \neq i} (R_{j})^{\theta_{ij}^{R}} \bar{R}_{ij}^{O} \ i = 1, \ldots, m.$

(A11b) $B_{i}^{T} + \bar{B}_{i}^{K} = 0, \ (R_{m} = \bar{R}_{m}^{O});$

$i = 1, \ldots, m - 1.$

Notation (m = number of countries; n = number of tradable goods; n' = number of goods total)

Endogenous Variables:

S_{ij}^{I} = supply of good j by country i, sector $I = X, H$.

D_{ij}^{I} = demand for good j in country i from sector $I = M, H$.

$P_{[i]}^{I}$ = price of good j on world market ($I = W$) [or, in country i, price of export ($I = X$), import ($I = M$), or home sector ($I = H$)].

E_{i} = final expenditure in country i.

B_{i}^{T} = balance of trade of country i.

R_{i} = exchange rate of country i (price of world currency).

D_{ij}^{L} = demand for labor by industry j in country i.

t_{ij}^{Meq} = tariff equivalent on good j in country i.

$N_{[i]j}^{I}$ = net exports of good j by the rest of world (I = row) [or by country i ($I = X$)].

Exogenous Variables:

$\bar{K}_{ij}^{I}$ = capital stock of industry j, country i, sector $I = X, H$.

$\bar{w}_{i}$ = money wage in counry i.

$\bar{t}_{ij}^{M}$ = one plus tariff on good j in country i.

$\bar{G}_{ij}$ = government procurement parameter in industry j, country i.

$\bar{E}_i^O$ = exogenous component of expenditure in country i.

$\bar{R}_i^O$ = exogenous exchange rate of country i.

$\bar{B}_i^K$ = capital inflow into country i.

$\bar{Q}_{ij}^M$ = quota parameter for good j, country i.

θ_{ij}^R = pegged exchange rate weight.

Explanation of Functions and Regimes

(A1): Supplies, $S_{ij}^I(\cdot)$, depend on price of output, prices of all home
and imported inputs, an exogenous country-wide wage, and
exogenous capital stocks that are specific to the home and
export sectors of each industry.

(A2): Demands, $D_{ij}^I(\cdot)$, depend on home and import prices, aggregate expenditure, outputs in all sectors (reflecting demands for
inputs), and a shift parameter for government procurement.

(A6a): With quotas covering part of an industry, the tariff equivalent,
$t_{ij}^{Meq}(\cdot)$, depends on the nominal tariff, other determinants of
import demand, and a shift parameter representing the quota.

(A6b): With import licensing, tariff equivalents are determined implicitly to hold import demands at licensed levels. The licensing
function, $L_{ij}(\cdot)$, allocates changes in net foreign exchange earnings, from exports and capital flows, to imports in proportion to
their existing levels.

(A7): Employment equals labor demand, $D_{ij}^L(\cdot)$, and depends on
output and sector-specific capital.

(A9): The rest of world contributes net supplies to world markets,
$N_j^{\text{row}}(\cdot)$, that depend on world prices and exchange rates, the
latter reflecting pegging by the rest of world to currencies in the
model.

(A11a): Some currencies in the model are pegged, either to particular
currencies or to baskets of currencies expressed as geometric
weighted averages.

(A11b): Other currencies are flexible and determined so as to maintain
zero balance of payments. One currency (the mth, usually the
U.S. dollar) is numéraire and its value is exogenous.

Functional Forms

The behavioral functions in (A1), (A2), (A6), (A7), and (A9) are
expressed as log-linear functions of the changes in the variables involved.
They were derived from the first-order conditions for utility and profit
maximation. The assumed utility and production functions were nested
composites of the Cobb-Douglas, CES, and fixed-coefficient functional
forms. Coefficients are calculated from data on production, trade, employment, and input-output transactions, plus published estimates of

demand and substitution elasticities. Details are contained in Deardorff and Stern (1981).

Notes

1. In our early applications of the model, we examined proposed Tokyo Round tariff reductions in Deardorff, Stern, and Baum (1977) and the effects of exchange rate changes in Deardorff, Stern, and Greene (1979).

2. The industries are identified by names and International Standard Industrial Classification (ISIC) number in the accompanying tables. The model originally covered the eighteen major industrialized countries: Australia, Austria, Canada, the members of the European Economic Community, Finland, Japan, New Zealand, Norway, Sweden, Switzerland, and the United States. We have since added sixteen major developing countries: Argentina, Brazil, Chile, Colombia, Greece, Hong Kong, India, Israel, South Korea, Mexico, Portugal, Singapore, Spain, Taiwan, Turkey, and Yugoslavia.

3. This section is based in large measure on Deardorff and Stern (1983b).

4. The role of imperfect substitutability in trade modeling has been addressed also in de Melo and Robinson (1981).

5. Corden (1971) has gone well beyond the simple formula of equation (5) in considering many of the general equilibrium complications that our model is designed to incorporate. We will associate the simple formula with his name only for ease of reference.

6. It is also common to assume fixed production coefficients. Our model is capable of handling either fixed or variable coefficients, and, as will be noted below, we have done the calculations both ways.

7. We have explored the sectoral impact of exchange rate changes in several papers, beginning with Deardorff, Stern, and Greene (1979).

8. The bilateral agricultural concessions were modeled as a relaxation of import quotas in each of the countries. For government procurement, we had information on the amounts of nondefense procurement that governments had tentatively agreed to open to foreign bidding. We assumed these amounts would be spent in proportion to the sector breakdown of each government's expenditures. Estimated government imports by sector were then determined by applying import shares from the private sector. This procedure will tend somewhat to overestimate the effects of procurement liberalization since, due to data limitations, no allowance has been made for existing government imports.

9. To make the reporting of our results somewhat less burdensome, we decided to concentrate only on the United States, EEC, and Japan. For this purpose, the EEC member countries have been combined using weighted averages for the particular measures noted. It should be noted, however, that all of our calculations have been done using the full thirty-four-country model and that detailed results are available for each country.

10. In calculating these effective rates, we did not attempt to make any adjustments in the input-output coefficients to correct for any biases in using actual rather than free trade conditions.

11. In Deardorff and Stern (1983b), we examined the effects of country size, exchange rate flexibility, and foreign tariffs, all of which had relatively much smaller effects than imperfect substitutability.

12. It is noteworthy that this is not the case in Japan, where the correlation between own-country and all-country protection measures is not significant, and New Zealand, where the correlation is negative. In correlations run between pairs of developed country vectors of tariff reductions, these two countries stand out as unusual.

13. It should be noted that our model is not able currently to incorporate differences between the capital-to-intermediate good elasticity, on the one hand, and the labor-to-

intermediate good elasticity, on the other. Our experiment using Cobb-Douglas technology should thus be interpreted with this limitation in mind.

14. This finding was least true for Japan, where neither simple nor rank correlations, though negative, were significant. Since our data on tariff offers reflected the unilateral tariff reductions made by Japan prior to the conclusion of the Tokyo Round negotiations, our comparisons for Japan may not reflect accurately the forces involved there.

15. De Melo and Robinson showed that across-the-board tariff changes are likely to have different effects on resource allocation than tariffs changed individually by sector. Our results, which involve comparisons of across-the-board tariff changes for the individual measures noted, are in agreement with their conclusion but show it to be the case even more strongly.

16. With only twenty-two tradable industries in our model, it is certainly possible that harmonization did occur but is obscured by our level of aggregation. Since we did find evidence of harmonization of nominal tariffs, however, such harmonization of true protection must have been relatively weak.

17. As we point out in Deardorff and Stern (1983a), the Tokyo Round tariff reductions will be beneficial to some developing countries involved currently in the exports of manufactures. But since many existing NTBs affecting a variety of manufactured exports from developing countries were left intact (e.g., textiles and apparel, footwear, etc.), the Tokyo Round may be of limited consequence for these countries.

References

Corden, W. M. 1966. The structure of a tariff system and the effective protective rate. *Journal of Political Economy* 74:221–37.

———. 1971. *The theory of protection*. Oxford: Oxford University Press.

Deardorff, A. V., and R. M. Stern. 1981. A disaggregated model of world production and trade. *Journal of Policy Modeling* 3:127–52.

———. 1983a. Economic effects of the Tokyo Round. *Southern Economic Journal*, 49:605–24.

———. 1983b. Tariff and exchange rate protection under fixed and flexible exchange rates in the major industrialized countries. In *Economic Interdependence and flexible rates*, ed. J. Bhandari and B. Putnam. Cambridge: MIT Press.

Deardorff, A. V., R. M. Stern, and C. F. Baum. 1977. A multi-country simulation of the employment and exchange-rate effects of post-Kennedy Round tariff reductions. In *Trade and employment in Asia and the Pacific*, ed. N. Akrasanee et al. Honolulu: University Press of Hawaii.

Deardorff, A. V., R. M. Stern, and M. N. Greene. 1979. The sensitivity of industrial output and employment to exchange-rate changes in the major industrialized countries. In *Trade and Payments Adjustment Under Flexible Exchange Rates*, ed. J. P. Martin and M. A. M. Smith. London: Macmillan.

De Melo, J., and S. Robinson. 1981. Trade policy and resource allocation in the presence of product differentiation. *Review of Economics and Statistics* 63:169–77.

11   Effects of Protection in Developed Countries on Developing Countries' Exports of Manufactures

Helen Hughes and Anne O. Krueger

The twenty-five years after 1945 witnessed the most rapid rate of sustained economic growth the world economy has ever experienced. An even more rapid expansion of international trade and capital flows accompanied and stimulated that growth. Whereas world real GNP grew at an average rate of about 5.2 percent over the period 1950–70, world exports in constant prices grew even faster—at 7.3 percent annually.

The expansion era was marked by a systematic and considerable reduction in barriers to trade and capital movements: declining barriers stimulated international economic relations and hence national productivity and income growth, and prosperity eased the further dismantling of barriers. The successive GATT rounds of negotiations were the principal instrument of freeing up trade, resulting in average tariffs on industrial products of less than 5 percent in the European Community (EC), the United States, and Japan at the end of the Tokyo Round.

The rate of growth of both real GNP and of trade, however, declined after 1973, and a widespread discussion of protectionist pressures followed. In part because of the continuing multilateral trade negotiations and the fact that they prevented the unilateral raising of tariffs, these pressures were generally for the erection of nontariff barriers (NTBs) and for nonborder protection. For a variety of reasons to be discussed below, some of the most visible pressures and public discussion were aimed at

Helen Hughes is professor of economics at Australian National University, Canberra, Australia. Anne O. Krueger is vice-president for economics and research, the World Bank, Washington, D.C.

The views and interpretations in this chapter are those of the authors and should not be attributed to the World Bank, to its affiliated organizations, or to any individual acting in their behalf. The authors are indebted to Ross Garnaut, Richard Snape, and participants in the Trade Relations conference for helpful comments on the earlier versions of this paper.

the imports of the developing countries (LDCs). To be sure, these pressures did not surface without a prior history: the Multifiber Arrangement had its origins in bilateral "voluntary export restraints" (VERs) negotiated as early as 1955; stainless steel flatware imports were subjected to VERs in the early 1960s; and, by the late 1960s, other commodities were either protected or there were threats of protection.[1] In the United States, the proposed Burke-Hartke bill of 1969 would have imposed strict quantitative limits on the levels and rates of growth of all imports into the United States. Although it was defeated by a narrow margin, it represents the most protectionist piece of legislation that would have had a reasonable possibility of being passed by the United States Congress in recent times.

Despite these earlier efforts to adopt highly restrictive measures, there is a widespread perception that protectionist pressures increased significantly in the 1970s, and that those pressures resulted in a pronounced increase in protection in the form of NTBs against manufactured imports from developing countries.[2]

It is the purpose of this paper to analyze the evidence on the extent of NTBs and their impact on manufactured imports from LDCs into developed-country (DC) markets in the 1970s. Section 11.1 sets forth the analytical problems that arise when direct measurement of NTBs is not feasible and provides a rationale for the indirect inferences used in the paper. Section 11.2 reviews the evidence on the incidence of protection by individual commodity groups. Section 11.3 examines the evidence on market penetration by LDCs. Section 11.4 evaluates the extent to which the data permit any inferences about the incidence of protection among developing countries. Section 11.5 then assesses the extent to which protection against imports of manufactured goods from developing countries may have increased in the 1970s.

11.1 Estimating the Impact of NTBs

In a world market for a given commodity which has substitutes in consumption or production, an effort by country A to impose a quantitative restriction on imports of that commodity from country B may fail to have the intended protectionist effect for a wide variety of reasons: (1) the NTB may be unenforceable; (2) the exports of country B may be diverted to a third market, while the previous suppliers of the third market may then ship their production of the good to the NTB-imposing country;[3] (3) the commodity in question may be a close substitute in production for similar, possibly higher-value items, and producers in the exporting country may shift their production structure toward those items while exporters in other countries shift their production structure toward the item protected from B's exports. While these last two would not be costless, they could substantially reduce the effects of protection.

For all of these reasons, it is not enough to say that DCs imposed NTBs in the 1970s. To be sure, there are a priori grounds for believing that restrictive trade measures impose some costs, but that is not to say that they completely achieve their intended purpose. An ideal methodology for dealing with this problem does not in practice exist. In principle, one might develop a general equilibrium model of world trade (broken down into relevant commodity groups) and then estimate what would have happened to individual trade flows, given price and income elasticities, in the absence of protection. The difficulties inherent in this approach are well known and need not detain us here: it would require a careful modeling not only of growth paths of developing countries but also of the evolution of their supply functions of various exports; substitution in production and among geographic origins is so important and difficult to estimate that any results would be highly suspect.

In this paper, therefore, an alternative, and indirect, approach is adopted. We first review the highly visible NTBs for the commodity groups for which protection against LDC products is thought to have been important. We then examine the rate at which developing countries were able to increase their shares of developed country markets in the 1970s as a whole and in each half of the decade. Thereafter, evidence on shifts in geographic origin of LDC imports is examined. These three pieces of evidence together provide a strong, although not conclusive, impression that the incidence of protection against manufactured exports from the developing countries was probably considerably less than is generally believed.

11.2 Protection against Manufactured Imports in the 1970s

As already noted, our focus centers on protection against manufactured imports from LDCs. We therefore ignore trade in agricultural products where EC actions have clearly increased protection in the 1970s. As a partial offset, it should also be noted that protection against some processed primary commodities—vegetable oils, builders' hardware and plywood, etc.—decreased in the 1970s.

We first examine trends in protection against manufactured commodities in which the LDCs have a special interest—clothing and textiles, footwear and leather products, electronics, etc. Thereafter, protection against developed country products that has spilled over to developing countries is examined. Finally, other policies affecting imports of manufactures from LDCs—export credits and domestic policies—are examined. The section concludes with an assessment of the overall balance.

11.2.1   Protection against Imports from LDCs[4]

Clothing and Textiles

High tariffs and quantitative restrictions on imports from developing countries date back to the 1920s, when the principal industrial countries imposed barriers against imports of labor-intensive goods from Japan into their domestic and colonial markets. These protectionist actions escalated in the 1930s, and protection was reintroduced in textiles as soon as the Japanese exports began to recover in the early 1950s.[5] Large shipments of low-cost (albeit low-quality) imports precipitated arguments of "unfair competition from cheap labor," and in many countries the textile industry, organized from the 1930s to press for protection, was successful in maintaining relatively high tariffs in this "sensitive" area in the face of otherwise declining tariffs. Rapidly growing clothing and textile imports from Hong Kong, Taiwan, and Korea led to further protectionist measures, notably to voluntary export restraints and orderly marketing arrangements in the early and mid-1960s. The administrative bargaining these arrangements entailed, originally principally between the United States and the Far Eastern exporters, became increasingly secretive and complex, and spread to more LDC and DC countries. The ensuing development of protection of clothing and textiles was very complex.

The producers' trade associations in the developing countries which were the main exporters favored the voluntary restraint form of restriction on trade (VERs), as contrasted with higher tariffs or quotas administered by importing countries. VERs enabled them to appropriate the rents arising from restrictions when the quota implementation rested with them. This also suited those producers and retailers in developed countries that had moved to subcontracting or direct investment in production in the LDCs, and had thereby encouraged more movement to production in the LDCs. The producers and importers (wholesalers and large retailers) who remained in the industrial countries countered by pressing for developed country import restrictions in addition to tariffs.

The higher prices of textiles in the developed countries induced protected producers to invest in capital-intensive production processes and so to compete (at the higher price) with the producers in developing countries in many product lines (Shepherd 1981; Isard 1973). In some cases such investment led to real competitiveness through greatly improved quality in the final product, although in other cases the domestic price increases resulting from protection were a contributing factor. One of the highest wage countries in the world, Switzerland, was thus able to increase its high quality textile exports through the 1970s. Design and marketing superiority also enabled some sectors of clothing and textiles to remain competitive in DCs. The Italian clothing industry, for example, was reorganized on the original lines of the Hong Kong industry, moving from integrated operations to subcontracting for high-quality products, just as Hong Kong was moving toward more integrated production for mass production low- and medium-quality goods.

Some countries—developing and developed—were not able to keep up with the changes taking place in the clothing and textile industries. Traditional clothing and textile exporters, such as India, had difficulties filling their import quotas into the DCs, and so did some of the new Latin American exporters (Morawetz 1981). But a number of LDC newcomers to exports did well (Havrylyshyn and Wolf 1981; Havrylyshyn and Alikhani 1982). Large producers in Hong Kong and Taiwan began to invest in production in Singapore, Malaysia, and Thailand, often in association with local entrepreneurs. Initially, this permitted them to avoid quotas, because new supplying countries were outside the restrictive agreements. Later, as exports from new geographic sources had increased, they obtained the right to a new quota as restrictive arrangements spread. Rents to the original producers increased because they remained the most efficient operators, and because they usually received the largest continuous (and thus most profitable) orders (Luey 1969). Investors from other developing countries, notably India, also began to invest abroad in Southeast Asia and farther afield, for example, in Mauritius, because export barriers prevented them from increasing such exports from their home bases. More European and Japanese firms began to produce offshore as developing country producers diversified their sales into new geographic areas.

The protectionist measures of the 1960s became consolidated into the Multifiber Arrangement (MFA) which, by 1978, contained provisions to control import growth by product and country according to bilateral arrangements, supplementing the continuing high tariffs that escaped the successive multilateral trade negotiations (table 11.1).

During the 1970s multifiber import quotas spread from the United

Table 11.1   Textile Tariffs after the Tokyo Round (percent of c.i.f. price)

	Textile Mill Products	Apparel and Miscellaneous Made-Up Products
Canada	15.1	21.2
EC	8.6	12.1
Japan	9.0	13.2
United States	11.4	21.1

SOURCE: Donald B. Keesing and Martin Wolf, *Textile Quotas against Developing Countries*, Thames Essays no. 23, London: Trade Policy Research Centre, 1980.

States to other countries and came to cover more products. In 1977–78 the quota systems were made more comprehensive and more restrictive, particularly in the EC. At the same time, growth rates of consumption and exports declined as DC growth fluctuated and slowed down (Keesing and Wolf 1981). Reductions in protection on clothing and textiles to the African, Caribbean, and Pacific Group of States (ACP) associated with the EC did little to offset the EC's growing restrictiveness because they provided that either the inputs used had to be manufactured in their own countries or imported from the EC. This meant that clothing manufacturers could not use low-cost East Asian textiles, severely limiting the advantages of their privileged market access. On balance protectionism in clothing and textiles increased in the 1970s in all respects: restrictions were applied to more products and more countries, and they were applied more stringently.

The producers' surpluses accruing to the established exporters became evident in the growth of legal and illegal auction and other sale systems for export and import quotas. In some cases, notably in Hong Kong and Taiwan, clothing and textiles were marginally priced in the highly competitive domestic markets, benefiting LDC consumers (and tourists). The cost of protection via VERs was borne by two groups. First, consumers in the industrial countries paid higher prices than those that would have prevailed in the absence of protection. Because competition from developing countries was greatest in low-cost mass consumption goods, the costs were borne primarily by low-income consumers (Jenkins 1980).

The second group was the developing countries, although the incidence was undoubtedly uneven within countries and between them. The developing countries' exports were restricted. The extent of the restrictions is moot. The existing leading countries moved up-market in clothing and textiles and diversified out of these products. Whether they would have moved more rapidly or slowly without the rents and restrictions of protectionism it is impossible to know. Export growth from "new" countries was also restricted, but some may have benefited from the limitations placed on the principal exporters. The new countries obtained investment, which combined capital with technology and marketing skills that they may not otherwise have obtained, and more generally were able to enter and compete in markets in which prices were raised by protection.

Overall, developed country consumers clearly were adversely affected by restrictions on textile and apparel imports. Developing countries as a group probably also lost, although they did receive the rents on VERs in at least partial compensation. One further factor relevant for assessing the probably future impact of protection should be noted: during the 1970s, Japan was reducing its net exports of textiles and apparel. This undoubtedly eased the impact of the MFA. This feature will no longer serve as a buffer in the future. To what extent it mitigated protection is difficult to evaluate.

Footwear and Leather Products

Footwear was also a "sensitive" industry in Europe, the United States, and Canada by the mid-1960s, with exports again first originating principally from the Far East and then diversifying rapidly across developing countries. Tariffs had remained relatively high through the 1960s, VERs and OMAs were common, and there was pressure to increase quantitative restrictions in the 1970s.

Protection was, however, less effective than in the clothing and textile industry. Footwear is a smaller industry than textiles, and it consists of smaller firms with frequent entry and exit. Many firms, including some of the larger ones, were not able to handle the major changes in taste to informal footwear that became marked from the mid-1960s, and pressure for protection eased with their exit from the industry. Some firms moved part of their production abroad or used imported components. Industrial country firms were able to continue to compete in the high-quality upper end of the market by using their advantages in design and craftsmanship, and there was little investment in new capital-intensive technology. Protection did not increase appreciably in the 1970s, and it is doubtful whether it had any effect on production trends in the industry in the United States (Mutti and Bale 1980). Thus when the principal NTBs were removed in the United States in 1981 there was relatively little organized opposition from the industry, and there seems to have been no major change in production trends.

Protection on other leather products such as handbags was probably even less effective. It has been even more sporadic than that on footwear. Some producers from industrial countries were able to compete effectively through design and craftsmanship at the top end of the market (U.S. International Trade Commission 1982), but protectionist efforts did not succeed in preventing rapid expansion in imports.

Electronic Products, Cutlery, Hand Tools, Etc.

As the developing countries widened their range of export products in the late 1960s, calls for protection were heard in response to increases in imports of a variety of goods. Manufacturers in Europe and the United States complained about growing imports of metal products, such as cutlery, hand tools, and even barbers' chairs. They were successful in having some partial, and often also temporary, restrictions imposed on imports, but the coverage was limited and it is doubtful whether restrictions were very effective. Then electronic products became the focus of attention.

Electronics assembly moved offshore in many developed countries in the late 1960s and early 1970s and, in addition, local entrepreneurs began to produce electronic goods in Taiwan, Korea, and Hong Kong in the 1970s. Large electronics firms in developed countries had conflicting interests: they wanted to encourage some types of imports, but they simultaneously wanted protection against others. In the United States, Zenith was the only major firm not to move production overseas until the early 1980s, when it too was forced to do so by competition from other U.S. producers and from Japanese and other imports. There were protests against imports in most of the industrial countries, and some restrictive actions followed, mostly of the VER-OMA type but with some increases in tariffs as well.

However, those measures were too partial and spasmodic to reverse the trend in the DCs toward the substitution of imports for local production in a growing range of products. Indeed, electronics firms, which had mostly started as assembly operations in LDCs, extended their activities deeper into manufacturing processes, even where this involved technology-intensive microprocessing. Although some observers forecast that the likely impact of changing electronics technology would result in the industry's relocation in the DCs in the mid-1970s, this has not happened. There was apparently more talk of an increase in VERs and OMAs in the mid-1970s than impact. The electronic, cutlery, hand tool, and other machine exports from LDCs were further diversified and expanded, but parts of these industries also remained competitively located in industrial countries. The trend was even more strongly toward intra-industry trade than in clothing, textiles, and footwear.

Miscellaneous Products

The miscellaneous group of manufacturing which includes toys, sporting goods, and musical instruments had a fairly large proportion of developing country exports from the 1960s, and it continued to grow rapidly in the 1970s. The competition these products faced in industrial countries came from relatively small industry groups and relatively small firms. In some cases the industrial country industry was practically wiped out. Baseball bats and gloves in the United States are an example. In others, such as musical instruments, developed country firms remained competitive. But little protectionist fervor was generated from the declining firms, and intra-industry trade largely developed on lines of comparative advantage in a widening circle of "industries."

11.2.2   Protection against DC Products That Also
             Affects LDC Manufactured Exports

In the mid-1970s, the focus of protectionist pressure swung from manufactured goods originating in LDCs to those from DCs. The bulk of protective measures taken were against imports of steel and automobiles.

Japan was the initial target, but in the late 1970s recriminations also arose between the United States and the EC over steel, petrochemicals, and associated industries. A few developing countries, notably Brazil and Korea, have been caught in these disputes because to a limited extent they are also competitors. This is particularly true in steel (Kamahito 1981).[6] And other developing countries are affected insofar as they are potential entrants or suppliers of raw material inputs whose demand is reduced by higher output prices.

The problems of these industries date back to the nineteenth century, and already once, in the 1930s, led to serious difficulties. It can plausibly be argued that the difficulties these industries are experiencing originate more in the domestic economies and structure of the industries than in trade itself. It is in defense of such industries that VERs, OMAs, and new protective measures such as the Trigger Price Mechanism for steel have spread.

The distribution of benefits and costs of these arrangements vary. With the Trigger Price Mechanism the protected countries' producers seem to have benefited, at least in the short run. The costs are very considerable. Protection for steel is inevitably followed by demands for protection in steel-using industries that compete internationally. Thus while the high cost of steel may be passed on to consumers by the construction industry, the competitiveness of producers of automobiles and domestic consumer durable goods suffers as consumers choose cheaper imports. Where the industry concerned has large employment but is dominated by a small number of firms, it demands—and often receives—further protection. But since the protected industries are large, the increases in costs are correspondingly high. To date, however, it would appear that those costs have been borne by the developed countries themselves and have not impacted significantly on LDC exports.[7]

11.2.3 Administered Protection

Another effect of the increasing pressures for protection has been the establishment of a considerable bureaucracy in the industrial countries. It sifts, interprets, sends through legal processes (in the case of the United States), and evaluates the demand for protection under dozens of different rubrics. In the EC two-fold layers of national and community bureaucracies deal with protection.

One of the reasons for the difficulty of evaluating administered protection is that its formats differ so widely. The more transparent the administration of protection, the less protective, but also the more public it is likely to be. Countries such as the United States and Australia appear to be relatively protectionist because they have more transparent systems of protection than Japan and the EC. Yet it is clear that Australia, except for clothing, footwear, and motor vehicles, reduced its protection substantially in the 1970s (Anderson and Garnaut). For the United States, requests for protection handled by such agencies as the International Trade Commission (ITC) and the Treasury were quite numerous, and the White House was involved in a number of trade policy decisions. Nonetheless, the overall impact of these measures was limited (Finger 1981, 1982; Finger, Hall, and Nelson 1982).

Evaluating EC trends is even more difficult. Apart from increasing protection against agricultural imports almost continuously, and against clothing and textiles in 1977, individual members of the EC, and the EC itself, introduced a large number of measures, many of them, however, of small effect and limited duration. Although all countries agreed to the several EC-wide increases in protection, not all implemented them. With the free flow of goods within the EC, imports flowed into member countries which did not implement the EC decisions to be sold also in those that did. A listing of the measures taken in countries such as Italy (Grilli 1980) would suggest that imports from developing countries were restricted. Yet overall, several analysts have concluded that there seems to have been little actual increase in the degree of restriction resulting from administered protection against imports from developing countries (Anjaria et al. 1981; Gard and Riedel 1980). If protection had significantly increased, the ACP States that received a great deal of preferential treatment might have been expected to have had booming exports, but this has not been the case.

Japan's system of administered protection is very opaque, even to Japanese scholars. However, discussions with Korean exporters indicate that the weight of administrative action in the 1970s was used to open markets to developing countries. The exception was traditional semi-handicraft products, especially silk, which was restricted. However, Japan's distribution system is heavily biased against imports (Yasugi 1980). The government began to plan reforms in the early 1970s but failed to carry them out because of reduced national growth rates and threatened unemployment. In that sense it failed to reduce protection with considerable costs to consumers.

11.2.4   Suppliers' Export Credit Subsidies

A major area of protection that has received little attention is export subsidies. These are protective of domestic producers when their magnitude permits producers to export profitably who would otherwise be unable to do so. In the context of protection against manufactured exports from LDCs, these subsidies may permit DC exporters to retain market shares when, in their absence, LDC exports would rise more rapidly.

Some export subsidies are granted directly to the exporting firm and these are impossible to trace. A significant, but also, unknown, volume takes the form of direct or indirect (through central bank discounts or public insurance) subsidies to exporters. Suppliers' credits grew in volume in the 1970s as trade grew, but the subsidy element declined as real interest rates fell, rising again as interest rates rose after 1979. The total volume of subsidy through export credits is estimated as having risen from $330 million to $3.5 billion from 1976 to 1980 (Fleisig and Hill, this volume).

Although export credit subsidies are always distortive of trade among industrial countries, it was argued in the 1950s and 1960s that the developing countries benefited because they were exporters of primary products and labor-intensive nondurable consumer goods, and importers of capital goods. This is, however, no longer the case. Developing countries appear to have a comparative advantage in producing "one-of" capital goods such as ships, oil rigs, hydroelectric generators, and specialized earth-moving machines (in contrast to mass-produced equipment). Those activities require relatively large inputs of skilled labor, such as draftsmen, technicians, and engineers whose wages are still low in developing countries. This type of export production has been developing for some twenty years, but the technological innovations that led to the use of numerically controlled machine tools have greatly speeded it up by enabling skilled workers to be trained in six months instead of six years.

Developing countries exporting such capital goods have to borrow abroad to finance exports in order for them to be competitive with the industrial country subsidies on suppliers' credits. This is clearly a case where the final consumers benefits, the taxpayers of exporting countries pay the cost of subsidy, developing countries' exports are disadvantaged, but developing countries importing capital goods may benefit.

11.2.5 Nonborder Protection

As protectionist pressures for high tariffs and quantitative and other import restrictions were mostly defeated in the 1950s and 1960s, protectionist interests sought subsidies for domestic production. The arguments for subsidies followed the traditional protectionist and mercantilist cases for import substitution and export growth, with a heavy weight being given to employment issues. This was particularly important in the case of "senile" industries such as textiles and shipbuilding. "Regional balance" became another rationale for local and national subsidies. Federal systems were particularly prone to this approach. Even the relatively liberal Federal Republic of Germany had many state subsidies (Donges 1980).

The principal forms of subsidy or nonborder protection were the following:

a) Favored tax treatment and other subsidies for research and development were used in an effort to stimulate technological advances, "pick the winners," implement "positive structural adjustment," and change the comparative advantage of senile industries.

b) Nationalization, initially advocated to take over the "commanding heights" of the economy, was used instead to take over floundering firms. It was either done directly with deficits in the public budget or the industries were instead assisted by subsidies, particularly in such oligopolistic sectors as steel and automobiles.

c) Regional taxation exemptions and cash subsidies were enacted to enable firms to move to areas where they otherwise could not operate efficiently.

d) Subsidy support was used in the mid-1970s for "senile" industries to avoid unemployment and maintain exports.

The extent of such subsidies is not known. Except for a few years and industries there are not even complete enumerations, and there are only very partial quantifications of the effects. The microeconomic impact was almost certainly more serious than the macroeconomic impact, but trading partners were deprived of markets and the industrial countries themselves were hence injured as exporters. There were high budgetary costs. For example, in the late 1970s it is estimated that it cost about $45,000 a year to maintain a job in the Swedish shipbuilding industry that paid a worker $20,000 (Hamilton 1981a).

In theory, subsidies may be preferred to their tariff equivalent or other import restrictions because they are more direct and more transparent. In practice this was not generally the case in the early and mid-1970s. Budgetary controls proved to be very lax in the boom years, and there is a marked absence of ex post analysis of the costs and benefits of R&D expenditures, subsidies to "pick the winners," and so on.[8] Budgets frequently lumped together subsidy sums for various purposes, leaving it to administrators to pick the "winning" firms or industries.

However, by the late 1970s, the available evidence suggests that under the pressure of declining national growth the peak of subsidization, and nonborder protection generally, had been passed (Hamilton 1981b; Yonezawa 1980). The pressure for budgetary restraints led to greater scrutiny, particularly where fiscally conservative governments were elected. In most countries, even if subsidy budgets were not actually reduced, they ceased to grow with other expenditures by the early 1980s.

Nonborder protection probably largely canceled out among the industrial countries. Indeed, the biggest effect may have been the costs of imposing protection and the reduced incentives for efficiency in the protection-imposing countries. If everything is protected, nothing is protected. Some firms may have obtained windfall rents from which capital, management, and labor benefited. But consumers had to pay more, and taxpayers had to support production. The developing countries probably gained in some cases but lost in others. Export competition may have been more difficult for potential LDC exporters in some industries, but to the extent that subsidies went to marginal, inefficient firms, the immediate impact was to make competition easier by raising prices. Shipbuilding is an example of an industry which shifted location despite massive subsidies.

11.2.6   The Balance

In the next two sections, we evaluate data on the behavior of LDC-manufactured exports in an effort to ascertain how effective protection may have been. Based on the evidence concerning the ability of the LDCs to maintain exports in the face of increased protection in the DCs, pessimists could conclude that export growth from developing countries was halted in the latter part of the 1970s. However, even pessimists might have expected the ACP countries to benefit by trade diversion from other developing country producers (although there are questions about supply elasticities in those countries). Optimists, on the other hand, might conclude that the underlying trends continued to be in the direction of liberal trade, mainly because of the success of the multilateral rounds of trade negotiation.

The threat of protection was considerable, but it can be argued that the cost of the protectionist measures taken was borne largely by the domestic economies of the industrial countries, with serious protective effects on the developing countries' exports confined to the textile and apparel industry.[9] Even optimists would, however, be likely to conclude that the Far Eastern exporters would have been most injured because the bulk of the protectionist measures were taken against them. It is clear that trade would have grown faster and everyone would have been better off with an even more rapid reduction of overall protection. Some of the losses, moreover, may have been through the impact on investment decisions of the uncertainty that was engendered in developing countries by protection.

11.3   Market Penetration Trends in the 1970s

One indirect check on the impact of protectionist measures is to examine the growth of LDC exports and their shares of developed country markets. The data used for this purpose combine production data in eleven industrial countries with export and import data to calculate apparent consumption for some 150 product groups[10] and classify trade origin and destination by principal trading groups. Table 11.2 shows the growth of LDC manufactured exports during the 1970s.[11]

LDC exports of manufactures to DCs grew at nearly 11 percent per annum in the 1970s, with the fastest growth occurring in metal products,

Table 11.2   Product Composition of Developing Countries' Manufactured
               Exports to Industrial Countries, 1970–80

ISIC	US$ (billion)		Average Annual Real Growth Rate[a]	Share of Total (percent)	
	1970	1980	1970–80	1970	1980
31 Food, beverages and tobacco	7.5	27.6	4.8	34.4	18.2
32 Textile, wearing apparel and leather industries	3.4	31.4	13.2	15.6	20.7
33 Manufacture of wood and wood products, including furniture	0.8	5.6	10.2	3.7	3.7
34 Manufacture of paper and paper products: Printing and publishing	0.2	1.6	15.0	0.7	1.1
35 Manufacture of chemicals and of chemical, petroleum, coal, rubber and plastic products	3.6	37.5	14.4	16.6	24.7
36 Manufacture of nonmetallic mineral products, except products of petroleum and coal	0.1	1.4	16.4	0.5	0.9
37 Basic metal industries	4.0	15.1	4.2	18.6	9.9
38 Manufacture of fabricated metal products, machinery and equipment	1.6	28.5	20.7	7.5	18.8
39 Miscellaneous manufacturing industries	0.5	3.1	11.7	2.2	2.1
3 All manufactured products	21.7	151.9	10.8	100.0	100.0

SOURCE: World Bank, Market Penetration research project data, for this and following tables.

[a]Growth rates were calculated by least-squares method. Deflated by industrial country GDP deflators.

machinery (including electronic products), nonmetallic minerals (particularly glassware and ceramics), paper and printing (from a low base), chemicals, and clothing, textiles, and leather. In gross output terms, chemicals became the principal product exported. However, textiles and metal products and machinery, which have a much higher value added in production, were economically more important. The relative share of food products declined, in part reflecting inelastic demand, but also because of high and increasing protection in the EC. Given the extent of protection against the clothing and textiles group, and its increase in the 1970s, the rapid rate of growth of textile exports is somewhat surprising.

It is even more surprising that the Far Eastern exporters, against whom much of the protection was directed, remained successful. Table 11.3 indicates that the Far Eastern exporters increased their share of total exports, largely at the expense of Latin American countries whose exports of food products (mainly coffee) declined markedly in real terms, but also at the expense of "old" southern European exporters and such countries as India and Pakistan. The ASEAN group made the principal gains in addition to the Far Eastern exporters (particularly if Singapore is excluded), and so did a number of small countries such as Mauritius and Malta. Among the Latin American countries Brazil did well in paper, nonmetallic mineral products, base metals and metal products, and machinery, but all from a relatively small base.

It may be objected that the 1970–80 data conceal the intradecade shift in trends. That this was not markedly the case is evidenced by the data in table 11.4. Imports into the industrial countries from developing countries grew rapidly, and much more so than imports from other industrial countries throughout the decade, although growth in developing country market penetration was more rapid in the early 1970s than in the later 1970s. The bulk of the decline in growth (except in textiles in the EC, see below) can probably be explained by faltering growth in the industrial countries. Market penetration growth of LDCs continued to be much faster than total import growth in the later period despite protectionist measures.

Table 11.5 shows the shares of the developing countries in developed country markets. With the exception of Australia and Canada, the industrial countries markedly increased the openness of their economy in the 1970s, as measured by import shares.

Market penetration varied considerably by country in 1970 and so did market penetration growth rates for the 1970s. The initial level of market penetration, a country's overall growth (and hence its growth of imports), and the overall impact of policies were clearly important, but so were supply conditions not captured by these data.

Japan had the lowest share of imports from all sources in its economy in 1970, and this was still true in 1980. Given its location in East Asia, moreover, it had a surprisingly low share of imports from developing countries and relatively low growth of such imports in the 1970s. Price comparisons suggest that for many goods this is not the result of the competitiveness of Japanese production, but rather that Japan's distribution system is a more effective barrier to trade than other forms of protection. However, the products that the Far Eastern LDCs were exporting were precisely those in which Japan was earlier preeminent. As

Table 11.3 Manufactured Exports of Developing Countries to Industrial Countries, by Origin and Product Groups, 1970–80

ISIC	All Developing Countries (US$ billion)	Percent Share of Exports from				
		Southern Europe[a]	Far East[b]	Latin America	Other Developing Countries	(ASEAN)[b]
31 Food, beverages and tobacco						
1970	7.5	9.5	2.7	50.0	37.8	(8.0)
1980	27.6	8.4	4.4	49.1	38.1	(12.1)
Growth rate: 1970–80	15.2	11.7	19.3	15.1	15.9	(20.1)
32 Textile, wearing apparel and leather industries						
1970	3.4	19.7	41.8	7.7	30.7	(2.5)
1980	31.4	18.6	44.5	9.0	27.9	(5.4)
Growth rate: 1970–80	24.5	22.9	25.6	27.4	23.0	(36.3)
33 Manufacture of wood and wood products, including furniture						
1970	0.8	20.3	29.9	13.7	36.2	(22.5)
1980	5.6	20.0	31.2	10.0	38.8	(31.3)
Growth rate: 1970–80	21.1	20.1	22.4	16.2	22.1	(25.4)
34 Manufacture of paper and paper products: Printing and publishing						
1970	0.2	57.9	14.2	10.7	17.2	(2.9)
1980	1.6	39.1	21.0	32.0	7.8	(2.8)
Growth rate: 1970–80	26.4	21.7	32.6	39.7	16.0	(23.7)
35 Manufacture of chemicals and of chemical, petroleum, coal, rubber and plastic products						
1970	3.6	10.4	10.9	54.4	24.2	(4.9)
1980	37.5	9.5	13.3	37.7	40.0	(10.4)
Growth rate: 1970–80	25.8	23.7	29.9	21.5	31.4	(33.9)

36 Manufacture of nonmetallic mineral products, except products of petroleum and coal	1970	0.1	50.2	17.0	27.5	5.3	(1.0)
	1980	1.4	39.4	36.4	13.5	10.6	(2.8)
Growth rate:	1970–80	27.9	23.8	40.2	20.2	48.0	(41.7)
37 Basic metal industries	1970	4.0	7.3	0.7	30.9	61.1	(7.4)
	1980	15.1	16.2	8.2	32.9	42.7	(13.2)
Growth rate:	1970–80	14.7	22.7	41.5	15.4	10.7	(22.0)
38 Manufacture of fabricated metal products, machinery and equipment	1970	1.6	25.8	35.5	16.5	22.2	(4.1)
	1980	28.5	22.9	43.7	14.9	18.5	(16.8)
Growth rate:	1970–80	32.8	28.9	34.6	31.0	37.2	(48.5)
39 Miscellaneous manufacturing industries	1970	0.5	4.5	85.2	3.3	6.9	(8.1)
	1980	3.1	4.7	79.7	4.5	11.1	(5.6)
Growth rate:	1970–80	22.8	21.6	22.1	25.2	28.5	(32.2)
3 All manufactured products	1970	21.7	13.1	15.5	35.3	36.1	(6.6)
	1980	151.9	15.2	25.7	27.1	32.0	(11.7)
Growth rate:	1970–80	21.8	22.1	27.9	18.9	20.5	(28.7)

[a]Southern Europe consists of Andorra, Cyprus, Gibraltar, Greece, Israel, Malta, Portugal, Spain, Turkey, and Yugoslavia.

[b]Far East: Korea, Taiwan, Hong Kong and Singapore; ASEAN: Indonesia, Malaysia, Philippines, Thailand, and Singapore. Singapore is thus included in both groups, and the other ASEAN countries are also included in "other developing countries." The ASEAN group is duplicative.

Table 11.4   Import Growth in Industrial Countries, 1970–75, 1975–80 and 1970–80 (average annual growth)

	Growth of Import Shares		
	Imports from Industrial Countries	Imports from Developing Countries	Imports from European Centrally Planned Economies
1970–75	4.9	9.7	10.9
1975–80	3.2	7.0	3.7
1970–80	3.6	7.2	6.3
Value of imports in 1980 ($US billion)	610	152	20

such the Japanese net export balance was diminishing and reductions in exports are not reflected in the data.

Belgium, Sweden, and the United Kingdom had the lowest growth rates in market penetration from developing countries in the 1970s, but they all started from relatively high initial levels. Australia, the Netherlands, France, and the United States had the highest increase in import penetration. The Netherlands also started at a high level of penetration in 1970. Its high growth of imports from developing countries thus reflected policy commitment and the effectiveness of its implementation policies. In France, the GSP and special bilateral arrangements with Southern Europe, the Maghreb, Africa South of the Sahara, and the Caribbean encouraged imports from those areas, which still accounted for more than two-thirds of imports in 1980. Yet despite policy biases in favor of the latter countries and against the Far East, the East Asian exporters continued to increase their share of French markets by 23 percent a year in 1975–80.

Most of the industry groups and subgroups show the same general patterns as the overall trends. This is reflected in the data presented in table 11.6. In all categories of manufactures, the LDC shares of DC imports increased. Despite protection, the increase was rapid for textiles, clothing, footwear, TV and radio, and the other groups subject to protection. As already noted, the developing countries' gains in processed food, beverages, and tobacco products were minimal. They increased their market penetration (table 11.6; Duncan and Lutz 1982) by only 1.5 percent a year in the 1970s in that category. For all manufactures, however, the rate of increase in share was over 7 percent a year—hardly evidence of trade restrictions having been highly effective.

One of the reasons why protective measures had relatively little impact on overall import performance was the diversification of developing

Table 11.5 Share of Developing Country Imports in the Apparent Consumption of Manufactured Goods, in Eleven Industrial Countries, 1970–80 (percent)

	Share in Apparent Consumption				Growth of Import Shares	
	1970		1980[a]		1970–1980[b]	
	All Imports	Imports from Developing Countries	All Imports	Imports from Developing Countries	All Imports	Imports from Developing Countries
Australia	22.3	2.1	25.9	5.5	2.6	11.0
Canada	27.0	1.3	31.1	2.1	1.7	5.0
European Community	20.4	2.5	31.8	4.6	4.8	6.7
Belgium	57.5	5.7	80.1	6.2	3.2	1.4
France	16.2	1.9	23.1	3.8	3.6	7.8
Germany	19.3	2.3	30.8	4.8	4.9	8.1
Italy	16.3	2.2	31.6	5.2	6.8	9.3
Netherlands	52.3	3.9	62.1	7.5	2.0	6.7
United Kingdom	15.8	2.8	26.6	4.1	5.8	3.8
Japan	4.7	1.3	6.2	2.4	2.4	5.8
Sweden	31.3	2.8	37.9	3.8	2.5	3.9
United States	5.5	1.3	8.6	2.9	4.5	8.6
Industrial countries	17.6	1.7	17.6	3.4	4.3	7.2

[a]Preliminary data subject to revision.
[b]Average annual rate of growth estimated by an ordinary least-square regression: growth rates are of the share of the market to avoid deflation problems.

Table 11.6   Share of Imports from Developing Countries by Product Groups, 1970 and 1980

ISIC	Total Imports (US$ billion)		Share of Apparent Consumption $\frac{M}{O+M-X}$ (percent)		Import Penetration Growth (percent per annum)
	1970	1980	1970	1980	1970–80
31 Food	7.5	27.6	3.5	3.7	1.5
32 Clothing, textiles and footwear	3.4	31.4	3.1	10.5	13.1
322 Clothing	1.4	16.6	4.0	16.3	15.0
321 Textiles	1.5	8.9	2.3	5.4	8.6
324 Footwear	0.2	3.2	2.6	16.3	18.9
323 Leather products	0.3	2.7	6.2	17.3	11.5
33 Wood products	0.8	5.6	1.9	3.6	7.1
34 Paper	0.2	1.6	0.2	0.5	11.9
35 Chemicals	3.6	37.5	2.0	3.8	5.7
36 Nonmetallic minerals	0.1	1.4	0.3	1.1	13.8
37 Base metals	4.0	15.1	3.5	4.1	2.1
38 Machinery	1.6	28.5	0.4	2.1	17.6
3811 Cutlery & hand tools	0.1	0.9	0.8	3.3	15.6
3812 Metal furniture	0.03	0.2	0.6	1.6	9.5
3832 Radio, TV, etc.	0.5	9.2	1.6	7.2	18.6
39 Other manufactured products	0.5	3.1	4.0	8.0	9.4
Total	21.7	151.9	1.7	3.4	7.2

country exports by product. The most rapid increases in market penetration came in machinery and nonmetallic mineral products (including china and glassware). Another high growth sector is the miscellaneous group that includes sports equipment, toys, and musical instruments. Nonetheless, clothing, textiles, and footwear still rank high on the list despite their relatively high market penetration in 1970 and despite textile protectionism.

The low correlation between the extensive import controls particularly designed to limit the growth of imports from the Far East and the increase in market penetration by the Far Eastern countries supports the hypothesis that administrative protection is not only costly, but also largely ineffective.

This is illustrated by the continuing strength of the Far Eastern exporters (table 11.7). Their market penetration growth was exceeded in 1970–75 and for the 1970s as a whole by the ASEAN group of the second-wave exporters and by some other newcomers (Havrylyshyn and Wolf 1981; Havrylyshyn and Alikhani 1982). However, when competition became tougher in more growing markets in the late 1970s, and although protection was mainly directed specifically against the Far Eastern exporters, they were able to compete and expand exports more rapidly than other countries, notably those of Southern Europe and Latin America.

11.4   The Impact of Protection on Suppliers

The primary and immediate impact of protection (to the extent that it is effective) is to reduce imports from those suppliers against which the protection is directed. But this is only the first step in a long chain affecting both demand and all sources of supply. As a first step toward disentangling these effects, table 11.8 indicates the changes in the share of imports of clothing, textile, and footwear markets into the United

Table 11.7   **Market Penetration Growth by Developing Country Groups, 1970–75, 1975–80, and 1970–80**

	1970–75	1975–80	1970–80	1970	1980
	(average annual growth rates)			(US$ million)	
Southern Europe	11.4	7.2	7.6	3	23
Far East[a]	16.4	10.0	12.7	3	39
ASEAN[a]	21.9	9.6	13.3	1	18
Latin America	7.2	4.3	4.7	8	41

[a]Far East: Korea, Taiwan, Hong Kong, and Singapore. ASEAN: Indonesia, Malaysia, Philippines, Thailand, and Singapore. Singapore is thus included in both groups.

Table 11.8 Clothing, Textile and Footwear Import Shares by Principal Exporting Groups and Importing DCs, 1970-80 (percent)

	U.S.				EC				Japan			
	1970	1976	1978	1980	1970	1976	1978	1980	1970	1976	1978	1980
ISIC 322 Clothing												
Imports from:												
Far East	42.9	62.0	60.7	64.0	12.4	19.5	17.2	17.9	55.4	70.6	65.3	50.9
Southern Europe	4.5	2.3	1.7	0.9	6.2	12.6	13.2	13.6	0.8	1.0	1.2	0.8
Latin America	4.3	10.5	10.3	9.2	0.1	1.0	0.9	0.9	0.2	0.2	0.2	0.1
Other developing	4.2	7.8	10.9	14.5	1.7	6.9	7.8	10.7	15.0	9.0	9.9	20.1
Industrial countries	43.9	15.8	14.3	10.2	75.9	53.9	55.4	51.8	27.8	18.9	23.2	27.9
Eastern European countries	0.2	1.6	2.1	1.2	3.7	6.1	5.5	5.1	0.8	0.3	0.2	0.2
(ASEAN)	(4.3)	(5.5)	(7.5)	(7.3)	(0.1)	(1.8)	(2.0)	(2.6)	(0.5)	(1.8)	(0.9)	(1.8)
Total share of imports[a]	6.4	11.9	16.3	16.7	20.6	40.2	43.0	48.0	4.4	10.4	9.4	10.7

ISIC 321 Textiles

Imports from:

Far East	6.4	14.0	11.5	14.0	2.2	3.1	2.7	2.7	26.7	36.0	37.4	29.9
Southern Europe	3.3	2.1	2.1	1.9	3.6	6.0	6.4	6.6	0.7	0.2	0.3	0.4
Latin America	4.5	9.3	10.7	9.7	0.9	2.5	2.3	2.5	2.1	3.1	2.0	2.3
Other developing	18.5	22.3	20.4	25.5	7.6	8.5	9.2	10.6	23.9	22.8	26.9	26.6
Industrial countries	66.7	51.1	53.8	47.3	84.0	77.7	77.3	75.7	44.3	36.2	32.2	39.9
Eastern European countries	0.6	2.2	1.5	1.6	1.7	2.2	2.1	1.9	2.3	1.7	1.2	0.9
(ASEAN)	(0.6)	(2.8)	(2.6)	(2.6)	(0.1)	(9.0)	(0.9)	(0.9)	(1.6)	(2.4)	(2.2)	(3.1)
Total share of imports[a]	4.5	4.1	4.7	4.4	17.4	27.2	30.5	33.7	4.0	6.2	7.3	7.4

ISIC 324 Footwear

Imports from:

Far East	3.0	29.3	32.9	38.1	5.0	5.6	5.4	8.1	27.4	67.0	74.3	60.3
Southern Europe	16.8	19.9	15.0	10.7	5.8	12.4	11.8	11.9	4.7	2.4	1.5	3.9
Latin America	3.5	15.2	13.5	15.7	0.3	1.5	2.7	2.3	0.0	1.2	0.4	2.3
Other developing	1.0	1.5	2.0	3.3	1.5	2.0	2.5	3.7	2.7	3.6	3.2	8.0
Industrial countries	74.2	31.0	33.2	28.4	83.4	73.9	73.7	62.5	64.5	25.6	20.5	25.4
Eastern European countries	1.5	3.1	3.4	3.8	4.0	4.6	3.9	2.5	0.7	0.2	0.1	0.1
(ASEAN)	(0.2)	(0.2)	(1.2)	(1.6)	(0.2)	(0.4)	(0.4)	(0.5)	(0.1)	(0.4)	(0.2)	(1.3)
Total share of imports[a]	13.3	26.9	38.9	35.7	19.7	37.5	40.9	47.9	2.4	7.1	7.2	9.8

[a]Total share of imports in apparent consumption.

States, the European Community, and Japan by principal suppliers in the late 1970s.

It is clear that despite the presumed intent to protect DC suppliers, the DCs on the whole continued to lose their share both of total markets as domestic suppliers and of other countries' markets. In some markets, notably U.S. textiles and footwear, the growth rate of imports as a share of apparent consumption declined, but at the high levels already reached, this may have been in part a consequence of market trends as penetration into high-quality markets became more difficult. The DCs also failed to make significant gains in their mutual trade except in clothing in Japan where their share of imports recovered to the 1970 level.

The primary impact of protection ought to have been to reduce the share of imports from the Far East, but this was true only to a minor degree in the EC in clothing, textiles, and footwear after 1976. In the United States the Far Eastern countries' share of clothing and textiles fluctuated, but it continued to rise in footwear. In Japan the Far Eastern exporters also lost clothing and textile shares but gained in footwear. In all three geographic markets, the Far Eastern exporters gained in other products.

It is impossible to determine the extent to which these trends resulted from protection and the extent to which they were the result of changing supply conditions. Where the elasticity of supply is high as in the Far East, entrepreneurs diversify exports geographically, move "up-market" to higher quality goods in the product group in question, and diversify their product range. The Far Eastern exporters were doing all this from the beginning of the 1970s, and it is impossible to gauge exactly how much the post-1976 protectionism accelerated such diversification.

In Hong Kong the diversification was largely the result of private initiatives, in Taiwan private initiative was supported by public liberalization measures, and Singapore and Korea made major, but very different, policy interventions. Singapore raised real wages between 1978 and 1981 by 10 percent a year to push entrepreneurs up-market and drive out marginal low-labor-productivity firms that were unable to make the move. Real wage increases, reflecting productivity gains, were having the same impact in Korea up to the mid-1970s, but then continued to rise rapidly largely because of the excessively capital- and technical-skill-intensive orientation of government policy. Whereas diversification in Hong Kong, Singapore, and Taiwan came smoothly, Korea's policy, combined with the lack of confidence arising out of political problems and failure to liberalize the economy, resulted in its lagging behind the other Far Eastern exporters in moving up-market within the relatively labor-intensive production categories (it led to other economic problems as well).

The principal expansion of labor-intensive exports came from three ASEAN countries—Thailand, Malaysia, and the Philippines—and from Southern Europe. The "old" developing country exporters—India and Pakistan—failed to take marked advantage of the protection against the Far Eastern countries, and so, on the whole, did Latin America. China began to make a major effort to increase exports at the very bottom of the low-quality, labor-intensive range at the end of the 1970s, and a large number of small new exporters such as Mauritius, Sri Lanka, and Morocco, and even including on a small scale a number of countries from Africa South of the Sahara (Ivory Coast, Botswana, Malawi) also began to export manufactured goods. The latter group benefited from ACP preferential treatment (though as already noted, their competitiveness was limited by lack of access to cheap raw materials under ACP rules). Investment in the "new" exporting countries (if they sought it) was also accelerated by the phenomenon of "quota seekers," as noted earlier.

These trends do not, however, mean that protection was costless, only that the costs to developing countries were less than might have been expected. Unrestricted markets could have led to even faster export growth because prices would have been lower without distorting rents, and living standards would have risen faster in the DCs and in the Far East. Given the considerable evidence of a high elasticity of substitution in production, up-market movement and other diversifications would have most probably occurred in the Far East in any case, together with investment in the second-echelon countries, so that an even greater effect would have been achieved than with protection and at higher standards of living. The ACP countries could have been assisted at lower cost and on a larger scale than has been the case to date.

11.5 Conclusions and Suggestions for Further Work

Based on the export performance of the developing countries in manufactured goods during the 1970s, it is difficult to infer that increasing protection was the dominant factor at work. To be sure, developing countries would have fared better (except possibly for the established exporters of textiles and clothing who received the rents under VERs) in the absence of protectionist measures. Yet, the overwhelming impression is that despite all the public discussion of protection and the political pressures for it, the effects on imports of manufactures from developing countries of protectionist measures were relatively small. The rate of increase of LDC market shares was sufficiently great that it is difficult to imagine that rates would have been significantly higher in the absence of any protectionist measures.

This leaves economists with an apparent puzzle: on one hand, protection is decried as necessarily welfare decreasing; yet it is difficult to infer sizeable effects on trade patterns, except possibly among sources of exports, to which we return below. Perhaps the answer lies in noting that the deleterious effects of interventions with free trade that are generally cited refer to the adverse welfare consequences for the protection-imposing countries. Insofar as there was a spread of protectionism in the 1970s, it would appear that the greater welfare losses were to the protecting countries, rather than to the rest of the world. It seems probable that this is the appropriate verdict on the protection of the 1970s: interventions in support of declining industries in the developed countries undoubtedly permitted the survival of some activities longer than would have been economically warranted. The economic costs of the survival may have been high, but they (and the consumption costs of protection) would have been borne by the developed countries themselves.

The geographic incidence of protectionist measures across developing countries remains an interesting and unresolved question. Would Korea have moved up-market in textiles more rapidly or more slowly in the absence of the MFA? Would Mauritius have entered the international textile market sooner or later in the absence of the MFA? Did VERs keep the newly industrialized countries (NICs) of the Far East exporting the same commodities longer than they otherwise would have? How important was the Japanese reduction in exports of the NIC commodities as a buffer to the impact VERs would otherwise have had?

On this score, the evidence is not yet in. Further research on the industrial organization of the exporting industries subject to protection in the NICs would undoubtedly shed further light on the issue. So, too, would research on the behavior of costs of the protected firms in developed countries, and the extent to which the industry structure changed under protection.

While there remain many unsettled questions, it seems reasonable to conclude that, at least in the 1970s, protectionist actions were not sufficient to prevent those developing countries with open economies from significantly increasing their share of world markets. How much more they could have done in the absence of protectionist measures is an open question. However, given the full employment that prevailed in those economies, it is doubtful whether expansion at a significantly more rapid rate could have occurred.

It is to be hoped that the peak of protectionist pressures already passed in the 1970s. Whether in the 1980s LDCs could continue this market penetration in the face of increasing protectionism is a difficult question. The Japanese reduction in net exports in the relevant commodity groups is bound to be less significant than it was. Likewise, there are those who believe that the protectionists may find more effective instruments.

Nonetheless, the experience of the 1970s suggests that the main brunt of protection falls on those adopting it, and that well-run, open developing countries maintain higher rates of economic growth, even in the face of protectionism, than developing countries that choose to protect their internal markets and rely on inner-oriented growth strategies.

Notes

1. See Frank (1977, chap. 1) for a discussion of the emergence of "strong protectionist pressures" in the 1960s.

2. Increases in protection against primary commodities exported by developing countries, such as sugar and meat, have, paradoxically, received less attention. They are not covered in this paper, but see Duncan and Lutz (1982).

3. This possibility also covers the case when B's exports are simply transshipped through a third country against which there is no quota. Relabeling the origin of clothing and textiles to indicate that they were produced in countries not subject to VERs under the MFA has been a frequent means of evading that agreement.

4. The secret nature of VERs and OMAs (orderly marketing arrangements) makes a detailed evaluation of their provisions impossible. Guesses as to the coverage of these restrictive arrangements center around 5 percent of all manufactured imports from developing countries, but much higher proportions for a number of products—clothing and textiles, footwear, and some electronic goods—in which developing countries have a particular interest (Hindley 1980).

5. An irony of the history of protection in this sector is that U.S. agricultural policy in the 1950s permitted exports of raw cotton—then the main textile fiber—at a lower price than American textile producers paid. This "unfair advantage" was the rationale for the initial textile protection. It, in turn, provided a rationale for the protection of clothing where producers suffered a disadvantage because of textile protection.

6. It is not clear whether industries such as steel represent a comparative advantage activity for these countries, or whether they are largely the creations of distorted policies and hence contributors to Brazil's and Korea's current problems.

7. In the case of "trigger" pricing, developing countries with competitive cost advantages (notably Brazil and Korea) may have had more difficulty entering new markets than they otherwise would have, but there were no legal restrictions.

8. This is as true for Japan as for other countries. For example, the electronics firms that received most government support in Japan were not the ones that were the most innovative and grew most rapidly.

9. Even then, there is the (partial?) offset that VERs gave the rents on import restrictions to the exporting countries.

10. The data are based on a four-digit International Standard Industrial Classification (ISIC), broken down to further subgroups for products of interest to developing countries. This enables production, import, and export data to be combined and comparisons to be made among the industrial countries. Trade data have been transformed from the Standard International Trade Classification (SITC) to ISIC. Production data for 1980 and in some cases 1979 are estimated. Note that these data include primary processed products, notably in the food, beverage, and tobacco category that is often excluded from LDC export data. Jewelry (i.e., precious stones) is excluded throughout.

11. Table 11.4 provides a breakdown of growth rates for the two halves of the decade.

References

Anderson, Kym, and Ross Garnaut. 1984. *Australian protection and trade with developing countries*, forthcoming.

Anjaria, S. J., Z. Iqbal, L. L. Perez, and W. S. Tseng. 1981. *Trade policy developments in industrial countries*. Occasional Paper no. 5. Washington, D.C.: International Monetary Fund.

Donges, Juergen. 1980. Industrial policies in an open advanced economy: The case of West Germany. Paper presented at the Symposium on Industrial Policies for the 1980s, Industry Committee of the OECD, Madrid, May.

Duncan, Ronald C., and Ernst Lutz. 1982. *Agricultural protectionism and import penetration by developing countries in industrial country markets*. Commodities and Export Projections Division Working Paper no. 1982-5. Washington, D.C.: World Bank.

Finger, J. M. 1981. The industry-country incidence of "less than fair value" cases in U.S. import trade. *Quarterly Review of Economics and Business*. 21, no. 2, 260–79.

———. 1982. Trade and the structure of American industry. *Annals of the American Academy of Political and Social Science* 460 (March).

Finger, J. M., H. K. Hall, and D. R. Nelson. 1982. The political economy of administered protection. *American Economic Review* 72:452–66.

Frank, Charles, Jr., with Stephanie Levinson. 1977. *Foreign trade and domestic aid*. Washington, D.C.: Brookings Institution.

Gard, Linda M., and James Riedel. 1980. Safeguard protection of industry in developed countries: Assessment of the implications for developing countries. *Weltwirtschaftliches Archiv* 116, no. 3, 471–92.

Grilli, Enzo. 1980. *Italian commercial policies in the 1970s*. World Bank Staff Working Paper no. 428. Washington, D.C.: World Bank.

Hamilton, Carl. 1981a. Public subsidies to industry: The case of Sweden and its shipbuilding industry. World Bank Market Penetration Project. Mimeo.

———. 1981b. Effects of non-tariff barriers to trade on prices, employment and imports: The case of the Swedish textile and clothing industry. World Bank Market Penetration Project. Mimeo.

Havrylyshyn, Oli, and Iradj Alikhani. 1982. *Is there cause for export optimism? An inquiry into the existence of a second generation of successful exporters*. International Trade and Capital Flows Division Working Paper no. 1982/1. Washington, D.C.: World Bank.

Havrylyshyn, Oli, and Martin Wolf. 1981. *Trade among developing countries: Theory, policy issues, and principal trends*. World Bank Staff Working Paper no. 479. Washington, D.C.: World Bank.

Hindley, Brian. 1980. Voluntary export restraints and the GATT's main escape clause. *World Economy* 3:313–41.

Hughes, Helen, and Jean Waelbroeck. 1981. Can developing-country exports keep growing in the 1980s? *World Economy* 4:127–47.

Isard, Peter. 1973. Employment impacts of textile imports and investment: A vintage capital model. *American Economic Review* 63:402–16.

Jenkins, Glenn P. 1980. *Costs and consequences of the new protectionism: The case of Canada's clothing sector.* Ottawa, Canada: The North South Institute.

Kamahito, Kiyoshi. 1981. Japanese steel in the American market: Conflict and causes. *World Economy* 4:229–50.

Keesing, Donald B., and Martin Wolf. 1980. *Textile quotas against developing countries.* London: Trade Policy Research Centre.

———. 1981. Questions on international trade in textiles and clothing. *World Economy* 4:79–101.

Kemper, Ria. 1980. *The Tokyo Round: Results and implications for developing countries.* World Bank Staff Working Paper no. 372. Washington, D.C.: World Bank.

Komiya, Ryuatoro. 1972. Japan's non-tariff barriers to trade in manufactured products. In *Obstacles to trade in the Pacific area*, ed. H. E. English and Keith A. J. Hay. Ottawa, Canada: School of International Affairs, Carleton University.

Kreinin, Mordechai E., and Lawrence H. Officer. 1979. Tariff reductions under the Tokyo Round: A review of their effects on trade flows, employment, and welfare. *Weltwirtschaftliches Archiv* 115, no. 3.

Luey, Paul. 1969. Hong Kong investment. In *Foreign investment and industrialization in Singapore*, ed. Helen Hughes and You Poh Seng. Canberra: ANU Press.

Morawetz, David. 1981. *Why the emporer's new clothes are not made in Colombia: A case study in Latin American and East Asian manufactured exports.* Oxford University Press.

Mutti, John, and Malcolm Bale. 1980. *Output and employment changes in a "trade sensitive" sector: Adjustment in the U.S. footwear industry.* World Bank Staff Working Paper no. 430. Washington, D.C.: World Bank.

Organization for Economic Cooperation and Development. 1976. Measures of assistance to shipbuilding. Mimeo.

Saxon, Eric, and Kym Anderson. 1982. *Japanese agricultural protection in historical perspective.* Research Paper no. 92. Australia: Australia Japan Research Centre.

Shepherd, Geoffrey. 1981. *Textile-industry adjustment in developed countries.* London: Trade Policy Research Centre.

U.S. International Trade Commission. 1982. *Economic effects of export restraints.* Washington, D.C.

Wall, David. 1980. Industrial processing of natural resources. *World Development* 8:303–16.

Yasugi, Yoneyoshi. 1980. *Access of exports to Japanese markets.* International Trade and Capital Flows Division Working Paper no. 1980/2. Washington, D.C.: World Bank.

Yonezawa, Yoshie. 1980. Analysis and evaluation of the adjustment process and policies of Japanese textile industry. World Bank Market Penetration Project. Mimeo.

Comment   Irving B. Kravis

The Hughes-Krueger Paradox

The paper by Hughes and Krueger is both informative and provocative. It documents the success of developing countries in expanding their exports of manufactured goods into the markets of the developed countries. It also points out that the developing countries' success in increasing their penetration of manufactured goods markets in the developed countries was achieved despite protective measures taken by the latter. The Hughes-Krueger paradox of increased protective efforts accompanied by increased import volumes is explored briefly in this note. It is suggested that the explanations may be partly in the dynamic restructuring of the world economy that has been in process during the past thirty years and partly in the arithmetic involved in the patterns of industrial country protection. These patterns are identified in terms of the United States, but they probably reflect those of other industrial countries as well.

Some Key Findings of Hughes and Krueger

To bring out these explanations, attention may be called first to three of the empirical findings of Hughes and Krueger:

1. Despite widespread efforts in the United States and other industrial countries to increase protection, including some efforts directed against products important to the developing countries, the penetration of manufactured goods imports from all sources into the industrial countries increased from 11.6 percent of the absorption of the manufactured goods in 1970 to 17.6 percent in 1980. At the same time the share of developing countries in the absorption of manufactured goods in industrial countries increased from 1.7 percent to 3.4 percent. About half of the developing country gain would have accrued had the developing countries merely maintained their share in the general expansion of imports in domestic markets, but the other half may be regarded as growth at the expense of imports from developed country suppliers (see table 11.4).

Irving B. Kravis is professor of economics at the University of Pennsylvania and a research associate of the National Bureau of Economic Research.

2. The gains in the exports of the developing countries appear to be widely dispersed among developing countries in general, although the Far Eastern developing countries did the best (see table 11.3). Of the four nonoverlapping developing regions given, the lowest growth rate in manufactured exports between 1970 and 1980 was 18.9 percent for Latin America.

3. The commodity composition of developing country manufactured exports to industrial countries shifted toward more sophisticated products (table 11.2). Between 1970 and 1980 the shares in exports of food, beverages, and tobacco and of base metals were down sharply while the largest increases in shares were for fabricated metal products, machinery, and equipment, and for manufactured chemicals, petroleum, coal, and rubber products. However, the share of textile and wearing apparel also increased, though not as much as the machinery and chemical categories just mentioned. Furthermore, these are trade-barrier-distorted increases; there is a strong presumption that developing country exports of textiles and wearing apparel faced larger barriers than their machinery exports. But the shift to machinery and chemicals through high growth rates did take place.

The Significance of the Hughes-Krueger Findings

As suggested above, these findings point to and are explained by great structural changes in the world economy on one side, and by the pattern of protection on the other.

The major change in the world economy is the spread of modern economic growth to most of the nations of the world. In 1950 the question could still be raised whether modern economic growth could be expected to spread beyond the countries of Northwestern Europe and their overseas offshoots. In the ensuing years there has not only been an unprecedentedly high rate of expansion in the real gross domestic product per capita of the well-established countries (3.2 percent per annum) but a growth rate in the developing countries that is not quite as high but still remarkable by historical standards (2.8 percent).[1] The rate of growth in the developing countries during this period exceeded that enjoyed by the developed countries in the heyday of their growth in the latter part of the nineteenth and early part of the twentieth centuries. The high growth rates of the last thirty years are also widely diffused. The countries in which the growth rate in real per capita GDP has been in excess of 2 percent per capita contain two-thirds of the world's population. This includes 75 percent of the people living in countries other than the score of industrialized market economies and nearly half of the people living in developing market countries. Most of the remaining people of the world live in countries that have per capita growth rates between 1 percent and 2 percent, still well above historical premodern growth rates.

The Hughes-Krueger results concerning the export performance of developing countries and their success in penetrating the manufactured goods markets of the industrial countries reflects the fact that this growth includes the production and export of manufactured goods. Their data show also that the industrial countries have been adapting their import patterns to these new facts of life. As pointed out above, the industrial countries have accepted both greater import penetration and larger shares in imports from developing countries. Among the three major industrial areas the share of imports coming from developing countries increased substantially in the United States and Japan. The increase in the developing countries' share of total imports taken by the European Community was much smaller (from 12 percent to 14.5 percent) (see table 11.4). For clothing, textiles, and footwear, however, the European Community did considerably better in accepting high import shares from developing countries.

The rapid growth in world GDP, the increased penetration of imports in the markets of the industrialized countries, and the expansion of manufactured goods exports of the developing countries have been associated with an extremely rapid growth in world trade. As the figures in my table C11.1 show, the expansion in world exports since 1963 has been more rapid than the growth of world commodity production. The figures in the table probably tend to underrate the real growth in world exports since current values are deflated by unit values rather than true

Table C.11.1   Growth in World Commodity Production and Trade, 1963–82 (average annual percentage changes in volume)

	1963–73	1973–82	1979	1980	1981	1982
All commodities						
Production	6	2	4	1	1	−2
Exports	8½	3	6	1½	0	−2
Agriculture						
Production	2½	2	1	—	3½	2
Exports	4	4	7	5	3	1
Minerals						
Production[a]	5½	½	4½	−1½	−3	−3½
Exports[b]	7	−2½	5	−6	−12	−7
Manufacturing						
Production	7	2½	5	1½	½	−2
Exports	11	4½	5	5	3½	−1½

SOURCE: GATT, *International Trade, 1982/83*, Geneva, 1983.
NOTE: Trade values deflated by unit value index.
[a]Mining.
[b]Includes fuels and nonferrous metals.

export prices. The tendency for unit values to exaggerate the price increase for manufactured exports and thus to underestimate the true value of expansion has been documented.[2]

This is not the place to try to explain the still more rapid growth of trade compared to the unprecedentedly high growth rates for output in general, but it is easy to believe that the rapid growth provides a hospitable environment for trade expansion. Some of the improvement in output is attributable to lower cost and more convenient means of communication and transportation. These changes facilitate the identification of newly emerging low-cost locations and the establishment of production at these new areas of comparative advantage. Some part of the expansion of world trade, indeed perhaps a substantial part, is through the mechanism of the multinational firm. Multinationals are equipped to scan the world more effectively for new advantageous locations and to take fuller advantage of the economies of scale by dividing the production of parts, models, and products among different locations. U.S. majority-owned foreign affiliates (MOFAs) in developing countries, for example, increased their exports from 8.4 percent of their sales in 1966 to 18.1 percent in 1977. The ratio of their 1977 to 1966 exports in current values went up 9.5-fold compared to a 6-fold increase for all firms, including the U.S. MOFAs, other foreign affiliates, and domestic firms.[3]

Another factor giving an impetus to the expansion of world trade since 1973 was the increase in oil prices. Higher prices for undiminished or even (for a time) expanding world oil exports gave the oil exporting countries greatly increased purchasing power in world markets, and stimulated oil importers to supply additional exports that would help meet their extra costs for imported fuel. This tended toward a shift from domestic absorption to exporting which raised the ratio of trade to production. Continued or expanded growth in some developing countries, and in some oil exporting countries as well, was supported by rapid debt expansion.

Why Protection Has Not Bitten Harder

The powerful tendencies producing the relative expansion of world trade may help explain the upward movement in imports in general and imports of manufactures from the developing countries by the industrial countries in particular. Other factors are associated with the pattern of protection:

(a) Products and product groups characterized by slow growth in consumption are more likely to be claimants for protection in industrial countries than fast growing products and product groups. The highly publicized list of troubled industries seeking protection might well be dwarfed by a list of product and product groups for which protection has not been sought. The latter would probably be dominated by sectors of moderate or fast growth products, for which import increases are apt to proceed without objection. Furthermore, the protective measures when applied are usually confined to a subset of commodities within the vulnerable product group, or designed to protect only one or a few geographical market areas rather than the national market, or, finally, (in the "voluntary" arrangements) aimed only at selected countries of origin. (U.S. protection for steel affords examples of these limitations in coverage.)

(b) For these commodities, market destinations, and market origins which are the actual objects of protection, the aim is usually to stop the growth of imports or to limit their growth. When there is a cutback, it is usually to a recent high level, though not necessarily the highest one. These points are illustrated in the papers in this volume. For example, Feenstra's table 2.1 (see chap. 2, this volume) shows that the number of automobiles imported under the voluntary export restraint in 1981–82, although 9 percent lower than the previous year, was 13 percent higher than in 1979 and 17 percent higher than in 1978.

Two reasons may be suggested for the restraints in the degree of protection. One is the desire to adhere to GATT principles and a liberal trading system, to some degree as a matter of principle and to some degree owing to fear of retaliation. The danger of retaliation may be perceived to be particularly high for products like steel and agricultural products, where the main contestants are often large industrial countries, each with considerable power to retaliate against protective measures taken by the other. While it is true that the developing countries have escaped the brunt of the protective drive, except in textiles and wearing apparel, their increased share in industrial country imports of textiles and apparel suggests that the importance of being unimportant is not the only factor operating in favor of the developing countries. As Hughes and Krueger point out, favorable supply capabilities probably have contributed to their success.

Another consideration constraining the resolution of the political struggle over the amount of protection accorded to each industry is a growing perception of the cost of protection. Hughes and Krueger offer the plausible hypothesis that the adverse welfare effects of protection are borne mainly by the protection-imposing country. This is more likely to be the outcome if supply curves in the countries of origin are elastic, and the tendency they describe for exporting countries to escape the effects of protection by shifting shipments toward higher quality goods betokens, in effect, elastic supply curves. Thus in the United States, the effects of protection of intermediate products like steel on the prices of other industries, particularly other export industries or on the prices of consumer goods like automobiles, seem to have commanded the attention of policymakers who have become more concerned with the general competitive position of the U.S. economy than ever before. The related estimates of the cost to the nation of saving a worker's job in the protected industries have also received wide circulation.

Even if these surmises trying to explain the Hughes-Krueger paradox are correct, there is little cause for complacency. If protection has not stopped import growth, it has surely restrained it and diverted imports away from channels that market forces would produce. Consumers bear extra costs owing to the restraint in import growth, the diversion of imports to other (though related) products, and the substitution of higher cost sources of imports as a result of quotas, some imposed on various sources of supply by various countries of destination and others "voluntarily" agreed to by the countries of origin. There is a trend toward the cartelization of the world economy in which decisions about the location of production for export are made increasingly by international political negotiation rather than by market forces. Often the private firms in an industry collectively play leading roles in the division of markets, either directly or by calling the shots in the official trade battles conducted by diplomats or political officials. In a world clamoring for faster growth, these spreading tendencies are clearly antigrowth in their effect; they diminish the efficiency of the world economy. Furthermore, a continuation of depressed economic conditions can be expected to lead to greater demands for protection and to broader and more deeply cutting measures of protection so that imports from all sources may be more sharply curbed in their growth and even in their level.

Hughes and Krueger did not set out to assess the ability of the developed countries seriously to cut back the import penetration of their markets, including the shares of developing countries. What they have done is to assess the impact of protective measures taken so far and to remind us of the diversity and complexity with which protective measures operate.

Notes

1. For further assessment and historical comparisons, see I. B. Kravis and R. E. Lipsey, "The Diffusion of Economic Growth in the World Economy, 1950–80," prepared for the Conference on International Comparisons of Productivity, American Enterprise Institute, Washington, D.C., 20 September–1 October 1982.

2. I. B. Kravis and R. E. Lipsey, "Price and Terms of Trade for Developed Country Exports of Manufactured Goods," prepared for the meeting of the International Economic Association, Athens, 31 August–5 September 1981.

3. R. E. Lipsey and I. B. Kravis, "U.S. Owned Affiliates and Host-Country Exports," NBER Working Paper no. 1037, Cambridge, Mass.: National Bureau of Economic Research.

List of Contributors

C. Michael Aho
Office of International Economic
  Affairs
Bureau of International Labor
  Affairs
U.S. Department of Labor
Washington, D.C. 20210

Robert E. Baldwin
Department of Economics
University of Wisconsin
Madison, Wisconsin 53706

Thomas O. Bayard
The Ford Foundation
320 East 43rd Street
New York, N.Y. 10017

William R. Cline
Senior Fellow
Institute for International Economics
11 Dupont Circle, NW
Washington, D.C. 20036

Richard N. Cooper
Department of Economics
Littauer Center
Harvard University
Cambridge, Massachusetts 02138

Alan V. Deardorff
Department of Economics
University of Michigan
Ann Arbor, Michigan 48109

Jonathan Eaton
Department of Economics
Rouss Hall
University of Virginia
Charlottesville, Virginia 22901

Zvi Eckstein
Economic Growth Center
Yale University
P.O. Box 1987, Yale Station
27 Hillhouse Avenue
New Haven, Connecticut 06520

Barry J. Eichengreen
Department of Economics
Littauer Center
Harvard University
Cambridge, Massachusetts 02138

Wilfred J. Ethier
University of Pennsylvania
Department of Economics
3718 Locust Walk CR
Philadelphia, Pennsylvania 19104

Robert C. Feenstra
Department of Economics
Columbia University
New York, New York 10027

Heywood Fleisig
The World Bank
1818 H Street, NW
Washington, D.C. 20433

Harry Grubert
Office of International Tax Affairs
U.S. Treasury Department
Washington, D.C. 20220

Catharine Hill
The World Bank
1818 H Street, NW
Washington, D.C. 20433

Gary N. Horlick
O'Melveny and Myers
1800 M Street, NW
Washington, D.C. 20036

Helen Hughes
Development Studies Center
The Research School of Pacific
    Studies
Australian National University
Canberra, Australia

Ronald W. Jones
Department of Economics
University of Rochester
Rochester, New York 14627

Irving B. Kravis
University of Pennsylvania
Department of Economics
3718 Locust Walk CR
Philadelphia, Pennsylvania 19104

Mordechai E. Kreinin
Department of Economics
Marshall Hall
Michigan State University
East Lansing, Michigan 48824

Anne O. Krueger
The World Bank
1818 H Street, NW
Washington, D.C. 20433

Lars Lundberg
Department of Forest Economics
SLU
S-90183 Umea
Sweden

Stephen P. Magee
Department of Finance
School of Business
University of Texas
Austin, Texas 78712

Rachel McCulloch
Department of Economics
University of Wisconsin
Madison, Wisconsin 53706

Tracy Murray
Department of Economics
University of Arkansas
Fayetteville, Arkansas 72701

John Mutti
Department of Economics
University of Wyoming
Laramie, Wyoming 82701

Joseph Pelzman
Department of Economics
George Washington University
Washington, D.C. 20052

Alfred Reifman
Senior Specialist in International
    Economics
Congressional Research Service
Library of Congress
Washington, D.C. 20540

J. David Richardson
Department of Economics
University of Wisconsin
Madison, Wisconsin 53706

André Sapir
CEME CP 139
Université Libre de Bruxelles
50, Avenue Roosevelt
1050 Bruxelles
Belgium

Robert M. Stern
Department of Economics
University of Michigan
Ann Arbor, Michigan 48109

David G. Tarr
Bureau of Economics
Federal Trade Commission
Washington, D.C. 20580

Hans van der Ven
Department of International Affairs
    and Government Relations
Hoogovens Groep B.V.
Beverwijk
The Netherlands

John Whalley
Department of Economics
Social Science Center
University of Western Ontario
London N6A 5C2
Canada

Martin Wolf
Director of Studies
Trade Policy Research Centre
1, Gough Square
Fleet Street
London, EC4A 3DE
England

Author Index

Subject Index